A SPECIAL PIECE OF HELL

The Untold Story of Peleliu— the Pacific War's Forgotten Battle

(published in hardcover as PELELIU: TRAGIC TRIUMPH)

BILL D. ROSS

ST. MARTIN'S PAPERBACKS

A Special Piece of Hell was previously published under the title *Peleliu: Tragic Triumph*.

Published by arrangement with Random House

A SPECIAL PIECE OF HELL

Copyright © 1991 by Bill D. Ross. Maps copyright © 1991 by William J. Clipson.

Cover photograph courtesy Wide World Photos, Inc.

Library of Congress Catalog Card Number: 89-43420

ISBN: 0-312-95004-7

Printed in the United States of America

Random House hardcover edition/August 1991
St. Martin's Paperbacks edition/May 1993

10 9 8 7 6 5 4 3 2 1

This book is dedicated
to the memory of the United States Marine Corps
Combat Correspondents and Photographers
whose last bylines were inscribed on white crosses
and Stars of David in a distant time of battle
on faraway Pacific islands and atolls.

Sergeant Lee F. C. Baggett II (Guadalcanal, November 1942)
Sergeant John Barberio (Iwo Jima, February 1945)
Staff Sergeant Solomon I. Blechman (Guam, July 1944)
Staff Sergeant James Gallagher (Guam, July 1944)
Sergeant William H. Genaust (Iwo Jima, March 1945)
Captain Eugene M. Key (Tulagi, August 1942)
Staff Sergeant Wesley L. Kroenung, Jr. (Tarawa, November 1943)
Second Lieutenant Ernest A. Matthews, Jr. (Tarawa, November 1943)
Corporal Howard McCue (Saipan, June 1944)
Sergeant James J. McElroy (Iwo Jima, February 1945)
Corporal William J. Middlebrooks (Iwo Jima, February 1945)
Technical Sergeant Richard J. Murphy, Jr. (Saipan, June 1944)
Staff Sergeant Donovan R. Raddata (Iwo Jima, February 1945)
Sergeant Robert W. S. Stinson (Bougainville, November 1943)
Staff Sergeant William T. Vessey (Iwo Jima, February 1945)

And in enduring remembrance of the late
Louis R. Lowery,
a legendary sergeant Marine Corps Combat Photographer
for *Leatherneck* magazine,
who landed with the initial assault wave
at Peleliu and later, at Iwo Jima, was with the
first patrol to fight its way to the summit
of Mount Suribachi, where he made the first
photograph of the raising of the Stars and Stripes.

Contents

Foreword

Millions of words fill thousands of pages of hundreds of books written about the war between the United States and the Japanese Empire. But very few accounts of the monumental clash of arms make more than passing mention of one of the most savage and costly struggles to seize heavily defended enemy islands that were the hard-won stepping-stones to ultimate victory in the Pacific.

This all but ignored battle was fought on a 6-mile-long, 2-mile-wide chunk of coral called Peleliu.

It began in the early morning of September 15, 1944, and raged in atrocious fury for nearly two months. Before the last shot was fired, 8,769 Americans—mostly in their late teens or early twenties—were killed, wounded, or missing in action. Less than 300 of the 13,000-man-plus Japanese garrison survived.

Why was Peleliu invaded? What did the conquest of the tiny island contribute to the unconditional surrender of the Japanese and the end of World War II?

Did pre-invasion aerial reconnaissance photographs result in a disastrous miscalculation of the island's brutal terrain and the strength and depth of enemy defensive fortifications? Was the battle plan too optimistic, based on this and other flawed intelligence, in assuming that the campaign would be short?

What was the impact of the start-to-finish eccentric behavior of the Marine major general who commanded the division spearheading the assault? How much did his actions contribute to the monstrous toll of casualties and the drawn-out length of the struggle?

Did his division, objectively viewed in its entirety, possess the combat efficiency required for another grueling amphibious assault? Were the 17,400 officers and men physically and emotionally in shape and sufficiently well trained and organized to attack and conquer a heavily defended objective? Especially some 4,500 replacements, mostly teenagers fresh from the States who had never been in combat?

Why was the terrible bloodletting on Peleliu all but forgotten almost before the shooting stopped?

Why was Peleliu invaded at all, since three days before the landing Admiral William F. Halsey had strongly recommended that it be bypassed as useless in the grand scenario to defeat Japan?

For that matter, where is Peleliu?

Other than the location of the battleground, the answers to these questions are often contradictory, confusing, and controversial.

Peleliu is a reef-fringed flyspeck atoll at the southern tip of a chain of some 200 mostly uninhabited islands called the Palaus. The 45-mile-long archipelago is roughly 550 miles due east of the southern Philippines and some 800 miles south by east from the Mariana Islands in the Central Pacific.

Except for a neck of flat ground across its southern promontory, Peleliu is a terrible landscape: jungle-covered sheer coral cliffs topped by saw-toothed ridges separated by deep boulder-strewn crevices, mangrove swamps, and impenetrable scrub undergrowth.

Water suitable for drinking is hard to come by. The main source is that collected in cisterns during violent typhoons and torrential rains, which frequently buffet the island. It is not unusual for the midafternoon temperature to reach between 110 and 120 degrees; the climate is made more unbearable by steaming humidity.

With that said, one must step through history's often murky looking glass to find the hows, whats, and whys of the basically untold story of the epic and arguably unnecessary struggle—to find verified facts from which can be set down an honest, candid account of the battle as viewed at all levels from teenage private to the highest command echelon.

That is the diligent intent of this book. It was written, however, with a realization expressed by Professor Harry Gailey in his *Peleliu: 1944*, one of the few books written about the battle: "Total objectivity may be a myth, but an historian always attempts to recognize the emotional components of his evaluation and not to confuse these with a set of circumstances long past. . . ."

The battle-tested 1st Marine Division spearheaded the amphibious landing, established the beachhead against an avalanche of opposition, lost 95 percent of the men killed during the campaign, and left the island only after it was conclusively under American control.

The reserve force was the Army's 81st Infantry Division, facing combat for the first time. Its mission was to capture Angaur, a lightly defended 2-mile-square atoll some 5 miles off Peleliu's southern tip, and reinforce the Marines if ordered to by the invasion high command.

The men of the 1st Division called themselves the Old Breed. They considered themselves members of the nation's "finest and fightingest" outfit, and they were ready to prove it anywhere or anytime, as often as duty demanded.

Most of the Old Breed, officers and men, had been in the South Pacific more than twenty-four months before the assault on Peleliu. They had achieved the first victory by American ground forces in World War II at Guadalcanal, an epic event considered by many historians the turning point in the conflict against Japan.

They also had conquered Cape Gloucester on New Britain Island, a success that was a major, if not determining, factor in enabling General Douglas MacArthur to begin his northward drive to recapture the Philippines as a step in the then projected Allied strategy leading to the invasion of the Japanese home islands and the ultimate unconditional surrender of the enemy.

Thus to some extent this is a chronicle of all three battles. Although it is mainly about Peleliu, what the 1st Marine Division had experienced earlier is integral, even crucial, to a fundamental understanding of the Palaus campaign and how the Old Breed accomplished their "tragic triumph."

It was not patriotism alone that bound together and motivated these men. It was faith in themselves and in one another in a way that is both unexplainable and unfathomable to non-Marines, even to family members and the closest of friends. Without this uncommon and indestructible bond of courage and dedication, fused in the crucible of shared hardships and good times, the invasion of Peleliu might have ended in a monstrous failure.

The obvious lack of high command coordination—Navy, Marine Corps, and Army—in planning and training for the assault sorely troubled knowledgeable 1st Division officers. The apprehension flowed upward from veteran company and battalion commanders to regimental colonels and key members of the headquarters staff.

Their worst fears were realized long before D-Day.

What emerged was a sorry litany of almost everything that can be done wrong in preparing for a major amphibious landing. The situation was especially acute and foreboding since the target was a heavily fortified island garrisoned by hold-or-die troops commanded by a shrewd, combat-wise Japanese colonel, whose ancestors had been renowned samurai warriors for generations.

Victory on Peleliu was bought and paid for by the élan, the bravery and self-sacrifice, the dedication and devotion to duty of the men in the ranks and the line officers who led the assault platoons, companies, and battalions.

The Marines of the Old Breed—and their Army comrades-in-arms—deserve much, much more than the fleeting mention they so far have received in the history of the struggle against Japan. The words that follow will, I hope, bring a more prominent and lasting recognition to them and the "forgotten battle" they so gallantly fought.

The phrase "tragic triumph" is more than justified by the horrible toll of killed and wounded and by the irony that after its capture, Peleliu served no offensive purpose in the defeat of Japan.

In the sober judgment of history, is there any reason to doubt or fault Admiral Halsey's wisdom in recommending that the island be bypassed as an objective without use in winning World War II?

Peleliu is the least accessible of the battlegrounds where the major Pacific campaigns were waged. Rarely visited by anyone except natives from nearby islands, it seems hidden away like a guilty secret—a tiny backwater atoll where nearly 15,000 men, American and Japanese, met violent death in a terrible conflict that should never have been fought.

If the conquest of the Palaus has any lasting meaning, it is this: To those who know the fiendish face of deadly man-on-man combat, it reinforces the nightmarish memory of the awful, stupid horror they know war to be. To those who do not, it is a legacy of what a now-aged generation of Americans were capable of in battle—even a needless and forgotten battle—when duty called.

B. D. R.
Somerset, New Jersey, 1993

A
SPECIAL
PIECE OF
HELL

ONE

Summit Decision

SHORTLY AFTER 3:00 ON THE SUN-DRENCHED AND BREEZY Wednesday afternoon of July 26, 1944, the heavy cruiser *Baltimore* docked at the mighty United States Naval Base at Pearl Harbor on the island of Oahu in Hawaii.

Aboard the gray-hulled 14,000-ton man-of-war was Franklin Delano Roosevelt, the nation's thirty-second President and Commander in Chief of its global fighting forces. Just six days earlier he had been nominated for an unprecedented fourth term by thunderous acclamation at the Democratic National Convention in Chicago.

The purpose of the top-secret voyage was a meeting of FDR with General Douglas MacArthur and Admiral Chester W. Nimitz. It would be a strange council of war—the only time the three would be together during the four years of World War II.

From their historic conference would come the decision for the 1st Marine Division's amphibious assault against Peleliu. While there was no specific decision involving the Palaus campaign, the fuse nonetheless was lit for the invasion.

A small coterie of the White House's inner circle of top military and civilian advisers made the trip from the States with the President—and his Scottie dog Fala, a traveling companion almost wherever he went at home or overseas.

A flotilla of six destroyers protected the *Baltimore* as it sailed south by west from California. Circling overhead from dawn to dusk were long-range Navy Catalina flying boats. Captain Walter L. Calhoun, skipper of the ship, was glad to have the sea-air escorts when a coded radio message was flashed at sunset a day before landfall.

It was from the Commander Hawaiian Sea Frontier: "Possible enemy task force located 200 miles north of Oahu. Alert all activities." Nothing further was heard. But it was a potent signal that the Pacific was far from being a peaceful ocean.

As the President's cruiser was slowly warped toward a berth behind the aircraft carrier *Enterprise,* a roaring throng of at least 25,000 servicemen, mostly sailors in spotless whites, jammed the piers from Tin Can Row to Ford Island. Brass-heavy Army, Navy, and Marine officers stood at ramrod attention in a special carpeted and roped-off area near where the ship would moor. Nimitz's flag secretary later said he counted 146 stars on the collars of the generals and admirals.

FDR unabashedly savored the tumultuous welcome. He had been Under Secretary of the Navy during World War I, before polio crippled his legs. From teenage years, helming a small seagoing sailing sloop had been his favorite recreation.

Pearl Harbor had risen phoenixlike from the devastating shambles of the Japanese sneak attack that propelled the United States into the war. Some grim reminders of what Roosevelt had called "a day that will live in infamy" remained in view: rusting hulks of sunken ships of the Pacific Fleet, burned-out skeletons of bombed airplane hangars and huge collapsed fuel tanks, bullet scars on buildings hit by strafing enemy planes.

But now the sprawling anchorage bristled with the greatest display of naval power FDR had ever seen. And it was just a small part of the reborn and battle-ready strength of the United States Navy: three recently commissioned battleships with turrets mounting 16-inch guns; six giant new aircraft carriers, decks crammed with planes; nineteen submarines; thirty-two destroyers and destroyer escorts; and more than 400 troop transports, tankers, and cargo ships. At least three times that number of vessels were at sea, carrying the war inexorably toward Japan.

Responding to the screaming and clapping multitude, the President lifted himself from his wheelchair. He stood at the starboard rail, his face beaming with a broad smile. Time and again, he doffed and waved his panama hat, the Commander in Chief's way of returning the pandemonious salute.

Victory in Europe remained the top priority of the United States and the Allied Powers. It had to be accomplished before their overpowering force of weapons and men could be shifted to the Pacific and unleashed against the Japanese.

The U.S. Joint Chiefs of Staff were certain that climactic battles just ahead would bring about the downfall of Adolf

Hitler and the liberation of the European continent. British Prime Minister Winston Churchill and his military high command shared the optimistic American outlook.

Churchill, however, was outspokenly concerned that the ultimate defeat of Japan would go down in history as a wholly American triumph. In a constant stream of correspondence with FDR, he was demanding that British and Australian forces have a prominent and highly visible role in the final victory. Otherwise, the voluble Briton adamantly contended, his outnumbered countrymen's sacrifices during the dark days in the Southwest Pacific would be quickly forgotten.

Shortly before leaving Washington, the President attempted to placate the irascible Prime Minister with a long, warmly worded handwritten letter. It said they would resolve the matter in a face-to-face meeting in the near future. But Roosevelt did not inform Churchill that he was en route to Hawaii to see personally what could be done to resolve what he deemed a vastly more vexatious problem in the master plan to win the Pacific war.

"Winnie seems hell-bent to put the cart before the horse," FDR said somewhat sardonically to Harry L. Hopkins, his closest confidant and adviser-at-large. The former Iowa schoolteacher was in the Oval Office offering suggestions on how to word the missive to 10 Downing Street in London. It had to be tactful and yet to convey its message in no uncertain terms.

The dilemma that had brought the President to Hawaii was the troubling knowledge that his Joint Chiefs were sharply split over two proposed strategies to crush the Japanese Empire.

One was the brainchild of General MacArthur. The other had been devised by Admiral Nimitz. Their differences were compounded by their longtime and thinly concealed mutual dislike for one another.

Each was firmly convinced that his design for victory was the most logical and rapid way to conquer the enemy and bring about the avowed Allied goal of unconditional surrender. And each sought, in approaches reflecting ingrained differences in temperament and personality, the mantle of Supreme Commander in the ultimate assault on Japan. Both agreed that Allied losses would be horrendously heavy—at least a million men killed or wounded to achieve success.

FDR had deliberately left the Joint Chiefs at home. Before leaving Washington he told Secretary of War Henry L. Stimson that he was acutely aware of and deeply concerned by the Joint Chiefs' divided stand on the towering differences between the opinions of Nimitz and MacArthur. Left unsaid was the President's decision that as Commander in Chief of the nation's armed forces, he wanted to hear firsthand both sides of the issue from the admiral and general.

Thus, as historian Samuel Eliot Morison has written, Mr. Roosevelt wanted to exchange ideas with his senior Army and Navy commanders in the Pacific, and if possible reach an agreement.

MacArthur's battle plan was both cautious and grandiose. It called for the recapture of the entire Philippines archipelago, followed by the seizure of Okinawa and Formosa, which, once in American hands, would become gigantic bases to launch a million-man landing on the Chinese mainland. The ultimate invasion of Japan would be mounted from there.

Nimitz's scenario was more direct and arguably less certain of success, but he was ready to take the gamble. It envisioned bypassing the Philippines and China as unnecessary, costly, and time-consuming objectives. Like MacArthur, Nimitz proposed the capture of Okinawa and Formosa, but not to make them jump-off points to establish a beachhead on the Chinese mainland; he merely wanted to prevent their use by the enemy for air and naval attacks against the main offensive—an amphibious landing operation against Kyushu, the southernmost of the Japanese home islands. The seaborne assault advocated by the admiral would surpass in naval firepower, aerial support, and ground troops anything in history, even D-Day in Europe.

The invasion of the Palaus, especially Peleliu, was part of the strategy of both the general and the admiral—but for different reasons. Nimitz, with approval of the Joint Chiefs, already had ordered the 1st Marine Division to prepare for the assault. Unless the outcome of the meeting with Roosevelt and MacArthur caused the admiral to change his plans, the operation would go ahead as scheduled.

2

While the *Baltimore* was steaming at flank speed a day from Pearl Harbor, MacArthur's plane took off from Army headquarters in Brisbane, Australia. The plush converted B-17 bomber, its name, *Bataan*, painted on the nose, was headed for Hawaii's Hickham Field, four time zones to the north and east across the equator.

It had taken a firm direct order from General George C. Marshall, head of the Joint Chiefs, to get MacArthur to attend the meeting. An aide who made the twenty-two-hour flight later said the general, between catnaps in his private quarters, spent much of the time pacing the aisle of the plane complaining frequently about flying to Honolulu for what MacArthur outspokenly called a "political picture-taking junket."

Admiral Ernest J. King, a member of the JCS as well as Chief of Naval Operations, agreed with MacArthur. It was King's view, according to navy historian E. B. Potter, that "the President's tour of inspection without the Joint Chiefs was a politically inspired grandstand play."

Master politician that he was, Roosevelt certainly was not unmindful of the impact on voters that being photographed with MacArthur and Nimitz would have on his quest for a fourth term. But the general seemingly had forgotten that only a few months earlier, he had ranted over the blunt refusal of the Joint Chiefs to let him journey 13,000 miles to Washington on what was, at least in part, a strictly personal political excursion.

Officially, MacArthur proposed the trip to lobby his case for the future conduct of the war before the Joint Chiefs and, if possible, the Commander in Chief himself. To his intimates, however, he made no secret of intentions to invigorate a badly sputtering "Draft MacArthur" campaign as the Republican Party's candidate to oppose Roosevelt for the presidency.

The scheme was fostered and promoted by powerful GOP members of Congress who decried FDR's fourth-term ambitions as a step toward creating a "Roosevelt dynasty." Support also came in the columns of newspapers owned by such anti-Roosevelt tycoons as William Randolph Hearst, Colonel Robert R. McCormick, and Eleanor "Cissy" Patterson. The idea was quickly and quietly abandoned when it failed to attract more than a smattering of other backers.

Although the *Bataan* had landed fully two hours before the *Baltimore* docked, MacArthur was determined to make the President await his arrival. The general was accustomed to the spotlight wherever he went, and knew how to make a grand entrance that would give it to him. This time he would make certain to be the last of the multitude of admirals and generals to board the cruiser to greet the Commander in Chief.

To kill time, MacArthur and his staff stopped at the Fort Shafter headquarters of Lieutenant General Robert C. Richardson. He was military governor of Hawaii and, subordinate to MacArthur, commander of all Army ground forces in the Pacific. The four-star visitor chatted amiably for several minutes with old friends. Then he had a leisurely shower, dropped off his musette bag in the three-room suite set aside for his stay, and left nonchalantly for Pearl Harbor some six miles away.

Samuel I. Rosenman, FDR's chief speechwriter, was in the presidential entourage. He recalled MacArthur's Caesar-like arrival.

" 'The Boss' had just asked Admiral Nimitz if he knew the general's whereabouts," Rosenman said, "when a terrific automobile siren was heard, and there raced onto the dock and screeched to a halt a motorcycle escort and the longest open car I have ever seen."

The limousine circled once around the carpeted area where the welcoming brass were standing, then stopped at the foot of the *Baltimore*'s gangplank. When the applause died down, the general strode rapidly to the gangplank. He dashed up the steps, stopped halfway to acknowledge another ovation, and was soon on deck to meet the President.

MacArthur wore his trademark regalia: dark sunglasses, a crushed Army officer's cap with visor emblazoned with tarnished "scrambled eggs" gold braid, a short khaki jacket, and starched khaki trousers, shirt and tie. Each side of his collar was studded with four highly polished and oversized silver stars.

Admiral William D. Leahy, the President's chief of staff, was first to greet the general. He remarked jokingly: "Douglas, why don't you wear the right clothes when you come to see us?"

The unsmiling answer: "Well, you haven't been where I came from, and it's cold up there in the sky."

Hardly an auspicious way to get a summit meeting off on the right foot, Nimitz thought. Always a stickler for military protocol and doing everything by the book, he wore the regulation starched white dress uniform of all naval officers—with its always uncomfortable buttonless high collar. The admiral's four, much smaller, stars were woven in gold thread on black shoulder epaulets.

The President was not surprised by MacArthur's late arrival. He was well aware of the general's legendary propensity for the theatrical. He took in stride, with unspoken and suppressed disdain, MacArthur's arrogance and eccentricities in dress and the personal animosity he had for the Commander in Chief.

After a brief conference in Roosevelt's stateroom, the threesome went ashore. The session had been more bantering and small talk than a taste of the major discussion to come. They departed with plans for a six-hour inspection of Oahu's defenses the next day.

Leaving the ship, FDR had groups of sailors on deck pose with him for pictures to be released after his return to the mainland. Always the showman, he also wanted to capitalize on the "photo opportunity," as later White House occupants would call such occasions, showing him waving to massive crowds with MacArthur and Nimitz at his side. There was no hint of objection from the general. In fact, several pictures show him with a broad smile.

As the chariot for the tour of military installations with the general and admiral, Roosevelt asked for and expected the seemingly impossible on wartime Oahu: a bright red convertible with its top down. Two of Nimitz's wheeler-dealer aides spent most of the night locating what FDR wanted. It was a 1941 Packard belonging to Honolulu's fire chief.

That evening the President learned there were two such vehicles on the island. He chuckled when told the other was owned by the madam of Honolulu's largest house of prostitution.

Wartime press censorship was rigidly enforced. Not one word or photograph was published in the *Honolulu Star-Bulletin* or *Advertiser*. No mention of the conference was made on radio newscasts. The small contingent of Washington correspondents who made the trip and the Hawaii-based wire service reporters abided by the news blackout.

Admiral Leahy felt little was gained by the inspection except the display of Oahu's massive buildup of manpower and countless acres of equipment and supplies being stockpiled for bat-

7

tles to come. He later told a close friend that the entourage reminded him of a "gaggle of vactioning mainland tourists enjoying the sights of the island's magnificent beaches and lush mountains" rather than leaders of a nation at war.

Leahy rode beside the driver, a Marine sergeant. MacArthur sat between Roosevelt and Nimitz in the backseat. Leahy later said FDR dominated the conversation, which was "mainly political gossip" with no mention of the monumental issues that had brought them together.

At one point MacArthur remarked that Roosevelt was "an overwhelming favorite with the troops for reelection." The President was silent for a moment and then threw back his head and laughed.

Leahy remembered his next words:

"I'll beat that little son of a bitch in Albany if it's the last thing I do," FDR said, alluding to New York's Governor Thomas E. Dewey, the Republican nominee for the presidency.

That evening the President hosted cocktails and dinner for twenty flag and general officers at his quarters in a three-story stucco mansion near Diamond Head. Its outside elevator faced the famed island landmark. Owned by millionaire industrialist Christopher R. Holmes, it had been requisitioned by the Navy for pilots on rest and rehabilitation leave from combat.

After dining on a main course of prime ribs, Roosevelt led MacArthur, Nimitz, and Leahy into an adjoining room, where a huge map of the Pacific covered the wall. The President picked up a long bamboo pointer and with it jabbed several islands. Then he suddenly spun his wheelchair around to confront MacArthur.

"Well, Douglas," he asked, "where do we go from here?"

The tone was one of challenge and authority. The general's immediate response: "Mindanao, Mr. President, then Leyte and then Luzon."

For the next three hours, MacArthur and Nimitz jousted as they took turns at the map to drive home salient advantages of their radically different strategies.

The general scored the most trenchantly when arguing that to bypass the Philippines would be to betray the Filipinos. In a dramatic reminder of his "I shall return" vow to liberate the archipelago, he declared that "promises must be kept."

Quiet, soft-spoken Nimitz was outmatched by MacArthur's eloquence. But he stood his ground and presented his case in a point-by-point methodical manner much as would the board

8

chairman of a blue-chip corporation. His argument was straightforward, laced with facts, and to the point.

Roosevelt listened intently and mostly in silence. He interrupted only when he needed clarification of some facet of the discussion or wanted to steer it in a way to placate the adversaries when he felt their comments were becoming overheated. Obviously fatigued, he called a halt shortly before midnight.

"Let's adjourn for now and get a good night's sleep," the Commander in Chief said in a voice with the overtone of an order. "We'll resume tomorrow morning at 10:30 for a final review, and then I'll give you my answer."

FDR had heard all the arguments of the Joint Chiefs in Washington. Now he had man-to-man knowledge of how MacArthur and Nimitz felt, and the reasons behind their thinking. While the President had veto power over any decisions the Joint Chiefs might make, he had no intention of imposing his authority over them after his meeting with the admiral and general. He was certain, however, that the nation's military high command would give serious consideration to his views and react in the best interests of their overall strategic plans to defeat Japan.

An exhausted Roosevelt chatted briefly with Vice Admiral Ross McIntire, his personal physician, before retiring.

"Give me an aspirin before I go to bed," he said. "On second thought, give me another to take in the morning. It's been a long day." The President slept soundly and awoke refreshed. He also had made up his mind.

The Philippines would be invaded with General MacArthur commanding the mightiest ground force the United States could muster in the Pacific at the time. Admiral Nimitz, however, would remain as his equal in rank and in full command of all naval support for the operation.

Roosevelt gave no hint, at the start of the ninety-minute morning conclave, that he had come to a decision.

Nimitz reiterated the logic of his plan. MacArthur replowed the emotional ground of "not betraying millions of Filipinos who looked upon the United States as their mother country." To him, recapture of the Philippines was more than a prime military goal; it also was a moral crusade. Time and again he used such words as "ethical" and "unethical," "virtue" and "shame" to bolster his arguments.

It was approaching lunchtime, and the protagonists had

begun to repeat themselves. But the President was still listening with what appeared to be rapt attention. He seemed especially impressed when the general said that "if the Philippines are left behind in the backwash of war, the Japanese army can live off the land and will slaughter, in revenge, thousands of prisoners, including women and children."

That was MacArthur's trump card, Roosevelt decided—a suitably dramatic curtain line for the historic occasion. Motioning with his hands for both sides to stop, he said without comment that he approved the general's plan. There was no outward show of elation or dejection from either MacArthur or Nimitz.

"Both had earlier vowed to work together in full agreement toward the common end of defeating Japan regardless of whatever strategy the President chose," Admiral Leahy recalled.

The President was in high spirits, obviously satisfied with the outcome. Before leaving the room, he called MacArthur aside and said jovially:

"Well, Douglas, you win! But I'm going to have a hell of a time over this with that old bear Ernie King!" Admiral King, as Chief of Naval Operations and one of the Joint Chiefs, was Nimitz's superior in the Navy chain of command and had been openly critical of any plan to retake the Philippines.

When photographers were called in to take pictures, a prankish Roosevelt noticed the fly of MacArthur's khakis was open. "Do you see what I see?" he chortled softly to one of them. "Quick! Get a shot of it!" The cameraman was focusing his lens when the general, with a look of icy annoyance, crossed his legs.

Lunch was casual—but without MacArthur's presence. Somewhat testily, he told the President that he must get back to his headquarters as soon as possible "to resume fighting the war." The *Bataan* was already warmed up, he said, and waiting for him on the tarmac at Hickham Field for the flight to Australia. If there was any conversation between Nimitz and MacArthur before the general left, there is no known record of it.

Only a press conference remained before the President began his return to Washington. He was cordial, smiling, and upbeat as he faced the media.

Frank Tremaine, Honolulu bureau manager of United Press and the news service's top correspondent in the Pacific, was among the corps of reporters and photographers. He was widely respected by his colleagues as the newsman who—with the help of his wife, Kay—had scooped all rivals with the first eyewitness report of the Japanese attack on Pearl Harbor to reach the United States. Their graphic dispatch was on teletypes to UP's client newspapers and radio stations across the country even before the shattering flash reached Washington through official channels.

Forty-five years later, Tremaine recalled the press briefing by FDR: "My recollection of the conference is that the President was seated, probably in his wheelchair, at the front edge of an open porch or lanai with several aides standing, flanking him on both sides. The correspondents and photographers—probably a dozen or two—lined up in front of him on the ocean side of a low retaining wall with the sea at our backs."

Little, if any, hard news came out of the meeting, and what was said could not be reported at the time because of censorship restrictions. Stories and photographs released for publication after the President was back in Washington showed and said only that he had met with MacArthur and Nimitz "to discuss future military moves in the war against Japan."

Reporters were allowed to quote FDR, however, as saying he "was absolutely delighted" to have visited military hospitals to meet "the brave young men in the wards," and that he was "greatly impressed and reassured" by the "bristling arsenal of democracy" he had seen on Oahu.

The *Baltimore* and her escorts were ready to cast off when the six-car presidential party arrived dockside at 6:45 P.M. Roosevelt sat for a few moments in Nimitz's limousine, chatting with the admiral. Then, smiling and waving and simultaneously smoking a cigarette in his customary long ebony holder, he was pushed up a red-carpeted ramp to the cruiser's deck. He paused there and whirled his chair around to deliver a snappy formal salute to the Stars and Stripes flying at the ship's stern.

Before retiring he told Dr. McIntire he was pleased with the way things had worked out with MacArthur and Nimitz. The President also said he was especially glad to have been wheeled slowly through hospital wards to banter with young men who had lost limbs in battle. He wanted them to know, without saying so, that he knew what it meant to have dead legs, and to realize the crippling handicap could be conquered.

Admiral Nimitz met that night with a small group of disconsolate members of his staff. He had invited them for cocktails and dinner in his personal quarters near the crest of an extinct volcano named Makalapa that towered above blacked-out Honolulu. A recording of Eugene Ormandy and the Philadelphia Orchestra played softly in the background.

The Commander in Chief Pacific (CinCPac) told his aides he had anticipated the President's decision and that he accepted it as final. He ordered all men and units of the Pacific Fleet to cooperate fully and without hesitation in seeing that it was successfully carried out.

"Almost as an afterthought," Navy Captain Waldo Drake, who was there, told *Newsweek* correspondent Bill Hipple months later, "Nimitz then directed someone to make sure an urgent dispatch was sent to the headquarters of the 1st Marine Division to let them know that Operation Stalemate was to proceed as scheduled. That meant, in other words, there would be no changes in plans for the Marines to attack Peleliu on September 15."

The 1st Division was nearly 4,000 miles away on tiny Pavuvu Island in the Southwest Pacific. The invasion date was little more than six weeks away.

3

Operation Stalemate had been on the Pacific war's invasion timetable for almost a year since President Roosevelt and Prime Minister Churchill approved it at a council of war convened at Quebec, Canada, in August 1943. With them were the Allied Combined Chiefs of Staff.

The main purpose of Quadrant, the secret conference's code name, was to chart a master long-range strategy to win the war. Topping the agenda was the still-to-come invasion of France. Crucial to this was the thrashing out of the thorny issue of whether the liberation of Europe would be led by a British or an American general.

An agreement was reached after twelve days that the Supreme Commander of Allied invasion forces would be an American yet to be named. To humor Churchill's nocturnal working habits, most of the often heated and frustrating talks began near midnight and went on until dawn.

There was no intention by Quadrant's decision-makers to lay down a firm and inviolate schedule for future operations in the Pacific. They hoped instead to devise a hazy but logical format that would pinpoint key objectives for massive naval and air strikes, and even amphibious assaults. The timetable was to be flexible enough to be revamped swiftly to capitalize on any unpredictable victories that could shorten the long and difficult road to Japan.

Minutes of the conference indicated that the American and British warlords felt General MacArthur had the situation well in hand in the South Pacific and was about to launch his island-hopping Army push northward toward the Philippines.

The minutes also indicated the optimistic judgment that Admiral Nimitz's Pacific Fleet was now calling the shots and had enemy naval power on the defensive. His battleships and wide-ranging aircraft carrier and cruiser task forces were tightening a ring of steel around the seaborne foe that severely restricted its movements.

Prowling submarines were torpedoing and sinking thousands of tons of irreplaceable troop transports and cargo ships. These losses were having a devastating impact on Japanese attempts to send reinforcements and supplies to outpost garrisons.

The Marine Corps soon would have enough combat troops overseas to invade Japanese-held islands whenever called upon. By early spring of 1944, its force would number nearly 175,000 men in four fully equipped divisions.

The purposely vague scheme to use this awesome and burgeoning war machine was relayed by Admiral King to Nimitz at his CinCPac headquarters in Pearl Harbor. King's instructions were more to the point. "The ball is in your court," he said. "Proceed as you see fit, but keep the Joint Chiefs informed of your plans."

Admiral Nimitz wasted no time. He immediately requested and quickly received authority from King and his fellow members of the JCS to "put more meat on the bare bones" of Operation Stalemate as it affected the role of the Pacific Fleet and the Marine divisions under his command.

Months before meeting with Roosevelt and MacArthur, Nimitz had ordered Rear Admiral Raymond A. Spruance to begin pondering the neutralization or capture of the Carolines. Known as the "quiet admiral," Spruance was Nimitz's brilliant right hand and trusted chief strategic brain.

Planning of the toughest and most complex operations was invariably assigned to him. His office was next to Nimitz's, and was bare of chairs or couches. He often spent eighteen hours a day standing at a specially built 12-foot-long, waist-high desk. Neatly stacked documents and maps covered the work space; he usually was developing plans for several campaigns at the same time.

The Carolines, at the moment, were Spruance's top priority. This necklace of 549 tiny islands and atolls is the longest in the world but its total land mass is less than 830 square miles. The chain is just a few degrees north of the equator, and extends across the Central Pacific from the Marshalls at its eastern tip to the Palaus, some 3,000 miles westward toward the Philippines.

Deemed at the time to have more military importance than the Palaus, and their bastion on Peleliu, were the islands of Truk, Yap, and Ulithi, which were the Japanese strongholds in the Carolines. Their location and massive defenses were a major and dangerous threat to U.S. fleet movements in the Central Pacific and a roadblock to future invasions by the Marines in the advance northward toward Japan.

Aerial intelligence photos showed them heavily fortified by at least a dozen big naval guns, several dug-in batteries of long-range artillery, more than 500 bombers and fighter planes, uncounted antiaircraft guns, a garrison of thousands of sailors and troops, huge steel storage tanks for fuel, and giant stacks of ammunition and supplies.

Months before the decision to invade the Philippines, Nimitz had decided to take Peleliu as a forward base from which to hit Truk, Yap, and Ulithi. Now the conquest of the Palaus, and more specifically the capture of Peleliu, had another purpose. To protect the eastern flank of General MacArthur's island-hopping drive, it was necessary, CinCPac felt, to retake the Philippines from Japanese air and naval forces based on the islands.

On March 26, four months to the day before he met with the President and MacArthur, Nimitz sent what military jargon calls a "Warning Order" to the commanding general of the 1st Marine Division. It said to invade Peleliu "no later than 15 September as directed in Operation Stalemate."

Neither Roosevelt nor MacArthur apparently was aware of Nimitz's earlier decision to seize the Palaus, although it was approved by the Joint Chiefs of Staff. The outcome of the Pearl Harbor conference, in the admiral's judgment, was merely another reason to proceed with Stalemate with all the resources at his command.

TWO

The Stuff of Legends

THE UNITED STATES MARINES WHO CRUSHED THE GERMANS in 1918 in the muddy blood-spattered trenches of Château-Thierry, Belleau Wood, Soissons, and St. Mihiel in France were a unique brotherhood of warriors.

Captain John W. Thomason, Jr., a legendary frontline combat officer turned author and artist, described his World War I comrades as "a number of diverse people who ran curiously to type, with drilled shoulders and a bone-deep sunburn and a tolerant scorn of nearly everything else on earth."

And he gave them a name and identity: "They were the Leathernecks, 'The Old Breed' of American regulars, regarding the service at home and war as an occupation, and they transmitted their temper and viewpoint to the high-hearted volunteer mass."

It was an attitude the 1st Marine Division quickly adopted as its own when the United States entered World War II.

On December 7, 1941, when the Japanese surprise attack devastated Pearl Harbor, the Marine Corps' total roster was 65,312 officers and men. They were scattered at duty stations around the world; 28,000 were deployed from Iceland to Hawaii and the Philippines, Guam, Wake, Midway, and other Pacific island outposts. Some 33,000 were in training or serving at Marine and Navy bases. Another 4,000 were aboard battleships, aircraft carriers, and cruisers at sea.

The 1st Division existed largely in name only. Its manpower was 518 officers and 6,871 privates, corporals, and sergeants, about a third of its authorized strength.

Despite constantly mounting signs that sooner or later, World War II would involve America in combat, growth had been slower than in the other armed forces. Because of the

Corps' unbending and high aptitude and physical standards, more eager volunteers were rejected than it signed up. Draftees were not accepted as Marines until mid-1943, and were then listed as "Selective Service Volunteers."

The division had first priority, however, on the best-rated recruits when they finished basic training at either of the Corps' boot camps—one at San Diego, California, and the other at Parris Island, South Carolina.

Newcomers were lucky to be assigned to the 1st Division, although most failed to realize it at the time. They were quickly integrated into units of hard-core career Marines who had seen action in France or were veterans of the nasty "little wars" of the 1920s in the jungles of Central America.

The old-timers, seasoned officers and salty noncoms, knew how to fight and survive, and they worked incessantly to pass along their expertise. Rugged physical conditioning and uncompromising discipline had top priority on the seven-days-a-week regimen that began before daybreak and ended well after dark. The youngsters also learned to become experts in the basic tools of their new trade, rifles, machine guns, mortars, flamethrowers, and hand grenades.

Man by man, the 1st Division was being molded into a self-contained, full-strength fighting machine of 19,000 Leathernecks. One officer, who had been a captain commanding a company in France, was now a major leading a battalion. He described his fledgling unit in a letter to his wife in California:

"The average age of the enlisted personnel is very low," he wrote, "possibly under twenty years. About 90 percent of them have enlisted since Pearl Harbor, but they are full of patriotism and have the 'up and at 'em' spirit. I am sure they will acquit themselves very well in combat, and I am proud to be their CO."

Major General Alexander Archer Vandegrift, a crusty World War I fighter known to old-timers as Archie, was the division's highly competent commander. He received sailing orders on May 19, 1942, and boarded ship the next day with an advance echelon of 152 officers and 1,719 enlisted men. They headed south without naval escort toward the Panama Canal through seas menaced by German submarines.

Following at regular intervals as rapidly as possible were hastily assembled convoys loaded with the manpower and equipment of the division's three infantry and one artillery regiments, and supporting units of tanks, special weapons, engineer, communications, and medical companies and battalions.

For some reason whose origin is lost in history, a Marine Corps regiment is often referred to by its numbered designation followed by the word "Marines." Thus the 1st Marine Regiment, for example, is the same outfit as the 1st Marines. The 1st, 5th, and 7th Marines were the 1st Division's ground troops, and the 11th was its artillery regiment. Support outfits were on call by any unit needing them in combat.

Wellington, New Zealand, was the division's destination. Six days after Vandegrift arrived, he and his staff were summoned by a Navy lieutenant messenger to an "urgent and immediate conference" at the headquarters of Vice Admiral Robert Ghormley. He was Commander South Pacific Area (ComSoPac) and, as such, was the Marine general's superior in the chain of command.

Vandegrift was hardly seated when Ghormley handed him a dispatch from the Joint Chiefs of Staff in Washington. It was short and to the point: "Occupy and defend Guadalcanal and adjacent positions in order to deny these areas to the enemy and provide U.S. bases in preparation for further actions."

Watchtower, the code name of the operation, was to be carried out by the 1st Division. "D-Day will be 1 August," the admiral said.

Vandegrift showed no emotion at the announcement. Inwardly he was extremely concerned about the combat-readiness of the troops, which he originally thought might take six months. He mentally calculated the new time frame: only thirty-seven days to do everything required to mount an amphibious assault against Japanese-held islands more than 1,000 miles away.

The vexatious situation was compounded by another serious problem. The last convoy of ships would not dock until July 11. It carried most of the division's troops, armament, and supplies—artillery, tanks, bulldozers and cranes, food rations, medical equipment, and other battle gear.

When Vandegrift patiently laid out these facts, Ghormley agreed to push back D-Day one week to August 7.

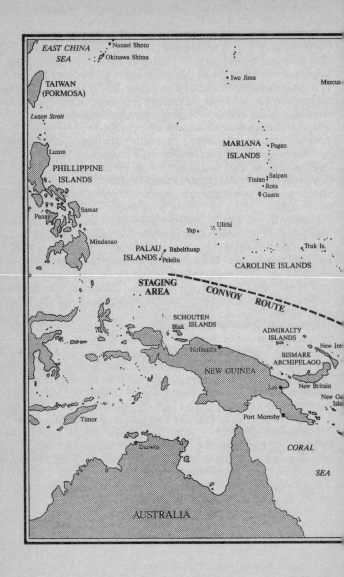

SOUTH PACIFIC AREA

• Midway

PACIFIC

OCEAN

• Wake

Eniwetok ∴ Bikini ⍩ Rongelap ⍩ MARSHALL
                 •Wotho   ISLANDS
        Kwajalein   •Wotje
            Namu Majuro •Maloelap
Ponape
            Jaluit   •Mili

•Kusaie

                    • Makin
                          GILBERT
                    • Tarawa   •Howland
                    • Apamama   •Baker
        •Nauru   ISLANDS

nville
hoiseul SOLOMON   •Nanomea
    Santa Isabel   ELLICE
        ISLANDS   ISLANDS
uvu   •Malaita   Nuku Fetau •Funafuti
l Is.   Guadalcanal
        San
        Christobal
                                        SAMOA
arine Division begins   Savaii Upolu
ing for Peleliu invasion Espiritu Santo   Tutuila
                    NEW HEBRIDES   FIJI   ISLANDS
                    ISLANDS   ISLANDS
                    Efate   Suva

2

In the tumultuous eight months since the Pearl Harbor attack, the United States and its allies in the Pacific had suffered disaster after disaster. The catastrophic events came with frightening speed as Japanese naval, air, and ground forces achieved an unbroken stream of victories.

"There was a haunting national nightmare at the time," one 1st Division officer recalled, "that the Japs were supermen, that maybe our American boys weren't as rugged as the Japs. What people wanted, what they needed in the summer of '42, was a hand-to-hand battle royal between some Japs and some Americans to see who would really win."

The historic clash of arms began in the overcast dawn of August 7, 1942.

It was D-Day for the 1st Marine Division to assault the beaches at Guadalcanal. Nineteen troop transports and cargo ships rounded the island's northwestern tip shortly after 3:00 in the morning. They were loaded with 956 officers and 18,146 enlisted men. At the time, the landing force was nearly one-third of the Marine Corps' total manpower.

Hardly a sound broke the stillness, only the muffled noise of hatches being opened and davits lowering landing craft for the run to shore. There was an eerie placidity over the calm tropical sea until 6:14.

Then came the thunderous blasts of last-minute pre-invasion bombardment from Rear Admiral Richmond Kelly Turner's covering fleet of twelve American and Australian heavy and light cruisers, twenty destroyers, and the new battleship U.S.S. *North Carolina.* Air support, commanded by Vice Admiral Frank Jack Fletcher, came from the carriers *Enterprise, Saratoga,* and *Wasp.*

No return fire came from Japanese artillery or naval defense guns. Not a single enemy plane appeared to challenge the assault.

The initial wave of Marines left the line of departure, some 2 miles at sea, right on schedule shortly after 8:30. The first troops—Lieutenant Colonel William E. Maxwell's 1st Battalion of the 5th Regiment—were on the beach at 9:10.

Miracle of miracles, surprise was complete! The landing was unopposed!

Some desultory bursts of small-arms fire came from the

palm groves a few hundred yards inland, but there was no strong enemy reaction; no chattering of machine guns; no shrill whine of falling artillery shells; no swishing sounds of incoming mortars.

By nightfall, 10,000-plus men were ashore with tank and artillery support on the 4-mile-long beachhead. A Navy doctor said the only man he treated on D-Day was "a character who cut himself trying to open a coconut." Thus was born the belief that the Old Breed were blessed with "landing luck."

General Vandegrift and his planners had the benefit of superb pre-invasion intelligence from a three-man team of intrepid British-Australian "coast watchers" led by one Martin Clemens, an adventurous Cambridge graduate. It was a message from Clemens that the Japanese were building a large airstrip on Guadalcanal that so shortened the time Vandegrift had been given for the 1st Division to go into battle.

Operation Watchtower's first and most important objective was the unfinished airstrip that the Leathernecks would name Henderson Field in honor of Major Lofton Henderson, killed while leading a squadron of Marine dive bombers in the Battle of Midway. The airstrip was overrun by sundown of D-Day plus one.

Martin Clemens had also reported that the Japanese were building up major defenses on nearby Florida, Tulagi, Gavutu, and Tanambogo islands. General Vandegrift thus ordered that they be assaulted simultaneously with the landing on Guadalcanal.

The importance of this phase of Operation Watchtower is reflected in the fact that Brigadier General William H. Rupertus, the 1st Division's assistant commander and Vandegrift's close friend and confidant, was personally commanding the attack on the four tiny coral strongpoints. Rupertus was given an elite force of four battalions, some 2,200 men, for the mission.

Tulagi was the largest of the islands, 2 miles long and a half mile wide with a 300-foot-high ridge down its center. Before the Japanese took over, it had been the administrative center of the British Solomon Islands Protectorate and now was headquarters and the radio communications hub for the occupying forces.

Clemens, using a high-definition telescope, had ascertained that it was fortified with caves, bunkers, and pillboxes manned by an estimated 500 troops. About 3,000 yards east of Tulagi were the twin atolls of Gavutu and Tanambogo.

Gavutu was a seaplane base, he reported, with a garrison of some 600, mostly air crewmen untrained for infantry duty. Tanambogo was a cluster of low-lying, sharp coral ridges where the Japanese had built a network of tunnel-connected defenses manned by up to 400 troops. Florida was the smallest, about half a mile square, covered with coconut groves defended by only fifty-plus troops.

H-Hour was 8:30 A.M., thirty minutes before the main assault hit Guadalcanal, and was intended to confuse the Japanese about where the Marines planned to land their major forces.

While Rupertus's troops churned toward the beaches in three lines of Higgins boats, the heavy cruiser *San Francisco* and two destroyers laced the islands with a five-minute bombardment. This was followed by ten minutes of strafing and bombing strikes from the *Wasp*.

Florida was overrun in less than an hour by the 1st Battalion of the 2d Marines at a cost of two men killed and six wounded. The 1st Raider Battalion found conditions distressingly different when they hit Tulagi.

They were caught in a concentration of savage machine-gun fire as soon as they crossed the beach and moved onto a coral ridge. It was one firefight after another throughout the day, as the Marines knocked out fiercely resisting positions, taking more and more casualties with each attack.

The 2d Battalion of the 5th Marines was in the same fix on their beach 2,000 yards to the east. What the two outfits encountered on Tulagi was the Marines' first exposure to tactics the Japanese used with devastating results in resisting many subsequent invasions. The technique was simple. Entrenched in cleverly concealed strongpoints, the enemy would let the point of the assault pass unmolested and then hit the advance from behind with machine guns, rifle fire, and hand grenades.

The Japanese dugouts, bunkers, pillboxes, and caves usually were covered with several feet of concrete or coral that could be penetrated only by lucky direct hits from naval shelling, heavy artillery, or air bombardment. Destroying the devilish positions was thus the messy and dangerous work of small infantry units—fire teams and squads attacking head-on with rifles, grenades, flamethrowers, and satchel charges of TNT.

Casualties were inevitably high, but there was no other way to do the job.

The 1st Parachute Battalion took on Gavutu and Tanambogo with only 397 men. The force was outnumbered by the dug-in defenders and was in a quagmire of trouble from the start. A frantic radio message to the *San Francisco* and *Wasp* brought in enough shelling and air strikes to relieve the pressure and enable the Marines to push ahead in what became a day-and-night forty-eight-hour battle.

Over on Guadalcanal, Vandegrift received his first direct communication from Rupertus at 7:00 in the morning of August 8, D plus one of the invasion. It bore the unmistakable overtones of desperation verging on panic. The 1st Division commander had to be very much troubled, if not alarmed, by the message. Rupertus reported staggering casualties of between 50 and 60 percent in the Parachute battalion and 22 percent in the Raider battalion. He also asked for immediate reinforcements—something that was impossible to provide.

There was no question that the Tulagi-Gavutu-Tanambogo operation had become a savage engagement, but the issue was never in doubt. And when the battalion commanders involved learned that Rupertus had, in effect, pushed the panic button, they were dumbfounded. His action, one said, "had to be based on misinformation, absence of firsthand knowledge of what was going on, or his well-known reputation of a lack of respect of the combat judgment of *all* subordinates."

The Stars and Stripes was raised above the shambles of the Governor's House on Tulagi shortly before 3:00 in the afternoon of August 8, 1942. The battle for the four key islands was over.

The cost to the Marines was 141 killed and 106 wounded. The losses were far from minor and insignificant, but might well have been much heavier considering the size of the determined Japanese garrisons and the strength and number of their well-fortified defenses. The some 1,500 enemy that Clemens estimated to be on the islands were annihilated or vanished while trying to swim to nonexistent safety.

3

When word of the invasion was flashed from Japanese Solomon Islands headquarters on Tulagi to Imperial General Headquarters at Rabaul, New Guinea, the reaction was massive and swift.

Admiral Gunichi Mikawa, Emperor Hirohito's commander in the Southwest Pacific, sensed instantly what the Americans were up to. The capture of Guadalcanal would give them a forward base for land, sea, and air offensive action against Japanese forces being massed for further island conquests and a projected invasion of northern Australia. He immediately dispatched an urgent and unmistakable order to all units of his command.

"Send with utmost speed all available combat vessels and aircraft to destroy United States naval forces in the vicinity of Guadalcanal," the coded message said. "Follow this by immediately sending all necessary ground forces necessary to exterminate the Americans on the island and those adjacent to it."

Within three hours the first of three powerful air strikes hit Admiral Turner's troop transports and cargo ships at anchor just offshore from Lunga Point, a few miles from the beachhead. The first wave of eighteen Zero fighters flew cover for twenty-seven Betty bombers.

Twelve Grumman Wildcat fighters from the *Wasp* tried to intercept the aerial onslaught, but they were no match for the much faster, more maneuverable Zeros. The enemy fighters repeatedly strafed the beachhead unmolested. Two more waves of Aichi bombers joined the Bettys in strikes against the transports and their escorts. Amazingly, only one cargo ship was sunk and two destroyer escorts seriously damaged.

This was only a prelude to the furious battle fought off Savo Island, some 1,500 yards from Guadalcanal's northwestern tip. In the rain-swept predawn darkness of August 9, seven undetected Japanese heavy and light cruisers all but wiped out Allied naval forces protecting the precarious Marine beachhead.

Sunk fathoms deep in what thereafter would be aptly known as Iron Bottom Sound were the American cruisers *Quincy, Astoria,* and *Vincennes* and Australia's *Canberra.* The cruiser *Chi-*

cago and a destroyer were badly damaged, still afloat but burning from stem to stern, and unable to fight or escape.

The engagement was over in less than thirty minutes. It was the most devastating defeat the United States Navy would suffer during the war and cost 1,250 dead and 709 wounded sailors.

Apparently not realizing the extent of their victory, the Japanese turned away undamaged and steamed back to Rabaul. Historians have speculated that Admiral Mikawa, who personally commanded the surprise attack, needlessly feared retaliation at dawn from American carrier-based planes.

Such action was far from the mind of Admiral Fletcher. He was worried over the safety of his carriers and felt that all three might be sunk if the enemy fleet struck again, or another massive attack came from Japanese planes. Fletcher signaled to Admiral Turner his intentions to leave the area, explaining that he "was seriously short of fuel" and that his aircraft "had been thinned down from ninety-nine to seventy-eight planes." The distressing message was relayed immediately to Admiral Ghormley in Wellington. He radioed approval of Fletcher's decision without questioning what it might mean to the success or failure of Operation Watchtower.

Kelly Turner, overall commander of the invasion, knew the consequences. They were bleak at best. At worst, they had the awful potential of total disaster. Without air cover and the firepower from warships at the bottom of Iron Bottom Sound, he had no option but to order all unloaded transports to leave for safe waters.

General Vandegrift was summoned to Admiral Turner's flagship shortly after midnight. He knew only that a savage sea battle had been fought off Savo, but expected nothing startling to come from the conference that vitally concerned the Marines. The general was escorted to the admiral's quarters and sat in silence for a short time before being told the reason for the meeting.

"At 6:00 tomorrow morning," Turner said while wiping his steel-rimmed glasses, "all transports and cargo ships will depart the area, not to return until an undetermined date in the future." Vandegrift later said the news "was most alarming," and that he did all in his power to make his senior officer "realize the demoralizing effect the action would have on the 1st Marine Division."

All to no avail. By midmorning of August 10, not one ship

could be seen off Guadalcanal, only scummy streaks of oil and floating debris marking the catastrophic one-sided sea battle off Savo.

Marines ashore were all alone without one solitary warship to protect their flimsy beachhead or any air power to ward off enemy attacks from the skies or sea. It would be difficult to find a phrase more cheerful than "abandoned and deserted" to describe the situation of the troops and their officers. Their outlook was even grimmer because the vanished ships carried more than a third of the division's manpower, armament, and supplies.

"It was as if the Marines held Jones Beach and the rest of Long Island was dominated by the Japanese," wrote correspondent Hanson Baldwin of the *New York Times* after the Joint Chiefs of Staff in Washington made public the crisis that faced the men on Guadalcanal.

An anxious corporal from North Carolina had his say to Staff Sergeant George McMillan, a Marine combat correspondent:

"I know I had a feeling, and I think a lot of others felt the same way, that we'd never get off the damned island alive. Nobody said this out loud. I was afraid to say it for fear it'd come true." A captain told McMillan that "there was an awful lot of talk about Bataan."

Twenty-four-year-old McMillan was one of the first of an organization unique to the Marines. Official rosters listed them as United States Marine Corps Combat Correspondents and although they, in fact, were public relations personnel, their duties were specified and different than those of counterparts in the Army and Navy.

All were volunteers, but to be accepted required a proven record as a full-time working journalist. Most were in their mid-twenties, and they came largely from small-town or big-city daily newspapers, nationwide press services, magazines or radio-station newsrooms. Many were qualified to serve as officers, but, not interested in rank of commanding other men, had chosen instead to cover the war as enlisted Marines.

Like all Marines the CCs, as they became known and respected throughout the Corps, went through the physical and mental rigors of boot camp, but by order of the Commandant all were made buck sergeants when they finished recruit training, and were issued special pocket-size laminated credentials similar to those of civilian newsmen. They lived and trained with the regiments to which they were assigned and invariably landed in early waves of an invasion, carrying portable Smith-Corona typewriters and carbines, and often fighting as combat troops or serving as stretcher bearers when the situation became frantic.

By midafternoon of August 10, General Vandegrift had fixed the priorities for Guadalcanal's last-ditch defense. The first was to establish as strong a perimeter as possible to protect the beachhead and airstrip from a counterattack landing by the enemy or a massive assault from Japanese forces already on the island. Next the cluttered beaches would be cleared and the slim stockpiles of supplies dispersed and camouflaged as much as possible. With these missions accomplished, all the 1st Division could do was to wait and see what the Japanese did.

The enemy's reaction was not slow in coming. Nor was it feeble, short-lived, or ineffective. Scarcely a day or night passed during the next two months when the Marines were not under attack. They were hit from the sea, air, and ground, sometimes in heavy, simultaneous, and coordinated actions. Few troops in history, certainly no other American forces in World War II, underwent a pounding so intense and sustained without relief or surrender.

As if operating on the schedule of a commuter train, the Japanese regularly sent reinforcements and a bombardment fleet to Guadalcanal. It was commanded by Rear Admiral Raizo Tanaka, who knew how to use pitch-black moonless nights as cover. His fast cruisers and converted destroyer-transports came and went so often that the Marines called them the Tokyo Express.

Each intrusion followed a pattern. Troops and supplies would first be quietly unloaded on unguarded shores miles from the beachhead perimeter, and would disappear silently into the jungle. Then Tanaka's ships would speed unchallenged past the Marines' besieged toehold with all guns firing.

Henderson Field was always the prime target, but the random shelling had little effect except to leave new craters that were patched up the next day, always in the hopeful anticipation of the arrival of American air support.

Troops took shelter in sandbagged dugouts and slit trenches. Few were wounded, but the thundering roar of the Tokyo Express made sleep impossible, and this took its toll on the desolate, weary Marines. In time, upward of 30,000 enemy reinforcements were delivered using the hit-and-run scheme of crafty Admiral Tanaka.

A carrier-based Zero fighter known as Louie the Louse came by occasionally to drop small bombs and flares on the airstrip, the signal that another naval shelling was soon to follow. "Washing Machine Charlie" caused more sleepless nights, but less damage. The nickname came from the irregular sound of the unsynchronized twin engines of his big flying boat. He scattered bombs at intervals just to keep the Marines awake and to wear down their frayed nerves.

Japanese destroyers moved about Iron Bottom Sound as they pleased, shelling the shore whenever they desired. They were virtually as safe as if in home waters; heavy artillery and coastal defense guns were aboard the ships Admiral Turner had ordered from the scene.

Ammunition was in such short supply that Marines constantly wondered if they had enough to beat off a massed and sustained enemy assault. Canned C rations were considered a rare gourmet meal to be savored whenever available. For days at a time, the men were hungry, barely subsisting on captured rice, seaweed, and dried fish.

In 1989, a retired sergeant major in his mid-seventies with combat duty in three wars behind him said: "To this day, I can't stand the thought of Jap food, much less smell or eat it. Hell, I won't even eat Rice Crispies."

At home in the States, people knew few details of the awful state of affairs on Guadalcanal, and what official statements reported was extremely bleak. A front-page story in the *Washington Post* said: "News from the Solomons is far from hopeful . . . it is omnious. Our forces may be dislodged from the precarious foothold they obtained on Guadalcanal. . . ."

Navy Secretary Frank Knox was asked at a news conference if the Marines could hold. He answered with a noticeable tinge of suppressed doubt: "I certainly hope so. I don't want to make any predictions, but every man out there, ashore and afloat, will give a good account of himself." Knox knew the only Americans "afloat" then at Guadalcanal were on four motor torpedo boats with barely enough fuel to start engines.

The fate of the Marines on Guadalcanal had become one of deepest national anxiety. The mounting concern was that they might, at any moment, be driven into the sea from their 9-square-mile beachhead and slaughtered to a man. The tragic prospect of another crushing defeat by the Japanese caused sleepless nights among the Joint Chiefs of Staff and at the White House.

President Roosevelt, in a coast-to-coast broadcast "fireside chat" from the Oval Office, assured millions of listeners that reinforcements were on the way and would soon arrive to turn the tide. The statement was patently untrue at the time, but the Commander in Chief had given a direct order to the Joint Chiefs: "My anxiety about the Southwest Pacific is to make sure that every possible weapon gets into the area to hold Guadalcanal."

The directive brought immediate movement from Admiral Nimitz at his CinCPac headquarters. Increasingly distressed over Admiral Ghormley's often bewildering handling of Operation Watchtower, he ordered him relieved of command of all South Pacific naval operations.

Vice Admiral William F. "Bull" Halsey was named Ghormley's successor. The shrewd, combat-savvy sea dog was already a legend, a fighter who knew how to get things done even if the odds were with the enemy. On April 18, 1942, he had carried Lieutenant Colonel James H. Doolittle and sixteen Army Air Corps twin-engined B-25 Mitchell bombers aboard the carrier *Hornet* to within 500 miles of Japan to launch the first American air raid on Tokyo. Halsey's widely publicized boast that he would "ride Emperor Hirohito's white horse down the streets of Tokyo" added to his luster, especially among the hard-pressed Marines on Guadalcanal, who were elated at his appointment as ComSoPac.

One of the admiral's first actions after taking over from Ghormley, a lifelong friend since midshipman days together at the Naval Academy, was to confer with the 1st Marine Division commander on Guadalcanal. Flying from Noumea, New Caledonia, in an unescorted Army Air Corps B-17 bomber, he landed at Henderson Field with two aides.

The trio were met by Vandegrift. For the next few hours, they inspected the beachhead perimeter and its defenses, a thin shield the Marines had built with the meager resources at hand. The group stopped several times for Halsey to talk with troops who had been under almost constant enemy sea and air attack since D-Day. Most were gaunt from malnutrition, fatigue, and recurring bouts with malaria and jungle-rot infections. Their young faces looked like those of old, worn-out men.

That night Halsey and Vandegrift discussed the grim outlook

29

for more than an hour before turning in. Both had hardly dozed off when a fast-moving destroyer or cruiser from the Tokyo Express started lobbing shells into Henderson Field. The admiral found it impossible to sleep. The next morning, in his typically self-deprecating and candid manner, Halsey said his wakefulness was not because of the noise but of fear.

At the airstrip, he decorated several officers and men before boarding the B-17. There was a reassuring twinkle in his eyes as he bid farewell and good luck to the 1st Division commander. Halsey's visit, Vandegrift recalled afterward, "was like a wonderful breath of spring." He had "Bill Halsey's promise that help was on the way, and Bill Halsey was always a man of his word."

4

Clouds hung low over Iron Bottom Sound at daybreak of August 15. Using the overcast as cover, four new fast American destroyer-transports appeared just offshore from the beachhead. They were loaded with 55-gallon drums of aviation gasoline, pallets of bombs and machine-gun ammunition, and some seventy Marine aircraft mechanics and ground crewmen. All were swiftly off-loaded and reached the beach without incident.

Four days later, shortly after 10:00 in the morning, Marines heard the drone of planes rapidly approaching from the northeast. Some men reacted instinctively by taking cover in slit trenches or dugouts. But spotters in Henderson Field's control tower, a flimsy open shack atop 15-foot wooden stilts, instantly recognized the silhouettes and circled stars on the fuselages and wings of the aircraft. At thirty-second intervals, they landed on the airstrip after a half-hour flight from the "baby flattop" Long Island about 100 miles at sea.

Now Guadalcanal had some long-awaited, desperately needed air support: nineteen Grumman Wildcat fighters (Marine Squadron VMF-223) led by Captain John Smith, and Major Richard Mangrum's twelve Douglas Dauntless dive-bombers (Marine Squadron VMBS-232). None of the pilots had been in combat, but several became "aces" by shooting down at least five enemy planes before their tours of duty ended.

Brigadier General Roy S. Geiger, commander of all Marine air operations in the battle zone, flew in near sunset. His pilots and planes were quickly dubbed the Cactus Air Force, since Cactus was Guadalcanal's code name. At the lowest ebb, less than a dozen of its aircraft were operational, some lost in combat, more destroyed on the ground by enemy air and naval bombardment, and others worn out from dawn-to-dusk flying and scavenged for parts to keep other planes airworthy.

Replacements were slow in coming at first. There were Navy planes from carriers sunk or damaged by enemy action, and a few long-range Army Air Corps twin-engined P-38 fighters from the big U.S. base at Noumea, nearly 500 miles to the southeast. But in time, Geiger's Cactus Air Force had more than 150 Marine, Navy, and Air Corps planes and air crews flying missions from Henderson Field.

Their role in winning victory in the Solomon Islands was undeniably major; 426 Japanese aircraft were shot from the skies and ten transports sunk, taking an estimated 11,000 ground troop reinforcements with them to the depths of Iron Bottom Sound. American losses were 103 planes shot down or missing.

The United States was now gaining control of the skies above and around the island. This meant that Japanese ships and planes no longer could shell and bomb Henderson Field and the beachhead without expecting fast and heavy retaliation.

Still, Admiral Mikawa had no thought of letting Guadalcanal fall into American hands as the battle entered its second month. His fleet still held a tight steel fist around sea-lanes in the Southwest Pacific—so tight, in fact, that only a trickle of American reinforcements and supplies was slipping through it.

From Imperial General Headquarters at Rabaul, Mikawa ordered that "all action be immediately intensified to recapture the airfield and annihilate the obstreperous Yankee invaders on Guadalcanal." It was only a question of time, the admiral was certain, until the enemy would be crushed.

5

Lieutenant Colonel Merritt Edson was an "Old China Hand" who had spent many prewar years on garrison duty in Shanghai and Peking. He was known throughout the Marine Corps as Red Mike because of his bone-deep sunburn and close-cropped reddish hair. Edson was also something more to his junior officers and troops: the perfect role model of a Marine combat leader, tough, fearless, trusted, compassionate, and dedicated to their well-being.

Colonel Edson and his command, considered elite even by other Marine outfits, left their mark on Guadalcanal mainly because of Admiral Mikawa's orders to wipe out American forces on the island. All of Edson's men had been specially trained to operate behind enemy lines after landing in rubber boats from submarines or dropping in parachutes from low-flying planes.

On Guadalcanal, however, they did neither. Instead, during forty-eight hours beginning on the black, moonless night of September 12, Edson's Raiders were repeatedly hit by a superior force of Japanese landed by the Tokyo Express. Some historians have attributed the outcome of this savage man-on-man struggle as saving Henderson Field and keeping the beachhead from being overrun.

Major General Kiyotaki Kawaguchi, considered by Mikawa to be his best troop commander, personally led the attacking force, estimated at some 6,000 well-trained jungle fighters. The first assault was preceded by heavy naval shelling on a low ridge about 1,000 yards long and less than a mile south of the airstrip.

This was where Red Mike and his battalion had dug in for the night. When the bombardment lifted, their positions came under a withering fifteen-minute barrage of mortars and artillery. Parachute flares lit the area in an eerie, brilliant brightness as they floated to earth. Then the first surge of Kiyotaki's men hit the ridge.

The Japanese made no attempt at surprise or concealment. They clambered up the open grassy slope, screaming and firing bayoneted rifles as they charged out of the dense jungle below. In passable English, they shouted a string of invectives adding to the noise of the constant gunfire: "Banzai!" "Marines, you die!" "Blood for the Emperor!" "Fuck Babe Ruth!"

Red Mike's men answered with their own obscenities and a curtain of machine-gun fire. The line was breached at several points, but the breaks were quickly closed in hand-to-hand combat. Some outposts were temporarily cut off, and there was wholesale infiltration by small enemy units.

One group even penetrated to within 50 yards of General Vandegrift's division command post, which was dangerously far forward. They were wiped out in a fierce mêlée before any

32

serious damage could be done. For two crucial hours, Colonel Edson held his CP with less than 300 men.

Slowly and stubbornly, with heavy losses to the enemy, the Marines were pushed back. The first faint streaks of dawn found them on the last knoll of the ridge above Henderson Field. There they held. At daybreak, nearly 500 Japanese corpses littered the ridge and its slopes.

September 14 was a day of relative calm as Red Mike's weary battalion consolidated its position. Stretcher bearers took constant sniper fire as they retrieved dead and wounded buddies from the battleground. The enemy, as usual, made no attempt to rescue their wounded and bodies were left where they had fallen.

The struggle cranked up in full fury again shortly after 6:00 that evening. From the Japanese side, it was a virtual replay of the previous night—naval shelling followed by mortar and artillery fire—except for a dense smoke screen, supposedly to cloak the attack. The tactic was a total waste.

This time the Marines were waiting with more firepower. During the day, every available artillery piece on the island had been sited to lay down heavy supporting fire for Edson's men on the perimeter line. Some infiltrators managed to get through, but they were few and were slaughtered within minutes. Firefights erupted throughout the night, and there were numerous and intense small unit scrimmages. By 5:00 in the morning it was obvious that the ridge would remain in American hands.

The Japanese tried one last desperate attack at dawn. It ended in what can only be described as a massacre. Artillery slammed into the now battle-drained enemy troops, and planes from Henderson Field riddled them with repeated low-level strafing and bombing runs. Pilots radioed that a completely disorganized, everyone-for-himself retreat was building momentum as the remnants of General Kawaguchi's forces fled into the jungles.

All was quiet by midmorning. Colonel Edson and his Raiders and Paramarines had held the ridge. A precise number of Japanese killed outright was impossible to determine, but it was more than 1,500. Those who died of unattended wounds probably were double that number. American casualties totaled 361, 109 killed in action and the others wounded or missing—a heavy toll of some 20 percent.

Marines later came up with different names for the battlefield—Edson's Ridge, Bloody Ridge, Raiders' Ridge. There is no known record of what the Japanese called it, but Deathtrap Ridge would seem appropriate.

Other attempts to break the perimeter still were to come. As late as mid-October, the Japanese mounted a major offensive with fresh troops in what was destined to be their last chance to push the Americans from Guadalcanal. This time Lieutenant General Harubichi Hyakutake, another of Admiral Mikawa's battle-tested stalwarts, had managed to land an estimated 8,500 troops—via the Tokyo Express—at Kokumbona, about 15 miles west of the beachhead.

They smashed headlong into a reinforced battalion led by another legendary Marine, Lieutenant Colonel Lewis B. "Chesty" Puller. In a roaring, climactic two-day battle, more than 3,000 Japanese were slain. The rest vanished, a defeated mass of leaderless stragglers, certainly hundreds if not thousands wounded, into the jungles and mountains, never to be heard from again. Marine losses were sixty-three killed and 204 wounded or missing.

Thus was destroyed the lingering but by then impossible Japanese hope of ever wresting Guadalcanal from United States forces.

6

Dawn.

September 18, 1942.

Rear Admiral Kelly Turner slipped past a strong picket line of Japanese patrol vessels with a seven-ship convoy of transports escorted by new 30-knot destroyers fresh from Stateside shipyards. Their arrival through the mists shrouding Iron Bottom Sound was further evidence of the military turnaround in the Solomons that had begun with the arrival of the first planes of the Cactus Air Force.

Under sky cover from Henderson Field's constantly circling Wildcats and P-38 Lightnings, the ships disembarked the 1st Division's long-awaited 7th Regiment and direly needed tanks, heavy artillery, ammunition, and supplies. Until then just two of the Old Breed's three infantry regiments—the 1st and 5th Marines—had been the only combat troops ashore.

Almost daily from then on, fast destroyer transports came with more reinforcements: elements of the 2d Marine Division and advance echelons of soldiers from the Army's Americal and 25th Infantry Divisions. The crisis in shortages of ammunition, food rations, and other supplies—even blood plasma and other medical necessities—was rapidly becoming a thing of the past as cargo ships appeared and were off-loaded.

Sometimes the "Canal," as Marines called the island, was as much an enemy as the Japanese. Ninety miles long and 25 miles across at its widest point, it was a microcosm of a primeval era. It was a weird and mysterious combination of lush rain forests and heavy jungles, disease-infested and stinking malarial swamps, and steep, treacherous mountains.

No air stirred in the incredible terrain. Unrelieved humidity and heat were so high as to defy description to anyone who never felt their debilitating agony. Rot was everywhere in the stifling atmosphere where overhead growth was so thick that sunlight rarely penetrated it. Freshly killed human or animal flesh decomposed within hours, giving off nauseating odors for hundreds of feet.

In more than a few ways, Guadalcanal's landscape resembled what Americans faced two decades later in Vietnam. Troops hacked through steaming, putrid undergrowth to get at the enemy. They forded streams, some knee-deep and others chest-high with murky crocodile-infested waters. They struggled through occasional patches of open ground of tough kunai grass taller than a man's head.

The threat of death-dealing ambushes and land-mine booby traps was always a worry. The torture and murder of captured Marines was not only an acceptable practice of the Japanese, but one in which they seemed to take great delight. Decapitated American prisoners, with the rest of their bodies hacked to pieces in "bayonet practice," were not uncommon discoveries.

Forgotten, or unknown to most Americans today, are most of the odd sounding names where Guadalcanal's battles were fought. Tassafaronga. Kokumbona. Point Cruz. Longa Point. The Tenaru and Matanikau rivers. And there are countless other nameless places where men struggled and died in savage combat.

At one of these, in the black night of October 24, Gunnery Sergeant John Basilone, of Raritan, New Jersey, single-handedly wiped out more than a hundred Japanese who surrounded his outpost. He was the first Marine in World War II to receive the Medal of Honor, and in recognition of his heroism he could have been assigned to Stateside duty for the rest of the conflict, selling war bonds or recruiting young Marines.

After a few months at home, however, "Manila John" Basilone asked to be sent back to combat duty in the Pacific. On February 19, 1945, he was in the first wave of troops of the newly formed 5th Marine Division assaulting the black sandy beaches of Iwo Jima. He was killed at water's edge by a Japanese mortar, the only Medal of Honor recipient in history to die in battle *after* receiving the nation's highest decoration for valor.

The Guadalcanal campaign was all but over for the 1st Division by late November. The reason, bluntly stated in General Vandegrift's battle diary, was that it was "no longer capable of offensive operations." The Old Breed's tragic condition wasn't the result of battles lost or of men killed or wounded by the Japanese. Malnutrition, malaria, and other crippling jungle diseases had done what the enemy had failed to do.

On October 1, there had been 1,941 Marines so stricken that they were hospitalized or evacuated. The number had skyrocketed an additional 3,215 by the third week in November—a total of 5,156 men so seriously laid low by tropical maladies that they could no longer carry on the fight.

To Vandegrift the situation was reduced to the simple, basic question of how soon his men could safely turn over their hard-won beachhead to replacements and leave the island. The Marine commander realized, of course, that Guadalcanal's final conquest was far from over; it would be another three months of grueling struggle before the enemy was vanquished and the last shot fired.

The final push and mop-up operations would be the difficult assignment of Army Major General Alexander M. Patch and his newly designated XIV Army Corps, a force growing larger almost daily with the arrival of more troops and armor. By mid-December it consisted of the Army's 25th and 132d Infantry Divisions and the 2d and 8th Regiments of the 2d Marine Division.

At sea the United States paid an extremely heavy price to break the back of the enemy's South Pacific fleet. More than two dozen American warships were sunk in Iron Bottom Sound and the waters near it, carrying with them nearly 8,500 officers and men. Japanese losses were approximately the same in both ships and crew. But the United States had the resources to replace losses. The rapid pace of new construction enabled the Pacific Fleet to more than quadruple its pre–Pearl Harbor strength in less than twenty-four months.

Losses suffered by Emperor Hirohito's navy, however, were another matter: all but irreplaceable. Japanese naval power was reduced, during the time of Operation Watchtower, to a point from which it was never able to recover.

If the 1st Marine Division had not held the Guadalcanal beachhead in the desperate days after the invasion, history books would record a far different chapter in the chronicles of World War II. If the Leathernecks had been wiped out or driven from the island, the epic sea engagements most likely would not have been fought.

7

Shortly before noon on December 9, the first contingent of the 1st Division began to leave the island. It was one year and two days after the Japanese attack on Pearl Harbor and 123 days since the invasion began.

The men were, as they often sardonically called themselves, "raggedy-assed Marines." Their dirty, sweat-stained, smelly, ripped and torn dungarees were graphic evidence of long wear in a messy campaign. Historian Robert Leckie described the departure years later in *Strong Men Armed,* a masterful book about Marines in the South Pacific. He knew the subject first-hand; he had been through his share of combat as a very young 1st Division machine gunner.

"They could not march. They stumbled," Leckie wrote. "They were ragged, sick, emaciated. They had not the strength to climb the cargo nets from Higgins boats that carried them from shore. Sailors had to pull them over the gunwales, fish them out of the water where they had fallen—doing it gladly and with open tears. They were sticks of men and their sunken eyes stared wonderingly at the island they were leaving."

The 1st Division cemetery was about a mile from Henderson Field, near the rubble of a native village on Lunga Point where several sharp scrimmages and a major battle had been fought. Men who could muster the strength visited the burial ground before they boarded ship.

The graves of the 1,242 Marines killed in action or dead from wounds were then still crudely marked. Most of them had a cross atop which was the dead man's mess gear and his identification tag with an inscription scribbled on the mess kit of the fallen comrade:

> To One Swell Guy
> Our Buddy
> A Great Guy and a Fine Marine
> The Harder the Going, the More Cheerful He Was

There was some verse:

> And when he goes to Heaven
> To St. Peter he'll tell:
> Another Marine reporting, sir,
> I've served my time in hell.

An additional 2,655 men had been wounded and evacuated to rear-area hospitals for surgery and other treatment. Another 5,601 were listed on medical records as "unsuitable for duty until further notice." They were the ones ravaged by serious cases of malaria, dysentery, bleeding "jungle rot" ulcers, and other cruel diseases found only in the tropics. If these Marines had been included in the final tabulation of casualties, losses of most 1st Division combat units would have been close to total.

General Vandegrift had one final official duty to perform before boarding a Navy transport plane for the long flight to the division's new headquarters in Australia. On December 11, at a brief ceremony near where the last 1st Marine Division troops were embarking, he turned over the United States command on Guadalcanal and its adjacent islands to General Patch and his XIV Army Corps.

On February 9, 1943, forward units of the XIV Corps reached the last-stand area at Cape Esperance. The soldiers found only empty barges and abandoned weapons and supplies left behind by an estimated force of some 10,000 disorganized, exhausted, bewildered, thoroughly defeated Japanese. They had been evacuated at night during the previous week by undetected submarines and small boats, the only ones to escape alive or uncaptured of more than 40,000 enemy troops hurled into the battle.

Admiral Halsey received a short message that night from General Patch. It read: "Tokyo Express no longer has terminus on Guadalcanal."

Not only did victory in the Solomons give American home-front morale a wonderful boost, but it signaled the end of Japanese advances everywhere. From then on, there was an inexorable island-by-island fall-back toward Japan in a United States offensive that could not be stopped.

To the Old Breed, Guadalcanal had a special meaning.

They had proved they had every right to be recognized as the proud new generation of the Marine Corps that Captain Thomason had written about in France in World War I.

8

"Where do we go from here?"

That was the bedeviling question, above all others, in the groggy minds of every man in the 1st Marine Division as its transports left Guadalcanal in convoy, sailing almost due south.

All of them knew the ultimate answer.

They would invade another miserable island, and fight another battle to drive the Japanese from a "rock" no one at home had ever heard about before the landing. More buddies would fall in action, and each man knew he himself ran a good chance of being wounded, possibly killed.

There was no official Marine Corps rotation policy until more than two years after Guadalcanal. Even then a man would not be sent home until a "suitable replacement" arrived. And since there was no specific definition of a "suitable replacement," this was a roadblock—a "Catch-22"—that sometimes took months to overcome.

In a few instances, some replacements for the Solomons campaign did not set foot in the United States from the time they left for the South Pacific until after the conquest of Okinawa, the last ground action of the war.

If a Marine was wounded badly enough for evacuation to the mainland for treatment, he usually was given thirty days of home leave after being released from the hospital. Then most likely he would be shipped back to the Pacific for more combat duty.

When American fighting men liberated villages or towns or cities in Europe, they were joyously welcomed and enjoyed the classic rewards of conquering heroes. It was a sorry and different story in the South Pacific islands. There were no towns or cities, and the villages were nothing more than a few dirty huts or shacks in a clearing surrounded by jungles. The few natives neither knew nor cared what the war was about.

As the 1st Division sailed toward its destination, there was a constant, fervent hope among the men. "God forbid that we end up on a mean little backwater island in the boondocks a million miles from nowhere" was the prevalent prayer of all hands.

Those who had small field compasses knew the convoy was not returning to Wellington. After six days on a zigzag course to avoid prowling enemy submarines, the fleet of transports and its destroyer escorts dropped anchor in the busy harbor of Brisbane, Australia.

Why Brisbane? It was a mystery to most officers and men. Brisbane was General MacArthur's headquarters, and this area of the Pacific was strictly his, and the Army's, domain. The answer was simple. The 1st Marine Division was now to be a part of MacArthur's command.

At the time, "Dugout Doug," as MacArthur was irreverently called by enlisted Marines and many of their officers, was in dire need of manpower. He hardly had enough troops to hold the small American beachhead on New Guinea's northern coast. A make-do camp had been quickly thrown together to billet the Marines while they refitted and took on replacements. Then, as soon as possible, the 1st Division was to reinforce the soldiers on New Guinea.

Two of MacArthur's aides got a jolting awakening when they went to the harbor to see the Marines disembark. One of General Vandegrift's staff was with them. "The men," he later recalled, "were ragged, still dirty, thin, anemic, sallow and listless. About one out of every ten fell, tumbling limply down the steep steps on their backs, landing painfully on the dock. I turned to one of the Army colonels and said, perhaps more bitterly than I should have, 'Well, here are your defenders of Australia.' "

The 15-mile trip by truck to the new base on Brisbane's outskirts took more than an hour. "Don't call it a camp," was the dour comment of a Marine battalion commander. "Just say we were dispersed in a flat swamp."

General Vandegrift was among the first to arrive at the site. He was livid at what he saw and gravely concerned about the morale and well-being of his battered troops in such bleak surroundings. He unhesitatingly made his views known to his new commander at their first conference.

"Vandegrift protested violently to MacArthur that the division, in its present condition, would be more of a drain than a help to the general and his plans," an aide to the Marine general noted in an official report on the meeting.

What must be done, Vandegrift said, was to send the outfit somewhere in southern Australia where the weather was cool and facilities in place. There the men could rest, take on fresh replacements, refit with new equipment, and train for whatever MacArthur wanted done. It was more of a forceful demand than a polite request.

MacArthur agreed after some thirty minutes of discussion that the 1st Marine Division would go to Melbourne. Then, almost as an apology, he said that if he had known about the condition of Vandegrift's troops, he never would have asked for them in the first place. But when the division regained combat readiness he would have plenty of use for it in campaigns already being planned.

So far as MacArthur was concerned, the Old Breed definitely were now "his Marines."

9

January 8, 1943.

Melbourne, Australia.

A month before, to the day, the first contingent of the 1st Marine Division had gladly left the battle-scarred beaches of Guadalcanal. Now their transports were moving slowly up the buoy-marked channel of a large harbor bristling with ships of all types and sizes.

A sergeant with an obvious talent for putting into words what he saw then later wrote in his diary:

"Around us lay a city of wide streets, taxis, trolleys, gas stations, department stores, bars, soda fountains, hotels, streetlights, factories, row after row of semidetached houses and thousands of friendly people. Around the city lay suburbs geometrically arranged along asphalt roads lined with gum trees, modern-styled houses of brick and stucco with lush green lawns and carefully tended flower gardens. . . . All this was something like home."

Melbourne's people also were something like home folks, as

the Americans rapidly discovered. The afternoon the first troops docked, a front-page story in the *Melbourne Herald* saluted them as "the Saviors of Australia" who, by the victory at Guadalcanal, had kept their country from being invaded. Within days the Australians were "Aussies" to every Marine, and the Americans were "Yanks" to every Australian.

A long-retired seventy-three-year-old master gunnery sergeant still had vivid and happy memories of Melbourne more than four decades later. "It was," he said, "like a wild never-ending combination of Mardi Gras in New Orleans and New Year's Eve in Times Square."

It was common for Aussies to walk up to small groups of Yanks aimlessly walking the streets of the city and buy them meals and drinks. Total strangers were taken into homes as overnight or weekend guests. No introduction or recommendation was needed; the fact the guest wore a Marine uniform was enough.

Steak and eggs became the standard breakfast for Marines on liberty. The menu was customary for the Australians, but it was gourmet fare to their guests. Thus a Marine Corps tradition was born, not only for the 1st Division but for all other divisions as well. Henceforth, on D-Day for an invasion, the final breakfast aboard ship was steak and eggs, usually served at about 3:00 in the morning.

Romance was inevitable, especially for young Marines who were half a world from home. The engagement rate soared, and there were a number of marriages, which required the permission of an enlisted man's commanding officer.

It was not all fun and games. As the division regained its collective strength, discipline became more strict and combat training more strenuous and demanding in a dawn-to-dusk schedule. Replacements from the States arrived almost weekly. They were scattered among units where combat-wise veterans schooled them in the unforgiving business of killing or be killed.

"Any resemblance between the 1st Division and the rest of the Marine Corps is purely coincidental," a seasoned company captain commented wryly to a young second lieutenant platoon leader fresh from officer training school in the States. In the minds of the men of the 1st Division, they *were* the Marine Corps.

Their feeling of membership in an exclusive, unbeatable clan of warriors was born in the early gloom of abandonment and desperation on Guadalcanal. It blossomed with the experiences shared in Melbourne. The mixture of awful memories in the jungle and the joyful associations with the Aussies was the common bond of the Old Breed in all their training and combat to come.

10

Operation Cartwheel was the next campaign to involve the 1st Marine Division. The Leathernecks would be part of Alamo Force, the code designation given to Army Lieutenant General Walter Krueger's 125,000-man Sixth Army, which would consist of four untested U.S. Army infantry divisions and two Australian brigades of veteran jungle troops. General MacArthur, of course, would be in supreme command.

Operation Cartwheel had two purposes, both crucial to long-range strategy. The first was to destroy or neutralize Japanese naval, air, and land forces that still were being massed on New Guinea for an invasion of northern Australia. Once this was accomplished, MacArthur could feel safe in beginning his long-planned island-hopping thrust northward toward the Philippines.

The 1st Division would have a new commanding general in its Alamo Force assignment. In early March 1943, Lieutenant General Thomas Holcomb ordered Vandegrift to Marine headquarters in Washington, where the 1st Division commander was informed that President Roosevelt wanted to see him at the White House. After a few minutes of small talk, a beaming FDR asked Vandegrift to come around his gadget-filled mahogany desk, where he awarded the general the Medal of Honor, and read the accompanying citation.

The nation's highest decoration, it said, was "for outstanding and heroic accomplishments above and beyond the call of duty as commanding officer of the 1st Marine Division in operations against enemy Japanese forces in the Solomon Islands during the period August 7, 1942, to December 9, 1942. . . ." There was more good news from the Commander in Chief: Major General Alexander Archer Vandegrift would become, on January 1, 1944, Lieutenant General Alexander Archer Vandegrift and, on that date, would succeed Holcomb as Commandant of the United States Marine Corps.

Vandegrift returned to Melbourne in late March. He wrote in

his autobiography, *Once a Marine,* that by late June "the division now stood in excellent shape. . . . I held no qualms in turning this splendid outfit over to Bill Rupertus, who had been through so much with me." And so on July 1, Brigadier General William H. Rupertus, assistant division commander since the division left the States, became Vandegrift's successor. The promotion carried with it the two stars of a major general.

With the passing of command, Vandegrift awarded Rupertus the Navy Cross, the highest decoration the Marine Corps can bestow, for bravery and leadership on Tulagi during the Guadalcanal campaign. "General Rupertus personally conducted the operations, exposing himself frequently and fearlessly to enemy fire, and setting an outstanding example of calmness and courage," the citation said in part.

The decoration and the tribute that accompanied it were in sharp contrast to what the troops and subordinate officers—the men who did the fighting—thought Rupertus deserved for his role in the assault. A retired brigadier general who had commanded a battalion at the time said years later: "He just sat on his duff in a bunker and let others do the dirty work."

On August 19, the first contingent of Leathernecks sailed toward Goodenough Island and Oro Bay, some 2,000 miles to the north. Here in remote jungle boondocks, the men would put the finishing touches to training for their role in Operation Cartwheel. By late October, the last echelon had departed from Melbourne.

The Old Breed's glorious, never-to-be-forgotten Australian idyll was over.

The ultimate destination of the division was an open secret. It would invade Cape Gloucester on the western tip of enemy-held New Britain, an island nearly twice as long and wide as Guadalcanal. The landing beaches were at a point just over the horizon from New Guinea and its powerful and still growing Japanese bases, where massive naval, air, and ground forces were being marshaled.

Getting to the staging area was an ordeal. The men were packed like canned sardines on the only vessels available, old mass-produced 6-knot, civilian-manned merchant marine Liberty ships that the Marines called, with ample reason, "rust bucket tubs."

When they finally reached the new campsites, the Marines were quartered in musty, leaky, worn-out pyramidal tents. Chow was as expected—bad and skimpy. The dismal plight of the Leathernecks was more grating because they were in areas next to Army encampments. A hard-bitten corporal who had earned his two stripes on Guadalcanal summed up the bitterness of his fellow "Jarheads"—a term that was used by Marines to describe themselves but meant trouble when uttered by outsiders. Said he: "Them fuckin' Doggies had every fuckin' thing better."

The problem was solved by "moonlight requisitioning." Such clandestine foraging was considered by understanding officers an ancient legitimate right and tradition of the Corps to get needed rations, supplies, and at times even such things as jeeps. Within days, most of the men were living much better, with chow, tents, and various amenities pilfered from Army supply dumps and ships anchored offshore.

Nightly broadcasts from Radio Tokyo carried the official Japanese version of the latest news from the area. Reports of American troop movements and military plans were surprisingly accurate much of the time.

In mid-December, sultry-voiced Tokyo Rose began broadcasts in flawless English beamed to the Alamo Force. To gain and hold listeners, she used every GI slang expression and played the hit recordings of America's immensely popular swing bands—Glenn Miller, Benny Goodman, Artie Shaw, Tommy and Jimmy Dorsey. How they were obtained remains one of the war's mysteries.

The music was interspersed with "newscasts." One was of special interest to the men of the 1st Division.

"This gang of degenerates, cutthroats, and assorted jailbirds has been thrown out of Melbourne because of their misconduct and are now staging off northern New Guinea," Tokyo Rose said. "Sometime during the week between Christmas and New Year's, they will attempt to invade the Cape Gloucester area of New Britain." The voice became an audible, contemptuous, confident smirk: "I am pleased to add that our soldiers are fully prepared to repulse this insolent attempt. The jungles will run red with the blood of the butchers of Guadalcanal."

Developments confirmed her predictions of the time frame for D-Day. And Alamo Force intelligence officers estimated that some 80,000 Japanese ground troops were on New Britain. The defenders were commanded by Major General Hori Matsuda, about whom little was known or ever learned—except, as Marines later discovered, that he was shrewd enough to take care of himself.

11

Sundown.

December 24, 1943.

H-Hour was 7:30 the next morning.

It already was Christmas Day in the States. Some men reflected on the irony of going into battle as Christians back home celebrated the anniversary of the birth of the Prince of Peace.

The Navy's prelanding-bombardment began at 6:00. Shells by the hundreds hammered the shoreline from the nonstop firing of guns from six heavy cruisers and eight destroyers on station less than 2,500 yards offshore.

Airpower went to work when the shelling ceased. Flights of Army Air Corps long-range, four-engined B-24 Liberator bombers first unloaded 2,000 tons of explosives on the beaches and the jungles and rain forests inland. Then formations of Army twin-engined Havoc and Mitchell attack bombers swept low to smother the landing zones repeatedly with flashing nose cannon and heavy-caliber machine-gun fire.

There was no answering ack-ack from Japanese antiaircraft guns. Nor did enemy artillery or mortars slam down among the landing craft carrying the first waves of Marines to the smoke-shrouded beaches.

The 1st Marine Division had been blessed again with "landing luck." The assault was unopposed.

By 8:30, some 5,000 Marines were on Cape Gloucester with more than enough firepower to hold the 1,500-yard-long beachhead and establish a perimeter to defend and expand it. Shortly after noon, the point of the advance was nearly a mile inland. The push had taken the assaulting troops through a belly-deep swamp, but they had been harassed only by infrequent small-arms fire. Japanese defenses in the area were feeble, and most had been hastily abandoned.

The 1st Marine Division beachhead on Cape Gloucester was a functioning reality by midday. Casualties so far were less than twenty men—six killed and most others not seriously wounded.

Everything was going too well to last.

The battle flared to blazing intensity shortly before 2:00 when the 1st and 3d Battalions of the 1st Regiment moved westward through the perimeter. The objective of the 2,000-

man force was the cape's airstrip. As had been the case at Guadalcanal's Henderson Field, its capture—and subsequent use by Allied air power—was the dominating reason for the New Britain phase of Operation Cartwheel.

Less than fifteen minutes after the Marines plunged into the dense jungle, the two companies leading the advance were hit by concentrated enemy fire. It came without warning from a cleverly camouflaged, strongly manned, heavily fortified roadblock. Both company commanders, young Marine Corps Reserve captains who had joined the division at Melbourne, were killed immediately. Nearly fifty men were hit before the sources of the deadly crossfire were spotted.

An amtrac loaded with ammunition arrived unexpectedly when the mêlée was at its peak. The three-man crew volunteered to use it as a tank, and charged two large bunkers that were causing the most trouble. With machine guns clattering and motor roaring, the amtrac smashed into the dense undergrowth until it became wedged between two trees.

Japanese instantly surged out of the jungle, screaming and firing as they came. Some were mowed down by the stalled amtrac's guns, but at least a dozen others swarmed over the machine before they could be stopped. One of the Marine crewmen was shot between his eyes. Another was dragged over the side and rapidly clubbed and slashed to pieces.

Somehow the driver, Private Paul E. Hansen, dislodged the amtrac and backed it to cover. His twin brother Leslie, also a private, was the man atrociously slaughtered. When General Rupertus learned they were the sons of a widow who already had lost an older son in battle, he immediately ordered Paul Hansen back to the States by top-priority air transportation. Hansen carried his service record book on the long trip home. It contained a signed directive from the 1st Division commander that the youth must never again be assigned to combat duty.

A pair of Sherman tanks rumbled onto the scene just as the amtrac broke free. The combined firepower of their 75-millimeter cannon and twin .50-caliber machine guns quickly silenced the concrete bunkers. Marines with hand grenades and flamethrowers made sure there were no survivors. Ninety-three Japanese bodies were sprawled in and around the smoldering emplacements. Marine casualties were nineteen dead and sixty-five wounded.

Only scattered resistance was encountered for the rest of

the afternoon, and when the Marines dug in for the night, they were 200 yards beyond their assigned D-Day phase line. Clearly visible ahead in the twilight were the twisted skeletons of the airstrip's hangars and other buildings. Demolished Zero fighters and Betty bombers were scattered in piles of useless junk.

That night General Rupertus was given the count of first-day casualties: twenty-five killed and seventy-nine wounded. He was grateful for the low number of losses and very proud of the men. "They're the best in the Corps," an aide heard him say. The situation map showed that every unit had moved well beyond its assigned D-Day objectives. More than 12,500 men were ashore, nearly two thirds of the division's total strength, with enough tanks and artillery to push ahead.

Not only had "landing luck" again been with the Old Breed, but D-Day weather was on their side, clear, calm, and relatively cool. It was the last time Cape Gloucester was not hit almost daily with typhoon-force gales and ceaseless monsoon cloudbursts of bone-chilling rain that were to plague the campaign.

Radio Tokyo had its own version of developments. A midnight broadcast said that "the invasion has been repulsed and bloodthirsty Marines wiped out on the beach or driven screaming into the sea to drown without a trace."

Back in Australia, the front-page banner headline of the *Melbourne Herald* proudly proclaimed: "OUR MARINES INVADE NEW BRITAIN!" The accompanying story carried Denis Warner's byline. He had landed with the first wave and now considered himself a full-fledged, albeit unofficial, member of the Old Breed.

The first night was quiet, the stillness eerie. No wild charges of massed rifle-firing Japanese screaming "Banzai!" or their usual string of death threats and profane insults. No sustained chatter of enemy machine guns. No loud explosions of constantly falling mortar and artillery shells coming from the jungle.

On D-Day plus one, the attack jumped off at 8:00 in a 3,700-man assault. The 1st Regiment's 1st and 3d Battalions continued the push to seize the airstrip. The reinforced 3d Battalion of the 5th Regiment headed toward Hill 660, about 8 miles southeast of the beachhead.

Steep-sided, rocky, and covered with dense undergrowth, Hill 660 was a natural fortress honeycombed with well-hidden concrete emplacements of heavy artillery. Some fortified caves on the slopes, as Marines later discovered, were huge enough to hold a company of ground troops. In Japanese hands, the mountain was a double-pronged threat. It could be used to shell the beaches and was the base for a possible massive last-gasp counterattack to smash the Marines' perimeter.

Shortly after 10:00, the push toward the airstrip ran into a few bunkers guarding the coral-topped road where the Marines were slogging forward in single file. The sparsely manned positions were quickly overrun without a casualty to the attackers. The invasion, so far, had been a virtual walk-over. Total division casualties for the second day were seven dead and twenty-one wounded, mostly from random mortar fire hitting scattered positions along the perimeter.

Monsoon weather was now becoming a much greater obstacle than the Japanese. Rain cascaded in what seemed a solid wall, and the howling wind was so strong that men often had to bend into it to keep from falling into the boottop-deep gooey mud. Everyone was drenched to the skin, and most wouldn't be completely dry anytime during the rest of the campaign.

Trucks that tried to move from coral-topped roads quickly sank hub-deep into muck and mire until they were dug out by laboring infantrymen. Only amtracs and tanks could maneuver in the jungle, and their movements were often stopped by huge trees uprooted by the gale-force typhoon.

On the infrequent days when the air was calm and skies were clear, the blazing sun and oppressive humidity brought another brand of misery. Swarms of disease-carrying insects came out of hiding to attack the men. The jungles, rain forests, swamps, and hills were smothered in a steamy hell. In George McMillan's words, "This is why the men who fought at Cape Gloucester remember the place more for the awful weather and nightmare terrain than for the Japanese."

Despite the brutal monsoon elements and the jungle's primeval landscape, the Marines slogged ahead. By sunset of their third day ashore, the advance was where the division's battle plan had projected it to be on the fifth day of the invasion.

Perhaps, after all, the weather actually had helped the Marines by pinning down Japanese defenders in shelters; their commanders were reluctant to order attacks against stupid Americans whose brutish leaders pushed them relentlessly ahead under impossible conditions.

The next two days were virtual carbon copies of the battle

so far, but with an important exception. Shortly after 1:00 in the afternoon of December 29, elements at the point of the two 1st Regiment battalions advancing on the airfield were ambushed by a strong, well-entrenched enemy force. The Marines had just rounded a bend in the road when they were clobbered by massed machine-gun fire and blasts of 75-millimeter cannon shells. Everyone scrambled for cover, pinned down by the violence erupting from nearly a dozen partly hidden bunkers and pillboxes.

It was an uneven firefight for the next two hours. The struggle was one of the most bitter of the Cape Gloucester campaign. Its site later would be known as Hell's Point.

Armed only with M-1 Garand rifles, several BARs (Browning automatic rifles), hand grenades, half a dozen bazookas, and a few Thompson submachine guns, the Marines were outgunned and fighting for their lives. Despite the murderous crossfire, they held most of their ground. At times, however, the issue was so critical that the Marines were in grave danger of being forced to retreat or, even worse, being overrun and slaughtered.

Help came about 3:15. The heavy roar of powerful engines was first heard above the noise of battle, followed by the unmistakable clank-clank-clank of the steel treads of four Sherman tanks. Like a cavalry charge in a John Wayne movie, they came to the rescue of the hard-pressed infantry.

The battle was over in a frantic half hour. One by one, the enemy emplacements were silenced by point-blank cannon and machine-gun fire from the monster machines. Charging Marines finished the job, tossing hand grenades and satchel packs of TNT into the apertures of the smoking debris, which reeked with smells of burning flesh and coconut logs. Nearly 400 Japanese bodies were counted in the bunkers and pillboxes. American losses were 172 men, killed or wounded.

At nightfall, there were no other obstacles to the seizure of the airfield, and it was in Marine hands by 10:00 the next morning. The seizure that afternoon of Hill 660 by the 5th Regiment's 3d Battalion removed the last threat to the beachhead at a cost of 466 dead Japanese. Marine casualties in swarming 660 were thirty-one killed and eighty-seven wounded.

The outcome of Cape Gloucester's invasion was now certain. General Rupertus sent an uncoded radio dispatch on December 30, 1943. It was marked "Urgent" and directed to the personal attention of Lieutenant General Krueger at Sixth Army headquarters in Brisbane:

"1st Marine Division presents to you as an early New Year gift complete airdrome at Cape Gloucester. Situation well in hand due to fighting spirit of troops, the usual Marine luck, and the help of God."

Krueger passed the good news to General MacArthur. He quickly called in civilian correspondents and read them a special press communiqué. It was more eloquently worded than Rupertus's message. He described the Cape Gloucester victory as his own personal New Year's present to the nation and all the people back home in the States.

12

The Stars and Stripes now flew above Cape Gloucester. But the conquered area was less than 5 percent of New Britain, which stretched nearly 200 miles from tip to tip and was some 60 miles across at its widest point.

Brigadier General Lemuel Shepherd, the division's assistant commander, was given the task of leading the conquest of the rest of the island. The task was far from a simple "mopping-up operation."

Alamo Force intelligence officers estimated that General Matsuda still had at least 70,000 well-armed troops. Thousands were believed scattered in steep hills within 25 miles of Cape Gloucester, and thousands more were thought to be in the rain forests and jungles, the swamps and mountains, stretching eastward to New Britain's tip.

General Shepherd immediately sounded the bugle for a grueling, sometimes deadly, game of hare and hounds. Of a certainty, Matsuda was on the run. When, and if, he would stop and fight was the big question. Or had he given up the defense of New Britain as a lost cause? The answer came on January 25, 1944.

After a heated but brief scrimmage that annihilated some 200 lightly armed enemy troops about 50 miles east of the airfield, a company from the 5th Regiment's 1st Battalion was amazed to find the most elaborate bivouac area encountered during a month of fighting. The complex was completely abandoned: barracks, mess halls, and offices.

The centerpiece was a skillfully camouflaged, spacious,

comfortably furnished house on stilts. It had been General Matsuda's headquarters, where he had lived in a style unequaled by anything the Marines had ever seen in the boondocks.

Some troops found great amusement in stretching out on the enemy commander's majestic four-poster bed. Others laughingly lined up to relieve themselves in his magnificent flush toilet. Several men took special delight in sitting in a pink wicker chair behind the general's huge black lacquered teakwood desk and barking out a stream of make-believe orders.

The surrounding ground was a gold mine of information for intelligence officers. No effort had been made by the Japanese to burn anything from office files. Important documents were strewn pell-mell for yards. Some contained complete rosters of forces deployed everywhere on the islands. Maps were found that pinpointed the location of the outposts, and they were quickly put to use. All had strange names—Gilnit, Agulupella, Suicide Creek, Aisega, Cape Busching, Umboi, Garover, Iboki Plantation—that would become vague memories in later years to the Marines who conquered New Britain.

General Shepherd's men had little trouble in swiftly destroying garrisons not already overrun and annihilating most of the defenders. Japanese dead were estimated at more than 2,500, while Marine losses were 173 men killed or wounded.

But the most startling find was a document in the unlocked center drawer of Matsuda's desk. It contained chapter and verse of the general's hastily conceived plan to move his headquarters to the village of Karai-ai, approximately 50 miles due east of the airstrip. A company-strength force immediately set out for the site, and met no opposition on the speedy trek through the jungle.

When the Marines got to Karai-ai, they found nothing but a few supplies and several hundred desperately sick, wounded, and dead Japanese—and no sign of the general.

A seriously hurt captain mumbled bitterly that Matsuda had taken a barge and vanished, saving just himself at least temporarily. He was never again seen or heard of. The physically able remnants of the army he deserted had fled east into the hilly jungles and putrid swamps, where they most likely perished of disease or starvation.

Marine patrols in pursuit of the Japanese found them more to be pitied than hated or feared. Every mile was strewn with dead and dying troops. Some were soaked with sweat and quivered uncontrollably with malaria. Others were wracked with dysentery. Some smelled sickeningly of rotting fungus infections. Many had open wounds oozing with blood and pus. Wretched individuals too weak to move waited stoically for Marines to appear, then blew themselves to pieces with hand grenades without a scream of pain.

The ordeal had been just as bad for the Marines in some ways. For nearly six weeks they had faced the same brutal weather as the enemy. They had moved in the same dreadful terrain. They often had been ravenously hungry, without hot chow for days and days. They were drenched and bone-weary all the time, and feared the ceaseless threat of a sniper's bullet or the mad fury of a full-scale ambush.

Another peril in the rain forests was falling trees, some as tall as 150 feet. The bark appeared as sound as a giant California redwood but the insides were so rotted that they collapsed without warning or apparent cause, killing nearly fifty Marines during the campaign.

This was the Cape Gloucester that the Old Breed knew and hated. They had faced an uninterrupted chronology of misery, of minute-to-minute danger of being wounded or killed in combat, of mental stress and debilitating jungle disease that would be the lingering legacy of the struggle for another South Pacific "rock" that nobody wanted except in time of war.

Orders reached General Shepherd on April 14 that the Army's 41st Infantry Division had landed. It was there to finish what now could be legitimately called the "mop-up" of New Britain.

The 1st Marine Division's role in Operation Cartwheel was coming to a victorious end.

13

April 17, 1944.

Two hundred yards off Hell's Point near the northern end of Cape Gloucester's airfield lay the heavy cruiser U.S.S. *Nashville.* It was the largest ship seen since D-Day. For a change, the skies were cloudless and the weather was cool.

A gangway, its steps covered by a brilliant red carpet, was put in place. Davits swung out a glistening white barge and lowered it quickly into the calm waters of the Bismarck Sea. A blue pennant, emblazoned with four gold stars, flew from the stern of the gently bobbing craft.

An easily recognized person rapidly descended, followed by a six-man entourage of Army and Navy officers. General Douglas MacArthur had arrived to extend personal congratulations to "his Marines" for their New Britain triumph.

Only a few troops were on hand to witness the event. General Rupertus and top members of his staff made up most of the small group of greeters. General Shepherd was not among them—not an oversight, but another display of Rupertus's bewildering disdain of and rudeness to his assistant division commanders.

"MacArthur shook hands all around," a Marine lieutenant colonel recalled years later. "He was very affable and gave you the impression that he was very glad to see you again, although he'd never seen you before. The handshaking and the picture taking—the general brought a covey of civilian and Army photographers with him—didn't take fifteen minutes. The party then departed for the beach to reembark."

Two weeks later, at the same place where MacArthur had come ashore, the first contingent of the Old Breed dragged themselves aboard amtracs to board ships to leave New Britain. Their farewell was a torrential downpour driven by heavy winds. Except for the still-to-come liberation of the Philippines, the 1st Marine Division had conquered the largest Japanese-held landmass during the Pacific war.

"The importance of the campaign was much more far-reaching than most people, even top military strategists, realized at the time," historian Frank Hough wrote a decade later. "Removal of this potent threat to his flank enabled General MacArthur to begin his brilliant advance which was to roll unchecked to the Philippines, and eventually find him in Tokyo as the Supreme Commander of Allied occupation forces in Japan and the entire Pacific theater of operations."

The Cape Gloucester campaign cost the 1st Marine Division 311 killed and 1,036 wounded. The dreadful price was even greater, for literally thousands of Marines were stricken with jungle diseases that would bring on suffering for decades to come; for some, for the rest of their lives.

Back in Brisbane, General MacArthur released a communiqué to newsmen. It said that 10,000-plus Japanese had been killed on New Britain. The figure was twice the number that the Marines were able to count.

What happened to the rest of the 80,000 Japanese that Alamo Force intelligence officers estimated were on New Britain on D-Day? No one seemed to know or care. Perhaps a few hundred made their way to New Guinea. Thousands more, like General Matsuda, simply vanished without a trace.

The last elements of the 1st Marine Division sailed from Cape Gloucester on May 4. The next sounds of battle the Old Breed would hear would be from enemy guns at Peleliu.

THREE

Island Beyond Belief

GENERAL RUPERTUS WAS IN AUSTRALIA WHEN THE 1ST DIVIsion finally left Cape Gloucester. He had been invited by General MacArthur, in a handwritten note, to spend several days relaxing at Army headquarters in Brisbane. Without hinting of his plans in advance, MacArthur intended to turn on the charisma and do some fancy arm-twisting.

The Marine commander quickly found himself in an extremely uncomfortable situation. MacArthur soon made it clear that he wanted to keep Rupertus's division as the prime assault force of the Sixth Army in future invasions of enemy-held islands blocking the way to the Philippines.

Rupertus knew the scheme would ignite a big blast at Marine Corps headquarters in Washington. He was equally certain of an identical violent and negative reaction from Admiral Nimitz at Pearl Harbor. CinCPac had definite ideas of his own about the 1st Division's future role in Pacific operations.

One of the little-known and seemingly strange things about General MacArthur is that he genuinely liked and respected the Marines as fighting men. The feeling did not include the Corps as an organization, nor did it extend to most of its brass. His admiration was restricted mainly to lower grades of line officers and the valiant young troops they led in combat.

MacArthur's affection for front-line Leathernecks went back to the savage trench fighting in France during World War I. As a thirty-eight-year-old brigadier general, he was the youngest soldier in U.S. Army history to hold such high rank. In less than a year, he was wounded twice and received seven American and French decorations for bravery.

During this period the future five-star general first saw the élan, *esprit de corps,* and devotion to duty of the original Old

Breed. Despite his rank, MacArthur was in the lines and fought side by side with Marine infantrymen. An incident that occurred shortly after midnight of September 15, 1950, showed his regard for Marines had not diminished.

General MacArthur stood silently at one end of the bridge of U.S.S. *Mount McKinley,* his command ship for the dawn invasion of Inchon, Korea. Another person was in the shadows several feet away. He was a newsman for the Associated Press and had been a Marine Corps combat correspondent sergeant in World War II.

"Good morning, General," the AP man said. "I hope all goes well with the landing."

"I'm sure it will," MacArthur replied. "My Marines never have let me down and they won't now. That's why I chose the 1st Division to spearhead the assault." Then, in what seemed an afterthought, he continued:

"I like the Marines and always have. They're fine soldiers, the best in the world. Yes, I like and respect the Marines. I'm proud to lead them in battle, any place and at any time."

MacArthur was turning to walk away when he said: "Of course, our conversation was strictly confidential and off the record. If a word of it is printed, I'll catch seven kinds of hell from every man in the Army and from all their fathers and mothers, brothers and sisters, uncles and aunts, nieces and nephews, and everyone they know. And you, young man, will no longer or ever again be accredited to my command."

A faint indication of a smile accompanied the last sentence, but the AP reporter knew MacArthur meant every word he said.

As General Rupertus expected, MacArthur's idea shook the walls of USMC headquarters in Washington. Commandant Vandegrift, like Rupertus, was ensnarled in a big bind without authority to intervene. Admiral Nimitz was his boss in the chain of command, and consequently, whatever happened to the 1st Division was a dispute to be thrashed out between Nimitz in Pearl Harbor and MacArthur in Brisbane.

Resolving the power play was not easy. Before the issue was settled, the Joint Chiefs of Staff became involved, as did some top aides to President Roosevelt. Admiral Nimitz was livid to the point of losing his customary soft-spoken composure.

"He really blew his stack, cussing like an old sea dog," Captain Waldo Drake, Nimitz's public relations officer, told *News-*

week correspondent Bill Hipple months later in a then off-the-record conversation.

"The 1st Marine Division was part of the Marine Corps and the Marine Corps was part of the United States Navy and, by God, he was the Navy's top enchilada in the Pacific, and he wanted the 1st Division back under his command now that Cape Gloucester was over," Drake paraphrased Nimitz's explosive tirade.

"An exchange of heated messages between Pearl Harbor and Brisbane didn't help," Drake added. "They were blunt and weren't couched in the usual polite gobbledygook of such dispatches between top brass. Neither side would budge."

Nimitz finally settled the issue with a direct order approved by Admiral King, Chief of Naval Operations, and his fellow members of the Joint Chiefs of Staff in Washington. MacArthur was told to "release the 1st Marine Division to Naval Command as soon as practicable." The general knew the wordage meant: "Do it now!"

The 1st Marine Division began taking its orders again from higher echelons of the Marine Corps, which took theirs from Nimitz. So ended another flurry of the clashes between MacArthur and Nimitz that were to flare up until the end of the war.

What would have been the destination of the 1st Division if it had stayed with the Sixth Army? There is no way of knowing. It certainly wouldn't have been where the Marines were now bound.

The 1,347 Marines killed or wounded on New Britain were gratifyingly fewer than planners had anticipated before the invasion. This gave some solace to all hands, but there was the other side of the coin. The Old Breed, as a combat division, left Cape Gloucester in almost as bad shape as when they departed Guadalcanal.

They were an undernourished, disease-wracked shadow of a Marine fighting force. Hundreds and hundreds of men were sick with recurring malaria and dysentery; uncounted others had emaciated bodies and rotting arms, legs, feet, and festering armpits. Many were low in spirit, suffering from acute depression, speaking only in raspy voices through jaundiced and swollen lips.

Without doubt, it would be months before the 1st Division would be fit for another campaign.

Scuttlebutt, the Marines' word for rumor, dies hard. Hope springs eternal and feeds upon itself among troops. For several days, a mixture of the two kept alive the happy dream that the division was headed for Melbourne. It was steaming, instead, toward a fiendish nightmare.

When official announcement of the convoy's destination was made, high hearts and wonderful wishes hit rock bottom. "Now hear this!" a voice with the timbre of doomsday blared from loudspeakers of every ship. There was a short pause as the men stopped whatever they were doing to listen:

"All hands! Listen up! We will anchor tomorrow at the island of Pavuvu, where Marines will disembark! That is all!"

From the Old Breed, there was only stunned silence.

2

Pavuvu?

Not a solitary soul in the division, with the exception of the tight-lipped top brass, had ever heard of the place.

"One thing was for damned sure. Pavuvu was to hell and gone in the boondocks," was the dour comment of Private First Class Henry Jacobson of Winnebago, Minnesota. He was nineteen at the time, but still vividly recalled his sad reaction on his sixtieth birthday.

The first transports entered the placid waters of Macquitti Bay from the choppy Pacific shortly after daybreak. Most of the men hadn't waited for the clanging gong of reveille to jar them awake.

Many had spent most of the sleepless night on deck, and the shoreside rails of every ship had been jammed for hours by troops anxious to catch a first look at Pavuvu. Haughty sailors, with access to navigational charts, eagerly flaunted their superior knowledge to the ignorant, disliked "Jarheads."

Pavuvu, the detested "Swabbies" told the Marines, was the largest of the Russell Islands, a remote chain of tiny dots on the map, located some 60 nautical miles north by west from Guadalcanal.

From shipboard, the island appeared pleasantly picturesque in the gray half-light of the cloudy, rain-threatening tropical dawn. One of the men, Corporal Bill Lundigan, said it reminded him of an elaborate movie set of a tropical island. He was a promising young Hollywood actor when he joined the Marine Corps to be a combat cameraman. In postwar years, he became well known as William Lundigan, a much-in-demand leading man and occasional star in feature films and television.

Neat rows of coconut trees could be seen across the smooth turquoise water. A gentle surf lapped the white sands of beaches on both sides of the bay. Narrow piers jutted out from several copra-drying sheds. A plantation house sat high on stilts a few hundred yards behind a palm grove on the southwest shore.

A short distance beyond the beach was a totally different picture—a forbidding landscape of dense jungles and deep, stinking swamps that were impassable by men or machines.

Pavuvu was 10 miles long east to west and 6 miles across at its widest north-south point. But except for 600 acres of beaches and groves along Macquitti Bay's shoreline, its terrain was totally useless as a base camp to train troops for battle. Just a few hundred yards inland from the narrow perimeter, most of the island was a thin crust of earth that concealed bottomless sinkholes of quicksand. The ground cover was barely thick enough to hold the weight of one man at a time, much less that of a platoon or company or a single Sherman tank or artillery howitzer.

This was not the first time Marines had been on Pavuvu. The 2d Raider Battalion had been there for several weeks a year earlier. Strands of barbed wire still hung along the beaches, silent and rusty sentinels of unneeded defenses hastily placed to guard against a possible Japanese reaction.

The Raiders had probed the beaches and nearby plantation groves, and one six-man patrol managed to scale the 1,500-foot crest of a cone-shaped hill that was the island's highest elevation. From there, with a powerful artillery spotter telescope, they repeatedly scoured Pavuvu from end to end. No signs of Japanese troops were spotted anywhere, so the Marines left the island. They had found only some 200 bewildered natives who wondered what all the fuss was about.

Aging survivors of the Old Breed continue, to this day, to seek an answer to a decades-old nagging question: "Why the hell did we end up on Pavuvu?" Enlisted men who volunteered only for wartime duty and career officers who retired as generals still harbor deep feelings of bitterness and resentment about the time they spent there.

"We marched ashore in the rain and slipped and slid up a mud-slicked slope into a coconut grove, and there sat down to contemplate our misery," a former sergeant recalled when he was interviewed by a television newswoman in the late 1980s.

"This was our new home. Pavuvu was to be our rest area. Here we were to make ready for our next campaign. To us, it was just another fuckin' example of the 1st Division having to do everything the hard way." His instinctive use of one adjective became a bleep when the tape was broadcast.

Several explanations have surfaced through the years of why Pavuvu was selected as the 1st Division's base camp to prepare for the invasion of Peleliu. Some are from little-known official documents. Others reflect the savvy personal instincts and wisdom of salty career Marines from sergeants to generals.

Regardless of the reason, Pavuvu was nothing short of unmitigated agony and privation during most of four months the division was there. It was a terrible place and time that to many men would be as nightmarish a memory as the fighting at Guadalcanal and Cape Gloucester.

An authorized but little-circulated Marine Corps monograph is surprisingly candid about what obviously was the thinking of top USMC headquarters brass in basing the 1st Division on Pavuvu:

"The theory is held in some military quarters that good treatment only softens first-rate assault troops; that the rougher they get it when not in combat, the rougher they will be when they are in combat. Thus the belief prevailed that the ubiquitous discomfort and privation which fell their lot was the result of deliberate policy."

Gene Sledge later recounted the more earthy observations of a comrade he described as a "philosophical Old Salt of prewar service." As Sledge recalled the conversation, the wizened veteran said:

"If they get us mad enough, they figure we'll take it out on the Nips when we hit the next beach coming up. I saw it happen before Guadalcanal and Cape Gloucester. They don't pull this kind of crap on the rear-echelon boys. They want us to be mean, mad, and malicious. That's straight dope, I'm telling you. I've seen it happen every time before we go on a campaign."

Precisely how Pavuvu was selected is no mystery. The decision was made by Major General Roy Geiger. The aviator, who was the sparkplug leader of the Cactus Air Force during the Guadalcanal fighting, also knew his stuff about ground combat. He had been given a second star and promoted to command the III Marine Amphibious Corps, of which the 1st Division was now an integral and important unit in dire need of rest and rehabilitation.

Without question, Geiger acted too hastily on the basis of haphazardly gathered information. He and a team of III Corps staff officers scouted the island from a Catalina flying boat borrowed from the Navy on Guadalcanal. The reconnaissance party never got closer than several hundred feet over the shoreline. They saw only the pleasant beaches, the symmetrical rows of palm trees with fronds being stirred by a fresh breeze, and the apparent tidiness of 600 acres of groves around Macquitti Bay.

If the general and his aides had landed and walked a half mile beyond the shoreline plantation, they would have realized that the jungles and swamps made Pavuvu an impossible campsite. It is surprising, too, that Geiger or someone on his staff failed to consult intelligence officers of the 2d Raider Battalion. They could have reported that Pavuvu was useless for anything but growing copra.

Geiger's heart was in the right place, and he had a valid military reason for not basing the 1st Division on Guadalcanal. The island already was overcrowded. The 3d Marine Division, also part of the III Amphibious Corps, was there training for the invasion of Guam.

Thousands of soldiers, nearly a hundred permanent buildings stockpiled with supplies, acres of tanks and trucks, and a 1,500-bed hospital occupied almost every foot of the once precarious beachhead area. Henderson Field had the look of a busy Stateside airport. A Quonset-hut terminal had a blackboard listing arrival and departure schedules of transport planes. Heavy B-24 bombers and long-range P-38 fighters flew hundreds of sorties daily to strike enemy shipping and land targets, some as distant as New Guinea.

Geiger felt, too, that being on the Canal again could have a demoralizing impact on the men. He didn't want to rekindle the memories of lost buddies buried there, and of the hardship and misery of the fighting to conquer the island.

The general had no doubt that Pavuvu would be a better rest camp and training area for the 1st Division, a place where the men would have a welcome period of sorely needed recuperation and refitting before shaping up for the next campaign. He passed along this decision, and the reasoning behind it, to Colonel John T. Selden. Selden was General Rupertus's chief of staff. In a postwar letter to a retired fellow officer, he wrote:

"Geiger informed me the night I reported in from Cape Gloucester with the advance party that we were being sent to Pavuvu because it was an ideal training area, that we would be by ourselves and would not be required to furnish a regiment a day to Guadalcanal's Army Island Command as stevedore working parties. He went on to say the roads were in, the wells had been drilled, that a Seabee battalion was there to assist us in every way possible, that the dock had been completed, and most other difficulties on Pavuvu overcome."

The source of Geiger's misinformation was never disclosed. If the culprit was known, his identity remains a secret. The 1st Division found that nothing on Pavuvu bore any resemblance to what Selden was told.

Two plantation houses and the copra sheds were the only buildings on the island. They had not been used since their British overseers, employees of the giant English conglomerate Unilever, had abandoned them three years earlier. The planters left behind only befuddled native workers to face an expected Japanese invasion that never came.

Roads were nonexistent. Until Marine engineers widened narrow and muddy jungle paths and covered them with coral, it was a struggle to get from one place to another. Wells that were drilled came from the sweat of Marine labor. The erection of screened-in, canvas-topped mess halls and other buildings was delayed for several weeks. There were no construction materials on hand, not even nails. Even if the supplies were available, the men were too bone-tired to do the job. Their time, thoughts, and efforts were totally consumed in a constant personal battle to survive.

The promised Seabees? They were there, all right, not a full battalion or even a company, but about fifty men from a skeletonized unit more concerned with taking care of themselves than with helping the Marines. A spitting-mad Colonel Selden contacted Navy headquarters on Guadalcanal and was told that "someone misunderstood what the Seabees on Pavuvu are supposed to be doing, and besides they are due for early transfer Stateside."

There is a brave sequel to the sorry start of the Seabees' relations with the Old Breed on the island. Another outfit, the 33d Construction Battalion, joined the division before it sailed for the Palaus.

Nearly a hundred sailors from the 33d landed with Marines

63

in the early waves of D-Day. They volunteered as riflemen and stretcher bearers until their equipment was brought ashore. It was risky duty, to say the least, for men untrained to assault a beach under withering enemy fire.

3

Bivouac areas were under water or ankle-deep mud. Tents were army rejects salvaged from Guadalcanal, piled like useless junk on the beach. They leaked like sieves and stank sickeningly of mildew and rot caused by oppressive humidity. Billy Joe Jackson, a teenage private raised on a farm near Lineville, Iowa, said: "It reminded me of a smelly barnyard swamped with dung and cow piss."

Most canvas cots were rotten and beyond repair. Some enterprising troops strung jungle hammocks between palm trees and made the best of it. A man was lucky to scavenge enough lumber from a discarded packing case to improvise a deck to keep his personal gear out of the muck.

Food was worse than what came from a Bowery soup kitchen for the homeless. Chow lines were outdoors, with messmen serving from huge metal pots atop empty barrels heated by burning coconut logs. Heavy rain was an unwelcome mealtime event. Food was a sloppy mixture carried back to dripping tents and eaten without a hint of enthusiasm but to dull the unceasing pangs of hunger.

Fresh meat and vegetables were the luxuries of dreams long after mess halls were built. The regular diet was a monotonous repetition of powdered eggs, dehydrated potatoes, Spam, and canned C rations. Chow was washed down with weak and lukewarm ersatz coffee or tepid synthetic lemonade called "battery acid" by the Marines. Whatever remained of this insidious concoction was dumped on the concrete slab decks of galleys to clean and bleach them, with excellent results.

DuWayne A. Philo became a prominent San Marcos, California, attorney after the war. He was a nineteen-year-old private first class on Pavuvu. He wrote a friend in 1989, recalling unhappy memories.

"The chow was so bad," Philo said, "that the cooks one time made a mistake and put a can of gasoline in the soup. It caught fire and burned down the mess tent. But nobody seemed to give a damn."

Rations were so short during one four-day spell that most of the division's menu was oatmeal, oatmeal, and oatmeal, morning, noon, and night. When bakers occasionally had ingredients to make bread, it was with flour so infested with weevils that each slice had more of the pests than there are caraway seeds in a slice of rye.

"It's a good deal," a philosophical corporal from Arkansas reputedly observed. "Them weevils mean more meat in your diet." He voiced no complaint, according to his buddies, that the bread was so heavy that each slice broke in two of its own weight.

Small herds of skinny cattle roamed among the palm groves, abandoned by the British when they left the island. Marines had high hopes that a do-it-yourself slaughterhouse would add fresh meat regularly to their food supply. A call went out for ex-cowboys to round up the beef and for butchers to do their job.

The system was just swinging into high gear when it was abruptly stopped. Word of the project reached a representative of Unilever on Guadalcanal. He immediately protested to the Army Island Command that the herds belonged to the British business combine, demanding "just compensation" then and there. Pavuvu's "Operation Slaughterhouse" was ordered out of business.

Some ingenious Marines supplemented their bill of fare with tough but palatable alligator steaks. Bagging the man-eating reptiles could be done only at night when they left the swamps in search of food. When a few hunters lost their way in the darkness and scattered rifle fire ripped into bivouac areas, a "do it now" directive from division headquarters ended the scheme.

Fishing the lagoons was tried; anything to get more food to fill growling stomachs. Casting with bamboo poles and safety-pin hooks was fruitless. Hand grenades and small dynamite charges were used with resounding success. Several men were seriously injured by coral fragments from the explosions. Stern orders came immediately from the top: "Terminate this dangerous practice at once!"

Shaving, bathing, and washing clothes?

All added to the burden of life on Pavuvu while wells were drilled, a job that took nearly six weeks to finish. Until then men bathed by dashing naked into rain showers, soaping madly, and hoping the downpour would last long enough for them to rinse. Water for shaving was caught in helmets.

The problem of laundering dungarees and skivvies was solved in different ways. Most men did it by hand in rainwater collected in helmets. A few enterprising ones strung their clothes on a rope and tossed them into the bay to soak. Some units found enough scrap lumber for communal washing tables, and scrubbed their garments in hot water from a cut-in-half oil drum heated by blazing palm fronds.

"There was one good thing about doing laundry on Pavuvu," an aging member of the Old Breed recalled at a 1988 reunion of Peleliu survivors. "You hardly got clothes on a line before they were bleached dry by the tropic sun. But you had to be damned fast and collect your wash. Otherwise it would be soaked again by more rain."

4

Tons of coral. Piles and piles of rotten coconuts. Thousands and thousands of land crabs. Vast armies of huge rats. Pavuvu had more than its share of these, much, much more than was needed or desired.

The coral was made useful with the help of dynamite, steam shovels, bulldozers, road scrappers, and trucks—and thousands of hours of back-breaking toil by sweat-drenched Marines.

The division's battalion of engineers dug deep quarries with explosives and heavy earth-moving equipment, then removed giant chunks of coral. Troops, stripped to the waist, broke them with sledgehammers into gravel-size rocks. Long lines of other men formed human conveyor lines. In the manner of slaving Chinese coolies, they passed buckets and helmets full of usable coral from man to man to load trucks. The work went on from early morning until dusk regardless of weather, burning sun or chilling rain.

From this hardened, determined work force came most of the basic raw material needed to convert Pavuvu's long-neglected shoreline plantation land into a small but functioning Marine Corps training base. The coral was the surface of a network of roads rolled out to connect bivouac areas with division headquarters, and to provide dry parks for amtrac

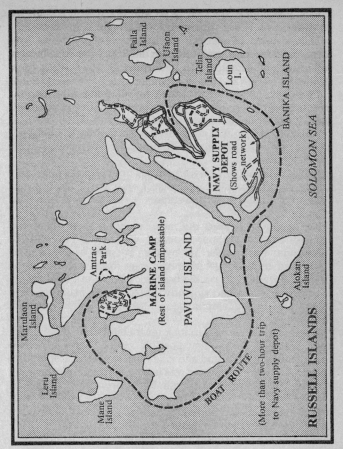

PAVUVU AND BANIKA

landing craft, artillery, trucks, and jeeps. In time, company streets and tent decks were covered with coral.

The coconuts?

This is a different story, not one of brutally hard labor, but one more onerous and vile. Every morning hundreds of men were detailed to gather up thousands of rotten shells that had been blown from trees during the wind- and rainstorms of the previous night. It was an obnoxious chore that had its hazards.

67

Falling coconuts frequently konked unsuspecting Marines on their heads. Few troops were injured, but the bristly objects usually cracked like an egg when they were picked up. The men were drenched in the sickening stench of rancid milk from the brittle shells, a smell so overpowering that many people vomited.

"We could even taste it in the drinking water, and you had to scrub like hell to get the awful smell from our clothes and body," one of the harvesters said in the late 1980s. "I'm still repulsed by the sight of coconuts in the supermarket, and I get sick to my stomach when I think about the smell of their damned milk."

Picture something with a blue-black body the size of a man's hand, an indescribably ugly object with sharp bristles and spines covering 6-inch-long spindly legs. That is what a land crab looks like.

No one ever figured out how many of them inhabited Pavuvu, but the number probably was in the hundreds of thousands. The hordes hid by day, roamed everywhere at night, and took refuge wherever they found themselves at dawn. Before putting on his boondock boots in the morning, everyone on the island violently shook them to make sure one of the slumbering vermin hadn't taken up temporary residence.

A pre-chow ritual was to look for the filthy creatures under cots, seabags, boxes—any possible hiding place in a tent. Some usually were found and killed before they scampered to safety. Any weapon at hand was used—bayonets, entrenching tools, K-bar combat knives, rifle butts, broomsticks, slabs of lumber. When the frenzied action was over, the stinking mess was shoveled up and buried. Otherwise a nauseating cloud of overpowering stench enveloped the area for hours.

Meandering battalions of land crabs were troublesome problems to jeep drivers, especially during twice-monthly mating rituals of the varmints. Massed thousands covered stretches of roads and were flattened under the vehicles' wheels, creating a gooey mess that was as difficult to navigate as a deep mudhole.

"Don't forget the rats!"

The admonition comes from Dr. Eugene B. Sledge, a professor of biology at Alabama's University of Montevallo, during one of many helpful talks about the 1st Division while this book was being written.

Sledge was a twenty-one-year-old private first class when he joined the division on Pavuvu, and was quickly nicknamed Sledgehammer by his comrades. The name has stuck with him through the years, not only with old buddies, but newer friends and countless students. His book *With the Old Breed* is a widely acclaimed personal memoir of experiences and recollections of the "rest camp" on Pavuvu and the bitter battles for Peleliu and Okinawa.

Forget the rats? Impossible!

Some of the evil-looking, long-toothed, snarling rodents were 2 feet long from fiendishly pointed snoot to whiplike tail. They were an indefatigable foe in an endless struggle of fury and frustration waged mainly at night. No one was ever sure where they spent daylight hours, but men speculated that the culprits had permanent nests in coconut trees.

Come dusk and they were on the move, marching as armies in tight formation on the tops of tents, their feet rat-tat-tat-tatting like drumbeats on the taut canvas. They would then slide down the ropes and charge through the tents, screeching loud and belligerent battle cries as they went in a determined search for food.

Members of the division's medical detachment came up with what they believed was a smart idea to decimate the enemy. One evening at twilight they smeared the foot of several trees with cyanide. The poison did its job. So many dead rats were around the trunks the next morning that working parties spent hours disposing of the putrid remains. Doctors shortly put a stop to the mass executions; the dead rats were too much trouble to clean up.

A squad of demolitions men tried a different approach. They made booby traps with dynamite percussion caps placed in boxes filled with moldy bread, and set them in several spots in a palm grove not far from their tents. The sappers didn't wait around to see what happened, but they knew when a rat took the bait.

"It made a satisfying explosion," one of the men said, "but getting rid of the bastards one at a time didn't make much sense. There were just too damned many of 'em, and we gave up the idea as a fuckin' waste of time."

A resourceful company commander and several willing troops with flamethrowers carried out a midnight expedition they hoped would produce results. "We killed upward of 400 on that foray," the captain reported. "But the next night I saw we hadn't even dented Pavuvu's rat population. I got discouraged and forgot about the scheme."

Despite their herculean, often wildly imaginative efforts to reduce Pavuvu's rat and crab population, the Old Breed finally admitted defeat. It was the only battle they ever lost, anywhere or anytime. But when the 1st Division left for Peleliu, the island probably was the home of more of the obnoxious pests than when the Marines arrived. The prodigious birth rate of the hardy tropical creatures was just too much to keep ahead of.

5

For weeks, Pavuvu's bivouac areas had the nighttime look of a Civil War encampment. Dim and flickering fingers of light came from primitive lamps in open tents. Dim shadows of men could be seen, aimlessly pacing muddy company streets. An occasional small campfire of palm fronds gave off dense smoke to ward away swarms of mosquitoes and other winged, stinging pests.

There was no place for off-duty troops to go, little or nothing to do to escape pangs of hunger, depression, boredom, and the deep weariness of day-long hard, furnace-hot heavy labor digging or breaking up coral. An official Marine Corps publication states with remarkable frankness: "The incidence of sickness shot upward, while morale plummeted to the lowest point it ever reached during the Pacific service of this elite outfit."

At first not even division headquarters had electricity. Most troop tents never did. Salty sergeants from World War I recalled something learned in France; they resurrected a way to provide feeble illumination, and passed their know-how along to the younger generation. Bottles and cans were half filled with sand and saturated with gasoline scrounged from fuel dumps. Pieces of tent rope were used for wicks.

Some men read and answered letters from home in the dismal half-light. Most of them stretched out on their cots, talking until taps. There was little else to do except chase rats, wish for a wholesome meal, and hope downpours of rain wouldn't come so heavy and so often.

Morning sick call for weeks looked like strange nudist camps in coconut groves. In bivouac areas across the island, there were bizarre scenes of hundreds of naked Marines having their buttocks painted with pink Merthiolate to ease painful ringworm infections. Other emaciated troops, sick with jungle rot in their armpits and on ankles and feet and hands, were given what treatment was available by overburdened corpsmen and doctors.

Marines painted themselves if they could reach their sores. Where buttocks were infected, men paired off and daubed each other. Some troops wore crude sandals to walk; their feet were so swollen that they could not wear boots. Many others were so seriously ill that they had been evacuated to the fully equipped naval hospital on Banika Island, less than 20 miles away.

The 1st Division was ravaged by another serious epidemic on Pavuvu: widespread and uncontrolled cases of severe mental illness. Doctors had different medical terms to describe the situation. Not so the Marines. To them, it was a galloping case of hundreds, even thousands, of comrades being "rock-happy" or "Asiatic." The terms were interchangeable descriptions of men whose oddball actions and flights of fancy would, in civilian life, most likely be considered unmistakable symptoms of insanity.

The miracle of the first months on Pavuvu was that so many people could function at all. Very few could pass even a cursory physical or mental examination, much less one as rigid as that required of hardy youngsters volunteering for Marine Corps duty. It is reasonable to state that no other division in the nation's World War II armed forces ever endured such a period of misery and privation knowing that it would soon face the enemy in another battle where casualties could be heavy.

Pavuvu pushed many men over the edge. A private in the 5th Marines, after an arduous and stinking day harvesting coconuts, darted from his tent and began to pound a palm tree with all the fury he could muster.

"I hate you, goddammit, I hate you!" the youth sobbed in uncontrolled anger. A non-jocular rejoinder came from a nearby tent: "Hit the fuckin' thing once for me!" The next morning two military police appeared with a straitjacket. They loaded the trussed-up, motionless, confused private into their jeep and drove away.

MPs grabbed another rock-happy youngster who had climbed undetected into one of the division's small artillery spotter planes. "Where do you think you're goin'?" the would-be pilot was asked when he tried to start the engine.

"Home," he answered quietly. "I'm gettin' the hell outta this fuckin' place." He was sent to the psychiatric ward of the naval hospital on Banika Island. His buddies never saw him again.

A well-liked captain in his late twenties, who had been in battle for the first time on Cape Gloucester, killed himself. He had been called to active duty from a reserve unit in Los Angeles, and appeared to be making the best of the sorry situation on Pavuvu. Inwardly, he was silently fighting a losing struggle to cope with present and future problems: mounting depression, the strength-sapping effects of malaria, the constant pain of jungle rot, the burden of training his demoralized company for the next invasion.

"He lay in his bunk one day, and without saying a word, he took a .45 pistol and blew his brains out," his battalion commander said. "It's a goddam shame to die in such a way on this worthless island."

A fifty-year-old gunnery sergeant had been a private in the 5th Regiment during World War I. On Pavuvu he was in the same company, battalion, and regiment that he was with in France a quarter century earlier.

A clean rifle was, and still is, an absolute order for all Marine infantry troops. The old gunny more than complied; he cleaned his weapon three times a day—before morning muster, at noon chow, and after his company was dismissed from duty.

He talked incessantly to himself, grinned frequently, and took slow drags on a cigarette until it was a half-inch nub. After the meticulous cleaning was finished, he reassembled the M-1, fixed bayonet, and went through several minutes of violent drill in thin air: thrust, parry, butt stroke. Then he lit up again, still chatting and smiling in his own private world.

"I felt that he was not a man born of woman, but that God had issued him to the Marine Corps," Gene Sledge later wrote. "To say that he was 'Asiatic' would miss the point entirely. He provided us with a direct link to the 'Old Corps.' To us, he *was* the Old Breed. We admired him. We loved him."

No doubt some men faked mental illness to escape Pavuvu's torment by appearing to be so rock-happy they would be sent to the States for treatment. The deceptions seldom worked, no matter how imaginative or zany.

"Doctors in the psycho ward on Banika saw to that," a battalion medical officer said. "They were all specialists who knew their stuff, and could quickly diagnose a trumped-up case of the loonies from the real thing. Men who required help got it, but the phonies were soon back with their old outfits or reassigned to others."

"What the hell," another doctor said years later, "virtually all of us on the island were rock-happy to some extent. Just being on Pavuvu made you that way."

Some of the rock-happy never made it to Banika for treatment, although it was desperately needed. One was a teenage private whose buddies were unaware of his deep mental troubles.

The youth finished four hours walking a sentry post, plodding back and forth in ankle-deep mud with a 10-pound rifle over his right shoulder. Relieved of duty, he trudged into a leaky tent. Without even nodding to anyone, he put the weapon to his mouth and pulled the trigger.

When told of the tragedy, the company's first sergeant said sadly and with bitterness: "Now I gotta find the padre. They won't even let a guy outta here *that* way without gettin' a pass."

Marine Corps records contain no count of suicides on Pavuvu, but one document lists more than a dozen "accidental deaths" with no precise explanation of causes or circumstances.

6

Ten miles of land and a shallow 100-yard-wide channel separated the 1st Marine Division base camp on Pavuvu from the Navy's 4th Base Depot on Banika Island.

A one-way journey by sea from one installation to the other was a choppy two-hour commute for the daily mail boat, a Marine LCM landing craft. It was a fifteen-minute flight by VMO artillery spotter planes that were two-seater, high-wing, fabric-covered, unarmed, single-engine military versions of the Stinson Sentinel, popular among civilian sports pilots in the States. They were used by the 1st Division as courier planes to carry urgent messages or ferry officers on official business to Banika.

For some arcane reason, Marines usually called the planes Messercubs or Piperschmitts. The nicknames apparently were derived from German Messerschmitt fighters, and from Piper Cubs used extensively for primary flight training in the U.S. armed forces and as personal planes for citizens who flew for a hobby back home.

An overland trip was impossible. An impenetrable maze of

jungles, swamps, and low-lying but steep ridges began just beyond the plantation groves surrounding Macquitti Bay. Amphibious vehicles tried repeatedly to navigate the primeval landscape. They made some progress in crossing the stinking crocodile-infested swamps, but bogged down when their weight broke through the thin crust of earth that covered bottomless sinkholes. How the 2d Raider Battalion had been able to scout the island was a constant source of wonder.

Banika, to the men on Pavuvu, was as distant as another planet. It had everything Pavuvu didn't have. It was a cornucopia of creature comforts the Marines dreamed about. Eight miles long and 3 miles wide, the island was indeed a tropical paradise.

A Seabee outfit of nearly 2,000 officers and skilled construction workers had arrived there in early 1943 with all the equipment and supplies needed to build a massive, modern forward naval base. Banika was, according to a report from the Navy Bureau of Yards and Docks, "highly favorable for the projected facilities. Well-drained shore areas, deep water, protected harbors, and a lack of malaria made it a good location. The gently sloping terrain and well-drained coral subsoil facilitated construction."

The Seabees did their job. When the 1st Division landed on Pavuvu, the 4th Naval Base Depot was a bustling 67-acre operation with asphalt roads, coral-covered equipment parks, and nearly a hundred permanent buildings. Eight 40-by-100-foot steel arch-ribbed structures were stockpiled with cartons of canned food; two were refrigerated to keep meat and vegetables fresh.

Fifty Quonset huts were used by base personnel for barracks and mess halls. One double-decked Quonset had air-conditioned quarters for visiting brass. Four hospitals contained nearly 2,000 beds, operating rooms fully equipped for major surgery, and a dental laboratory.

Three outdoor movie amphitheaters nightly showed first-run films flown from the States. Several flavors of ice cream were available at Red Cross canteens. Cold beer, two bottles per man, was served three times weekly at the recreation hall for enlisted sailors. Officers' clubs poured hard liquor during Happy Hour each afternoon.

Post exchanges were treasure chests of luxuries that evoked memories of distant times and places to the Marines on Pavuvu. Shelves were jammed with candy, chewing gum, chewing tobacco, cigars, all brands of cigarettes, Zippo lighters, shaving lotion, mouthwash, toothpaste, handkerchiefs, socks, comic books, newspapers, magazines, even postcards of unspecified tropical islands and other souvenirs of the South Pacific.

More than a hundred women were stationed on Banika, Navy nurses and Red Cross workers whose quarters were behind high barbed-wire fences patrolled night and day by guards. Two armed sailor police escorted pairs in jeeps to and from duty.

Except for those requiring hospital treatment, very few field Marines ever set foot on the island. Those who did were on one-day assignments to pick up rations that the Navy reluctantly and infrequently doled out.

"I went to Banika a few times on working parties," Gene Sledge wrote a friend in 1989. "The Navy watched us like we were a bunch of convicts who would steal anything classified as food—which was true—and rape the nurses, which was not true. We felt stealing from the rear echelon was legitimate 'moonlight requisitioning' from people who lived and ate like civilians and griped about boredom."

An official document in the archives of the Marine Corps Historical Center contrasts food supplies on Pavuvu and Banika.

"Rations had been bad throughout the protracted Cape Gloucester operation, as is to be expected in an active combat area," the text reads. "At Pavuvu, the amply stocked 4th Base Depot on neighboring Banika was only ten or fifteen minutes away by cub plane, yet any change for the better was purely coincidental."

Brigadier General Oliver P. Smith, who became the 1st Division's assistant commander after the New Britain campaign, later described the Marines' plight on Pavuvu.

"The men were not in very good physical shape," he said in an interview. "Authority was granted to increase the ration 25 percent. It was assumed that fresh provision would be furnished from Banika. We built reefer boxes on the beach to receive these stores, but the reefer boxes were generally empty."

A retired three-star Marine general who had been a lieutenant colonel on Peleliu was told of Smith's statement in a 1989 conversation with several other veterans of the battle. His reaction was blunt: "In other words, the Navy brass didn't get the word, or they didn't gave a damn if the Marines starved. And don't forget the possibility that the order for additional rations might have been overruled by higher authority for some reason or another."

Was it the official policy of Marine Corps headquarters? Was it a deliberate means, as the China Hand gunnery sergeant said, "to make us mean, mad, and malicious for the next battle"? Most of the Old Breed thought then, and survivors believe today, that that was why they were on Pavuvu. If documented proof exists, one way or the other, its location is unknown.

Two members of Gene Sledge's outfit had a difference of opinion about the cruel situation. He remembers their views in these words:

"I think the Marine Corps has forgotten where Pavuvu is," one man said.

"I think God has forgotten where Pavuvu is," came a reply.

"God couldn't forget, because He made everything."

"Then I bet He wishes He could forget He made Pavuvu."

7

Bob Hope was one of the few people ever to venture to Pavuvu unless ordered to do so.

"I guess that's true," the eighty-seven-year-old entertainer quipped forty-five years later when reminded of the incident. "But I didn't want to be lonesome, so I *ordered* five other suckers to come along."

What actually happened is this:

Hope and a small troupe of his show business sidekicks were on a USO tour of South Pacific bases. Banika was one of the stops on the schedule. When Hope learned the 1st Marine Division was on a nearby island, he prodded Navy brass into letting him sandwich in a morning performance there before an afternoon show for 4th Base Depot people.

Hope and Company included Jerry Colonna, a comic whose trademark was bulging eyes, a long black handlebar mustache, and a screaming voice that sounded like a fire-alarm siren. Tony Romano, a quick-witted and talented guitarist, provided backup music. The entourage of volunteer vagabonds was rounded out by Frances Langford, a shapely well-known screen-star singer, and Patti Thomas, a sexy young red-haired and scantily clad dancer.

Despite Hope's well-deserved reputation as the favorite entertainer of millions of GIs everywhere, the singer and dancer were the unmistakable hits of the impromptu show. The magnificent duo not only were top-notch performers, but they were the first *American* women most of the men had laid eyes on for more than two years.

Getting to Pavuvu and landing on its make-do airstrip was itself an adventure for the troupe. The short flight from Banika was made in a V-formation of six of the 1st Division's Piperschmitts and Messercubs. It was a low-level bumpy trip through several minor rainsqualls.

The island had no airfield, only a makeshift runway that doubled as a road when the little artillery spotter planes were not landing or taking off. Then a loud siren let loose, and red lights flashed a bright blinking warning from the jeeps of MPs as they cordoned off all vehicular traffic.

"It was tricky getting in there," a Marine master sergeant pilot recalled. "You had to make a steep bank around a large grove of palms and then line up, come down, and hit the middle of the road. It had a high crown, and if you didn't hit it just right you'd ground-loop into the ditch."

For ninety minutes, thousands of Marines forgot their sorry plight on Pavuvu, laughing, cheering, whistling, applauding as loud as they could. The only ones who missed the show were on guard duty or sacked out, too sick with malaria or some other jungle malady to get up.

Early birds climbed trees, perching in fronds to get an unobstructed view. Most men were able to sit, in a shoulder-to-shoulder mass, under bright skies near Macquitti Bay. Division brass, officers with at least a major's rank, sat in canvas-back folding chairs down front and close to the well-built stage near the dock.

Here was a memorable slice of home to all hands. The Old Breed, from private to general, savored every moment of it and clamored for more. Whether the performance would have drawn even a mediocre response from a sophisticated Stateside audience is questionable, but it was a howling success that day on Pavuvu. A sample of the bantering that brought unrestrained, thundering paroxysms of laughter:

"How was the flight over from Banika?" Hope asked Colonna.

"Rough sledding!" was the answer.

Hope: "Tell me why?"

Colonna: "No snow!"

Frances Langford sang a medley of nostalgic ballads. Patti Thomas was a show-stopper with a sizzling dance routine backed by Tony Romano and four musicians from the division band.

Maestro Hope closed the performance. He sang "Thanks for the Memory," his theme for nearly a half century of entertaining millions of civilians at home and millions more American servicemen, in the States and overseas, during three wars. He and the USO troupe were back in the civilization of Banika an hour later.

Their impromptu appearance was almost the only thing Marines talked about for the next several days. A curious reaction came from one man reminiscing with a buddy in a chow line:

"Man, what a show! One of them every day and we could fight this damned war with a smile!"

"Yeah, but I wish I'd stayed in my sack, and never gone near it."

"You gone nuts? You rock-happy?"

"Oh, them girls! Until I seen 'em prancin' out there, I'd clean forgot there was such a thing as an *American* woman. Now I could swim home!"

8

Things were looking up by the end of July. First and foremost was the arrival, during the month, of 4,860 replacements. This meant that slightly more than half of the division's veterans with two years of overseas duty *might* be sent home.

"This was very cheering news to those actually returning to the States," a document in Marine Corps Historical Center archives says, adding a "Catch-22": "But it did little to raise the spirits of those left behind, many of them key specialists for whom *competent replacements might never be available.*"

The official report also contains a curious mixture of concern and optimism:

"The new men, fresh from the amenities of Stateside life, were poorly conditioned for the wretched life into which they had been so rudely pitched. Yet, despite all the discouragement and hardships, such was the spirit and resiliency of this veteran combat outfit, passed on by the old-timers to the infusion of new blood, that morale rebounded progressively as the prospect of going into action again became more imminent."

Slowly and determinedly, Pavuvu was day by day taking on the look of a *real* Marine base camp where men could train for another invasion. The Old Breed again was doing it the hard way. They claimed that distinction, along with the "landing luck" legacy, belonged exclusively to the 1st Marine Division and wouldn't be shared with any other outfit.

Seventy-two-year-old retired Master Sergeant Everett H. Shults of Lakeview, Oregon, recalled Pavuvu's transformation during an interview in 1990. He joined the Marine Corps in 1936 when he was eighteen and, in his words, "was damned good and hungry because I couldn't find a job during the Great Depression."

He was in combat on Guadalcanal and Cape Gloucester, and was the ranking noncommissioned officer of the 1st Platoon of L Company, 3rd Battalion, Fifth Marines on Pavuvu and Peleliu. "Working like hell, and making do with whatever the Marine Corps gave us, and whatever we begged, borrowed, or moonlight requisitioned from the navy depot on Banika, we managed the hard way to turn things around on Pavuvu," Shults said.

Rations arrived more often, not of the quality of the Navy's 4th Base Depot's daily fare, but in sufficient quantity to let skinny, hungry men regain some lost strength and pounds. The number of Marines hospitalized on Banika dropped to less than 200. Once it had been nearly 1,000.

Coral-topped roads girded the coconut grove bivouac areas. Trim rows of patched tents still leaked in places, but their decks were covered with plywood or coral. Company streets were no longer mudholes. Small rocks, neatly raked twice daily, replaced the muck and mire. Each battalion had its own screened mess hall. Movies were shown nightly on screens hung between palm trees. Marines could shower during limited hours as more and more wells were drilled. Corpsmen could now handle morning sick call without men daubing each other's hind ends.

Brief rain showers still blew across the islands almost every day, but the monsoon season was over. The battle against rats and land crabs continued, but the obnoxious chore of harvesting putrid old coconuts was over. The copra crop was all new and growing.

"Sometime around the end of July—the day or hour is impossible to fix—a strange and subtle change came over Pavuvu and its inhabitants," George McMillan wrote. "So quietly did it come that the men themselves hardly realized what was taking place."

What happened was a rekindling of spirit that came from within; a return of the supreme sardonic sureness of the Old Breed; the resurgence of the men's belief that, by God, the 1st Marine Division was an elite outfit of warriors, the best in the Marine Corps, and that it always would be when left to its own devices.

Sullen and silent men began to spout more profanity than usual and to joke about conditions, always a sure sign that morale was on the upturn. Everyone became more aware of how his dungarees looked and started to shave and shower more often. One man would find a broom and voluntarily sweep out the tent. Another would scrounge a packing crate and make a foot locker of it, and soon others would join the spic-and-span spree.

Basketball and volleyball courts appeared overnight. In off-duty hours, give-no-quarter competition—backed by substantial bets—broke out between squads, platoons, companies, and battalions.

The Old Breed had shared together the good life of Melbourne. They had conquered together the bad life of Guadalcanal and Cape Gloucester and Pavuvu. Now everyone felt he was a better man, a better Marine, because of it.

Robert Leckie was a witness to what happened. "The great thing is abroad again," he wrote. "The fighting spirt is unfurling like a banner on the winds of pride, and all that remains is to draw up the plan of battle."

FOUR

Battle Born in Confusion

ADMIRAL NIMITZ AND HIS HIGH COMMAND OF NAVY AND Marine officers often differed sharply on many issues when planning and mounting an amphibious assault against Japanese-held islands. They always were in solid agreement, however, that any seaborne invasion was the most complex and difficult of all military operations—and that casualties among the landing force could be extremely heavy.

The Palaus campaign was destined to be an epic example of all these diverse factors coming to a head in one savage battle, a struggle that would leave behind many controversial unanswered questions about the wisdom of a plethora of crucial command decisions made before and during the fighting. Major General William Henry Rupertus was and is at the vortex of much that happened.

The Washington, D.C., native received the bars of a second lieutenant on November 14, 1913, his twenty-fourth birthday. He spent the next three decades at duty stations that were customary for ambitious young Marine career officers: aboard warships or fighting the Germans in World War I, chasing revolutionary "bandits" in Central America in the 1920s, filling Stateside administrative and training billets, and serving overseas at American embassies and legations during the following years.

By mid-June of 1929, Rupertus was a China Hand major at the United States legation in Peking. Within weeks, his wife and young son and daughter were dead, victims of a scarlet fever epidemic that took thousands of lives in the city.

Lifelong Marine associates said that Bill Rupertus never fully recovered from the tragedy, that his personality changed from constant affability to the demeanor of a demanding introvert.

The rest of his thirty-one years in the Marine Corps would seem to verify their observation.

As the fifty-five-year-old commanding general of the 1st Marine Division, he had the reputation of being a strange, complex, moody man, difficult to know and even unlikable. He seldom smiled, usually kept his thoughts to himself, and was seemingly unconcerned over the fact that he had the respect, admiration, and affection of very few, if any, of his subordinate officers.

In the outspoken, earthy jargon of the men in the ranks, he was "Rupe the Dupe" or "Rupe the Stupe," and their opinion was shared if not voiced by the commanders of the division's platoons, companies, battalions—even, at times, by its regimental colonels and headquarters staff members.

No one questioned the general's dedication to the Marine Corps. Many officers, however, were confused and upset by his apparent unwillingness to recognize their combat accomplishments and those of the troops. Seldom did he voice a "well done" to anyone; even more rare were the occasions when he would write a formal letter of commendation or award a medal for bravery or outstanding performance of duty.

Nonetheless, Rupertus willingly accepted the Navy Cross, the second highest decoration for valor, personally awarded by General Vandegrift for what subordinates considered his highly questionable role in the capture of Tulagi in the Guadalcanal campaign. And he treasured the Army's Distinguished Service Medal he had received from General MacArthur "for outstanding performance of duty" at Cape Gloucester.

Now "Bill" Rupertus, as "Archie" Vandegrift always referred to him in conversations or correspondence, was about to lead the 1st Marine Division to Peleliu. The battle would mark the abrupt eclipse of his hope of becoming USMC Commandant, the capstone ambition of virtually all Marine generals young enough that the Corps' mandatory retirement age of sixty-five didn't concern them.

Most had known one another, and one another's wives and families, since days as shavetail lieutenants. This is not to say they all were cordial friends; some soundly detested one another. But because of its small size compared with the other branches of the armed forces, the Marine Corps was indeed a "family" and its officers had developed a strong "old buddy network" of mutual support in good times and bad.

It was an understandable consequence that there were few

secrets, personal or professional, among them. A majority of fellow generals, in fact, viewed Rupertus as Vandegrift's protégé and the odds-on choice to succeed him as the Marine Corps' next occupant of "the Head House." This was, and still is, the commonly used name of the Commandant's office suite on the second deck of USMC's unimposing command center on a hill adjacent to Arlington National Cemetery and overlooking Washington, across the Potomac River.

2

Warning signals were flying as plans for the Peleliu invasion took final shape at 1st Division headquarters on Pavuvu. They were quickly recognized by lower-echelon officers powerless to influence the planning because of the rigid military chain of command. Two things were at the heart of the troubling situation.

One was the increasing complexity of the Pacific war and the fast-moving events that made it necessary for Navy and Marine brass at CinCPac headquarters in Pearl Harbor to interweave as many as a half-dozen operations being planned at the same time.

The second and more vexatious obstacle was the absence of input from General Rupertus and his lack of knowledge about what was going on. The man who would command the 1st Division in the rapidly approaching campaign was 15,000 miles away in Washington. A crucial six weeks passed before he returned to Pavuvu, nearly a third of the time his troops endured the island's misery.

Why had Rupertus been ordered to Marine Corps headquarters?

Under most recognized practices of military doctrine, the commanding general of some 20,000 men about to mount a seaborne assault against a well-defended enemy beach was expected to be personally masterminding the training, strategy, and battle tactics of his outfit.

True, it wasn't unusual for a Marine division CO to spend a few days with superiors in Pearl Harbor, resolving last-minute problems just before an invasion. Nor was it out of the ordinary for a general to be granted a short Stateside rest *after* a hard-fought campaign. But there is no known case to match that of Rupertus.

Several different, confusing, and contradictory reasons have emerged to explain Rupertus's long absence from the Pacific war zone. General Vandegrift's memoirs cover the situation in a single paragraph:

"Bill Rupertus and his chief of staff [Colonel John T. Selden] flew to Washington . . . furnishing us with valuable firsthand information on the fighting [at Cape Gloucester] . . . and explained in detail a thorny personnel problem. . . . The extremely primitive and uncomfortable living conditions of his new rehabilitation camp on Pavuvu were not conducive to high morale and with his help we worked out a plan whereby 260 officers and 4,500 enlisted men [all overseas for more than twenty-four months] were rotated home." Vandegrift makes no mention of, or reason for, the general's lengthy stay in the States.

The official monograph on the Palaus campaign contains one sentence about the trip: "Major General William H. Rupertus, and Colonel John T. Selden, his chief of staff, obtained orders to proceed Stateside to place their needs [for replacements] before Headquarters Marine Corps, and hence were absent during the planning phases." Again, there is no reference to how long the division's top brass were gone.

A copy of Rupertus's travel orders was found after a time-consuming search in 1989. The radioed dispatch from Washington to Pavuvu is dated May 8, 1944, and carries a large RESTRICTED notation stamped above the message:

REQUEST MAJGEN W. H. RUPERTUS USMC 0852 BE DIRECTED PROCEED BY AIR WASHN DC X REPORT MARCORPS TEMPORARY DUTY COMPLETION WHICH DIRECTS RETURN BY AIR REGULAR STATION AND DUTIES X FOR AIR TRAVEL ABROAD CLASS TWO PRIORITY CERTIFIED X WHILE ABSENT FROM STATION IN AIR TRAVEL STATUS MAJGEN RUPERTUS WILL BE ALLOWED PER DIEM SEVEN DOLLARS IN LIEU SUBSISTENCE.

Documents in Marine Corps archives reveal that Rupertus and Selden reported to USMC headquarters on May 17 and, as Vandegrift wrote, conferred with him about the status of the 1st Division. The following day the Commandant directed Rupertus be issued the following order:

You are hereby assigned to temporary additional duty as President of an Advisory Board ordered to convene at this Headquarters at 1000 on 20 May, 1944, to recommend officers for temporary promotion to the grades of colonel and lieutenant colonel.

It was an unusual assignment for the commanding general of a division slated for a soon-to-come battle; some military experts and historians, considering the circumstances, even believe it unique.

A decorated combat Marine company commander, who was a young reserve officer called to active duty in early 1943, said that much later he heard disturbing reports that Rupertus's long sojourn in Washington also had another far different and serious aspect. The man was, by then, a nationally known author and editor who was acknowledged and respected by fellow journalists for the accuracy and objectivity of his reporting and writing.

"After V-J Day, I was in Washington and heard from several highly placed and reliable people that the general was ordered to Marine Corps headquarters to explain the alleged shortage of a huge amount of money from post exchange funds," he said. "But the war was over and Rupertus was dead. I decided nothing of a positive nature could be accomplished by pursuing the matter, so I dropped it."

In 1990, in an effort to determine, once and for all, the official explanation of Rupertus's lengthy sojourn in Washington, the author obtained open access to the general's personnel file detailing every official important event and order involving his Marine Corps career from second lieutenant to major general.

There is no hint of an investigation of financial or other irregularities involving the 1st Division's post exchanges while the unit was under Rupertus's command. Nor, for that matter, do the documents explain his long Stateside stay except with the seemingly unprecedented directive of the Commandant to chair the selection board for the promotion of senior officers while Rupertus's division was on the threshold of an invasion of a strongly defended Japanese-held island.

However, some senior officers aware of the close personal relationship between Vandegrift and Rupertus speculated later that the 1st Division commander's inordinately long absence from Pavuvu was because of the Commandant's untimely and indiscreet show of compassion for his old friend. Rupertus had remarried shortly before shipping out for the South Pacific and had an infant son he'd never seen.

General Rupertus and Colonel Selden returned to Pavuvu on June 21. They found that Brigadier General Smith, acting commander of the division during their absence, and the headquarters staff had already worked out a detailed plan for the invasion of Peleliu.

It called for the division's three infantry regiments to land abreast across five designated beaches along a 2-mile stretch of the island's western shore. The 7th Marines, less one battalion in reserve, would swarm and isolate the southern tip of the objective. The 5th Marines, hitting the center, had the mission of seizing the airstrip. The 1st Marines would assault the northern beaches and execute a leftward movement to attack the 6-mile axis of the island.

"We gave Rupertus a briefing on the plan and he approved it," General Smith said in a taped interview for the Marine Corps' Oral History Section. Smith was quiet and reserved, yet friendly and open-minded—the diametric opposite of the usually sullen Rupertus in dealing with people. During the postwar recording session, about his relationships with Rupertus, Smith indicated they were "at best aloof" and "sometimes confusing and strained." He continued:

"Rupertus told me when we got to Pavuvu, 'Now I am setting up this new command post up on the hill here. I've got sixteen mess attendants that have been sent for duty with the division. You can take your choice, and I suggest you set up a separate mess over in the plantation house.' I went over there, but I told the general: 'I think I should keep abreast of what's going on in the division, so you should let me take some junior members out of the division staff sections to live with me so I can keep abreast.'"

Rupertus agreed that Smith should have a staff made up of the division's younger, lower-ranking officers at his headquarters. There is an ironic twist to Rupertus's approval of Smith's suggestion: Development of the Peleliu invasion plan was almost entirely the work of the assistant division commander and his make-do staff.

When asked to elaborate on his pre-Peleliu duties after Rupertus returned from Washington, Smith responded:

"I went around, inspected the training, and periodically I'd come in and tell the general what I saw. . . . I was only a guest at Division Headquarters. . . . The only time I ever went over to the general's mess was when some VIP was there and he thought he ought to have me over, I guess."

Smith felt the cavalier treatment reflected not personal animosity but instead the general's unwavering attitude toward *all* subordinates. "Our relations weren't 'buddy-buddy,' but there was no bitterness or anything like that."

Bill Rupertus clearly had an intractable aversion to assistant division commanders. He had treated Major General Lem Shepherd in an identical manner when he held the same unenviable billet during the Cape Gloucester campaign.

"It was one helluva way to run either a railroad or a Marine division, especially one getting ready for an assault landing," said a retired brigadier general, a veteran of Peleliu and three other invasions, when he discussed the Palaus campaign in a 1989 interview.

A fascinating footnote: Both Smith and Shepherd retired as four-star generals. Smith had later commanded the 1st Division in Korea, and Shepherd had led the 6th Division on Okinawa and ended his career as Commandant of the Marine Corps.

3

So far as General Rupertus was concerned, the 1st Division had an assault landing plan for Peleliu that he was absolutely convinced would be successfully executed. He was enthusiastic enough about the outcome that he openly predicted the Palaus campaign would be over in less than a week.

The forecast was contained in personal notes to civilian news correspondents and several ranking Marine officers. The envelopes bore instructions that they weren't to be opened until the invasion armada was at sea.

"It will be a short operation, a hard-fought 'quickie' that will last four days, five days at the most, and may result in a considerable number of casualties. You can be sure, however, that the 1st Division will conquer Peleliu," the contents said.

Rupertus never revealed why he was so optimistic, but he was sorrowfully mistaken on all points except one. The Old Breed did, with help from Army troops, take Peleliu. But the furious battle lasted nearly six weeks for the Marines, and the "considerable number of casualties" reached a terrible total of more than 6,000 officers and men killed, wounded, or missing in action.

Having a well-conceived assault plan is a major part of what is necessary for the success of a massive amphibious operation. But countless other serious and perplexing problems must be solved before combat troops can storm an enemy-held beachhead. Many of these vital obstacles were not overcome until a few days before the 1st Division loaded ships for Peleliu. Some never were.

The major and crucial stumbling block was a monumental lack of coordination and communications between CinCPac headquarters at Pearl Harbor and the 1st Division staff on Pavuvu. Back in Hawaii, 3,990 nautical miles away, the admirals and generals and their staffs had to determine how much naval firepower—battleships, aircraft carriers, heavy and light cruisers, destroyers, rocket-launching craft—was needed to support the invasion and assure its success.

Pearl Harbor was also the logistics nerve center where Navy transportation staffs had the responsibility of seeing to it that literally hundreds of other noncombatant ships were at the right place at the right time—an armada of transports and cargo ships to carry troops, artillery, tanks, trucks, bulldozers, rations and drinking water, ammunition, and other equipment and supplies from Pavuvu to Peleliu.

CinCPac headquarters, too, was where schedules were made for Navy hospital ships to be offshore at dawn of D-Day with doctors, corpsmen, and nurses to treat the wounded. Arrangements also had to be made for prefabricated grave markers to be somewhere among the cargo along with blood plasma, pain-killing morphine, splints and bandages, and other medical supplies.

The latest intelligence reports, air and submarine reconnaissance photos, and combat maps of Peleliu were *supposed* to come from designated Navy sources at Pearl Harbor. All of this was vital to the division's commanders, but communications between Pavuvu and CinCPac's planners were an endless nightmare.

"It was almost like jungle tribes talking to each other with tom-toms," one of General Smith's aides said.

There was no high-powered radio link between the 1st Division and Hawaii. Urgent dispatches from Pavuvu were ferried to Banika by officer couriers in one of the small artillery-spotter planes, and sent from there by the Navy's long-range short-wave transmitters. Important messages from CinCPac to Pavuvu were received by reversing the same slow, inefficient procedure.

Photographs, maps, and documents were flown to Banika, but it was a two-day flight for transport planes from the naval air station on Oahu. By the time the material was ferried to Pavuvu, it usually was three days since it left CinCPac.

Some crucial last-minute intelligence from Pearl Harbor failed to reach 1st Division headquarters until after the troops had embarked for the assault. It all added up to a massive state of confusion about what was happening and who was doing what.

Another factor further compounded the situation. The invasion of the Marianas was going full-blast, a decisive battle designed to crack Japan's main line of defense in the Central Pacific.

Major General Geiger, who was Rupertus's immediate superior in the Palaus campaign, was there commanding the III Marine Amphibious Corps, whose troops were spearheading the bitter fight to seize Saipan, Tinian, and Guam. With him were Admiral Nimitz's three highest-ranking and most knowledgeable experts on amphibious warfare: Rear Admiral Raymond Spruance, Vice Admiral Kelly Turner, and Lieutenant General Holland M. "Howlin' Mad" Smith, the overall commander of Marine forces in the Pacific.

Subject to CinCPac's approval, they were the final tactical decision-makers on everything connected with the Peleliu assault. At the moment, they were totally involved in achieving victory in the Marianas. Until those islands were in American hands, it was impossible for them to give much more than passing attention to Operation Stalemate.

The result? More uncertainty and confusion about logistics and the amount of naval firepower and carrier-based air support for the Peleliu invasion. Without consulting with Nimitz's "Big Three," lower-echelon naval planners at Pearl Harbor hesitated to make firm commitments lest their judgment be proved wrong.

4

Another rankling and major concern to Marine commanders on Pavuvu was the designation of the 81st Army Division as part of the Palaus invasion force. The primary assignment of the Army was to seize Angaur, a small atoll 7 miles south of

Peleliu, and to reinforce the Marines when and if General Rupertus thought they were needed.

What most disturbed the Marines was that the 81st had never been in combat, although the division had been activated in June 1942 at Camp Rucker, Alabama. It trained there and elsewhere in the States for the next two years, involved in war games and maneuvers in Florida, Tennessee, Arizona, and California.

The first echelon of the 81st sailed for Hawaii from San Francisco on June 29, 1944. In mid-August, the division shipped out for Guadalcanal for amphibious landing exercises. It left for the Palaus on September 8.

The 81st was listed on War Department records as "Regular Army." Its "Wildcat" nickname—and shoulder-patch likeness of the snarling predator—were legacies of the division's active role in World War One. A substantial number of its troops were from the midwest and south.

The 81st's training had been rugged, extensive, and far from easy. But the fact remained: from the commanding general down through the men in the ranks, the outfit still hadn't been battle-tested.

There were no face-to-face meetings between officers of the 81st and their Marine counterparts on Pavuvu until three weeks before D-Day. How would the self-proclaimed Wildcats react when they came under enemy fire for the first time? The question worried the Leathernecks, who soon probably would be depending on their courage and support in battle.

The sessions, arranged to discuss Marine and Army roles in the invasion, were held in a climate of simmering suspicion and hostility, not only because the Marines questioned the 81st's leadership and its soldiers' combat know-how but because of the sorry state of bickering and interservice rivalry that usually existed, from generals to privates, between the Army and the Marine Corps.

5

The 1st Division still had more than a handful of big problems six weeks before H-Hour on Peleliu.

"Perhaps the best way to describe the situation is to quote the old adage 'The spirit was willing but the flesh was weak'" was the observation, made in 1989, of a retired brigadier general who had been a lieutenant colonel on Peleliu. "Morale of the troops was getting better every day, and the will to fight as an elite outfit was visibly returning," he said. "Living conditions and rations had reached a tolerable stage, and the camp had the tidy look of an honest-to-god Marine Corps boondocks base."

So what were the remaining problems? Pavuvu's shortage of land where troops could be trained topped the list; there was a total area less than that covered by many of today's shopping malls, and smaller than the parking lot of Dodger Stadium in Los Angeles. Shortages of equipment, especially tanks and amtracs, warned of extreme—possibly catastrophic—difficulties in landing the invasion force and supporting it in battle.

Enough new men had arrived to bring the division up to full battle strength of 19,000-plus officers and men. But a matter of highest concern was integrating the newcomers with combat-wise old-timers and seeing that the replacements learned as much as possible about killing the enemy and surviving to talk about it.

Roughly 80 percent of the nearly 5,000 youngsters were between eighteen and twenty-five. Some were draftees, but all had volunteered for Marine Corps duty. Most could think of nothing better than being with the 1st Division. Private First Class Gene Sledge later expressed his feelings, which matched those of a majority of his comrades. He wrote:

"If I had had an option—and there was none, of course—as to which of the five Marine divisions I served with, it would have been the 1st Marine Division. . . . Of regiments, I would have chosen the 5th Marines. . . . The fact that I was assigned to the very regiment and division I would have chosen was a matter of pure chance. I felt as though I had rolled the dice and won."

From beginning to end, training on Pavuvu was little short of pandemonium and frustration.

Company streets were the only areas where men could engage in mock attacks. It was routine to see one outfit charging full-tilt between rows of tents into other troops in formations standing at rigid attention for rifle inspection, or other units practicing close-order drill.

"This would have been fine if we were getting ready to fight Nips hiding in tents, but it was useless as hell as a training exercise if you were expected to blast the little bastards from caves or fortified bunkers," a battalion commander sadly observed.

A primitive rifle range was set up at the edge of one of the palm groves. It was largely ineffective in sharpening the marksmanship of troops. No conventional bull's-eye targets were available, so the men took potshots at coconuts lined up on sand bags.

Whenever tanks and infantry attempted joint maneuvers in the jungle, the lumbering Shermans rapidly bogged down in the quicksand. Artillery batteries fired at imaginary targets in the hills, but it was impossible to determine the accuracy of their shelling. Mortar and machine-gun crews were rusty from lack of activity. Flamethrower and demolition teams could only hold dry runs; there simply was no place for them to use their equipment without endangering other Marines.

General Smith made daily rounds of the camp, and—as Rupertus had directed when he returned from Washington—made his "occasional reports" to the division commander about what was happening. Smith was very pleased with the obviously improved morale of the troops, but remained deeply disturbed about their overall combat readiness and efficiency.

Rupertus, Smith later said, "never commented on the renewed spirit of the men, and seemed unconcerned about our training problems."

If there was any sound basis for General Rupertus's optimistic forecast of a quick victory on Peleliu, it was the battle record of the 1st Division's three infantry regiments—the 1st, 5th, and 7th Marines.

6

The 1st Division's infantry regiments were commanded by colonels. Lewis B. Puller led the 1st Marines, Harold D. Harris the 5th Marines, and Herman H. Hanneken the 7th Marines.

Two were swashbuckling Leathernecks who had enlisted as privates in the early 1920s and literally fought their way, step by step, up the ranks by dint of bravery and leadership under fire. The other was recognized by top Marine Corps brass, including Commandant Vandegrift, as a brilliant military planner and intelligence officer. Peleliu would be his first campaign as a regimental commander.

Colonel Puller, known for years even then as a legendary

Marine Corps character, was the snorting, cocky, barrel-chested, jut-jawed, raspy-voiced, pipe-smoking, bigger-than-life but bantam-size—5-foot-eight—personification of the Old Breed. He was at his best, truly in his element, in the heat of battle, a rip-roaring, totally fearless holy terror anytime and anywhere he met the enemy.

From boyhood in rural Virginia, where he was consumed by tales of ancestors who fought for the Confederacy in what he always called the "War Between the States," Puller spent his life in preparation for wars and fighting them. He was forty-six when he went to Peleliu and had been a Leatherneck for more than a quarter century.

He was "Lewie" to old comrades and friends, all of whom respected his outspoken aggressiveness and personal courage. But he also had his detractors, including more than a few high-ranking Marine Corps officers, who believed him too brash, flamboyant, and wasteful of his men. He had a passionate dislike for most Navy officers—especially the top brass. His disrespect was so deeply ingrained that he persisted in calling Admiral Nimitz "Ninmitz."

Most of Puller's men called him "Chesty"—but not to his face. Then he was Colonel Puller, a CO they were proud to serve.

Some others had mixed emotions, and he was simply "the Old Man" to them. A few saw him in an entirely different light and fervently wished they were in some other, any other, outfit, where they believed chances of survival were infinitely better. One man, a platoon sergeant on Peleliu, was asked his opinion of Puller at a postwar reunion of former 1st Division members. The answer: "He was a sonofabitchin' butcher and warmonger."

Puller's first taste of action came in the 1920s in Haiti and Nicaragua, where he survived more than a hundred small but spirited scrimmages with insurgent "bandits." The natives gave him the nickname El Tigre, and accused him of paying a bounty for the ears of captured revolutionaries.

He served under Rupertus as a rambunctious captain of the "Horse Marines" in Peking. In Shanghai, shortly before World War II, he stared down a well-armed force of Japanese and led his outnumbered troops in a bayonet charge that chased them from the grounds of the beleaguered International Settlement without a shot being fired.

Puller was a lieutenant colonel and battalion commander on

Guadalcanal, where his men had earned two Medals of Honor; five Navy Crosses, including Puller's third; eleven Silver Stars; twenty Bronze Stars; and 364 Purple Hearts. At Cape Gloucester he took personal command of two confused and stalled units and led them to quick victory.

A curious relationship existed between Rupertus and Puller. It probably began when they served together as Horse Marines and expert marksmen on the championship rifle team of China Hands that competed in Peking with military shooters from other nations posted to legation duty in the city's foreign compound.

Both were avid students of tactics and strategies of long-ago battles, and occasionally engaged in friendly chit-chat about these and other subjects—something Rupertus rarely did with other subordinates.

One evening the general stopped by the colonel's tent on Pavuvu for a quiet talk. As Rupertus was leaving, he turned and said to Puller:

"Lewie, you should make general on Peleliu. It's tailored for you. Your performance of duty should bring you another Navy Cross and a brigadier's star, too."

Puller took a big pull from his corncob pipe and smiled through the billow of smoke without uttering another word. He cherished the unspoken hope that the next campaign might also bring him the Medal of Honor, the nation's highest award for valor and the only one that he didn't already possess.

Colonel Hanneken, the stalwart, dedicated, dependable, nononsense commander of the 7th Marines, already possessed the Medal of Honor. His Marine Corps career closely paralleled Puller's in many ways, and his record of personal bravery was second to none, not even that of his old comrade-in-arms Lewie.

They parted company, however, when it came to flamboyance and other personality traits. Hanneken was stoic and something of a loner. At fifty-one, he was older than most regimental colonels.

To fellow ranking officers and old friends, he was "Herm" or "Hank." Subordinates had two nicknames for him: "HotHeaded" or "Hard-Headed" Hanneken. Both reflected his Germanic background and philosophy. He was a rigid disciplinarian, trained his men with a firm hand, did everything by the book, and his mind was locked once he made a decision on anything.

"He never smiled very much," his sergeant major once said. "I think if someone tickled him with a feather he still wouldn't smile. He had to be one of the toughest COs of all time, but he was greatly respected and didn't know the meaning of fear."

Like Puller, he was a mustang officer; he joined up in 1914 at a recruiting station in St. Louis, Missouri, his hometown. The twenty-one-year-old private missed World War I duty in France, as did most Marines of that era. He earned a sergeant's stripes within four years. It was a somewhat remarkable accomplishment because of the Marine Corps' snail pace in doling out promotions in those days.

Hanneken saw his first action in the jungles and hills of Haiti in 1919, fighting "rebel bandits" bent on overthrowing the American-backed government of the island. Its top officials were under the thumb of the vast banana-growing combine controlled by the Boston-based United Fruit Company.

Hanneken came out of the expedition with the bars of a second lieutenant and the Medal of Honor. He was awarded the coveted decoration for leading a two-man raid against the main base of the insurgents and slaying their leader, Charlemagne Peralte. On another behind-the-lines mission, this time alone, Hanneken used his jungle know-how to elude numerous patrols and kill Osiris Joseph, the insurgent native chieftain who succeeded Charlemagne. His single-handed foray effectively quelled the revolt, and he received the Navy Cross for the daring action.

Hanneken was the first regimental commander selected by General Vandegrift when the 1st Division was formed in 1941. He served on Guadalcanal, where he was awarded the Silver Star for "conspicious gallantry and intrepidity in action against the enemy." He led the 7th Marines during the Cape Gloucester campaign and received the Bronze Star for "outstanding bravery and leadership." Peleliu was the next stop for the craggy, combat-wise veteran and his regiment.

How the 5th Marines would perform in the upcoming invasion was a troubling question. There was no doubt about the capabilities of its battle-tested battalion commanders, their junior officers, and the men in the ranks. The reason for concern was the newly appointed commanding officer of the outfit, Colonel Harris. The disturbing situation was not of his making and was beyond his control.

Colonel William S. Fellers, a much-decorated and highly regarded officer, had been made CO of the 5th Marines after the

Cape Gloucester campaign. Less than a month before the division embarked for Peleliu, he was relieved and sent back to the States under what, at the time, were mysterious circumstances. His totally unexpected replacement was Harris.

It was later revealed that Fellers was plagued with ravaging attacks of malaria, seizures so severe that he was almost constantly laid low with shaking tension and virtually uncontrollable depression. On one occasion, according to Lieutenant Colonel Lewis W. Walt, his executive officer, Fellers "became hopelessly confused" during a regimental training exercise.

Walt knew something must be done, and fast, to remedy the increasingly desperate situation. But what and how? He found himself in an onerous bind; not only was Fellers his immediate superior but they were close friends.

The regiment's three battalion commanders were acutely aware of Fellers's serious physical and mental condition and had openly told Walt of numerous instances when the colonel had "goofed up." All were fearful of deadly consequences to the 5th Marines on Peleliu unless Fellers was relieved of command. As to be expected, rumors of the "looney colonel" were prime scuttlebutt that circulated throughout the division.

Unless it was adroitly handled, any action on Walt's part could mean the end of the brilliant military careers of both men. To report Fellers's obvious unfitness to General Rupertus was in direct violation of Marine Corps regulations on such matters. And if a medical and psychiatric examination found Fellers unsuitable for duty, he most likely would be dismissed from the service.

Walt agonized over the decision, but he knew his only option was to confront the 1st Division's commander with the hard-to-face facts. As Major Gordon D. Gayle, CO of the 5th Marines' 2d Battalion, later said, "Colonel Walt went up and laid his career right on the line."

Walt subsequently told Gayle of the tense meeting. In the major's words:

"I wasn't there, of course, but Lou said General Rupertus looked at him in what one might call an intimidating fashion and said, 'You know, you can get a general court-martial for this?' Walt said, 'Yes, sir. I know that, but I think it would be worse for me to think this way and not do something about it.'"

There was no further discussion. The meeting had lasted less than five minutes. As he left the general's quarters, Walt nodded somewhat grimly to two of Rupertus's aides who were seated beside his desk during the sobbering exchange of words—Colonel John T. Selden, Rupertus's chief of staff, and Captain Paul Douglas, the division adjutant.

Douglas commented years later that he "expected to be called in and to write orders for Walt to go home." Instead, Fellers was evacuated the next day to Banika with a directive from General Rupertus that the colonel be immediately flown to the States for treatment.

When Commandant Vandegrift at Marine Corps headquarters in Washington was informed of the sad chain of events, he remarked that he had known for some time that Fellers was "quite sick and showing the effects of malaria," but had "left him there [on Pavuvu] against my better judgment."

Thus arise several never answered questions about myriad decisions and actions of Rupertus before and during the Palaus campaign:

If General Vandegrift knew of the sorry state of affairs with the 5th Marines, why didn't General Rupertus? If he did, why didn't he relieve Fellers without Walt's prodding? Did Rupertus knowingly intend to send one of his infantry regiments into battle under an obviously ill—physically and mentally—commanding officer? Or was he simply out of touch, as many of his subordinates—and some superior officers—believed then and through the years, with what was happening day to day as the 1st Division prepared to invade Peleliu?

Unlike his fellow regimental commanders—Puller and Hanneken—Colonel Harris wasn't a mustang who had climbed up the arduous ladder to become an officer from the enlisted ranks.

He was quite the opposite, not a born-to-battle warrior but a dedicated intellectual who had finished in the top 10 percent of the 1925 class of midshipmen graduates of the Naval Academy at Annapolis. His instructors were impressed with his brilliant scholastic record and predicted an outstanding career for him as a Navy planner and strategist.

The twenty-two-year-old Harris opted instead for Marine Corps duty and happily accepted a commission as a second lieutenant, something more likely to provide challenge and adventure. Before the outbreak of World War II, he had done the obligatory tours of foreign duty in China and Latin America. Stateside, he had held a variety of recruiting and administrative billets.

Overseas, he had been mainly a very junior planning and intelligence aide. Superior officers were so impressed with his performance that he was assigned as one of a handful of young Americans to attend the Ecole Supérieure de Guerre in Paris. It was France's most prestigious academy for those headed toward high rank in the armed services of member nations.

He was Major Harris when he joined the Old Breed for the Guadalcanal invasion. For a time he was executive officer to Chesty Puller, then a lieutenant colonel commanding a battalion in the 1st Marines.

General Vandegrift was quick to spot Harris as a comer, and made him the assistant chief of staff for intelligence. He held the same post under Rupertus at Cape Gloucester, and that was his assignment on Pavuvu before he was named to replace Bill Fellers.

Two mysteries surrounded Harris. One was the source of his nickname, Bucky. The other was why he was selected to lead the 5th Marines. Both ultimately were solved to a degree that satisfied the curious.

"Bucky," they surmised, could be traced to his upbringing in the wild turn-of-the-century cattle country around Laramie, Wyoming, where he was born in 1903.

Why, without long experience leading an outfit in combat, was he given command of a regiment about to invade a fortified Japanese island? The most logical answer was that he was the only colonel available in the division to fill the void created by the relief of Fellers.

There was also another and more significant reason. Harris was one of the very few subordinates that Rupertus respected and trusted, an instinctive reaction based largely on Vandegrift's assessment of Bucky Harris's potential to take on any job and successfully fill it.

At Peleliu, his mettle as a regimental commander would be fiercely tested and not found wanting.

In the final analysis, however, it wouldn't be the brass who could claim credit for winning the battle. The victory would be won, at a ghastly cost, by valorous enlisted Marines and the dedicated lower-ranking officers who were at their sides in the battalions, companies, and platoons that invaded the Palaus.

7

The high-echelon chain of command of a Marine invasion of a Japanese-held island is difficult to explain to anyone not fully acquainted with the subject.

The first thing to understand is that no one in the Marine Corps, including the Commandant, had any say in determining the objective. This was a decision made at CinCPac by Admiral Nimitz and his staff, subject to the strategic aims and approval of the Joint Chiefs of Staff in Washington.

Point number two: Even after planning was completed and a beachhead was established by Marine assault forces, admirals offshore from the fighting still maintained strong overall command of the operation. From the conception of a campaign until its completion, Navy officers made the final decisions with or without the concurrence of Marine Corps generals and their staffs.

Point three: Under the command structure, development of the D-Day landing plan was usually the responsibility of the general leading the division selected to spearhead the invasion. The scenario would then be scrutinized and approved by the general commanding the higher-echelon Marine Amphibious Corps to which the assault force was attached. Once a beachhead was established, the tactics and use of troops was the job of the division CO and his regimental commanders.

There were, of course, constant communications and conferences between the admirals and generals during the planning of an operation. These often resulted in bitter, openly expressed differences of opinion, especially regarding the extent of pre-invasion naval bombardment and carrier-based air attacks needed to soften Japanese defenses before Marines hit the beach.

Major General Julian C. Smith, who commanded the 2d Division in the extremely costly invasion of Tarawa, once put the picture in sharp focus in a turbulent session with Nimitz's admirals.

"Even though you Navy officers do come in to about 1,000 yards," he said, "I remind you that you have a little more armor. I want you to know that Marines are crossing the beach with bayonets, and the only armor they'll have is a khaki shirt."

"Howlin' Mad" Smith (not related to the major general) was

much more caustic in comments about the Marines' relations with Navy brass. The obstreperous, outspoken Old Warrior (he was sixty-four at the time of Peleliu) is quoted on the Tarawa campaign in his biography:

"If the Marines had received better cooperation from the Navy our casualties would have been lower. More naval gunfire would have saved many lives. I had to beg for gunfire, and I rarely received what the situation called for. . . . The Navy transported us, landed us, and protected us against Japanese naval attack. We could not have reached the islands without the Navy, but at that point their duties should have ended. Instead they tried to continue running the show. . . . It was the admirals who wanted to be generals who imperiled victory among the Pacific islands."

It is debatable whether a tighter, more unified liaison between Navy and Marine high-echelon brass would have had a significant impact in reducing the tragic American losses on Peleliu. There is no doubt, however, that the battle was born in confusion—and that the agonizing birth pangs continued until D-Day and for weeks to come.

Some critics of the Navy's participation in the Palaus campaign have contended that it was led by Admiral Nimitz's "second team." The view has a shadow of logic, since CinCPac's acknowledged top-ranking invasion commanders—Admirals Raymond Spruance and Kelly Turner, and General Holland Smith—were in the Marianas, winding up that strenuous and crucial conflict.

The bottom line of the Navy's role at Peleliu, however, is that it performed exceedingly well under very difficult circumstances. The admirals in command were not, by any measurement, passed-over mediocrities or incompetent misfits. They all knew what they were doing, and had the credentials from earlier amphibious operations—both in Europe and in the Pacific—to prove it.

Fifty-six-year-old Vice Admiral Theodore S. Wilkinson commanded the Third Amphibious Force, the official designation of all ships and men involved in the operation. He had a chestful of battle ribbons and decorations, including the Medal of Honor, earned in other battles.

Rear Admiral George H. Fort commanded the convoys of transports and flotilla of armed escorts carrying the assault forces to the landing beaches. At fifty-four, he was a much-decorated sea dog whose World War I destroyer had sunk a German submarine.

Rear Admiral Jesse B. Oldendorf, fifty-seven, led the Fire Support Group of battleships, cruisers, and destroyers, whose task was to soften up—and with luck obliterate—Japanese defenses before the shock troops landed. His assignment had been the same in three earlier Marine invasions. He was destined to leave the Palaus under a cloud of criticism that, justified or not, he drew entirely on himself.

Considering the size of the primary targets of the operation—Peleliu and Angaur—Admiral Oldendorf's armada was deemed more than adequate to handle the job of pre-invasion bombardment and provide support for the Marines once they were ashore.

The fleet included five battleships, eight heavy and light cruisers, twelve destroyers, seven minesweepers, and fifteen seagoing landing craft converted for use as close-to-shore rocket launchers. Air cover came from some 300 Dauntless dive-bombers and Hellcat fighters on three heavy and five escort carriers. Several surfaced submarines patrolled 50 miles at sea, their radar working to warn off possible enemy naval reaction or air attacks.

A thick file of sailing orders, all marked "Top Secret" and locked in a steel cabinet when not being consulted, were kept up to date at CinCPac headquarters. It showed that nearly 400 ships were assigned to Operation Stalemate. A distressing number never made it.

The battleships *California* and *Tennessee* collided in Iron Bottom Sound ten days before the invasion. Damage was severe enough to keep them from adding firepower to the softening-up bombardment at Peleliu. Two fleet oilers, loaded to the gunwales with precious fuel for aircraft and tanks, rammed each other and limped back to port.

Potentially more serious was the collision of a destroyer and a troopship. The transport went to the bottom in waters 1,000 fathoms deep, and the escort was heavily damaged. But amazingly, no lives were lost.

As the first troops were embarking for the battle, Admiral Wilkinson sent an urgent signal to General Rupertus. One of his transport divisions—seven ships with space for more than 6,000 Marines and their combat gear—wouldn't be available. A mix-up in orders had sent them elsewhere.

Most likely the sorely needed bottoms were thousands of

miles away, floating empty with bewildered skippers wondering what to do next. Space was found for the troops on ships already jammed with men and equipment.

A more serious foul-up was the shortage of vessels to lift the division's tank battalion to Peleliu. Only two tank-carrying ships (LSDs) showed up. These ungainly, bulky, 458-feet-long vessels were designed as floating dry docks to repair damaged smaller ships at sea, but had been adapted for invasion duty.

There was room on the LSDs for only thirty of the division's forty-six Sherman tanks, so sixteen were left on the docks. The loss of their cannon and machine-gun armor would be keenly missed from beginning to end of the struggle for Peleliu.

Fifty long-awaited amphibious trucks (DUKWs) arrived just as the first troops were shoving off. Space was somehow found for the vehicles, but a fingernail-biting problem still remained. DUKWs were complicated to operate and required skilled drivers, none of whom were available in the division.

Men from the 1st Motor Transport Battalion were drafted to fill the void, and were given crash courses as DUKW operators en route to the target. Considering their total lack of experience, the new drivers did their dangerous jobs courageously and surprisingly well during the landing and in the following weeks of battle.

Military historian J. A. Isely, a professor at Princeton University, later wrote: "Thoughtful observers might well regard these unhappy incidents as harbingers of calamities yet to come."

8

With D-Day less than a month away, General Rupertus apparently was the only officer in the 1st Division's high command who was satisfied with the state of affairs. Most certainly his staff was not—and nor were the regimental, battalion, and company commanders.

With the approved Peleliu landing plan as their guide, all hands at all levels in the assault regiments went over, again and again, what was expected of them during the campaign. The scheme had the element of simplicity in its favor, but surprise was impossible.

The Japanese had long been certain that the some 2 miles of beaches on the island's southwestern shore were the only place the Americans could possibly use for a full-scale invasion. The enemy had reacted by meticulously targeting every yard of the strip within easy range of artillery and mortar fire and had constructed a network of dug-in fortifications and trenches to beat back the assault before a beachhead could be established.

Brigadier General Smith and his staff, who had planned the invasion during General Rupertus's long absence in Washington, were fearful from the beginning that the landing would be "hot"—that it would be a tough fight to get ashore. What they had no way of knowing, however, was that much of the pre-invasion intelligence was seriously flawed.

Hundreds of reconnaissance photos were made of the island by Navy carrier-based planes and long-range Army bombers during a five-month period before D-Day. The submarine *Seawolf,* in early June, photographed the landing beaches through its periscope. But all the shots were taken before close-in pre-invasion shelling and aerial bombing stripped the island of its dense coverage of trees, jungle, and undergrowth.

The photos led the 1st Division planners to believe that most of Peleliu was low and flat, not the insidious labyrinth of steep hills, coral ridges, sheer cliffs, deep crevices, and hundreds of fortified caves and camouflaged bunkers and pillboxes that made Peleliu the killing ground for thousands of men.

"Maps of Peleliu," an official Marine Corps battle report said, "were deficient and found to be extremely inaccurate as to the figuration of terrain, especially as far as the ridgelines and other elevations were concerned."

The assault plan for D-Day called for Colonel Puller's 1st Marines to swarm ashore on White Beach One and White Beach Two at the north end of the landing zone. When these pieces of sand were seized, the regiment would drive inland 500 yards and swing left to attack low ridges dominating the shoreline.

Colonel Harris's 5th Marines would hit Orange Beach One and Orange Beach Two on Puller's right flank in the center of the beachhead. Once ashore, the regiment was to push straight ahead eastward as far as it could toward Peleliu's airstrip, the main objective of the operation.

Colonel Hanneken's 7th Marines would land on Orange Beach Three and smash across the island in a movement to protect the flank of Harris's outfit. Then the 7th would wheel to

103

the right to take on Japanese troops on the island's southern tip.

Nearly 400 ships were in the giant invasion armada destined for the Palaus. It included vessels of every size and category needed by ground forces to assault, seize, and hold the chain of fortified enemy islands and atolls.

Assembling enough transports to lift thousands of men and tons of equipment and supplies to a Pacific beachhead was always a big problem. Until Hitler's downfall, the liberation of Europe had first priority on shipping, manpower, and all the other needs of carrying the war to the enemy.

Troopships and cargo vessels required for a Marine invasion always seemed to be at the distant end of the pipeline, some as far away as West Coast Stateside ports. Others were on permanent duty with General MacArthur's forces in the Southwest Pacific.

The always complex situation became a full-blown mess for Operation Stalemate. Pavuvu's scarcity of docks (it had two) was largely to blame. There simply weren't sufficient facilities to combat-load ships more than two or three at a time.

The result? Nearly half of the 1st Division's troops and combat gear, as well as tanks and artillery, were ferried by landing craft to other islands with enough dockage to embark. Some went to Banika, others 60 miles away to Guadalcanal and Tulagi.

So far so good?

Not really.

Still to come were two days of "dry runs," the final dress rehearsals for D-Day. It was another case of confused birth.

The 1st Division had never crossed a reef in its previous invasions. Peleliu was surrounded by one that was 200 yards wide at some points. What was needed for the ultimate rehearsals was an island that had a reef and was roughly the size of Peleliu with some of the target's supposed terrain features.

General Smith was given the task of finding such a place nearby, if one did indeed exist. He scouted the area for hours in a low-flying artillery spotter plane. The nearest islands he could find with the elusive characteristics were Florida and Malaita in the Solomons. He decided Malaita was the best bet.

"But the Australian government objected strenuously because they would have to move the natives out, and they didn't want to do that," Smith said years later. "So we ended up at Cape Esperance on Guadalcanal."

The landing site didn't resemble Peleliu in any way, nor was it protected by a reef. Crossing the one at Peleliu was critical to the D-Day landing. The Marines had learned the hard way that only tracked landing craft, amtracs, had a chance of navigating the treacherous coral barriers.

At the invasion of Tarawa the old reliable Higgins boats were stopped, high and dry, by the reef. Many of the 2d Division's 3,056 casualties in that savage seventy-two-hour struggle came when troops were forced to abandon their trackless landing craft. They waded ashore as sitting ducks in waist-deep water, nearly a mile of it, through a murderous torrent of Japanese artillery, mortar, and machine-gun fire.

Without question, the same thing would happen to the 1st Division at Peleliu unless amtracs were used for the final dash to shore from the island's reef. Nonetheless, the rehearsals were held.

Special flag-flying control vessels indicated an imaginary reef where troops on Higgins boats transferred to amtracs for the last 2,000-yard run to the beach. Again more confusion and uncertainty. Many of the 9-ton monsters were of a new design, untested in combat, and most of the three-man crews had less than a month's training in their operation.

"A lot of us were beginning to feel the whole operation, maybe the division, was jinxed," a youthful second lieutenant platoon leader said. "I felt like we were going into action on a Greyhound bus with an inexperienced driver at the wheel."

If there was a jinx, it recognized no rank.

General Rupertus suffered a broken ankle before the final rehearsals began. General Smith later described what happened:

"I took him around to see what was going on and observe the training. . . . He started to climb up into one of the amphibian tractors and the handhold gave way and he fell backward onto the rough coral rocks, and he badly fractured his ankle. It was a bad fracture and he was in bed for quite a while."

More confusion.

When General Geiger learned on Peleliu that Rupertus's ankle was still in a cast, he told General Smith: "If I'd known [before the landing], I'd have relieved him."

General Vandegrift obviously had a different opinion on the matter. His memoirs contain a paragraph recounting a visit to Pavuvu shortly before the invasion. There isn't the slightest hint that the Marine Corps Commandant had any thought of relieving the division commander.

"I found Bill Rupertus on crutches, his ankle fractured by a fall during a recent landing maneuver," Vandegrift wrote. "He was in excellent spirits and proudly showed me the camp which the 1st Division had hacked out of mud and coconut trees, the prominent features of this wretched island which swarmed with huge rats and slimy land crabs."

It is a matter of conjecture what effect, if any, Rupertus's broken ankle had on his capability to command on Peleliu. It should be noted, however, that it was necessary for him to use a heavy cane to walk around most of the time he was on the island.

Like all invasion dry runs, the 1st Division's rehearsals at Cape Esperance had their good and bad effects. The troops learned some of the intricacies involved in crossing Peleliu's reef, but the new men gained no real feeling of what a combat landing was like.

No thundering sounds of bombardment from the Navy's battleships and cruisers as the troops approached the beach. No ear-piercing noise of roaring rockets. No deafening explosions of bombs or loud clatter of machine guns from carrier-based planes softening enemy defenses before the first waves of the assault landed. No torrential downpour of enemy artillery and mortar shells wreaking death and destruction on the incoming amtracs loaded with Marines and their combat gear.

That would come soon enough.

Four days before the first ships of the invasion armada lifted anchor for the journey to the Palaus, General Rupertus called a meeting of most of the division's officers. He exhorted a supreme confidence not shared by many of his more knowledgeable and concerned troop commanders, nor by General Smith.

"We're going to have some casualties," he said, "but let me assure you this is going to be a fast one. Rough but fast. We'll be through in three days. It might take only two."

His last words were an outlandishly serious order that would, under different circumstances and issued by a different general, have been taken as uproariously facetious: "Someone find and bring to me the sword of the Japanese commander on Peleliu."

Then the assemblage broke up, and the officers returned to their units to finish the last-minute chores of boarding ship.

"It wasn't a critique at all," a staff officer remembered. "It was a pep talk." Word of the general's optimistic forecast spread like a tidal wave through the enlisted ranks:

"Three days, maybe just two and it'll be all over" was the happy and welcome division-wide scuttlebutt. One sardonic China Hand platoon sergeant put it to his men: "It's gonna be an in-again-out-again-Finnegan fuckin' match with the Japs as the fuckees."

Major Gayle, CO of Bucky Harris's 2d Battalion, was one of the combat commanders who had deep misgivings. Years later, after his retirement as a highly esteemed brigadier general, he recalled his ominous feelings in a lengthy taped interview for official Marine Corps archives.

". . . I never understood why he [Rupertus] said a thing like that," General Gayle asserted, "because it was pretty obvious from the [available] terrain information that we *might* make the assault in seventy-two hours and *might* establish ourselves in a position so that there was no question about the outcome . . . [but] the terrain was such that inevitably there would be an awful lot of Japanese to dig out. . . .

"I think it [Rupertus's pep talk] had a very negative effect because some people believed it, and if you were in my position you couldn't discredit the division commander's statement, but neither could you believe it. Later on, during the course of the campaign, there got to be a lot of wry and bitter cracks about 'What would you rather have? A two-week vacation or a Rupertus seventy-two [a weekend liberty pass]?' . . .

"Obviously, he believed what he said [about the length of the battle] or he wouldn't have said it, but I couldn't see why he did. . . ."

All that remained now was the 2,100-mile trip to the Palaus. Thirty tank landing ships—the blunt-nosed, ugly, slow-moving, 328-feet-long LSTs—lifted anchor in the early-morning mists of September 4. They were loaded with troops, Higgins boats, and amtracs. Escorted by destroyers, the convoy departed the rehearsal area at the tip of Iron Bottom Sound.

Seventeen 20-knot transports and the tank-loaded LSDs, also screened by destroyers, sailed four days later after picking up troops and cargo at Pavuvu and Banika. Two "baby flat-top" aircraft carriers and a flotilla of rocket-launching gunboats were along to provide protection as they steamed to rendezvous with the 30-mile-long invasion fleet at a point 50 miles due south of the Palaus.

D-Day was one week away.

The men of the 1st Marine Division, the Old Breed of "the few and the proud," were as ready as they would ever be for the invasion of Peleliu.

FIVE

Battleground Chronology

FOR MORE THAN TWO CENTURIES, NO ONE HAD MUCH IN-
terest in Peleliu and the 200-plus tiny atolls and islands that
make up the Palaus. Seafaring adventurers claimed them for
Spain in 1712, but officials in Madrid did virtually nothing to
exploit or develop the distant backwater archipelago. Only a
few European ships, tracking the great schools of whales in the
Pacific, stopped off to replenish supplies of fresh water.

Trade was of little concern to the already moribund Spanish
kingdom, and the islands were sold to Germany in 1899. The $4
million in gold was sorely needed by the nearly bankrupt national treasury to continue financing Spain's ill-fated war with
the United States.

Under Kaiser Wilhelm's ambitions for a global empire, the
Palaus were viewed from a different perspective. Naval officers
and merchant marine interests in Berlin envisioned the islands
as ideal mid-Pacific coaling stations for German warships and
cargo vessels. Prussian business cartels saw opportunities for
economic development, perhaps as an offshore hub for commercial trade with the Philippines, Southeast Asia, and mainland China.

But higher priorities were given to the expansion of heavy
industry in the Fatherland, frantically building armaments for
the soon-to-come World War I. Thus little was done to fulfill
Germany's original schemes for the islands.

Japan acquired the Palaus in 1920 under a mandate from the
League of Nations that was part of the Versailles Treaty after
Germany's surrender on November 11, 1918. The Japanese had
opportunistically, albeit passively, joined the Allied Powers
within a month after the outbreak of war. They immediately
occupied Germany's Pacific island possessions and "conces-

sions" in China, but sent no ground troops to Europe. Japan's armed forces contribution was limited to a flotilla of destroyers that, late in the war, did convoy duty in the Mediterranean.

Tokyo's officialdom of the 1920s considered the Palaus to have only commercial potential and no military value. They

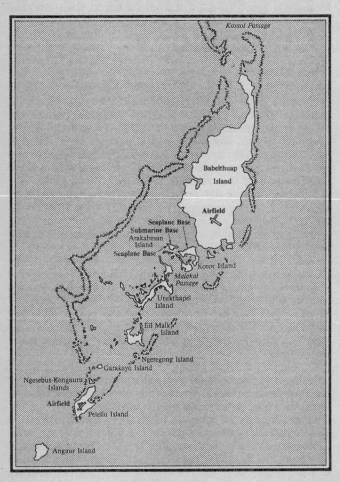

THE PALAUS

would be developed as a source of phosphate, their only known mineral, and as bases for fishing fleets to harvest the rich ocean waters.

The Japanese went to work with customary determination and energy. As the first step, they established administrative control of the some 30,000 natives—a blend of Polynesian and Melanesian stock—who lived on Koror Island, the traditional capital of the chain.

By the mid-1920s, Koror was a bustling commercial center. The daily catch of fishing boats kept four new canneries busy from sunrise to sunset. Concrete breakwaters had been built to protect the harbor. Roads were paved, and several airy two- and three-story concrete structures were constructed. Trees and electric lights lined the main streets. Koror had a well-equipped hospital, a radio and cable communications center, and several fish hatcheries and agriculture research facilities.

Several thousand Japanese were resettled on Koror and nearby Babelthuap, the largest and northernmost of the Palaus. The immigrants held all the better positions in government and business. Only the most menial tasks went to the natives, and very little was done to change their way of life or their living conditions, a policy that seemed not to disturb them in the least.

Peleliu, 25 miles south of Koror, had been unchanged since the Japanese came to the Palaus. To them it was nothing but a small atoll of swamps, jungles, and rugged coral ridges not worth bothering about.

Angaur, the most southerly of the chain, was 7 miles from Peleliu and even smaller. Some 300 natives inhabited the two islands, eking out a primitive living from fishing and communal gardens.

2

Lieutenant Colonel Earl Hancock Ellis was the first Marine to die in the Palaus. He wasn't killed in the Peleliu invasion, but died nearly a quarter century earlier under circumstances still shrouded in mystery.

Ellis was known far and wide to charter members of the Old Breed as Pete. He was a gregarious, rambunctious, brave, and brilliant intelligence officer with fire in his belly when it wasn't full of booze. One time during World War I, Brigadier General

John A. Lejeune sought him out for advice on a planned attack against the Germans.

When the highest-ranking Marine commander in France was told Ellis was "indisposed," the general reputedly answered: "Hell, Ellis drunk is better than anyone else around here sober. Fetch him!" There is no question that he was a world-class alcoholic, or that he was convinced that Japan and the United States would go to war against each other, sooner or later, in the Pacific.

After the Armistice ended the conflict in Europe, Lejeune became Marine Corps Commandant. In 1921 he ordered Ellis to write what the general called a "blueprint for the future," and saw to it that his aide stayed dry until the assignment was completed. The colonel came up with a 30,000-word document that proved amazingly accurate in its predictions. Two paragraphs summarize what emerged from Ellis's crystal ball:

> Japan is a World Power and her army and navy will doubtless be up to date as to training and material. Considering our consistent policy of nonaggression, she will probably initiate the war, which will indicate that, in her own mind, she believes that, considering her natural defensive position, she has sufficient strength to defeat our fleet.
>
> In order to impose our will upon Japan, it will be necessary to project our fleet and land forces across the Pacific and wage war in Japanese waters. To effect this requires that we have sufficient bases to support the fleet, both during its projection and afterward.

Ellis's bouts with the bottle became more frequent, often landing him in curious and embarrassing circumstances. With a passport identifying him as a "Commercial Traveler," he showed up stumbling drunk in Tokyo in late April 1923. Marine sentries repeatedly turned him away at the gate of the United States embassy because of his condition.

Back in Washington, Lieutenant Colonel Earl H. Ellis was officially posted as "absent without leave," although Marine Corps headquarters had been informed through Navy channels that he was drying out in the U.S. naval hospital in Yokohama. Unofficially, the word was leaked to a few fellow officers at HQMC that Ellis was on a "special mission." He knew, they were told, that he was under close surveillance by

Japanese counterintelligence agents and was using drunken stupor as his cover.

Ellis somehow arranged passage aboard a tramp steamer and arrived in the Palaus the first week in May. Exactly what happened after that has never been determined. A Polynesian woman, who claimed they had lived together for ten days, reputedly told Japanese authorities that Ellis swilled down 400 bottles of native beer during the period.

On May 23, U.S. embassy officials in Tokyo were informed that police on Koror had reported the recent death there of an American whose passport said he was "Earl Hancock Ellis, Commercial Traveler." The Japanese said he died of a tropical fever, a claim never disproved.

American correspondents sent short cables to their Stateside editors. To them, it was a minor news item worth no more than a paragraph or two in print. When the dispatch reached Washington, however, it created something approaching a national furor when the deceased was identified.

A front-page headline of one of the capital's newspapers read: "MARINE HERO DIES MYSTERIOUSLY ON JAPANESE PACIFIC ISLAND." A New York tabloid carried a five-column photo of Ellis in his formal "dress blues" with four rows of ribbons denoting various decorations for valor and distinguished service during his Marine Corps career. "WAS MARINE MURDERED BY JAPS WHILE ON U.S. SPY MISSION?" captioned the picture that filled the paper's first page.

Navy and Marine intelligence officers began an undercover search for the full story of Ellis's final days in Japan and the Palaus. The quest lasted ten years, but the investigators always came up empty. Marine Corps headquarters maintained a discreet silence, saying only that Ellis was "on personal leave" when he died.

If Lieutenant Colonel Earl H. Ellis was, indeed, on a spy mission to scout Japanese defenses in the Palaus, it was a futile expedition from the start. At the time, in the early 1920s, the Japanese had no military presence in the islands—no troops, no aircraft, no naval vessels. It would be a tragically different picture, especially on Peleliu, two decades later.

The fate of Pete Ellis and questions about the reason he was in the Palaus soon were forgotten by the public. Very few Americans knew the islands existed, and most of those who did had no interest in them.

Sheer but fascinating speculation: Maybe Ellis realized—a

decade and a half before the Japanese did—the strategic importance of the Palaus in a war with America. In the light of history, such conjecture is meaningless.

The United States at the time had neither the military power nor the national consensus of millions of peace-minded citizens to do anything about the situation. Most Americans clung to the optimistic belief that the surrender in 1918 of Kaiser Wilhelm's armies in Europe ended what President Wilson called "the war to end all wars."

3

Japan's Imperial General Headquarters in Tokyo had different ideas about the future. Emperor Hirohito's inner circle of high command admirals and generals shared Pete Ellis's opinion that a war with the United States was inevitable in the not too distant future.

Despite the lack of concern of the average American, the top echelons of diplomatic and military officials in Washington were increasingly troubled by a stream of deteriorating relations between the two nations. Substantial reasons existed for the pessimistic outlook.

In September 1931, a 500,000-strong force of Japanese steamrolled across Manchuria, China's highly industrialized northern province, rich in iron ore and coal deposits. Three months later, 70,000 Japanese troops seized control, without firing a shot, of Shanghai, China's nerve center of banking, manufacturing, and international trade and a city of more than 8 million.

A major blow fell in March 1933. Tokyo announced that Japan was withdrawing from the League of Nations. It would no longer honor the League's limitations on the size and number of battleships, aircraft carriers, and cruisers the Japanese could build for its fleet.

Japan's saber-rattling first struck home across the United States in mid-December 1937. The U.S.S. *Panay* was sunk in China's Yangtze River by a squadron of carrier-based Japanese dive-bombers. The small, lightly armed gunboat, flying a large and clearly visible American flag, was on routine patrol under a longstanding international agreement recognized by Japan.

Norman Alley, an American newsreel cameraman, just happened to be aboard. He filmed the entire surprise attack. News of the sinking reached Washington within a few hours.

President Roosevelt, fuming with anger, reacted immediately. He threatened a total trade embargo with Japan and the freezing of the nation's assets in the United States.

It took several days of strong persuasion from Secretary of State Cordell Hull and Secretary of War Henry L. Stimson to cool down FDR. Now was not the time, they successfully argued, to aggravate an extremely delicate situation the United States was virtually powerless to change.

An audience of millions saw Alley's dramatic footage when it was shown in thousands of theaters across the country. They were astounded and shouting mad, but the tumultuous reaction was short-lived. Most of the viewers still believed that World War II wouldn't come—and that if it did, the United States wouldn't become directly involved.

Japanese Prime Minister Fumimaro Konoye, a prince of the royal family, ultimately issued a formal apology for the sinking of the *Panay*. He blamed "the unfortunate incident" on an obscure admiral, who was allegedly court-martialed and cashiered out of the Imperial Fleet "as punishment for his unauthorized action."

American intelligence officers didn't believe a word of the explanation. Neither did President Roosevelt, Secretaries Hull and Stimson, nor their aides. To them it was a Japanese show of force, a blatant dare to the United States not to interfere with Japan's military moves or plans to expand the Empire of the Rising Sun.

Within weeks after Prince Konoye sent his "so sorry" note, he summoned his cabinet's War Minister, Marshal General Fumio Sugiyama, to the Prime Minister's office in a building on the grounds of the Imperial Palace. They conferred for several hours with advisers, poring over maps of Pacific islands considered strategic in a war with the Americans.

The Palaus, some 2,000 miles almost due south of Tokyo, were selected as a stronghold for immediate development. Contrary to the thinking of Japan's military planners in the 1920s, the island chain now was viewed as a major outpost for ground forces, naval anchorages, and aircraft operations.

Fifteen years after Pete Ellis's spy-novellike death on Koror, give or take a month or two, Japan began its massive buildup of the Palaus. The heaviest activity was concentrated on Peleliu.

By April 1939, a naval force of 3,000 officers and sailors were ashore there with steam shovels, bulldozers, cranes, heavy earth-packing rollers, and trucks. The Japanese had brought along 500 Koreans to do the forced labor, backbreaking pick-and-shovel work.

Two excellent hard-packed coral runways were completed within six months. One was 6,000 feet long, the other 3,500 feet. The strips crisscrossed at the center to permit takeoffs and landings regardless of wind direction. Along with ample taxiways, sandbagged dispersal revetments, and paved turning circles, the installation was a first-class facility for both offensive and defensive air operations.

A complex of permanent cinder-block and prefabricated metal structures was erected at the northern edge of the airfield. The area included nearly a dozen hangars and barracks, a two-story concrete headquarters building, a radio and cable communications center, an electricity-generating power plant, and machine shops. Several cisterns were dug to catch and store rainwater, a scarce necessity on the island.

Ground was cleared for a fighter strip and barracks on tiny Ngesebus, some 500 yards north of Peleliu. A causeway was built connecting the islands, and a single-lane coral-topped north-south road was laid down from Ngesebus to the southern end of Peleliu 6 miles away.

While Koror remained the command headquarters of the Palaus, little was done there except to increase the power of its radio communications. Several new long-range transmitters with 300-foot-tall masts were installed to relay messages between Tokyo and other islands and naval ships at sea. A two-ramp seaplane base was built, mainly for the convenience of high-ranking officers on inspection tours.

Babelthuap, the Palaus' "big island," became a base and staging area for an ever-increasing number of ground troops. By mid-December 1941, the garrison totaled nearly 12,000 well-trained officers and men.

A small carrier task force was anchored in the harbor of Malakal, an atoll 12 miles north of Ngesebus, when Pearl Harbor was attacked. It steamed immediately to preassigned battle stations off the Philippines, 600 miles to the west, to join other carriers and Formosa-based bombers in massed attacks on American naval installations and airfields.

United States air power in the Philippines was wiped out in less than a week, in some part by the planes from the Palau-based carrier force and fighters and bombers from Peleliu's airfield. Assault troops from Babelthuap were among the spearhead force of the Japanese juggernaut that conquered the islands.

For all intents and purposes, however, this was the beginning and end of the Palaus' role as an offensive jump-off point in Japan's ambitious plans for the conquest of the Pacific. After mid-January 1942, the chain served mainly as a funnel for men, planes, and supplies headed elsewhere.

Peleliu's airstrip was a refueling stop for new Zero fighters and Betty bombers coming from aircraft plants. Babelthuap was a staging area for ground troop reinforcements. Planes and men usually were South Pacific–bound to help in the increasingly desperate struggle to derail the Allies' version of the Tokyo Express. Island by island, the American-led offensive was picking up speed and momentum in the northward journey to the Japanese home islands.

4

Admiral Nimitz never considered the conquest of the Palaus to be the grand prize of Operation Stalemate. True, he apparently felt that American control of the islands—especially Peleliu—was necessary to protect the eastern oceanside flank of General MacArthur's invasion of the southern Philippines, or was at least a commitment made at the Pearl Harbor meeting with FDR.

In CinCPac's view, however, the downfall of Truk, Ulithi, and Yap were of far greater strategic importance in the ultimate defeat of Japan. Truk was at the top of the admiral's priority list of targets. It was almost at the center of the Carolines, about 1,200 miles east of the Palaus.

Several important reasons were behind his wanting the island removed as an obstacle to future operations in the mid-Pacific. One was that it was headquarters for Admiral Mineichi Koga, commander of the Japanese Combined Fleet, the enemy's equivalent in rank and authority to Nimitz.

Truk's huge lagoon also was the main offshore anchorage and supply depot for Japan's navy. It was defended by at least 400 fighters and bombers based on four airstrips, planes that were a constant threat to U.S. fleet movements in the area. The island also was fortified with at least a dozen batteries of big naval coastal guns and heavy artillery.

A garrison estimated to number more than 3,500 Imperial Marines, the elite of Japan's ground forces, was poised to repel any invasion attempt. Communications facilities were unsurpassed by any others, American or Japanese, in the Pacific except those at Pearl Harbor.

The second week in February 1944, Admiral Nimitz issued orders to Rear Admiral Marc A. Mitscher: "Proceed immediately with Task Force 58 to Truk with the objective of destroying all enemy facilities on and around the island."

The attack began at daybreak of February 17 and continued almost constantly for two days. Mitscher's fleet can only be described as "mighty." It consisted of twelve aircraft carriers with more than 600 planes, eight new fast battleships, and some thirty cruisers and destroyers.

Each air strike was more powerful than either of the two waves of Japanese planes that hit Pearl Harbor—more bombs, more torpedoes, more machine-gun strafing. Nearly 2,000 shells struck areas designated for bombardment by the big guns of the task force.

The tally of Japanese losses: more than 250 aircraft destroyed and two light cruisers, four destroyers, two submarines, and twenty-four cargo ships sunk. Thirty American planes were shot down and one carrier damaged.

The destruction of communications and other facilities was so complete, the island so in jeopardy to more massive attacks, that Koga decided immediately to move his headquarters to Koror Island in the Palaus. Imperial General Headquarters in Tokyo was in turmoil over the decision, but had no option other than accept it—or strip the admiral of his command.

Task Force 58 not only had shattered the myth that Truk was invulnerable, a view previously shared by the Japanese high command and some American intelligence officers, but had made it possible to bypass Truk as an invasion objective of Operation Stalemate. It was later occupied by Navy and Marine Corps personnel after V-J Day.

Hard-driving, gutsy, diminutive Marc Mitscher wasn't about to give up the chase now that Admiral Koga was on the run. Task Force 58 followed him to the Palaus and showed up there at daybreak of March 2. Mitscher's objective, however, was not to attack the admiral's new headquarters on Koror. Instead, he had his eye on the enemy's installations on Peleliu and Angaur, targets he deemed of greater importance for the time being.

For the next forty-eight hours, the islands and the reef-protected anchorage off Malakal received the same devastating treatment that obliterated Truk—but with a shift in tactics. Mitscher decided to use his planes as the major thrust of the attack while the battleships and cruisers occasionally bombarded Babelthuap. Otherwise, the big guns would remain silent with crews at battle stations until a large Japanese naval force appeared to challenge the action. None did.

Seventy-two Hellcat fighters from the carriers *Lexington*, *Hornet*, and *Bunker Hill* began dawn-to-dusk strikes on Peleliu's airstrip. They tangled in virtually nonstop dogfights with intercepting Zeroes, shooting down ninety-three and destroying thirty-six more on the ground.

Wave after wave of Dauntless dive-bombers blasted the runways into a checkerboard pattern of gaping holes. Hangars and barracks were blasted into smoldering heaps of steel, coral, and cinder-block rubble. The communications center was leveled, and its tall antenna was a zigzag tangle of metal lying across one of the taxi strips. Only the walls of the roofless headquarters building remained standing.

Avenger torpedo planes repeatedly came in less than 50 feet above Malakal harbor to strew it with several hundred magnetic mines, an operation designed to bottle up anchored naval and cargo vessels.

The scheme worked. Thirty-two ships—destroyers, tankers, transports, fleet oilers—stayed inside. When the American dive-bombers and torpedo planes had nothing better to do, they sank most of the trapped vessels. Those still afloat were abandoned and smoking hulks.

Sea dog Mitscher's Task Force 58 left Peleliu's air power a useless shambles. The enemy's airworthy planes numbered less than a dozen. Malakal's harbor was a graveyard of ships, no longer an anchorage capable of supporting the Japanese fleet.

Six months before D-Day for the invasion, the Palaus were out of business as a base for effective offensive operations, either naval or air. The islands, from then on, were only a link in the crumbling chain of outposts defending the approaches to the Japanese homeland.

Admiral Koga remained aboard the battleship *Musashi*, anchored off Koror, during the devastating attack. Between infrequent catnaps, the sixty-three-year-old commander constantly paced the flag deck as reports of mounting destruction came from Peleliu.

It was a repeat of the Truk disaster. Koga again was in a desperate quandary. What to do next?

It was obvious that the Palaus were no longer a reasonably tenable headquarters for the commander of the Japanese Combined Fleet. Several times Hellcat fighters buzzed the *Musashi* and Koror, but, for reasons never explained, neither was attacked. Nonetheless, the admiral must have felt the same frustration as the Americans had at Pearl Harbor—bewildered and powerless to stop the onslaught of enemy military might.

After several hours of agonizing consultation with senior aides, Koga made up his mind. He told Tokyo the grave news of what had happened and said he was leaving as soon as possible to establish a new command center on Davao Island in the southern Philippines.

Koga apparently was unaware that General Hideki Tojo had engineered a palace coup by Emperor Hirohito's most ambitious admirals and generals. Tojo's successful plot not only elevated him to Supreme Commander of Imperial General Headquarters, but also made him Prime Minister and unchallenged head of Japan's civilian government.

Wearing his hat as the empire's top warlord, Tojo responded immediately to Koga's urgent dispatch. He not only understood the gravity of the Palaus disaster but was in complete agreement with the move to the Philippines. There, Tojo said, the admiral would be in a better position to marshal Japanese forces to beat off General MacArthur's long-expected invasion of the islands.

Koga and his staff took off the next morning in two flying boats for the four-hour flight to Davao. They never made it.

About thirty minutes from the destination, the four-engined prewar airliners were struck by typhoon-force winds and plunged out of control into the sea. There were no survivors.

Admiral Koga was the Japanese navy's second Combined Fleet commander killed in an aircraft disaster. Fleet Admiral Isoroku Yamamoto, the mastermind of the Pearl Harbor attack, had died two years earlier in the flaming wreckage of a Betty bomber. The plane was downed by Army Air Corps P-38 fighters while Yamamoto was on an inspection tour of installations in the South Pacific.

5

The Japanese garrison on Peleliu was little more than a token force during the first twenty-nine months of the war; about 3,000 men, all naval personnel, were on the island when Task Force 58 struck. One third were attached to the 45th Ground Force and were trained as combat troops or antiaircraft gun crews. The other 2,000 were counted as noncombatants, men from air support units and construction outfits. When the invasion came, all fought as infantry.

Very few were casualties of the bombing and strafing that obliterated the airstrip. When sirens warned of the first strike by Mitscher's planes, the Japanese took cover in deep underground concrete shelters. It was a nerve-racking and deafening ordeal, but roofs of the fortifications were thick enough to withstand a direct hit from a 500-pound bomb or a 16-inch naval shell.

As soon as the American fleet disappeared beyond the horizon, the stunned Japanese surveyed the ruins. Officers immediately ordered working parties to repair what they could with picks and shovels and the few pieces of heavy equipment still in operating condition.

Back at Imperial General Headquarters in Tokyo, General Tojo had a difficult decision to make. Should he leave the Palaus to their fate as a walk-over objective for a Yankee invasion that he was certain would come? Or should he immediately send reinforcements to at least hold Peleliu—or die, to the last man, in a savage battle with the Americans?

Tojo was a devout believer in the ancient Japanese military code of *bushido,* which held that the highest honor any soldier of the Rising Sun Empire could have was the privilege of sacrificing his life for the Emperor. He decided that was the best thing to do in the Palaus, not only for the sake of samurai tradition, but also to kill as many hated Yankees as possible.

Lieutenant General Sadae Inoue was Tojo's instant choice to lead the 12,000 reinforcements—his veteran, battle-tested 14th Infantry Division—and take command of all Japanese forces in the islands. These included naval and air personnel on Peleliu, as well as army garrisons—largely untrained troops and inexperienced officers—on Babelthuap and Angaur.

Inoue had the physical looks of Hollywood's version of a Japanese general officer. A strict disciplinarian in his mid-fifties, he was medium-tall, husky, balding, myopic, stern-voiced, and fiercely dedicated to the heritage of five generations of ancestors who had been military officers. As a twenty-year-old sublieutenant, he was decorated for valor during the Russo-Japanese War, and he had risen step by step to command the 14th Division in Manchuria.

General Tojo and his staff considered Inoue thoroughly competent and temperamentally suited for the unenviable post of commander of the Paulus. "He was the type of senior officer who would carry out his tasks without flair, but with tenacity," said one authority on the capabilities of Japan's wartime brass. "He wouldn't crumble under the most adverse circumstances."

There is no documented record of what was said when Inoue was summoned by Tojo to discuss plans to reinforce and defend the Palaus. But because of one of the most bewildering oddities of World War II, a firsthand report of the conference exists.

Inoue was at his headquarters on Koror when the Marines invaded Peleliu, and he remained there throughout the battle and thus survived. One of the first actions of U.S. Army occupation forces, when they seized Koror without opposition, was to capture the defeated general.

He was immediately flown to Guam for questioning by Navy intelligence officers. After lengthy interrogation, it was determined that Inoue possessed no information of value that could be used in future operations against the Japanese. The general was held in the island's war prisoner stockade until after V-J Day, when he was sent to Tokyo to face war crimes charges for actions committed in North China.

While awaiting trial in Sugamo Prison, Inoue renewed a thirty-year close acquaintance with Navy Captain Tsunezo Wachi.

During countless hours of conversations, the longtime friends talked about their military careers and families. Allied intelligence officers learned nothing of significance from constant eavesdropping.

Wachi's story was, by far, the more interesting. From the Japanese embassy in Mexico City, he was the spymaster controlling the enemy's prewar espionage network in the western hemisphere, including the United States. He was interned, along with top officials from the Japanese embassy in Washington, for nearly a year at White Sulphur Springs, West Virginia, after the Pearl Harbor attack.

The war prisoners were repatriated to Japan on the Swedish liner *Gripsholm* in late 1942. The ship returned to the United States with 200 American embassy officials, news correspondents, business executives, and their families.

Captain Wachi was recalled to active military duty almost immediately and sent to Iwo Jima as the island's commanding officer. For the next eighteen months, he directed construction of hundreds of fortified tunnels that were the major defensive strongpoints used by the Japanese during the February 1945 invasion that claimed nearly 26,000 Marines, dead or wounded.

Six months before the Iwo Jima operation, Wachi was ordered to Imperial General Headquarters in Tokyo as a senior member of General Tojo's intelligence staff. He held the same post when the war ended. After a year's imprisonment and interrogation, war crimes charges against Wachi were dropped and he was freed from Sugamo. Inoue, however, was found guilty and returned to Guam, where he served a ten-year sentence.

There is a reason for recounting Wachi's background in a book about Peleliu, an island he never saw. After publication of a history of the Iwo Jima battle, the author visited Japan for ten days in 1986. He sought out Iwo's former commander for comments on the accuracy of the book, which had been published in a Japanese edition—and to inquire if Wachi knew any Japanese survivors of the Palaus campaign.

Wachi, who had become a Buddhist priest in 1952, told of his friendship with General Inoue. He said, with the trace of a sly smile, that he was "blessed with total recall, something of great value during my tour of duty in Mexico City." He vividly remembered numerous conversations with Inoue about Peleliu.

"Did he ever mention a meeting with General Tojo before he left for Koror?" Wachi was asked.

"Yes, he did," was the response in easily understood English. "Inoue said Tojo bluntly told him that the Palaus no longer were of offensive use to either naval or air operations against the Americans, and that he doubted their defensive capabilities."

"In other words, General Inoue and his troops were being assigned to what amounted to a kamikaze mission?"

Wachi paused for a few moments, then he replied with a wan, sorrowful nod: "I guess that sums it up."

He went on to say that Inoue said Tojo told him:

"There is no possible way we can use our limited air power on Peleliu to disrupt Yankee landings in the Philippines. Your objective is to hold the island as long as possible to deny its use by the enemy to support their future plans, and kill as many Americans as you can before the last Japanese soldier dies at his post."

Inoue and his chief of staff, Colonel Taokuchi Tada, left for Koror on a flying boat the day after the general's meeting with Tojo.

By week's end, sixteen transports and cargo ships had left Yokohama with the 14th Infantry Division's troops, artillery, tanks, ammunition, and other equipment and supplies needed in battle. The convoy took a wide zigzag route to escape the threat of torpedo attacks from prowling U.S. submarines constantly on patrol between Japan and the Palaus.

6

When General Inoue departed from Tokyo Bay, he was certain that much must rapidly be accomplished to make his new command a well-fortified stronghold capable of holding off an invasion and, possibly, driving the enemy landing force back into the sea.

He wasn't, however, prepared for what he found. Beyond doubt, he was stunned and dismayed.

Very little had been done to prepare an adequate network of defensive positions. If an overall strategic plan had been made to ward off a seaborne assault, it was not evident.

The only thing Inoue could do was to start from scratch. His first step was a two-day tour of the major islands in the chain.

Koror was of little military value to the enemy, except to destroy its use as a communications relay center between Tokyo, the embattled Japanese fleet, and other island outposts. Its 30,000-plus civilian population and commercial functions were insurmountable obstacles to effective fortification.

Babelthuap had served its purpose well as a training base and staging area for ground forces during the halcyon days of Japan's South Pacific conquests. Inoue found some 20,000 men still there.

For his purposes they were more of a burden than an asset: young, recently inducted, ill-trained, poorly led, disorganized replacement troops awaiting ships to carry them elsewhere to do whatever they could in suicidal attempts to halt the unceasing Allied push toward their homeland. Besides, the island was too large, and its terrain unsuited, for the last-ditch defense of the Palaus.

Peleliu and Angaur, the general decided, were the only places where there was even a remote chance to beat back an invasion.

He also correctly surmised why Peleliu had been the principal target of Task Force 58's massive attack: Its airstrip would be the major object of any amphibious assault in the Palaus. He knew that, beginning at Guadalcanal and continuing with almost every other invasion, the basic underlying U.S. strategy was to seize new air bases to strengthen and expand American control of the skies.

Most of Inoue's 14th Infantry Division reached Koror by the last week in April. Seven ships hadn't taken time to dock, but were sent on immediately to Peleliu for unloading.

That convoy carried Colonel Kunio Nakagawa and 6,500 troops of his elite 2d Infantry Regiment. The outfit was well armed for its assignment: more than two dozen 75-millimeter cannon, twelve tanks, fifteen 81-millimeter mortars, some thirty high-velocity antiaircraft guns that could be cranked down for flat-trajectory fire against tanks and infantry, and nearly a hundred .50 caliber heavy machine guns.

Nakagawa, in his early forties, was a veteran of Japan's Kwangtung Army and had received nine medals for bravery and leadership in fighting the Chinese. He was recognized by his superiors as a brilliant planner and combat commander destined to become a high-ranking general. Most of his subordinate officers and soldiers had served with him in Manchuria and were battle-tested and emotionally ready for the battle to come.

Inoue dispatched Major Ushio Goto and two battalions from the 59th Regiment to defend Angaur. The 1,500-man force had been under Goto's command in numerous engagements in China and were comparably equipped with armor and *bushido* for the battle they were certain was coming.

Colonel Nakagawa spent most of his first day on Peleliu in a reconnaissance of the island. Using the Japanese equivalent of a jeep, he drove up and down the 6-mile coral-topped road from the airstrip to Ngesebus at the island's northern tip. Then he inveigled the airbase commander, an obviously irritated admiral, to provide him with a pilot and one of his few operational dive-bombers to make several low-altitude swings around the atoll.

What Nakagawa observed convinced him that he had two major favorable factors in planning and executing a prolonged and costly defense of the island. The terrain was on his side, and he was certain the Americans could use only one strip of its western beaches for their invasion—the same ones General Smith and his 1st Division planners logically had chosen.

The next morning the colonel ordered work to begin on implementing his hastily conceived strategy. But his army construction crews immediately ran into an unexpected obstacle: The navy refused to cooperate in providing manpower, material, or equipment to build or strengthen strongpoints as directed by Nakagawa.

The reason was long-existing interservice rivalry, a factor that would plague the Japanese war effort until the final months of the Pacific conflict. Simply put, the recalcitrant rear admiral commanding naval forces of Peleliu resented an army colonel's superseding his authority.

General Inoue settled the issue by dispatching Major General Kenijiro Murai, superior in rank to the admiral, to assume overall command of all forces on the island. From then on, the fortification of Peleliu proceeded with dawn-to-dusk urgency under Nakagawa's unhindered direction.

Murai, fifty-three, was the youngest officer to hold such high rank in Japan's armed forces. His military acumen and courage were highly regarded in Tokyo, where he wielded heavy influence with the high command. He quickly recognized Nakagawa's abilities without ever questioning his decisions. During the battle they fought as equals, leading close-in combat with the Americans.

7

Nakagawa had no intention of conceding Peleliu's beachhead to the Marines without bitter resistance. He realized, however, that the massive firepower of the U.S. battleships, cruisers, and destroyers would make it impossible to prevent a landing.

Further, he knew he would have neither surface naval support nor air cover while literally hundreds of enemy carrier planes bombed and strafed the landing zone in ceaseless strikes just prior to H-Hour on D-Day. But with the limited resources available to him, and the obstacle of crossing the treacherous reef, he was determined that the invaders would pay a heavy cost to gain a foothold on the island.

Weeks before the invasion, Nakagawa's engineers had carefully measured the distance to the reef from artillery and heavy mortar emplacements in the high ground behind the beaches. This enabled the defenders to aim their weapons precisely to assure accurate fire on the coral barrier when landing craft attempted to cross it.

His next line of defense was a string of some 500 mines placed a few feet below the water between the reef and the shoreline. It was a good idea that, fortunately for the Marines, had little effect.

The reason? Most of the mines weren't naval mines at all. They were aircraft bombs to be triggered by cables stretching to Japanese positions ashore. When time came for the explosives to be detonated, troops were too stunned by pre-invasion shelling to jerk the wires.

More than a hundred V-shaped obstacles were implanted a few yards offshore. They were several feet high but were poorly put together with logs and steel salvaged from destroyed aircraft hangars, and did little to hamper the landing. The meager supply of barbed wire was strung closer to land, but there wasn't enough of it to cause concern.

Contrary to pre-invasion reconnaissance photos and intelligence reports that described most of Peleliu's terrain as "low-lying and flat," the ground rose sharply less than 100 yards inland from the invasion beaches.

A long 6-foot-deep tank trap was dug at the base of one of the rises near the center of the landing zone. Numerous concealed sandbagged machine-gun positions were scattered along the adjacent slopes facing the beach. At least thirty mortar pits were positioned just beyond the ridgeline.

The 1st Division would find the Peleliu landing far from a "walk-over." Colonel Nakagawa's defense plan had decreed otherwise. Just getting ashore was the toughest struggle the Old Breed had so far faced in the Pacific—and the battle would be more bitter and costly in the weeks to come.

Less than 2,500 of Nakagawa's estimated force of 10,500-plus troops were committed to repelling the invasion and holding the airstrip. The rest were in Peleliu's hundreds of caves and other fortifications in the inland hills and narrow cliff-lined valleys, where they fought to the end. Counting the some 3,000 naval personnel, the island's garrison totaled about 13,500. Less than 300 survived the battle.

Peleliu's northern highlands and the deadly approaches to the enemy's well-hidden and heavily fortified caves were also where Marines suffered most of their losses. Without question, the terrain was on the side of the Japanese—it was a maze of strange geometrical patterns and grotesque geological formations ideal for last-ditch defenses.

The landscape gave the false impression of a solid plateau blanketed with dense foliage along its 6-mile north-south axis and the 2 miles across its widest point. An entirely different picture emerged after pre-invasion naval shelling and aerial bombardment stripped away nature's camouflage.

Centuries of typhoon winds and monsoon rains had left their mark on Peleliu, forming a bewildering kaleidoscope of unconnected hills, jagged crags, countless swamps and patches of quicksand, deep cavities with sheer limestone and coral walls. Peleliu could have been a science fiction scene of a distant planet.

There is no way of knowing how many caves were on Peleliu, but at least 500 were counted after the fighting ended. Some 200 were blasted out by naval construction crews, who had reinforced the entrances, walls, and ceilings with thick layers of concrete. The others were creations of nature, and all the Japanese did was to camouflage the mouths.

The redoubts ran the gamut in size and design. They ranged from one-man "spider traps" used by snipers to vast fortified installations large enough to serve as hospitals or to base a fully equipped company of combat troops. Some were artillery emplacements where guns were rolled to the entrance to fire several 75-millimeter shells, then pulled back out of sight.

One of the most elaborate burrowed more than 300 feet from its mouth and had five 150-foot-long spokelike offshoots. A squad of Japanese were discovered there five months after the battle, well fed and wearing fresh uniforms from an ample stockpile of supplies. The cave apparently had served as a headquarters for a unit of navy combatant forces.

Entrances to all caves were small and well concealed. Most sloped steeply downward or had sharp turns just inside their mouths—protection against flamethrowers, satchel packs of demolition charges, tank attacks, or direct artillery hits. Paths that had to be used by Marine infantry to assault the larger installations were covered from several directions by positions sited to unleash devastating machine-gun crossfire.

The Marines quickly gave aptly descriptive and, to them, unforgettable names to the convoluted highlands killing ground. Bloody Nose Ridge. Death Valley. The China Wall. The Five Sisters. The Five Brothers. The virtually unpronounceable Amiangal and Umurbrogol cliffs and ridges.

There were also uncounted and unnamed other places where men fought and were wounded and were killed in give-no-quarter combat to conquer an island that, in the light of history, never should have been invaded.

8

By the first week in July, Colonel Nakagawa was convinced that everything possible had been done to prepare Peleliu for invasion. He knew there were countless other things that could make the island's defenses more formidable and its capture more costly to the Americans. But he lacked the troops and armor to do anything more. Now it was a matter of waiting for D-Day.

Major General Murai concurred in his judgment. So did Lieutenant General Inoue at his headquarters on Koror.

On July 11, Inoue issued a lengthy proclamation designed to bolster the *bushido* credo of his command. The statement contained little optimism about the ultimate outcome of the impending clash of arms, but it bristled with the belligerent words of a samurai battle cry. Its contents can be summarized in a few sentences:

". . . We must recognize the limits of naval and aerial bombardment. . . . Every soldier will remain unmoved by this, must strengthen his spirits even while advancing by utilizing lulls in enemy bombardment and taking advantage of the terrain without incurring damage or exposing other areas too quickly or thoughtlessly. . . . We are ready to die honorably . . . but even if we die delivering our territory into the hands of the enemy it may contribute to the opening of a new phase of the war. . . ."

Like the Old Breed, the Japanese were as ready as they would ever be for the Peleliu invasion.

SIX

Point of No Return

SEPTEMBER 12, 1944.

D-Day minus three.

A soft breeze barely rippled the gentle offshore swells of the dark blue predawn ocean. The turquoise waters between the reef and Peleilu's beaches were as smooth as a mammoth man-made swimming pool. A dark low-lying cloud bank promised an early-morning shower such as is common among the Pacific islands.

The scene was one of tropical tranquillity, destined shortly to vanish in the thundering, deadly turmoil of war.

Rear Admiral Jesse Oldendorf appeared on the bridge of the battleship *Pennsylvania,* on station 7,500 yards west of Peleilu's shoreline. Arrayed with it in formation along a 2-mile-long line were four other battlewagons: the *Maryland, Mississippi, Tennessee,* and *Idaho.*

The gray-hulled 23,000-ton vessels were the venerable "old ladies" of the United States Navy, relics now modernized and refitted for action against the Axis Powers in either Europe or the Pacific. Between them, their turrets mounted forty-eight 14- and 16-inch guns.

Two thousand yards closer to shore were the heavy cruisers *Columbus, Indianapolis, Louisville, Minneapolis,* and *Portland* and the light cruisers *Cleveland, Denver,* and *Honolulu.* Some 15 miles to the southwest were three large carriers and five "baby flattops" with nearly 400 planes to add air power to the armada.

Oldendorf's Fire Support Group was ready for action.

At 5:30 A.M., the admiral flashed the order:

"Commence firing!"

The three days allotted to the pre-invasion softening-up of

Peleliu began precisely on schedule. Each ship had specific targets assigned to it in Oldendorf's operational plan, and every known major fortification was marked on a master chart in the combat information center aboard his flagship. He had commanded the pre-invasion bombardment before the Marine assaults on Kwajalein and Saipan, and was acutely aware how much naval gunfire could mean to the success of establishing a beachhead.

Every gun crew on every battleship and cruiser had known for days the enemy strongpoints they were expected to demolish, the number of shells to fire to complete the mission, and the exact time to send them on their way.

Peleliu's beaches and highlands were lambasted for the next half hour by nonstop shelling from the armada's big guns. Every ship seemed to be firing at the same time, and the bombardment mounted in intensity with each passing minute as tons of hot steel and explosives ripped into the island in a rolling, roaring pattern of destruction.

The trajectories of the 5-foot-long shells could clearly be seen as they arced through the sky. Each impact made a bright orange flash that was instantly swallowed in an ugly shroud of grayish-black smoke and billowing clouds of dust. The beaches and the high ground behind them and to the north were engulfed in cascades of falling dirt and debris, leaving giant craters where the heavy explosives landed.

All firing stopped at 6:00.

It was the time scheduled in Oldendorf's plan to give the battleships and cruisers a rest and let the carrier planes take over. Twenty-four Hellcat fighters and thirty-two Dauntless dive-bombers appeared as the first streaks of sunlight broke through the scudding squall line.

Flying four abreast in a miles-wide circle 12,000 feet above the island, wave after wave peeled away from the formation and plunged earthward into action.

The planes made low-level 300-mile-an-hour passes, dropping 500-pound bombs and napalm canisters, unleashing rounds of screeching rockets, and strafing with firehose streams of .50 caliber machine-gun fire. They crisscrossed the beaches, buzzed the ridges inland, plastered the northern highlands, then zoomed up with full throttle to swing around and make more passes.

The mad aerial circus continued until the pilots had spent their firepower and fuel gauges approached red-line warnings that tanks were nearly empty. Then it was back to the carriers to take on more fuel and fresh supplies of bombs and bullets and await the signal for another round of attacks.

When Peleliu's skies were clear of aircraft, the surface fleet resumed its bombardment. The precisely timed scheme of alternating sea-air softening-up strikes went on until dark.

Just before sunset, three reconnaissance planes made repeated passes over the island. Flying at a 500-foot altitude, they photographed the length and width of the target. Results of Day One of the pre-invasion operations were quickly relayed by Rear Admiral William Sample, commander of the carrier force, to an anxious Oldendorf.

The admiral was gratified, but still deeply concerned, by what the strike photos showed. His apprehension was justified.

Nearly 300 targets had been demolished or heavily damaged during the day. All but a few of the enemy's above-ground fortified positions were leveled. The airfield's patched-up runways and taxi strips were pocked with huge new craters. Skeletons of wrecked planes showed that Peleliu's small air force had been further reduced to almost nothing. Whatever the Japanese had done to repair the hangars and nearby complex of buildings was again in shambles.

What disturbed Oldendorf was that there had been no counterbattery fire from coastal defense artillery and giant mortars that Navy aerial reconnaissance photos, made several weeks earlier, had shown to be on the island. The admiral logically and correctly surmised that Colonel Nakagawa had since wisely moved these heavy weapons to underground bunkers and deep caves. There his troops waited—without sustaining serious losses to themselves or the armor—for the shelling and bombing to lift.

The Fire Support Group commander was on the *Pennsylvania*'s bridge at dawn, scanning the island through powerful binoculars. He was amazed by what he saw. Peleliu's terrain looked totally different from the previous morning.

Then it had appeared to be a relatively flat piece of real estate covered with an undergrowth of thick bushes and low trees. Now it was virtually barren of greenery, an unearthly scene of steep isolated coral hills and sheer cliffs that began just a few hundred yards beyond the shoreline and extended over the length and breadth of the island.

September 13 was a dawn-to-dusk repeat of the preceding

day's action. The battleships and cruisers again opened fire at 6:30 and bombarded virtually the same areas they had wracked before. The carrier planes followed the same bombing and strafing patterns as yesterday.

Still no reaction from Japanese shore batteries. Still no sign of enemy planes. Still no hint of opposition from the Imperial Fleet. And Nakagawa and his troops were still dug in, waiting to strike back in full fury when the Americans tried to storm the island's beaches, something they were convinced was certain to happen within hours.

By early afternoon, the last of the predetermined targets had been crossed off the master chart in the combat information center of the *Pennsylvania*. But the shelling and carrier-plane strikes continued for the rest of the day in what Oldendorf considered little more than a gigantic display of the fleet's sea and air power.

That evening, after conferring with his aides, the admiral radioed an urgent dispatch to Pearl Harbor. He asked that its contents be relayed to all senior Navy and Marine officers involved in Operation Stalemate.

The terse message said the fleet had "run out of targets" and was ceasing operations despite the fact that another day still remained on the pre-invasion softening-up schedule. If Admiral Nimitz disagreed with Oldendorf's decision, there is no record of his questioning its wisdom.

Generals Geiger and Rupertus were at sea en route to Peleliu and sailing, for security reasons, under a radio communications blackout. So if the Marine commanders objected, there was no way to let higher echelons know about it.

General Murai and Colonel Nakagawa must have been bewildered, if not thoroughly amazed, by the next morning's eerie stillness. Not a solitary ship could be seen in the calm seas off Peleliu, nor was there a single plane in the cloudless skies.

The Japanese commanders hadn't the vaguest idea why the Americans had broken off the engagement and sailed somewhere beyond the horizon. They were certain, however, that they would be back with a bigger armada—one determined to conquer Peleliu—very soon.

Shortly after midnight, General Inoue had called Murai from Koror on the still-operational underwater telephone cable that connected their headquarters. Inoue said a patrolling submarine had sighted and was tracking a large destroyer-escorted convoy of American troop transports. It was then some

200 miles south of the Palaus and steaming due north. The generals agreed that this was the invasion fleet—that the assault was imminent.

Did Admiral Oldendorf blunder in cutting short the pre-invasion bombardment and air attacks? Was the belief that his ships and planes had "run out of targets" the logical consequence of using flawed maps made before the island was stripped of its jungle cover? If he believed, as he had indicated to aides, that the Japanese had moved their heavy armaments to underground installations, why did he not keep seeking them out for destruction?

So far as the men of the 1st Division were concerned, it was an unforgivable blunder. Regardless of the admiral's reason, they believed the fact that the Fire Support Group left Peleliu with ammunition still in lockers cost them heavy and unnecessary casualties on D-Day—and during the battle that followed.

An interesting but supremely insignificant statistical facet of the two-day pre-invasion action is contained in an official Navy document.

Compiled by a nameless "bean counter" at CinCPac headquarters, it meticulously reports the amount of firepower expended: 519 rounds of 16-inch shells from the battleships; 1,845 rounds from the cruisers' 6- and 8-inch guns; 1,793 500-pound bombs from carrier planes; 73,412 .50-caliber machine-gun bullets in strafing attacks.

There also is a remarkable and odd footnote to Admiral Oldendorf's personal reaction to the concept of Operation Stalemate. In a postwar statement, he said:

"If military leaders—and that includes Navy brass—were gifted with the same accuracy of foresight that they are with hindsight, then the assault on Peleliu should never have been attempted."

2

The scenario of Operation Stalemate now became more complex and confusing. The next developments were crucial and can best be recounted by using the motion-picture "flashback" device to connect widely separated actions and to focus their importance on the final outcome of the script.

The principal characters were Admirals Halsey and Nimitz, General MacArthur, and the Joint Chiefs of Staff. The scenes ranged from the newly commissioned 45,000-ton battleship *New Jersey* on combat duty off the central Philippines to CinC-Pac's headquarters at Pearl Harbor, and to Canada, where the military high command of the United States and Great Britain were again meeting with President Roosevelt and Prime Minister Churchill.

The plot, assuming the word is appropriate for the occasion, involved a final decision about Peleliu.

Should the island be invaded? Or should it be bypassed as unnecessary to the success of MacArthur's plan to retake the Philippines? The question had taken center stage because of an urgent last-minute recommendation from Admiral Halsey.

During the two days of pre-invasion bombardment and aerial attacks on Peleliu, Halsey's Third Fleet had been having a merry time lambasting the Japanese on and above Samar Island, some 700 miles northwest of the Palaus.

The results were so overwhelming and one-sided that the admiral was convinced the central Philippines were, as he put it, "a hollow shell with weak defenses and skimpy facilities." His analysis was backed by solid evidence. From sunrise on September 12 until sundown the next day, Halsey's planes—designated as Task Force 38—flew more than 2,400 sorties.

Most of the carriers and flight crews had been attached to Admiral Mitscher's Task Force 58 during the early-March attacks that had devastated Peleliu's airstrip and all but wiped out Japanese air power on the island. The pilots knew their business; they had a combination of courage and flying skill that future generations of airmen would call "the right stuff."

Nearly 250 Japanese planes were shot down or destroyed before they could take off. Countless ground facilities and lightly armed fortifications were leveled. A dozen cargo ships and a tanker were sunk. Task Force 38 lost eight planes, but three pilots were rescued.

Did the impressive tally of Japanese losses and the apparent lack of defensive capabilities represent a true picture of the enemy situation in the central Philippines?

Halsey pondered the question. For nearly an hour, alone in a far corner of the *New Jersey*'s bridge, he sat on the high leather-backed admiral's chair, silently mulling over possible answers about what to do next. In the words of a close friend, "the old master of the calculated risk saw opportunity."

Why not recommend to Admiral Nimitz the scrapping of what remained on the schedule of Operation Stalemate?

Why not propose to CinCPac the scrubbing of the plans of General MacArthur to invade Mindanao Island in the southern Philippines as a base for future operations?

Why not attack and seize Leyte Island, the key to success in the overall strategy to retake the Philippines, months ahead of schedule?

Halsey had made up his mind, and was convinced his idea was a workable scheme that could shorten the still long and difficult route to Tokyo—and thus speed up the downfall of the Japanese Empire and the end of the war. He realized that Admiral Nimitz—and others at the top level of the military high command—must approve such a sweeping change in strategy.

Before informing Nimitz of what he had in mind, Halsey called his staff together. They pored over the latest combat reports, reconnaissance photos, and intelligence data. They checked and rechecked their estimates of the strength of naval, air, and ground forces available to Nimitz and MacArthur.

Their unanimous conclusion: Halsey's plan could be carried out with a reasonable chance of success.

"I'm going to stick my neck out," he told his aides. "Such a recommendation," he later said, "would upset many applecarts, possibly all the way to Mr. Roosevelt and Mr. Churchill."

The admiral then began working on his message to CinCPac. He was assisted in its meticulous wording by Captain Robert B. Carney, his chief of staff, and Lieutenant Commander Harold E. Stassen. Stassen had been governor of Minnesota, the youngest in the state's history when elected in 1938 at the age of thirty-one, and was serving a third term when he resigned in 1943 to volunteer as a Navy lieutenant. He was Halsey's assistant chief of staff, commanding the Third Fleet's combat information center.

Following V-J Day, Stassen was the United States delegate to the 1945 San Francisco Conference that marked the foundation of the United Nations. He later was president of the University of Pennsylvania, and also served as President Eisenhower's Mutual Security Administrator. In years to come, he became known as the "Grand Old Warrior" of the Republican Party after three unsuccessful campaigns to become the GOP's presidential nominee.

Forty-five years later, in 1989, eighty-one-year-old Stassen recalled vividly how the crucial event was resolved. "It didn't take very long," he told a friend. "Admiral Bill knew what he wanted to say. He just wanted to make sure that all points were covered, and that his recommendations were perfectly clear and understood."

A copy of the dispatch, until recently classified as secret, is in the files of the Navy Archives Center in Washington.

It asserts, in essence, that as a result of Task Force 38's attacks in the central Philippines, the Japanese had very few serviceable aircraft in the area, that most of their oil storage tanks had been destroyed, and that there was "no shipping left to sink."

The "enemy's nonaggressive attitude was unbelievable and fantastic," the text continues. No Japanese installations were seen on Leyte nor was any air opposition encountered, "thus the area is wide open for assault." Moreover, a downed Navy pilot reported that Filipino guerrillas, who rescued him, insisted that there was only a token ill-equipped Japanese garrison on Leyte.

The message concludes with Halsey's unmistakable strongly worded recommendation that Operation Stalemate be canceled—including the invasion of Peleliu—and that all naval forces involved, including the 1st Marine Division, be immediately placed at General MacArthur's disposal for use in his campaign.

3

Admiral Nimitz had not anticipated Admiral Halsey's proposed changes in strategy. In fact, the sweeping recommendations placed him in a perplexing dilemma. Nimitz had learned from past events to respect Halsey's brilliant strategic judgment as well as his fearless combat leadership. His previous experiences involving "the old master of the calculated risk" had resulted in a string of sometimes unexpected naval victories.

This, however, was a vastly different matter. Halsey's proposal, Nimitz felt, was a far-reaching change in strategy that he lacked the authority to make. Since the recommendations directly concerned MacArthur and his scheme for the recapture of the Philippines and the ultimate invasion of Japan, CinCPac believed that the matter had to be resolved by the Joint Chiefs of Staff.

They were then again in Canada attending a conference in Quebec (code-named Quadrant) with their British counterparts and President Roosevelt and Prime Minister Churchill. Nimitz thus forwarded Halsey's proposal to them, saying that he approved of the plan—with one exception. He was not willing to cancel the Palaus operation and thus bypass Peleliu.

General George C. Marshall, chairman of the Joint Chiefs, immediately sent Nimitz's message by radio to MacArthur, asking his reaction to the proposed changes. The general, however, was at sea leading his troops to attack the first island in the Philippines in the campaign to recapture the archipelago. The convoy, for security reasons, was under a communications blackout. MacArthur, therefore, was unable to respond.

Lieutenant General Richard K. Sutherland, his chief of staff, answered in MacArthur's name from Army headquarters in Brisbane, Australia. He radioed back that Halsey's information about the absence of Japanese forces on Leyte was incorrect. But with the additional sea, air, and ground support offered by the Navy, he approved the plan that called for advancing the date of Leyte's invasion.

When Sutherland's ex officio reply was received in Quebec, the Joint Chiefs were at a formal dinner hosted by Canadian military brass. The American high command excused themselves, stepped outside the banquet room, and conferred.

"Having the utmost confidence in General MacArthur, Admiral Nimitz, and Admiral Halsey," JCS Chairman Marshall wrote afterward, "it was not a difficult decision to make. Within ninety minutes after the signal had been received at Quebec, General MacArthur and Admiral Nimitz had received their instructions [approving the changes in Operation Stalemate]."

D-Day for Peleliu was less than twenty-four hours away.

4

Admiral Nimitz never revealed, either publicly or in any known private correspondence or conversation, why he rejected Admiral Halsey's recommendation to bypass the Palaus and cancel the Peleliu invasion.

Halsey also kept discreetly silent about the decision, declining even to speculate on it. While most biographies of both make passing mention of the matter, none questions Nimitz's reasons for not fully agreeing with Halsey's recommendations.

Harold Stassen, however, shares the opinion of an increasing number of military analysts and historians who find no logic to support Nimitz's position on Operation Stalemate. In a long telephone conversation, followed by a lengthy letter, Stassen in late 1989 detailed his views to the author.

"The invasion of Peleliu was," he bluntly asserted, "a terrible mistake, a tragedy that was needless and should not have happened." When asked if Halsey held the same opinion, he said: "I don't know. We never discussed it after that night in his quarters on the *New Jersey.*"

Considering the fact that General Eisenhower, when he was elected President, thought enough of Stassen's acumen and credentials to make him the ranking military adviser on the White House staff for three years, Stassen's opinion merits a place in the background and history of the Palaus campaign.

Another outspoken critic is historian Charles Bateson, who wrote in his book *The War Against Japan*: "The tragedy of the Palaus was that the Americans had no need to take them. They could have and should have been bypassed."

Some of Nimitz's former aides and other retired high-ranking Navy and Marine Corps officers, as well as World War II news correspondents, have said the CinCPac's personality and temperament were often at wide variance from his public image as a soft-spoken, understanding, compassionate, brilliant combat planner and commander.

Their views were summarized on one occasion by Lieutenant General Holland M. "Howlin' Mad" Smith, the senior Marine in the Pacific at the time of the Peleliu invasion. Smith's scathing remarks were not specifically directed at Nimitz's decision on the Palaus campaign, but reflected the private views of many people who served under the admiral or had dealings with him.

"Never an exuberant man, he could work up, in his quiet way, an extremely pessimistic mood," the truculent general said. "Admiral Nimitz was riding to fame on the shoulders of the Marines, so what did he have to worry about? The Japanese were on the run. Nimitz couldn't lose. He knew the Marines would win. If we didn't, he probably would be yanked out of his job and perhaps the Army would be in command."

There is no doubt that General Smith was extremely biased in his assessment of his superior, the Commander in Chief

Pacific. Nor is there any doubt that Nimitz harbored a personal aversion to the flamboyant Marine general.

A sorry final display of Nimitz's attitude is the fact that "Howlin' Mad" Smith was the only three-star United States officer in the Pacific who was not on the quarterdeck of the battleship *Missouri* in Tokyo Bay when the unconditional surrender of the Japanese was signed. Stunned and heartsick, he listened to the broadcast of the ceremonies in his headquarters at San Diego, 8,000 miles from the historic event that he and his Marines had done so much to bring about.

Rear Admiral Harry W. Hill, a friend of both men, was responsible for making up the list of Navy and Marine brass who would witness the formal end of World War II. When he petitioned Nimitz to invite Smith, the strongly worded written request was returned with "Negative!" scrawled across it in CinCPac's unmistakable handwriting.

But the question remains: Why did Nimitz reject Halsey's recommendation to bypass Peleliu? With the benefit of hindsight, there are several answers that, in themselves, are best posed as possibilities.

Was the admiral motivated by the assurance given President Roosevelt during the trio's meeting at Pearl Harbor that he would do everything possible to support MacArthur's strategy? Did he believe, as General Rupertus did, that the Palaus campaign would be a quick, albeit costly, victory? Was he concerned about the possibility that MacArthur might encounter an unexpected disaster in the Philippines and blame CinCPac for not providing enough Navy support to stave it off?

Recalling the problems in getting the 1st Division returned to naval jurisdiction after Cape Gloucester, was Nimitz determined not to chance a repetition of such a contretemps? With all of the elements of the assault virtually within sight of the target, and Admiral Oldendorf's pre-invasion bombardment a *fait accompli,* was it simply too late to abort the landing?

If the invasion was canceled, would the Japanese claim they had defeated the Americans and driven the assault force from the island? What effect would this have on undermining U.S. home-front morale and boosting that of the Japanese, both military and civilian?

Persons who observed Nimitz's actions throughout his tenure as CinCPac—high-ranking admirals and generals, subordinate junior officers, news correspondents, Washington's officialdom from President Roosevelt to congressmen and senators—agreed that he rarely, if ever, did anything of significance without a definite purpose.

What Chester William Nimitz's purpose was in rejecting Admiral Halsey's recommendation to bypass the Palaus will never be known. Nimitz carried the answer to the grave when he died in San Francisco on February 20, 1966, after a lingering illness triggered by a series of strokes. He was eighty-one. During his forty-seven years of military service before retiring as Chief of Naval Operations in 1947 he had risen from a seventeen-year-old plebe at the Annapolis Naval Academy to become the third five-star fleet admiral in American history.

SEVEN

A Special Piece of Hell

TROOPS HEADED FOR AN INVASION IN THE PACIFIC ALWAYS found a monotonous sameness to daily shipboard life.

The pattern was an unchanging and burdensome mix of physical and emotional discomfort: cramped berthing quarters, invariably bad chow, constant squabbles with annoying "Swabbies," mounting boredom, and creeping anxiety about chances of making it through the looming battle in one piece.

Each man of the 1st Division had his own way of coping with the situation as the Peleliu-bound convoy churned inexorably toward the objective.

During daylight hours, some sunbathed or did calisthenics. Others slept, read whatever they could find interesting, played checkers and sometimes chess, gambled at poker or blackjack or dice. Old buddies recounted shared pleasures of ancient weekend liberty passes back home or in Melbourne. Here and there, squad leaders huddled with their men, reviewing training maneuvers and studying maps of the island.

Activities shifted belowdecks at sundown, mainly because the ships were blacked out topside and smoking there was strictly forbidden. Until "lights out" blared through loudspeakers, most men talked or wrote letters. All hands, at some point each evening, cleaned rifles and other weapons and checked and rechecked ammunition and other personal gear.

Once the berthing compartments were dark, most men moved outside to escape the stifling heat and sleep on deck. Except for a few nights, the skies were clear, the sea was calm, and the temperature was pleasantly cool. The last evening before D-Day a yellowish quarter-moon failed to dim the luster of millions of stars.

The final hours before an amphibious landing were always a

period of lonely reverie for Marines about to storm the beaches of a Japanese-held island. It didn't matter whether it was the first time or the second or third or, for some, even more. In his own way, each man faced the brutal truth that he might die before another night fell.

Few slept soundly, some not at all. Even those who had been through it before, and had some idea of what to expect, felt unspoken but gnawing fears.

"Anyone who claims he ain't afraid is either lyin' or don't know the score." The words are those of a Guadalcanal and Cape Gloucester survivor quoted in a news story written by Sergeant Donald A. Hallman, a Marine combat correspondent, a few hours before D-Day. It is completely accurate to say that the sentence reflected the no-nonsense feelings of the Old Breed's veterans.

"Reveille came at 5:30," Hallman's dispatch continues. "On some ships it was a recorded bugle call trumpeting through loudspeakers. On others it was signaled by a clanging bell and someone turning on blinding lights in berthing compartments, followed by a loud shout of 'Hit the deck! Hit the deck!' Only the most hardy and hungry took more than a few bites from the traditional steak-and-eggs breakfast. A couple of slices of toast washed down by steaming black coffee filled the appetites of virtually every Marine."

During the night, the hundreds of vessels of the landing force had moved from the rendezvous area 20 miles at sea. Each ship—regardless of size or function—was now at its assigned battle station, waiting for H-Hour to come at 8:30.

The *Mount McKinley*, command ship and communications center for the operation, was 3,000 yards offshore. The invasion's top Navy and Marine brass—Rear Admiral George Fort and Major Generals Julian C. Smith and Roy S. Geiger—paced her bridge, ticking off the minutes until the assault began.

Major General Rupertus and his staff were aboard the 1st Division's floating headquarters, the specially converted APA troop transport *DuPage*. It also was the operation's standby command and communications ship, and was 500 yards closer to the beach.

The *Elmore*, an APA fitted out like the *DuPage*, carried Brigadier General Smith, assistant division commander, and his aides. It was in position 1,000 yards beyond the reef, near the center of the landing zones. Smith had been designated to be the first general officer to land and to set up the 1st Division's beachhead command post.

The LSTs and APAs, loaded with the first waves of assault troops, were some 2,000 yards at sea in front of the reef. Straight ahead beyond the deadly coral barrier were the specific beaches where the division's infantry regiments were to land.

It was almost curtain time for a tragic drama—the needless and deadly struggle for Peleliu.

2

Weather was ideal for the invasion.

Predawn ocean swells were so slight outside the reef that ships appeared to be motionless, as if securely moored to a dock. Small clusters of brilliant morning stars appeared between slow-moving clouds that floated leisurely to the west, pushed along by a soft tropical breeze. Navy meteorologists predicted that the day's temperature wouldn't exceed 90 degrees.

H-Hour was three hours away.

Topside on the APA transports, sailors opened hatches and swung out booms to unload wooden pallets of supplies and equipment. They lowered Higgins boats on their davits and slung nets over the side for Marines to clamber down to the landing craft.

The descent was always clumsy and dangerous. Each infantryman's rifle was slung over his shoulder, and he was further burdened with at least two heavy backpacks of personal gear and rations, a web belt carrying ammunition, two full canteens of water, and an emergency kit of bandages and sulfa powder.

It was not uncommon for a man to lose his grip and plunge backward into the sea. Lucky ones were quickly fished out by comrades; a few others disappeared like huge rocks falling from a cliff, dragged to their deaths by the weight of the loads they carried. Some were seriously injured or killed, crushed between a ship's steel hull and the heavy side of a landing craft.

When the Higgins boats were loaded, they pulled away to form a giant circle and wait for the signal to move abreast to the reef. There the men transferred to amtracs for the final run to the beach.

Men on the LSTs made up the first three waves designated to hit the beaches. They carried the same heavy loads as the other infantrymen. Instead of using cargo nets, they backed down steel ladders from troop compartments to the cavernous hulls of the LSTs. Then they climbed up and over the 3-inch-thick steel sides of the amtracs that, like monster alligators, could move across the reef and carry them direct to the shore.

That was the way things were *supposed* to work according to the landing plan. Colonel Nakagawa and his troops, however, had different ideas that soon became devastatingly obvious.

Despite Admiral Oldendorf's dispatch that all known enemy targets had been destroyed twenty-four hours before D-Day, the Fire Support Group was again in action as H-Hour approached. It was now-or-never time for the big guns of the Navy's battlewagons and cruisers to clear the beaches and their approaches of any undiscovered or new defenses.

At 5:50 A.M., Oldendorf again flashed the order:

"Commence firing!"

This time the bombardment wasn't as heavy or concentrated. The mission now was to keep the Japanese pinned down until the first waves of Marine assault troops landed and established a functioning beachhead. When fifteen-minute spasms of 14- and 16-inch shelling stopped, carrier planes took over with dive-bombing and strafing runs.

The nonstop combination of sea-air support continued for two hours. At 7:50, sixteen rocket-launching LCM landing craft moved to the edge of the reef and unleashed a screaming stream of flaming 5-inch projectiles.

It was time for the first wave of amtracs to head for the reef.

Tom Lea, a correspondent-artist for *Life* magazine, later wrote: "In the first gray light I saw the sea filled with the awe-inspiring company of our ships. Out on the horizon in every direction were lean men-of-war, fat transports, and stubby landing craft, gathered around like magic in the growing light."

Thousands of anxious Marines, waiting to disembark, jammed the rails of transports, transfixed by the sights and sounds of what was happening. They, and other thousands in bobbing amtracs and Higgins boats, wondered how anyone on shore could survive the doomsday torrent of explosives.

Colonel Chesty Puller was in the lead string of the amtracs churning toward White Beach Two. The doughty commander of the 1st Marines had a different view—that of a combat veteran who had been through too many landings to remember. He was sure this one would meet heavy resistance.

"We'll catch hell is my guess," he told First Lieutenant Frank Sheppard, a platoon leader at his side. "One of these days we're going to be caught on an amphibious operation and be driven into the sea."

High tension clearly showed on the faces of many Marines—especially the young and frightened replacements—as their amtracs approached the onerous coral barrier that guarded Peleliu's shore. Normal conversation was impossible; only loud yells were audible over the roar of engines.

Most men tried to stifle their simmering but obvious anxiety and mounting fear. One might smile at his buddy, but it was a self-conscious, tight-lipped grin of faked bravado. Shouted bits of confidence-building banter were ignored or acknowledged with a solemn nod. Even battle-hardened veterans knew *no one* ever got used to hitting an enemy beach.

Troops silently prayed that the Old Breed would be blessed once again with "landing luck"—that the landing would be unopposed, or that resistance would be minor with only a few casualties.

The answer came as the lead amtracs clanked out of the sea and onto the reef, and were met with a searing curtain of Japanese mortar and artillery fire. Giant geysers of water and huge chunks of coral spewed skyward as a hail of shells slammed down among the landing craft.

All that could be seen from the bridges of the command ships was clouds of dense black smoke and flaming debris. When the screen began to dissipate after several minutes, stunned admirals and generals knew the invasion would be far from the "walk-over" that the 1st Division commander had predicted.

Hulks of burning amtracs littered the length and breadth of the reef along the landing beaches. Twenty-six had taken direct hits during the first ten minutes. In the next hour and a half, sixty were damaged or destroyed.

General Rupertus, his broken ankle still in a cast, watched what was happening from a canvas-back chair on the deck of the *DuPage*. "He was obviously concerned," one of his aides said years later, "but he was still optimistic. I remember him saying something like 'This won't stop us. We'll take the island on schedule, a week at the most.'"

Lieutenant Colonel H. C. Tschirgi, the division's transportation officer, was appalled at the destruction. "I'd never seen combat before," he said, "and the first thing that struck me was this was a hell of a way to treat $40,000 equipment." The comment was an obviously facetious attempt to conceal deep apprehension, but it was answered with stone-faced glares from bystanders.

To them, and most certainly to the Marines under fire, what they were witnessing couldn't be measured in dollars and cents. It was a grim question of survival for troops in amtracs caught in the firestorm on the reef, and the others approaching it.

Somehow they had to make it across the deathtrap.

Somehow they had to make it to shore and establish a toehold beachhead.

The assault landing force was committed beyond the point of no return.

3

There are only two ways to explain how the invasion was saved at its most crucial stage. One was the courage and determination of the Marines to cross the reef despite all the firepower the Japanese unleashed to stop them.

The other was something of a miracle. When the situation was most desperate, the intensity of enemy shelling diminished to sporadic artillery and mortar barrages. The timing of the let-up in the reef's bombardment has given rise to much speculation over the years.

Was it a deliberate part of General Murai's and Colonel Nakagawa's strategy to hold Peleliu as long as possible? Had they accepted the inevitable conclusion, long before D-Day, that the Marines would establish a beachhead regardless of cost? Now that heavy American losses had been inflicted on the reef, wasn't it by design that resistance shifted to shore, where thousands of well-armed Japanese were waiting in hundreds of fortified caves, bunkers, and pillboxes?

Admiral Oldendorf, offshore on the *Pennsylvania*, was unaware of what was happening just off Peleliu. However, his ships again joined the fray when the reef problem was at its worst. The timing was an unpredictable circumstance, the likes of which have often changed the outcome of battles through the years of military history.

Oldendorf's orders called for one final mission before the 1st Division hit the beaches.

The attack began precisely at 8:00, and was minor in comparison to previous shellings and air strikes. The action was planned as a short last-minute sea-air shellacking of the beachhead and nearby high ground. Its purpose was to keep the Japanese underground or in dug-in emplacements while the first assault waves landed, and to lay down a dense smoke screen to black out enemy observation of their approach.

With Colonel Nakagawa's shoreline defending force pinned down and the smoke screen covering the reef, the amtracs were able to form lines inside the coral barrier. Preceded by six newly developed waterproofed amphibious Sherman tanks, armed with twin .50-caliber machine guns and a 75-millimeter howitzer, the leading wave of infantry-carrying amtracs churned toward Peleliu.

The first troops were on the beaches at 8:32 A.M., two minutes behind the timetable made months before on Pavuvu.

Radio circuits throughout the invasion armada crackled with minute-by-minute reports from an air spotter:

". . . *Playmate* [*code name for General Rupertus's command ship*], *this is Spider. The first waves are on the beach! Repeat: the first waves are on the beach! Over.*"

"*Spider, this is Playmate. What resistance do they seem to be meeting? Over.*"

"*Playmate, this is Spider. Hard to tell much through this smoke. Over.*"

Knots of tense, restless, mostly silent men stood at the rails of transports, ready to descend into bobbing Higgins boats to carry them to the reef. Swarms of other landing craft, jammed with troops, circled in a seemingly endless and aimless pattern as far as the eye could see. Closer to shore, other boats moved toward the transfer line at the reef's edge to board amtracs for the final run to the increasingly violent beaches.

". . . *Playmate, this is Spider. Resistance moderate to heavy, I'd say. There are amtracs burning on the reef. Repeat: there are amtracs burning on the reef. Over.*"

"*Spider, this is Playmate. Where are our front lines? Over.*"

"*Playmate, this is Spider. Lines well inland on the right and center, but Spitfire [Puller's regiment] is still on White Beach One. They seem to be pinned down. Over.*"

"*Spider, this is Playmate. Can you see what's holding them up? Over.*"

"Playmate, this is Spider. There's heavy fire from the point just north of White One. They seem to have both beaches enfiladed. More amtracs are burning on the reef. I'm going lower to try and see what's to their front. Over."

Captain Frank Hough, the 1st Division's public relations officer, was aboard the *DuPage*, awaiting orders from Rupertus to land. As Hough looked toward Peleliu and listened to the battle reports from the ship's loudspeakers, several Higgins boats returned from the reef.

"As they drew alongside, it was seen that many carried wounded," he recalled years later. "Those capable of standing on their own feet were assisted up the gangway. For the more serious cases, tackle was lowered from the davits and the boat was hoisted to the deck, where stretchers were transferred with a minimum of discomfort to the sufferers."

Marines at the rail watched in silence. Then, as their turns came, they went down rope cargo nets to make the run to the beach. In Hough's words, "Peleliu was rapidly becoming one of the grimmest spots ever seen in the whole Pacific."

A new voice, young and excited, broke a silence of several minutes on the battle report radio circuit:

"Playmate, this is Spider Two. Spider One has been shot down. Lonewolf [Harris's regiment] is on the edge of the airstrip in several places. Mustang [Hanneken's regiment] making good progress, too, but resistance is heavy behind White Beaches. Over."

"Spider Two, this is Playmate. How are things on the reef now? Over."

"Playmate, this is Spider Two. Damned bad! Boy, the stuff is sure hitting the fan now! Some big stuff! There's about twenty amtracs burning off the White Beaches, and I make about eighteen off Orange Three. They got that one enfiladed, too. Ow! I see 'em. Six of 'em with a field gun! Request permission to attack. Over."

"Spider Two, this is Playmate. Your request . . . negative. Over."

"Playmate, this is Spider Two. Please, just one little strafing. Over."

"Spider Two, this is Playmate. Negative! Repeat: negative! You're supposed to be an aerial observer. Stay in the air and observe."

"Oh! Goddammit to hell!"

The scene was one of mounting chaos. All along the reef,

anxious Marines waited in Higgins boats for fewer and fewer amtracs to shuttle them across it and head for the raging maelstrom on shore. It was a mind-bending nightmare, especially to bewildered and undertrained teenage replacements being hurled into battle for the first time.

Flaming and smoldering wreckage of vehicles and floating combat gear were everywhere. Bodies bobbed sluggishly in the shallow water or were draped grotesquely across protruding coral outcroppings. Those who survived the battle, newcomers or combat-wise veterans of other invasions, would never forget the reef. It would always be a special kind of hell to haunt them for the rest of their lives.

Nineteen-year-old Private First Class Joseph Moskalczak was a coal-breaker in a mine near Blakely, Pennsylvania, before enlisting.

"The work was dirty, hard, and sometimes dangerous," he told friends on his sixty-fourth birthday, "but it was like a Sunday-school picnic compared to Peleliu, where I've often thought I was probably the first Marine to land."

Through the years numerous others have expressed the belief that the historic distinction belonged to them—an understandable belief created by the awful feeling of loneliness of all men in the first wave of any assault against a bitterly contested beach.

"This was my first and last time in an amtrac," Moskalczak said. "When it stopped on the beach, the rear ramp slammed down and I scampered out and ran to the left and jumped into a large shell hole about 50 yards inland. Then I looked to my right and saw no one. I looked to my left and saw a lone figure behind me on the dead run. He joined me in the hole and soon several other Marines were with us.

"No one knew what to do next, so we just hugged the sides of the hole and waited for something to happen. About this time my sergeant, a BAR man named Frank Minkewicz, crawled into the shell hole. 'Let's go!' he yelled, and we ran up the sandy incline of the beach. Near the top we hit the deck, because I heard the crack of machine-gun bullets overhead.

"Reaching the top of the slope, we saw eight or nine Japs. They were pulling and pushing a large cannon, one of the old-fashioned kind, with wooden spokes and 3-foot wheels. A line formed on my right, but I still saw no one on the left. We opened up on the Japs and killed 'em all.

"We went down to look at the enemy. 'Hey, this one is still

breathing!' someone yelled. One man plunged a bayonet into his chest and couldn't pull it out. He fired his rifle and the recoil made the job easy."

Jack McCombs, now retired in Palm Beach Gardens, Florida, joined the Navy when he was seventeen. His first combat as a medical corpsman came at Peleliu eighteen months later. It was an experience he would never forget:

"I was somewhat aghast after watching the bombing of the island by the Navy before we landed. I thought all the Japs would be dead. Archie MacKecknie, one of our machine gunners who had fought on Guadalcanal, told me: 'You're nuts. You'll see plenty of action.' When we got within fifty yards of shore, I found out how right he was. Enemy shells were falling everywhere. The beach was littered with dead and wounded men.

"That night the Japs hit us in the dark, and it created a helluva mess. I patched up the wounded by feeling my hands for blood, because many of the men didn't know where they were hit."

McCombs was wounded in five places by rifle and mortar fire on D plus four. He spent fifteen months recovering from several operations, and later graduated from the University of Wisconsin with a degree in accounting.

Charles H. Owen, of Lafayette, Georgia, retired as a master sergeant after thirty years in the Marine Corps in World War II, Korea, and Vietnam. On Peleliu, he was a sixteen-year-old private first class rifleman facing enemy fire for the first time. His recollections of D-Day?

"I was in an amtrac in one of the first waves. When we hit the beach, I went over the side. It was a long jump . . . like falling into hell. The beach was being hit by heavy small-arms fire and mortars and artillery. There were bodies and parts of bodies all around. I was terrified.

"We had always been told to get off the beach. It was the most dangerous place to be. But many troops were still there and not moving. Out of nowhere came a major I never saw before or again.

"He ignored all the torrent of enemy fire, and was busy kicking asses and screaming at us. All I could think of was to get off the beach before that crazy sonofabitch shot me.

"Years later, while serving as a senior drill instructor at boot camp in San Diego, I had a fellow DI who babied and talked his recruits through training. I was told this was psychology. All those years, I had thought what that major on Peleliu was using was psychology. But whatever it was, he saved our lives."

At forty-one, John C. Boyd could lay claim to being the oldest private first class to land early on D-Day. He was thirty-eight, too old for the draft, when he volunteered in time to see action as a machine gunner on New Britain. He also was huge—the biggest man in his outfit, well over 6 feet tall and weighing at least 200 pounds.

Boyd was a radio jeep driver, but he abandoned the vehicle when it sank in the surf. He was wading to shore when the Marine in front of him was hit by shrapnel and collapsed in the chest-deep water. He pulled the man from below the surface, tucked him under one arm, and carried him ashore.

Later, on Okinawa, Boyd killed a bayonet-wielding Japanese in hand-to-hand combat. But his most vivid memory of the war was D-Day at Peleliu, where, he said, "the sea was red with the blood of Marines." He was discharged in November 1945, still a PFC, and still forever proud to be one of the Old Breed.

Private First Class Don MacIvor landed in the fifth wave on White Beach with a platoon from the 2d Battalion of the 1st Marines. He ultimately retired as a major and settled in Yuba City, California. What happened to his unit is etched in memory:

"I don't think anyone really knew how bad things were until the fifth day, when we were brought off the lines into reserve. We hadn't eaten except for the C rations we had in our packs. I remember some Navy guys, carrying large containers of hot chow, finally located us. A chief petty officer said he had food for fifty men and asked, 'Where the hell are the rest of your guys?'

"It was then we looked around and counted the group. There were eighteen of us left. We had lost two thirds of our outfit, but we were lucky compared to some other units in the battalion."

4

The concept of amphibious landings as a strategy of modern warfare was born in 1915 during World War I. It was the brainchild of Winston Churchill, then Great Britain's First Lord of the Admiralty, and was first used against strongly entrenched pro-German Turkish forces on the Gallipoli Peninsula in the Middle East.

The operation ended in a bloody defeat for British and French troops and resulted in Churchill's political eclipse until World War II erupted. It wasn't that the concept was basically unsound. It failed because its planners hadn't recognized the complexities and cost of *any* seaborne assault against *any* well-defended objective.

Now, three decades later on Peleliu, the 1st Marine Division *knew* what it faced. Like the Allied troops at Gallipoli, it was ensnarled in an amphibious landing in which victory or defeat was always an unpredictable and costly gamble.

Through the years beginning in 1918, and during earlier World War II Pacific battles, the Marine Corps had painstakingly developed and refined the techniques of ship-to-shore operations. The major lesson learned was that success or failure hinged on what happened during the first crucial minutes after the troops landed against heavy enemy opposition.

Despite the hellish shelling of the reef, despite the deadly machine-gun and mortar fire on the beach, the Old Breed did what was expected of them. Now, on Peleliu's blazing shore, individuals began to form up in their assigned fire teams and squads, then in platoons and companies and battalions of combat Marines.

Corporal Lewis K. Bausell was one of the first to locate his squad in the turmoil of the beach. Eight days after the Japanese attack on Pearl Harbor, he had quit his job as a seventeen-year-old apprentice bookbinder in Washington, D.C., to join the Marine Corps.

Bausell earned his stripes for service on Guadalcanal and Cape Gloucester, and had observed his twentieth birthday aboard ship en route to Peleliu. If anyone ever was destined to be forever remembered by his buddies in the 1st Battalion, 5th Marines, it was Bausell.

Shortly after 10:00, less than an hour after hitting Orange Beach Two, he and several other Marines had fought their way to the top of a small coral ridge about 100 yards inland. As they reached the crest, they found a second lieutenant and a flame-thrower team attacking a cave with entrances on both sides of the slope. The action was fierce, with enemy machine-gun fire and incoming mortars.

Bausell and about a half-dozen other men crouched at the open mouth, waiting to cut down any Japanese trying to escape the deadly stream of flame coming from the other end. Moments later, one of the enemy charged out. He was holding a hand grenade against his body, and lunged forward as it exploded. Four Marines were wounded, and the Japanese was blown to pieces.

"Another Jap came to the entrance and was shot," one of Bausell's comrades said in describing what happened. "Then a third appeared and threw a grenade into the band of Marines. There wasn't any cover and no place to run, so Corporal Bausell threw himself against it."

He was mortally wounded saving the lives of his comrades, and died three days later on the hospital ship *Bountiful*. "We did all we could to pull him through," a grim-faced Navy surgeon told one of Bausell's buddies, "but it wasn't enough. He fought to the end, but he was torn apart in so many places that we couldn't stop the bleeding."

On June 11, 1945, Navy Secretary James Forrestal presented Bausell's parents with their son's posthumous Medal of Honor at a ceremony in Washington. President Roosevelt had personally approved the hero's award and signed the accompanying citation, just before the Commander in Chief's unexpected death two months earlier.

By 11:30 of D-Day, three hours after the first wave of Marines landed, the beachhead still looked like a battlefield junkyard. Smoldering hulks of landing craft were scattered along the shoreline. Dozens of wrecked vehicles were everywhere. Piles of supplies, pallets of ammunition, and 55-gallon drums of fuel and water remained where they had been dumped from landing craft. Out on the reef, gray smoke plumes pinpointed damaged or destroyed amtracs.

But the scene was deceiving; the most crucial stage of the invasion was over. Again, as had been the case so many times in the past, all the ingredients came together: *esprit de corps,* training, discipline, dedication to comrades, leadership—everything that made the 1st Division a unique elite clan of fighting men.

The Marines now had momentum on their side. Nearly 6,000 troops were ashore, pressing the attack against heavy resistance that was becoming more intense by the minute.

Chesty Puller had landed and set up the regimental command post for the 1st Marines on White Beach One near the northern end of the beachhead. Bucky Harris was in his CP on Orange Beach Two, calling the shots for the 5th Regiment in the center of the battleline. Herm Hanneken was keeping track of what was happening to the 7th Marines from his foxhole headquarters on Orange Beach Three near Peleliu's south tip.

No one had any thought that the beachhead was secure; it was, in fact, taking frequent heavy and accurate artillery fire. No one believed, as General Rupertus apparently still did, that the campaign would end in a quick victory. And casualties? Except for the horrendous losses at Tarawa, they already exceeded those suffered on D-Day during any previous Pacific invasion.

Although he didn't know it at the time, Chesty Puller's 1st Marines were in serious trouble even before the first wave was on the beach.

While crossing the reef, five of its amtracs took direct mortar hits and were badly damaged. Not only were several men killed or wounded, but most of the regiment's radio communications gear and operators were lost. For several hours, contact was virtually nonexistent between Puller's CP and other units.

"Remember I told you that one of these days we'd get the shit shot out of us during a landing," the fuming Puller remarked to Sheppard. "I guess all we can do now is fart in the wind and see if anybody answers. Meantime, let's see if we can kill a few fuckin' Nips." It was a typical Puller reaction to a bad situation, Sheppard said later.

Several hundred yards down the beach, Lieutenant Colonel Steven V. Sabol and his 3d Battalion of the 1st Marines were in a desperate firefight that had erupted within minutes after the landing.

They had first been bracketed by precisely targeted and timed heavy artillery and mortar barrages that caused serious losses. Then, after surviving the bombardment by scampering from one shell crater to another, leading elements advanced slightly more than 100 yards inland. Directly in front was a long, rugged coral ridge about 50 feet high, a formidable obstacle not shown on the flawed combat maps.

Japanese machine gunners and snipers opened up with a curtain of withering crossfire from countless caves and dug-in positions that honeycombed the precipitous face of the coral fortress. Three of the few Sherman tanks ashore were called up to do what they could to silence the blistering enemy firestorm. Their approach brought down another roaring mortar and artillery bombardment, and the tanks were forced from the scene.

A platoon of Marines managed to crawl to within a few yards of the base of the ridge, and found themselves tumbling into a wide, deep tank trap. Diving for whatever cover they could find, the men were pinned down, unable either to attack or to withdraw.

Nineteen-year-old Private First Class Braswell D. Dean, Jr., was one of those snared in the rock-strewn no-man's-land. Peleliu was his first campaign, and since landing he had passed through the stage of sheer fear to a feeling of virtual hopelessness.

"Late in the afternoon, with mortars dropping down from all directions, it seemed like most of our platoon was either killed or wounded," Dean recalled forty-five years later. "Death and devastation were everywhere."

The youthful attorney-to-be made it through the battle, and the invasion of Okinawa, safely. In 1989, while serving as presiding judge of the Georgia State Court of Appeals, he wrote about September 15, 1944.

"The first day on Peleliu was a nightmare that will remain with me forever," he said.

The close-in combat continued for almost eight hours. About an hour before sundown, Colonel Sabol considered the battalion's position so precarious that he feared a strong Japanese night attack could crack the Marines' thin perimeter and sweep across the beachhead to the sea.

Such a breakthrough in force would certainly create, at the time, serious chaos all along the division's 3,000-yard foothold on the island, and possibly jeopardize chances of the invasion's success. Since all organized reinforcement units already were committed elsewhere, non-infantry troops were ordered forward to help meet the threat.

Some one hundred men from the 1st Engineer Battalion, twenty or thirty division headquarters personnel, a dozen or so cooks and bakers—anyone who could be spared—grabbed rifles and grenades to dig in with Sabol's shot-up platoons.

For whatever reason, the Japanese didn't attack. A senior Marine intelligence officer later speculated that the enemy was unaware of the shallowness of the Marine defenses.

"Furthermore," he wrote in an official combat analysis, "the plans for the defense of Peleliu, as was later discovered, did not envision a major counterattack in this particular sector.

"Never overgifted with the resourcefulness to capitalize on a fluid tactical situation, the Japanese were in no position to do so now . . . and so as happens so often in the confusion of battle, the golden opportunity slipped through their fingers."

5

Colonel Nakagawa's defense plan may not have been flexible enough to improvise an attack to overrun the Marines' flimsy line at the foot of the ridge. But the shrewd enemy commander wisely placed his key fortified positions where they could inflict the most telling damage on the invaders.

Captain George P. Hunt found this out within minutes after he led the 235 officers and men of the 1st Marines' K Company ashore at the northern end of White Beach One. The unit's objective wasn't large. But its sheer, rock-strewn terrain and heavily armed strongpoints made the tiny isolated promontory an almost impregnable coral fortress.

Maps and reconnaissance photos of the sector identified it as "The Point," but both were miserably lacking in vital details.

The most glaring deficiency was the failure to spot the 47-millimeter antitank-antiboat gun that was causing constant havoc up and down White Beaches One and Two. Until it could be knocked out, the weapon endangered every movement of the 1st Regiment.

What K Company faced is graphically described in a small, highly acclaimed book, *Coral Comes High*, written by Hunt in 1946:

"The Point, rising 30 feet above the water's edge, was of solid, jagged coral, a rocky mass of sharp pinnacles, deep crevices, tremendous boulders. Pillboxes, reinforced with steel and concrete, had been blasted in the base of the perpendicular drop to the beach. Others, with coral and concrete piled 6 feet on top, were constructed above, and spider holes were blasted around them for protecting infantry. It surpassed, by far, anything we had conceived of when we studied aerial photographs before the invasion."

Colonel Puller, with his keen awareness of the dangers of *any* amphibious assault, recognized the potentially disastrous threat of the Point to the 1st Regiment's landings on its assigned beaches.

His concern was so strong that before D-Day, he asked Admiral Oldendorf to make sure that the target be given special attention by the big guns of the Navy's bombardment fleet. Despite assurances from one of the admiral's top aides that "the matter will be taken care of," the 130-foot-high promontory was unexplainably left untouched by the battleships and cruisers.

Because the steep western sides of the Point descended to the sea, it was necessary for K Company to land on the exposed shore a few hundred feet to the north. The two platoons at the point of the assault scrambled inland, where they intended to swing to the right to attack the objective head-on.

Only about half of the troops advanced more than 50 yards before they were pinned down in a tank trap. The rest were cut to pieces in typhoonlike waves of heavy machine-gun and mortar fire as they desperately sought cover. To make matters worse, the platoons became separated in the fierce mêlée, leaving a gap in the lines.

Captain Hunt knew K Company was in deep trouble, the likes of which it never before had encountered. The 2d and 3d Platoons had lost nearly half their men, killed or wounded, in less than an hour. The lieutenant commanding one of the units was dead, and his second-in-command had been seriously hurt in a mortar blast.

Hunt later described the scene of the savage and ongoing struggle:

"I saw a ghastly mixture of bandages, bloody and mutilated skin; Marines gritting their teeth resigned to their wounds; men groaning and writhing in their agonies; men outstretched or twisted or grotesquely transfixed in the attitudes of death; men with their entrails exposed or whole chunks of body ripped out of them. . . ."

K Company's only chance to survive and seize the Point, Hunt knew, was to commit his last reserves: Second Lieutenant William Willis's 1st Platoon. While the Japanese concentrated on completing the annihilation of the other pinned-down Marines, Willis and his men managed to push around the base of the Point and hit it from the eastern side without being spotted by the enemy.

The make-or-break, do-or-die tactic worked.

Attacking the death-dealing Japanese pillboxes from their blind sides, the Marines systematically destroyed them one by one by lobbing hand grenades into the steel-and-concrete positions. In the process, Lieutenant Willis located the 75-millimeter gun that was the source of all the destruction on the 1st Marines' beachhead. The weapon was in a well-hidden, heavily constructed bunker in the coral rocks near the base of a sheer cliff facing to the south.

Willis, moving swiftly in a low crouch, dropped a smoke canister just outside the emplacement's aperture. Its dense cloud covered the approach of a corporal armed with a powerful rifle grenade launcher. The Marine took careful aim and fired the missile straight at the gun barrel. The direct hit blew the cannon to smithereens and triggered a thunderous, flaming blast of stacked artillery shells. A choking curtain of acrid smoke swept the interior of the bunker.

Screaming Japanese, many with uniforms afire from head to foot, groped to escape the inferno through a rear exit. The ones who made it were slaughtered by waiting Marines positioned for that specific purpose.

Shortly before 10:30, Captain Hunt and the survivors of the two other platoons stormed to the crest of the Point. They quickly established a defense perimeter anchored by a captured Japanese machine gun.

K Company now existed in name only. It consisted of just thirty-four effectives. And their ordeal was far from over.

During the hectic turmoil of the assault on the Point, the Japanese discovered the gap in Marine lines facing the objective. The enemy seized the opportunity to move several hundred heavily armed troops into the breach, and they completely cut off the Point from the rest of the 1st Regiment. Despite repeated attempts to dislodge the Japanese, it took another thirty hours of fierce fighting before a tank-supported charge achieved a breakthrough to relieve the isolated handful of K Company's survivors.

Captain Hunt and his tiny band of Marines, all exhausted and several seriously wounded, somehow beat back repeated daylong counterattacks. By nightfall, they were low on ammunition and short of water and medical supplies, and casualties one by one further reduced their thin ranks.

At one point, with the muffled sound of Japanese infiltrators clearly audible everywhere around them in the pitch-black darkness, Hunt was holding the Point with eighteen men. It was nothing short of a miracle, combined with courage and determination, that they made it through the night—but they did.

In many respects, K Company was a microcosm of all Marines on Peleliu. Ethnic backgrounds, personalities, civilian jobs, physical characteristics, mental attitudes, individual desires and ambitions were a cross section of every outfit fighting on the island.

Lieutenant William Sellers, Hunt's executive officer, was a twenty-seven-year-old farmer from Clayton, Alabama. He was nearly 6 feet tall by the time he was twelve and knew, in his words, "how to plow a straight furrow." If he made it through the war, he planned to study agriculture at Alabama Polytechnic Institute and put his knowledge to work "on a piece of my own land."

Big and brawny, tough as nails, highly explosive and brave beyond belief, everyone called him "the Bull." Sellers was sincerely respected and admired by all hands. "It wasn't just because of his rank or size or any crap like that," Corporal Clyde McComas said after the battle. "The Bull's bark was worse than his bite, and he was always right there when things were the roughest."

McComas was a twenty-year-old miner from Mifflin, West Virginia, and joined the Marine Corps to escape the poverty of the coal fields. He once told his buddies: "I'm never goin' home after this fuckin' war is over. The reason is mighty simple, and I'll make it simpler just so you yardbirds can understand it. I live in the worst goddamn dump in the world, worse maybe than the hellhole we're in now."

The corporal left Peleliu with shrapnel in his legs, and a Bronze Star Medal for bravery when he knocked out a Japanese mortar pit with a rifle grenade. Later, on Okinawa, he earned the Silver Star for a similar exploit, and was given a spot promotion to platoon sergeant. He left that island with more shrapnel wounds, this time in the neck.

Private First Class Fred Fox, a seventeen-year-old from Houston, planned to become a petroleum engineer after the war. He was tall and blond and spoke with a Texan's drawl. Peleliu was his introduction to battle, and he was very lucky to live through the tumultuous night on the Point.

Shortly before midnight, Fox heard the faint sound of rocks rolling down the slope in front of his outpost. Almost before the young Marine knew what was happening, he was bayoneted in the chest and neck by an infiltrator.

"I shouted 'Japs!' and twisted the rifle out of his hands, and stuck the bayonet in his stomach," Fox later said. "When I was pulling it out—you know, just the way we did it in boot camp, pushing with your foot at the same time—something exploded next to me, probably a grenade, and I felt my left side go numb.

"The next thing I knew I was rolling down the cliff toward the water, and damned if another Jap wasn't stabbing me with a bayonet. He got me in the back, but I kept rolling. I don't remember anything after that until I saw a corpsman bending over me in the daylight."

Fox survived and ultimately realized his prewar ambition: a master's degree in petroleum engineering from the University of Texas. Like his comrades, he would never forget Peleliu—especially because he had eleven deep scars to remind him of the awful night on the Point.

It was years later that the Texan learned he owed his life to Corporal Andrew Byrnes, a K Company buddy from New York.

Andy Byrnes was from the Bronx, a fact quickly discernible as soon as he spoke. He had quit his job as a twenty-two-year-old dump truck driver to join up in early 1942 and intended to buy his own rig after the war. Captain Hunt described him as "a likable, conscientious individual, whose large capacity for hard work was equaled only by his mastery of growling or gum beating or teeth clicking. This made him, of course, a good Marine and good member of Company K."

Byrnes was a machine gunner and had shredded a large group of Japanese trying to overrun his one-man outpost at the base of the Point. At dawn he saw Fox sprawled, apparently dead, in the shallow water a few yards away. But Byrnes wanted to make sure, so he waded out and, under heavy sniper fire, carried Fox back to shore. This was where Fox opened his eyes and saw the corpsman bending over to treat his many wounds.

Corporal Byrnes received the Silver Star for his life-saving act of valor. And after V-J Day, he went back to the Bronx, where with $800 in savings he bought a used Mack dump truck and went into business for himself.

Twenty-two-year-old Sergeant Richard Webber was in the 2d Platoon, a squad leader from Beverly, Massachusetts. He was one of K Company's most popular men—imperturbable, quietly humorous, inconspicuously brave, and highly skilled in combat.

During the first few hours of the assault on the Point, all of Webber's superiors were killed or wounded. He took command of the platoon and, in the words of Hunt, "managed it brilliantly for the rest of the battle." They ran across each other three years after the war.

Webber had held a variety of jobs after being discharged. He was unemployed at the time, and was trying to decide whether or not to enter college under the GI Bill of Rights. He told his former captain:

"When you think of those guys in my squad, wearing dirty dungarees, batting the breeze, drinking jungle juice, fighting like hell when the chips were down—with never a care in the world—well, I just miss all that. People are too 'one-way' now, grabbing for themselves, not caring about the next guy."

"Why not go back into the Marine Corps?" Hunt asked.

Webber's answer: "No, it would be changed—peacetime stuff, spit-and-polish, parades, rank-happy bastards."

Platoon Sergeant Emil Macek, twenty-seven, was an enigma to his buddies, a mysterious and impenetrable person whose changing moods and philosophy of life baffled them. He was a machinist in a Detroit automobile plant before enlisting, and lived with his Czechoslovakian immigrant parents, who understood very little English.

Macek made no secret of the fact that he didn't believe in either God or the power of prayer. He took fantastic chances in battle, as though challenging death to come and get him. He saw fear distorting the faces of the other men who prayed regularly and said they believed in God, but he knew his face was as calm as ever.

"I think I became an atheist in the early thirties," he told Hunt one evening aboard the LST carrying them to Peleliu. "It was during the days when nothing—not even prayer or tears—could bring so much as a crust of bread to us, when charities refused to give us any help, and the only clothes we could get were castoffs from our neighbors."

Sometimes, back on Pavuvu, the gaunt, blond, hook-nosed Marine would serenade his buddies with an ancient Czech ballad. His haunting baritone voice invariably cast a strange nostalgic stillness over K Company's area. The song was always the same: "Dobu Noc Moja Mila," meaning "Goodnight, My Love."

Macek once wrote his parents: "The work out here has to be done, and if my faith and belief make me the strongest, then I feel it my duty to do the jobs that others fear."

On D-Day on Peleliu, a machine-gun burst ripped through his right shoulder. As he slumped to the ground, the look on the face of one of his sergeants helped to ease Macek's awful pain.

"What in the hell are we going to do without you, Emil?" the teary-eyed Marine asked.

6

Captain Hunt was handed a message shortly after dawn on the third day of the invasion. It was from Lieutenant Colonel Sabol, his battalion commander: "I Company will take over your positions at 8:00 and continue the advance. You will go into reserve and get a rest."

As the replacements moved in, man by man, to take over the Point, Hunt had a last look at the monstrous killing ground. He later described the scene:

"Along the shore Jap dead washed in with the tide and bled on the sand. . . . In the countless gullies and basins, the Jap dead lay four deep, and on the level stretches they were scattered in one layer . . . sprawled in ghastly attitudes with their faces frozen and lips curled in apish grins.

"Many were huddled with their arms around each other as though they had futilely tried to protect themselves from our fire . . . horribly mutilated, riddled by bullets and torn by shrapnel. . . . Seeing this I could think of no more scathing and ironic symbol of their disastrous efforts to drive us from the Point. . . . On the beach, in the woods, and on the coral rocks, we counted over 500 of them—dead. . . ."

K Company paid an atrocious price to take and hold the Point. Seventy-eight men remained alive, the survivors of 235 Marines who had landed on White Beach One forty-eight hours earlier.

The fortunate few who left Peleliu with Captain Hunt later complained bitterly when he was awarded the Navy Cross for his bravery and leadership. They thought, to a man, that he should have received the Medal of Honor.

EIGHT

Day One in Purgatory

THE TIME AND PLACE ARE LOST IN HISTORY, BUT SOME-where and somehow the men of the 1st Marine Division found themselves feeling that their outfit was destined always to do everything "the hard way." Dog Day at Peleliu further confirmed the belief.

True, the first assault waves landed just two minutes behind schedule. True, a functioning beachhead was established within an hour despite the devastation on the reef. True, more troops and firepower were coming ashore in increasing numbers, and the attack was slowly building up momentum in some areas.

But . . .

Although the situation was under control, it was far from an ideal state of affairs. All along the shore it was increasingly apparent that the operation was caught in the troubling tenets of Murphy's Law: "Anything that possibly can go wrong, will go wrong."

Brigadier General Smith learned firsthand of the imbroglio some thirty minutes after H-Hour when he and his staff left the troopship *Elmore* to set up the division's beachhead command post. A Higgins boat carried them to the edge of the reef, where they boarded the destroyer *Hazelwood,* expecting to find an amtrac to immediately make the final dash to land.

No such luck. So many of the amphibians had been hit while crossing the barrier that none was available. It was an anxious wait of nearly ninety minutes before, in the general's words, "we were able to hail an LVT, and it came alongside and picked us up.

"I asked the youngster who was driving it if he knew the way into the beach, and he said yes, he had been in two times, so

I said, 'Okay, we want to go into Orange Two.' He started toward shore, and there was heavy mortar fire falling in the water. . . .

"There was a barbed-wire fence about halfway from the reef, and he turned north instead of going right through the wire, which he should have. . . . After several minutes going the wrong way, I told him, 'Look, son, you're going to run out of beach pretty soon, and we've got to move in here and now. . . .' "

Whether it was because of the amtrac driver's inexperience or fear of crashing through the threatening but flimsy barricade, or whether the general's beachhead map was inaccurate, the result was the same.

The division's advance command post landing party went ashore at the wrong place. Instead of being on Orange Beach Two, as the operational plan called for, it was on the northern edge of White Two, less than 300 yards from the tip of the airstrip's east-west runway.

General Smith's first order of business, obviously, was to find a suitable site for the CP. It didn't take long for a two-man reconnaissance team of lieutenant aides to locate one in a nearby abandoned tank trap, but the mission had its bad moments.

"A Japanese popped up out of the sand and took a shot at one of the men," Smith recalled. "The lieutenant took a shot at him with his pistol; both of them missed. The matter was quickly settled when the other Marine bumped off the Jap with a Tommy submachine gun."

Despite the 1st Division's self-imposed and arguably imaginary "hard way" jinx, General Smith's command post was in business shortly after 11:30—just a few minutes behind the timetable of the battle plan. The news was immediately flashed to General Rupertus on the *DuPage*, and radio contact was quickly made with the regimental CPs of the 5th and 7th Marines.

All attempts to reach the 1st Regiment were fruitless for several hours; its radio gear lay in the sunken or burning hulks of the communications amtracs hit by artillery and mortars while crossing the reef.

Colonel Selden, the division's chief of staff, said Smith's first situation report to Rupertus ended in a heated flare-up.

"On the way to Peleliu," Selden asserted, "the Old Boy got ants in his pants and started talking about landing on D-Day.

. . . as the situation progressed on that fateful day, he became more obsessed with the idea of an early landing. . . . It was all I could do to keep him from going in immediately."

Selden's major and logical concern was more than justified. What would be the catastrophic results if all the division's senior officers were concentrated on a hotly contested beach, and were wiped out by a heavy artillery or mortar barrage?

General Smith had equally valid reasons for Rupertus staying afloat for the time being: ". . . Although he tried to get me to tell him to come ashore, I knew he shouldn't be ashore. . . . he had a tremendously large staff, and to move them ashore would have taken a lot of amphibian tractors and we just didn't have them."

Left unsaid was Smith's instinctive hunch that he was much better able to handle the present situation than Rupertus, a conclusion later verified by most of the division's regimental and battalion commanders, who were often confused by Rupertus's curious behavior toward subordinates.

Smith had more immediate and crucial problems to worry about than how the division commander felt. First and foremost, he had to find out firsthand from the infantry regiment commanders what their situation was—what progress, if any, their battalions were making. Were they in trouble? What was the outlook for reaching D-Day objectives? How many casualties had they suffered?

Reaching Colonel Harris at the 5th Marines CP was an easy matter, thanks to a newly developed experimental amtrac designed to provide several channels of radio telephone links with units ashore as well as offshore command ships. Likewise with Colonel Hanneken and the 7th Regiment. But it was impossible to get through to Colonel Puller, whose 1st Marines were in a horrible mess, a fact unknown to Smith for several hours.

Bucky Harris reported shortly after 1:00, saying, in effect, "So far, so good." His battalions had landed on Orange One and Two, and "met only scattered resistance on the beaches and not much more immediately inland." The cautiously optimistic outlook turned into a spectacular and crucial battle later in the afternoon when the Japanese launched a heavy tank-led counterattack against the 1st and 2d Battalions, which were trying to seize the airstrip.

The word from the 7th Marines CP on Orange Beach Three wasn't a cause for the slightest jubilation. Herm Hanneken's men, especially the 3d Battalion, had their hands full from the start. Because of the devastation and clutter on the reef, its assault amtracs were forced to approach shore in a one-by-one column. It was a slow-moving parade of inviting targets for antiboat and machine guns as the vehicles dodged floating mines and underwater obstructions.

Once ashore, the Marines found themselves in a deadly man-made and natural obstacle course. The beaches were strung with barbed-wire entanglements and a dense minefield, behind which was a system of mutually supporting trenches and reinforced pillboxes dug into the coral. For some unknown reason, however, the enemy's heavy reaction was short-lived, and the battalion took cover in an abandoned tank trap, where Hanneken set up the regiment's command post.

Regardless of circumstances, Hanneken had learned in his days as a sergeant in Haiti never to be either overly concerned or unduly optimistic about what would be the ultimate outcome of a combat situation in its early stages. Thus his first report to General Smith:

". . . We've got our hands full with problems. . . . Right now, we're pretty much pinned down . . . and we need some help from reinforcements and tanks to clear out the south piece of the island. . . . Our losses are about what were excepted, but not too heavy. . . . Over and out."

But what about Chesty Puller and the 1st Marines?

For easily discernible reasons, they were fighting a savage battle separate and apart from the rest of the struggle to consolidate the beachhead. The landing of the assault waves wasn't especially difficult or costly—except for the serious loss of the amtracs carrying the regiment's communication section.

Once ashore, however, everything fell precipitously into the 1st Division's "hard way" scenario.

Lieutenant Colonel Sabol's 3d Battalion was ensnared almost immediately in supporting Captain Hunt's K Company attack on the Point. The 2d Battalion, commanded by Lieutenant Colonel Russell E. Honsowetz, found itself facing a firestorm of machine-gun and mortar fire from a well-fortified ridge less than 200 yards inland. Major Raymond Davis's 1st Battalion, on Honsowetz's right, was caught up in a very similar situation.

In the words of George McMillan: "One thing was plain. If

there was danger on the beachhead it was where Puller and his men stood."

"The fact that we were, for all practical purposes, cut off from the rest of the division didn't bother the Old Man at all," one of Puller's men said afterward. "In thinking back, it was a made-to-order situation for Chesty. He liked nothing better than to do things his own way, without the brass breathing down his neck.

"I imagine if he'd had been with General Custer fighting the Sioux Indians at Little Big Horn, his last order would have been 'Charge! Goddammit, charge!' He'd probably have done the same thing with Kit Carson at the Alamo, and General Pickett at Gettysburg."

Not only was General Smith unable to contact Puller's CP by radio, but for nearly two hours he hadn't the vaguest idea of where it was. Not until shortly after 1:00 was he able to get an approximate fix on the location of the colonel's tenuous front-line command post.

The word came when a trembling, sweat-soaked, out-of-breath lieutenant—Puller's liaison officer—stumbled over the lip of Smith's tank-trap headquarters. He said the 1st Marines' CP was at the foot of a ridge some 300 yards to the northeast, and taking heavy fire from artillery, machine guns, and mortars.

With the still shaken-up lieutenant leading the way, Smith immediately sent a communications wire team to lay ground lines to Puller's besieged position. A phone link was working within thirty minutes.

"I asked Chesty how he was coming and he said, 'All right,' " Smith recalled. " 'Do you need any help?' He said he didn't need any help. I asked him about casualties, and he said, 'Maybe as many as forty killed and wounded.' "

Whether Puller's report of losses was based on misinformation has never been determined, but the verified official count was distressingly higher—nearly 500 men killed or wounded on D-Day. The figure totaled more than a sixth of the 1st Marines' regimental strength.

Twenty-five-year-old Lieutenant Carlton H. Rouh, from Lindenwold, New Jersey, was one of the casualties who somehow survived. Staff Sergeant James E. Moser, Jr., a 1st Division combat correspondent and former reporter for the Washington, D.C., *Times-Herald,* later described what happened.

"Rouh was moving his mortar platoon near the top of a small

ridge looking for a place to dig in for the night," Moser wrote. "He found what apparently was an abandoned Japanese bunker, but decided to inspect it before settling in with his men."

Minutes earlier, a Marine flamethrower squad had seared the position and two enemy dead were sprawled near the entrance. Rouh skirted around the scorched bodies and, with carbine level for action, crept into the dark interior where he saw no sign of life.

"Suddenly a shot rang out," Moser's dispatch continued, "hitting the lieutenant in the left shoulder. Several Japanese, hurling hand grenades, followed as he stumbled back toward his waiting men. Fragments filled the air as one grenade landed about four feet from Rouh and two of his platoon members."

Blood gushed from his wound, but the lieutenant mustered enough strength to shove his men to the ground. He was down on his elbows and one knee when the sputtering missive exploded. His abdomen and chest took the full impact of the blast, and he slumped to the ground. His men were unhurt.

More from Moser's story:

"Still conscious, Rouh could half hear and see the rest of the fight. 'Tommy' guns spurted death at the Japanese as one of his men stood over him. Soon it was all over, and Rouh's Marines had their cover for the night."

What saved Rouh's life was the fortunate fact that a battalion aid station was nearby, and a surgeon was able to keep the lieutenant from bleeding to death. With enemy mortars and artillery falling around them, a stretcher team of black Marines carried the critically wounded lieutenant to the beach where he was evacuated to the hospital ship *Solace*.

While recovering in a Melbourne hospital, Rouh found one of his nurses was Army Lieutenant Phyllis Rowand. They had been high school sweethearts and married a few months later. Among the wedding gifts were Rouh's promotion to captain and word from Marine Corps headquarters that he had been awarded the Medal of Honor for his valorous D-Day action on Peleliu.

General Smith had an unexpected visitor in his tank trap command post a few hours before Rouh's heroic episode. It was Major General Geiger, commander of the III Marine Amphibious Corps. Smith never forgot the incident:

"About 1:00, I looked up and here came Geiger over the bank, with mortar shells falling in the area. He came to see me, and I said: 'Look here, General, according to the book, you're not supposed to be here at this time.' He said: 'Well, I wanted to see why those amtracs were burning, and I'd like to see the airfield.' I said, 'That's simple—all you have to do is climb up this bank and there it is.' "

Then they had a brief discussion of casualties, and came up with a figure of some 250 in the 5th and 7th Regiments. At the time, Smith hadn't been able to reach Puller, and had no estimate of the losses so far suffered by the 1st Marines.

More conversation.

Geiger: "Where's Rupertus?"

Smith: "He's still out on the *DuPage* with his broken ankle."

Geiger, with a surprised and concerned look: "If I'd known that, I'd have relieved him [before the landing]."

There are different versions of where and when Smith informed Geiger of Rupertus's disabling injury. Some assert that it was back on Guadalcanal during the final rehearsals for the invasion. But one of Geiger's top aides, now a retired brigadier general, who was in the tank trap with the twosome, has said *that* was the place and time where Geiger first learned of Rupertus's accident.

To maintain objectivity, it should be mentioned that Geiger had an obvious but generally unspoken personal dislike of Rupertus and questioned his military acumen. The statement is verified by several official Marine Corps documents, and by conversations with persons, civilian and military, who knew both men.

2

Everyone who landed at Peleliu on D-Day has a different story to tell, but a brutal consistency is common in all of them. It is like a tightly woven rope with the strength of a hangman's noose.

Horrible fear and mind-boggling bewilderment. Awful sights of blown-to-pieces corpses. Mortally wounded men grotesquely sprawled in screaming agony. Explosions louder than doomsday's thunder as artillery and mortar shells fell in torrents. A narrow strip of sand cluttered with the wreckage of destroyed vehicles. Men desperately pushing inland, darting from shell hole to shell hole to survive machine-gun fire and hand grenades that seemed to come from every direction.

Navy Lieutenant Edward J. Hagan was in the third wave to

hit Orange Beach Three. The twenty-seven-year-old doctor from Williston, North Dakota, was the combat surgeon attached to the 7th Regiment's 3d Battalion, and had been awarded the Silver Star for valor in treating wounded troops under heavy fire on Cape Gloucester.

Forty-five years later, Hagan wrote a long letter to a retired Marine friend recalling mainly his vivid recollections of D-Day on Peleliu. The doctor said he returned to his hometown after V-J Day and was "still practicing family medicine and, like any small-town medic of my generation, still making house calls to patients who can't make it to my office." The letter was more sobering and reflective about September 15, 1944.

"I can't imagine how anything could be worse," he wrote. "After more than forty years, there isn't a single day that I haven't thought about Peleliu. I thought I'd forget, but I haven't. . . .

". . . Lying on the beach there, the first thing I felt was a horrible feeling of being all alone, the continuous high pitch of all calibers of guns punctuated by the continuous 'whap' of mortar fire and thunderous roar and then detonation of 150-millimeter mortars made it impossible to hear anything. . . . In turning your head from side to side lying on the beach, you could see dead Marines on both sides. . . .

"Horribly wounded Marines were staggering toward the beach, some apparently not wounded physically, but mentally out of it. . . . There were geysers of water all around the incoming amtracs [and] many were burning on the beach and in the water. . . . There is no way that one can exaggerate the intensity of the combined mortar, artillery, and small-arms fire. . . . A fair question would be to ask, 'How did anyone get through such a concentration of firepower and be able to cope with it?' I think that question is impossible to answer."

Tom Lea, the combat journalist-artist for *Life* magazine, was in the same amtrac as Dr. Hagan. He earlier had been with other Marines on other flaming beaches, but none were as hot as the hell of Peleliu.

"Mortar shells swished and whopped through the air over our heads," Lea wrote of the landing. "They hit without apparent pattern on the beach and in the reef at our backs. Turning my head seaward I saw a direct center hit on an amtrac. Pieces of iron and men seemed to sail slow-motion into the air. As bursts began to creep steadily from the reef in toward the beach, the shells from one mortar rustled through the air

171

directly over our heads at intervals of a few seconds, bursting closer and closer.

". . . A flat, cracking flash nearly buried me with sand. . . . Wiggling out, and trying to wipe the sharp grains from my sweating eyelids, I saw in the clingling gray smoke that a burst had hit about 6 feet from my left foot. . . . As I looked over my shoulder a burst smashed into a file of Marines wading toward our beach from a smoking amtrac. Jap machine guns lashed the reef with white lines and Marines fell with bloody splashes into the green water. The survivors seemed so slow and small and patient coming in there. . . ."

Assault landings were nothing new to *Newsweek* correspondent Bill Hipple. He was working for the Associated Press in Honolulu when the Japanese attacked Pearl Harbor, and had been among the first waves when the Marines hit Guadalcanal, Cape Gloucester, Bougainville, and Guam. Like Tom Lea, he never had seen such fury as D-Day on Peleliu.

The September 20 issue of *Newsweek* carried his eyewitness account of landing on White Beach One with Chesty Puller's 1st Marines.

"A heavy mortar shell splashed fifty yards away. . . . I was packed in so tightly with twenty Marines, weapons and gear that both of my legs were asleep and I wondered whether I could jump over the top at the propitious moment. . . . We couldn't see anything, but we heard the continuous 'whoomph-whoomp' of enemy mortars and artillery. . . . We clumped on the beach and halted. My sleeping feet needed no urging. I vaulted 6 feet to the beach and flung myself into a large shell hole.

". . . Snipers' bullets and mortars kept coming and an officer yelled: 'Spread out, everybody!' Some of us pushed into the underbrush—a onetime forest now a mass of tangled foliage, stumps and holes. . . .

"A Marine major somehow adopted several of us. 'Come on, I'll show you around,' he said. 'There's a Jap plane a little way up.' We followed him, inching 100 yards through the brush and wondering where the front lines were. . . . Near a limestone knoll I looked over the battle landscape and saw the upthrust tail of the Jap plane. . . . Just beyond, the forward elements were fighting for a toehold on the airstrip. . . ."

Lisle Shoemaker, a twenty-seven-year-old United Press (now called UPI) correspondent from San Diego, landed in the same amtrac with Hipple. As a former sportswriter, he had written often about "battles" between football teams, horses racing head to head in the final furlong of a major stakes race, and boxers slugging desperately to knock out one another in a championship prizefight.

Now he was writing about a battle in which the stakes were not money or glory, but life and death. And, for the first time, he also was part of it. Four decades later, he told his story in the present-tense idiom of Damon Runyon, the idol of young sportswriters of the era:

"This is my first combat landing. I am apprehensive but not really scared. I am doing what I had tried so hard for. I am an accredited United Press War Correspondent and I am covering a battle between the Marines and Japanese defenders.

". . . Our amtrac clunks to a halt. Hipple vaults 6 feet and flings himself into a large shell hole. I walk ashore upright, carrying my bulky portable typewriter that Bing Crosby gives me in 1939 at his Del Mar racetrack. For perhaps five glorious seconds, I am reveling in the thought that I am really in action and 'Hey, where the hell is the war?'

"My flash reverie is shattered whem I am assaulted by yells of 'Get down, you dumb bastard.' Just before I hit the sand, I hear a single shout, a familiar voice. 'What the hell took you guys so long?' asks the voice, a laughing voice.

"It belongs to Associated Press photographer Joe Rosenthal. He later takes the most famous picture in history on Iwo Jima as I am watching goggle-eyed from the beach 500 feet below as the Stars and Stripes snap in the wind on the summit of Mount Suribachi. . . . Doesn't take a genius to figure out that Joe lands in the first or second wave on Peleliu because Hipple and I land in the third. Joe takes photos of Bill and me landing, proof of his earlier arrival.

". . . Several of us start down the beach, crouching low like groundhogs looking for a convenient rock to hide under. We keep glancing around like racetrack touts, dodging booby-trap land mines and hoping we do not see a Jap pillbox with its snoot sticking out our way. . . . I am about 5 yards from Gene Sherman of the *Los Angeles Times*. He is confused and scared as I am. It is his first combat landing, too.

"A zzzzzzz sound whizzes right between us. 'Jesus Christ, Shoe,' shouts Sherman, 'that was a bullet!' Or a shell, I think. Whatever the temperature is, the searing heat gets to me. . . . I crawl up under a scrubby tree and collapse. I can't move an inch and I am not carrying loads like the Marines. I am toting only my typewriter. . . . I remember thinking I really don't care if I am captured or wounded. . . . It is no matter so long as I am not killed. . . .

"I do not know how long it takes, but I pull together enough strength and am staggering like a skid-row drunk down toward the beach. . . . Two Australians are there, Denis Warner of the *Melbourne Herald* and Damien Parer, a newsreel cameraman for Paramount News. 'You look to be done in, cobber,' one says. 'We'll fix you right up.' They build a fire under a tin can, get the water boiling, throw in a lot of tea and a lot of sugar. I drink half a canteen cup of this strong sugared tea and feel my strength come right back.

"I give the Aussies my sincere thanks and set out to find Hipple. . . ."

Obviously, the most dangerous part of a correspondent's job on D-Day was making it to the beach and moving up and down the front to get news copy or combat photos. But getting the stories and pictures off the island and on the way to civilization was often as difficult and frustrating.

The first step was to somehow get the material to the *Mount McKinley,* some 5 miles beyond the reef. This required finding an available amtrac with a coxswain who knew where the invasion's command ship was anchored, usually a hit-or-miss time-consuming thing to do. Most of the seaworthy LVTs had more pressing duties, like bringing in additional troops, ammunition, equipment, and supplies or evacuating wounded men to either the *Bountiful* or the *Solace,* the two glistening white and Red Cross–marked hospital ships lying 2,000 yards offshore.

Newsmen were understandably reluctant to entrust their day's work, for which they had risked their lives, to some youngster they'd never seen before and probably wouldn't again. So most usually served as their own couriers.

Once aboard the *McKinley* the precious stories and negatives were turned over to Navy Lieutenant Tom Lambert, who was the operation's press coordination officer. A team of censors then went over the dispatches, blue-penciling taboo material or sometimes killing the entire story for seldom-explained "security reasons."

After that, copy was radioed to CinCPac headquarters at Pearl Harbor for further review and, finally, cabled to anxious editors. Still photo and newsreel negatives were sent daily by Navy PBY flying boat to Hawaii, where they were developed and, if they passed the sharp eyes of pictorial censors, sent to their ultimate destinations.

From Peleliu's beachhead to newspaper headlines usually took more than twelve hours; generally photographs and newsreel footage took a day or more.

"A trip to the *McKinley* was never a total loss even if the censors spiked your story," Robert "Pepper" Martin of *Time* magazine observed. "You could always get a hot cup of coffee, and maybe some decent chow and a shower. The Navy sure as hell knew how to live."

While three dozen civilian correspondents and photographers were offshore on various ships at H-Hour, only six landed in the terrible tumult of D-Day. It wasn't fear or a lack of courage that kept most of the others afloat, but rather an understandable decision of the invasion high command.

Simply put, the brass had learned from previous amphibious assaults that having too many newsmen on a hotly contested beachhead could cause problems. Many had made other D-Day landings, but in a tight situation the unarmed and untrained civilians often endangered their own lives—and those of Marines concerned for the survival of the correspondents.

When beachhead conditions stabilized, any newsman who wanted to go ashore was allowed to do so. At one time or another, most did for several hours, and then returned to the *McKinley* for a variety of reasons. The most compelling was that they had been assured by General Rupertus that the costly battle would be won within a week at most and thus Peleliu would no longer be a major news story.

Correspondents relayed the 1st Division commander's highly optimistic prediction to their editors in brief and not-for-print messages passed by censors. The response was to be expected.

Most of the reporters and cameramen were told by bosses to immediately find ways to join General MacArthur's forces already at sea en route to invade small fringe islands of the southern Philippines. That operation, the editors said, was now the "big story."

By week's end, just five civilian newsmen were still on Peleliu to cover the fighting. As it developed, the worst of the savage struggle was yet to come. Thus it was a largely "forgotten battle" even before it reached its climax.

Daily dispatches from the remaining correspondents quickly vanished from the front pages of most newspapers.

Daily news communiqués from Admiral Nimitz's headquarters in Pearl Harbor began to have less and less to say about the Palaus, often devoting only a few sentences to what was happening there.

After the first week, most eyewitness accounts of the battle were written by Marine combat correspondent "writer-fighter" sergeants assigned to the 1st Division's combat regiments. Of the thirteen CCs who were on Peleliu, five were wounded. Of a total of less than 200 who served in the various divisions during the war, some sixty were wounded and fifteen were killed in action.

3

By late afternoon, General Smith felt he had a handle on the situation, albeit a tenuous one. He knew, at least, where the division's regimental command posts were and had a general idea of what was happening with the assault battalions. But he was deeply concerned about two critical questions: Where was the main body of Japanese beachhead defenders, and when were they going to counterattack in force?

The devastating bombardment of the reef and the heavy resistance the assault troops met after landing convinced him that the enemy had no intention of letting the Marines establish an unbreakable foothold on Peleliu without a major last-ditch D-Day effort to push them back into the sea.

The first sign of Colonel Nakagawa's well-prepared plan came shortly after 4:00 from a Navy carrier-based observation plane. By then two-way air-ground radio links were working, and the pilot immediately flashed an alert to Smith's command post that he had spotted several Japanese tanks moving forward from low-lying ridges north of the airstrip.

This was a sector several hundred yards inland from Orange Beach One, where the assault battalions of Bucky Harris's 5th Marines were advancing against determined but so far surprisingly light opposition.

Moving abreast were Lieutenant Colonel Robert Boyd's 1st Battalion and Major Gordon Gayle's 2d Battalion, both with the support of several Sherman tanks. Their D-Day objective was to drive a wedge across the southern tip of the airstrip's north-south runway and reach the island's eastern shore before digging in for the night.

(Above) D-Day: 0832 hours. Navy spotter plane reports: "First troops are on the beach!" as following amtracs cross reef where, at bottom, razor-sharp coral marks the treacherous barrier. (JOE ROSENTHAL/ASSOCIATED PRESS/WIDE WORLD)
(Below) Fierce resistance from dug-in Japanese pins down troops on Orange Beach One while the entire beachhead is hit by artillery from the Point, center, where Captain Hunt's K Company attacks concealed fortifications.
(CORPORAL ROBERT BAILEY, USMC)

Positive identification of dead is made on the beachhead *(above)* by checking dogtags and taking fingerprints before burial. (CORPORAL ROBERT BAILEY, USMC) Wounded evacuated to hospital ship *Bountiful (below)* had a 90 percent-plus survival rate. (SERGEANT LAWRENCE JOHNSON, USMC)

Japanese tank hulks and bodies of nearly 500 enemy dead *(above)* mark the end of the disastrous D-Day counterattack on the airstrip. (STAFF SERGEANT HARRY VASICSK, USMC) *(Below left)* Marines, under skeleton of a Betty bomber, call in artillery and pinpoint targets for Sherman tanks during the battle. (CORPORAL MAX ROEMER, USMC) *(Below right)* Wounded Marine receives solace and water from a buddy while waiting for stretcher bearers. (SERGEANT JAMES WASDEN, USMC)

A tank-supported platoon of 5th Marines, with Corsairs circling on call at 2,000 feet for low-level bombing and strafing strikes, advance warily into Peleliu's Pocket. Captain Frank Hough's words reflect the essence of this remarkable panoramic photo of Colonel Nakagawa's last-stand redoubt. "In broad daylight," he wrote, "one could stand at the mouth of Horseshoe Valley and study at leisure the precipitous slopes and sheer cliffs that were

its walls. It was eerie. You could almost physically feel the weightless presence of hundreds of hostile eyes watching you. Yet there was no sign of the enemy: no movement, no shots, only a lonely silence." Wisps of smoke on ridge and cliffs are from 75-millimeter shells fired at suspected Japanese cave entrances by Sherman tanks. (CORPORAL MAX ROEMER, USMC)

(Above) General Rupertus, right, maintains a stoic attitude for General Smith in the tanktrap CP as Marines complete mop-up of airstrip a hundred yards behind them. (STAFF SERGEANT THOMAS GAMBILL, USMC)

(Below) Beachhead, still under mortar and artillery fire, is a bedlam of incoming men, equipment, and supplies while wounded wait on stretchers to be evacuated. (JOE ROSENTHAL/ASSOCIATED PRESS/WIDE WORLD)

Ground crewmen *(above right)* clear away a destroyed hangar's debris for 2d MAW's aircraft as Seabees *(above left)* make Japanese headquarters suitable for the 1st Division CP. (SERGEANT FRANKLIN FITZGERALD, USMC), (SERGEANT JOHN CLEMENTS, USMC)

(Below) General Rupertus, right, and General Geiger discuss the battle's progress in obviously heated confrontation. (SERGEANT HUBERT WEST, USMC) *(Bottom)* Chesty Puller, shirtless and with his left leg swollen from an old wound, greets Geiger at the 1st Marines' frontline command post. (SERGEANT LAWRENCE JOHNSON, USMC)

(Top) Corsairs buzz the airstrip before landing after a low-level bombing and strafing sortie against enemy strongpoints in the Pocket.
(STAFF SERGEANT HENRY SIDERMAN, USMC)
(Above left) Ground crew quickly rearm a plane with a napalm canister for the next mission. (STAFF SERGEANT WILLIAM WILSON, USMC)
(Above right) Another aircraft, armed with a 1,000-pound bomb, taxis to the take-off point. (STAFF SERGEANT WILLIAM KAPPEL, USMC)
A target on Bloody Nose Ridge is hit *(below)* within thirty seconds—before the Corsair's landing gear can be retracted. (STAFF SERGEANT T.C. BARNETT, JR., USMC)

Three things are certain about what happened next.

One is that the counterattack began at 4:50. The second is that it started as a well-organized tank-infantry assault, not resembling in any way a typical Japanese banzai charge of tightly bunched hordes of sword-swinging, screaming fanatics. The third is that the short, tumultuous action ended in total disaster for the enemy.

Precisely who did what is a different matter. Recollections vary all over the lot, depending upon the memories of individuals about where and how they were involved. When all the pieces are put together, however, a broad-scope, reasonably verified picture emerges.

The enemy force was estimated at between 400 and 500 men, later identified as a battalion of Colonel Nakagawa's best troops. They started the advance with the cool discipline and determination of combat-savvy veterans, keeping widely dispersed, taking advantage of the scanty cover of shell holes and coral rocks, opening fire only when they came within effective range.

Some troops, armed with Nambu automatic rifles, clung to the turrets of several tanks, ready to jump off and start firing at the opportune moment. This time never came for most of them.

As soon as the counterattack reached the edge of the airstrip, Gayle's battalion opened up with everything it had. Almost immediately, Boyd's outfit joined in the furious action.

"We got about halfway out into that open field and then the Japanese tanks came roaring in on us," Gayle recalled. ". . . Very fortunately, I had my tank platoon right at hand, a matter of 50 yards or so from where I was, and was able to send them into the fray at the critical time. . . . The Japanese tanks were no match for our tanks and didn't last very long, although some did get into our front lines between the 2d Battalion and the 1st Battalion on our left. . . . Of course, everybody claimed credit for knocking out the tanks because everybody was shooting at them. . . ."

Private First Class Eugene Sledge's sharpest memory of the attack hasn't the slightest connection with tactics, but is merely bewildering and thankful wonderment that he lived through the battle. The future college professor was about to fire a mortar at the advancing Japanese when, in his words, "a Marine tank to our rear mistook us for enemy troops."

As the Sherman let loose with its 75-millimeter cannon at

point-blank range against an enemy field gun around a bend of the trail, Sledge's position came under a curtain of heavy machine-gun fire, obviously from confused Marines.

"My God, when that tank knocks out that Nip tank he'll swing his 75 over thisaway, and it'll be our ass. He thinks we're Nips," Sledge remembered a fellow mortar man saying.

More words from Sledge:

"A surge of panic rose within me. In a brief moment our tank had reduced me from a well-trained, determined assistant mortar gunner to a quivering mass of terror. It was not just that I was being fired at by a machine gunner that unnerved me so terribly, but that it was one of ours. To be killed by the enemy was bad enough; that was a real possibility I had prepared myself for. But to be killed by one of my own comrades was something I found hard to accept. It was simply too much."

Just as the Marine reaction was reaching its crescendo, a Navy carrier plane swept down in a screaming dive and dropped a 500-pound bomb on a concentration of several tanks and their supporting troops.

Then and there the counterattack began to look more like a nineteenth-century cavalry charge than anything so far seen in the Pacific war. What had started out with all the signs of a coordinated push suddenly became a pell-mell panorama of mass confusion and sudden death for the Japanese.

Enemy tank drivers opened their throttles and, in the words of an observer, "lit out for the American lines like so many of the proverbial bats from hell, too fast to support their assault troops or for those troops to support them."

The onrushing Japanese machines began exploding and burning under blistering Marine firepower, an impenetrable curtain of 37-millimeter guns, bazookas, antitank grenades, artillery, mortars, and machine guns. The troops that some were carrying plunged for cover, and were slaughtered by machine guns almost before they hit the ground. Those caught in the open were easy targets, and most died in the nonstop shelling and small-arms crossfire.

Without the impossible element of complete surprise, the enemy's action had little if any chance of success. The only plausible reason for the attack was to fulfill the suicidal code of *bushido,* and to kill as many Marines as possible before they captured the airstrip.

The Japanese machines were flimsy, obsolete "tankettes" with half-inch-thick steel sides—small, lightly armed reconnaissance vehicles whose only weapons were a 37-millimeter cannon and one .30-caliber machine gun. They most certainly were never intended for use in massive head-on combat against prepared positions or Sherman tanks.

The exact number of enemy tanks involved remains a mystery, but there weren't very many. The number was from thirteen to nineteen, depending on who made the count and where and when it was made. The discrepancy most likely stems from the mind-boggling confusion of the battle itself, and from the fact that the tankettes were so demolished that it wasn't possible to tell which parts belonged to which mass of smoldering junk.

A division intelligence officer with a flair for figures calculated later that "if every individual claim of a Jap tank knocked out was counted, there would have had to be 179½ of them." However, all tabulations agree on one point: Just two tanks escaped, badly damaged, into the scrub jungle north of the airstrip.

Marine casualties from both battalions were fifty-nine men killed or wounded. It was impossible to count the Japanese dead for the same reason that enemy tank losses couldn't be confirmed, but Marines disposed of nearly 450 bodies.

The most significant thing resulting from the disastrous counterattack wasn't immediately evident to the Marines. Only as the campaign wore on did they realize that resistance from enemy tanks was never again encountered.

The explanation was simple. Japanese tank strength was wiped out in the late afternoon of D-Day.

Grayish acrid smoke and coral dust still hung in patches as Gayle and his battalion resumed their determined push across the airstrip runway. They reached Peleliu's eastern shore, their Day One objective, shortly before dark and dug in for the night.

The twenty-seven-year-old commanding officer of the 2d Battalion of the 1st Marine Division's 5th Regiment was awarded the Navy Cross for his memorable performance of duty. His citation stated in part:

". . . Immediately after repulsing a strong Japanese counterattack, Major Gayle seized the critical moment to lead the attack of his battalion across the Peleliu airdrome. . . . With utter disregard for his own safety, he placed himself with the forward elements of his command and personally led the assault. . . . His courageous leadership and gallantry were an inspiration to his men and enabled his battalion to seize and hold a major portion of the airfield. . . ."

International News Service correspondent Howard Handleman came across Gayle in his command post the next morning.

"I don't know what fighting you've seen before," the major said, "but this is a sonofabitch." Handleman agreed. The newsman was an old hand who had landed before with other Marines on other beaches: Sitka in the Aleutian Islands, Bougainville, Kwajalein, Saipan, and Guam. He told Gayle he'd never seen anything like Peleliu and "I hope to hell I never do again."

4

Tom Lea had watched the volcanic airstrip erupt with General Smith less than 100 yards from the action. At one time an enemy tank roared to within a stone's throw of the division command post before it was destroyed by point-blank fire from a 75-millimeter pack howitzer. "It was rather upsetting," the intrepid general commented.

With dusk rapidly approaching, Lea decided to return to the beachhead for a final look at what had happened there on D-Day. He saw sights of unforgettable carnage.

"Jagged holes in the scattered stone and dirty sand," he wrote, "splintered trees and tangled vines made a churned, burned wilderness. Strewn through this chaos were not only the remnants and reminders of the Marines' advance, but also the new men and new gear that had poured ashore to back up the front lines.

"These men were digging in, making holes for themselves for the long night ahead. We jumped over foxholes, climbed around and over smashed trees, sidestepped tapes denoting mines and booby traps, walked gingerly around those yet unmarked. Telephone lines in crazy crisscross mazes were stretched along the broken ground. . . .

"Scattered everywhere were discarded packs, helmets, rifles, boxes, rubber life belts—the debris of battle. Lying on the seared leaves and hot sands were dead bodies yet ungathered by burial parties. . . ."

Lea found Lieutenant Hagan, the Navy surgeon he had landed with, in a shell hole that was a combination medical aid and evacuation station a few hundred feet inland from Orange Beach Two. He was giving a blood transfusion to a seriously wounded wide-eyed but silent Marine from a plasma bottle hanging from the limb of a shattered tree.

"Glad to see you're okay, Tom," Hagan said with a weary half-smile of recognition. "We've got our hands full here, as you can see."

Another young surgeon, Lieutenant Frank Stewart from Edgar, Nebraska, was at the bottom of the crater, doing what he could for another man. Padre John Malone, the 7th Marines' Catholic chaplain, kneeled with Bible in hand over a youngster lying on the ground at the lip of the hole.

Every few minutes another casualty arrived. The stream of suffering Marines was endless. Some were walking wounded. Others were draped over the shoulders of compassionate and worried buddies. Stretcher bearers carefully toted still more fallen men.

Teams of blood-spattered, bone-tired corpsmen methodically applied tourniquets and bandages, doused open wounds with sulfa powder, gave shots of morphine—did everything they could to treat and comfort their Marine comrades.

"We didn't have the facilities or time for any surgery on D-Day," Hagan recalled years later. "All we would do was to try to stop the bleeding, give plasma, sprinkle huge amounts of sulfa, dress wounds and apply splints, and do whatever we could to lessen the pain. Once that was done, we tried to get the men evacuated as rapidly as possible."

Getting the wounded to fully equipped shipboard operating rooms was a major problem because of the shortage of amtracs. The situation was compounded by the fact that the locations of evacuation points were improperly marked and thus hard to find. And some of the operational amtracs didn't have ramps, so the wounded had to be lifted over the side, a difficult task at best and excruciatingly painful for badly shot-up casualties.

Chaplain Malone had never been in battle before, a fact that Lea noted with compassion in describing the oppressive scene on Orange Beach Two:

"On this dot of earth he was deeply affected by the continued stream of resignation, suffering, and death. Amid the frenzy, the wreckage, and the snipers' bullets the Padre looked very lonely, very close to God, as he intoned his prayers over the shattered men . . . as the dead were covered with a shirt, a poncho, a blanket or anything that was handy [and] were placed in rows to wait the digging of graves."

The shattering brutality, the primeval savagery, the mind-crippling horror of it all hit everyone, even those who had been exposed many times to the grisly sights and the malefi-cent stench of the dying and dead. One of the surgeons, who had performed brilliantly and with unflinching emotion on Guadalcanal and Cape Gloucester, found he could no longer cope with the gruesome realities of Peleliu.

"I just happened to look up about 3:00 on D-Day," Dr. Hagan recalled, "and noticed him standing upright on the beach, staring blankly into space, twirling a pistol in his right hand and, I'm certain, contemplating suicide."

The surgeon was evacuated and honorably discharged with a Silver Star for valor after lengthy psychiatric treatment in a Stateside hospital. Hagan saw him years later. "He didn't have the vaguest recollection of the incident," the doctor said. "He had completely recovered and was again practicing medicine in his hometown."

It was four days before the division's field hospital was func-tioning on the island. It relieved the brutal situation, but not very much. Daily losses were mounting so rapidly by then that there weren't enough operating-room tents and surgeons to handle all of even the most serious cases—so much of the major surgery still was performed aboard the hospital ships or APA troop transports specially equipped to treat casualties.

The light of Peleliu's D-Day was rapidly becoming a dismal short-lived twilight soon to be followed by the fearful black of night. George McMillan wrote:

"The first day did not become the second until daylight. The hours of tension and danger did not stop with dusk; every man lay taut in his shallow foxhole through the night, beseeching the sun to hurry, to restore to the battlefield its bright, accus-tomed focus."

Parachute flares fired from offshore destroyers lit the beach-head in an eerie greenish pallor. Intermittent shelling from the Navy's big guns sounded like freight trains rumbling out of control down a mountainside. Every few minutes enemy mor-tars and artillery would blast away. Marine and Japanese ma-chine gunners constantly dueled, their tracer bullets marking the exchange of fire. Grenades exploded with disconcerting frequency, and any sound of movement was certain to draw sniper fire.

There wasn't a Marine on the island who wasn't nervously expecting a big banzai attack. Fortunately, none came. With the exception of the savage struggle for survival that Captain Hunt and his K Company were waging on the Point, the first night on Peleliu could be described in military terms as "relatively quiet."

Before closing up shop in his command post, General Smith messaged General Rupertus out on the *DuPage*: "All regiments are in contact and dug in for the night, and the attack will resume at 0800 in the morning."

The beachhead averaged about 300 yards inland from north to south. The deepest penetration had been made by the 1st and 2d Battalions of Bucky Harris's 5th Marines, who had driven about 700 yards across the airstrip to the eastern shore. The shallowest was zero yards where the Japanese held the shoreline on the Point, cutting off K Company from the rest of the invading Marines.

Total casualties weren't known until shortly before dawn. The figure was appalling. Day One on the narrow beachhead had cost 1,298 Marines—1,148 wounded, ninety-two killed, and fifty-eight missing. General Rupertus had estimated to correspondents that the total figure wouldn't exceed 500.

Robert Shaplen, one of Bill Hipple's fellow correspondents for *Newsweek,* had written a dispatch for the magazine earlier that day. It read in part:

". . . As soon as they hit shore, the troops fanned out and moved up along both sides of the overgrown Jap airstrip, which runs diagonally up the cape between the two beaches. . . . This is being written as I sit on a log at the main landing beach. . . . Bulldozers and tanks are busy helping unload men. . . . A hot sun beating down on us isn't making the job any easier, and although there are many complaints, there still isn't a sign of the Nips. . . . the general has just come ashore and he had to wade through water up to his thighs. But otherwise he was as immaculate as ever. . . ."

Obviously, Shaplen was writing about another invasion taking place at the same time as D-Day on Peleliu: General MacArthur's Sixth Army landing on Morotai, a 695-square-mile "stepping stone" island off the southernmost Philippines, the ultimate target of MacArthur's offensive at the time. The assault was unopposed and the objective abandoned by the Japanese. The only casualty was a major who stumbled into a hole.

It would appear that Admiral Halsey had been right in urging Admiral Nimitz that Peleliu be bypassed—that it was unnecessary to protect MacArthur's forces from Japanese naval or air attacks, at least from the Palaus.

NINE

Into the Boiling Caldron

MARINES ON PELELIU'S BEACHHEAD WERE TORMENTED BY uncountable and agonizing thoughts as Day Two of the invasion dawned. They were understandably thankful to have made it through the savage action of D-Day, but they knew without question that the worst was yet to come.

The furious resistance to the landing and the ferocity of the struggle to advance a few hundred yards inland had subjected them to the deadly realities of an amphibious assault, the likes of which most—whether combat-tested veterans or youngsters not long from the States—had never experienced.

It was, as General Geiger later said, "one hell of a hot beach." The word "hot" was used, in this instance, as a military term. It had an additional and devastating meaning to the men under fire. To them, "hot" also meant Peleliu's boiler-room temperature.

By noon of D-Day it was between 110 and 120 degrees. At 10:00 of the second day, it already had reached 100 and was getting hotter by the minute. With the possible exception of Army troops who fought the Germans in the deserts of North Africa, no other Americans encountered such an unrelenting and debilitating battlefield climate during the war.

According to pre-invasion intelligence reports, Peleliu's highest temperature from July through October averaged 90 degrees. The prediction apparently was based more on guesswork than on solid information, and would have a sorry impact on the first few days of the battle.

It was an inviolable practice for assault troops to carry two freshly filled canteens of drinking water and a packet of salt tablets when hitting an enemy beach anywhere. Throughout training it was drummed into the men, especially the newcomers, that—second only to firearms and ammunition—these could be vital to survival.

Water conservation was also stressed. Experience from prior invasions had shown that potable water was scarce, if available at all, on a beachhead. But clear thinking vanished fast under Peleliu's boiling sun and soaring temperature. D-Day conditions worsened by the minute, became more torrid and suffocating from the frying-pan heat of sun-reflecting coral and throat-parching dust and acrid smoke from shell holes blasted by naval bombardment and enemy artillery and mortar fire.

By noon, hundreds of men had drunk every drop of water they carried. The consequences were an inevitable disaster.

As if struck by invisible science fiction ray guns, scores of troops collapsed one by one everywhere along the shore. From helmets to boots, they were a stinking mass of dehydrated men in green dungarees drenched in steaming shrouds of sweat.

The stricken Marines, unconscious and defenseless victims of sunstroke, were easy targets for Japanese snipers.

Exhausted but still functioning comrades dragged as many fallen men as possible to whatever cover and shade they could find, crouching low and moving from shell hole to shell hole as fast as weary legs would carry them to the rescue.

"It was a sight I'll never forget," Dr. Hagan, the surgeon from North Dakota, said. "I especially remember the bravery of the black Marines who volunteered as stretcher bearers to retrieve the casualties and bring them to our aid station for whatever we could do for them—patch them up and evacuate them as fast as possible."

At the time the Marine Corps, and all branches of the armed forces, had a rigorously enforced official policy of segregation. Whites and blacks went through different boot camps when they entered service and never trained or served in the same units in the States or overseas.

Most black Marines were assigned to so-called noncombatant but labor-intensive outfits whose principal duties were to manhandle backbreaking crates of ammunition and supplies. A very few became cooks and bakers, and some served as mess attendants for generals. All black units were commanded by white officers.

Because of the heavy casualties and the unceasing need for manpower on Peleliu, they brilliantly performed a different—

and to most of them a welcome and long-sought—role as combat Marines in frontline action. Frank Hough later wrote of their valorous part in winning the battle:

"The black Marines of the 16th Field Depot distinguished themselves throughout the operation serving as stretcher bearers or carrying ammunition and supplies, and sometimes helping to man the outposts," he said. "They worked under the heaviest fire and most difficult conditions with courage, pa-

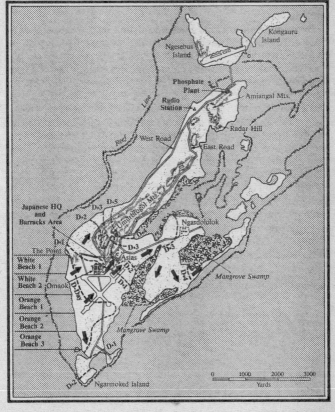

**SOUTHERN LANDING BEACHES AND ADVANCE TO
D PLUS FIVE**

tience, and cheerfulness notable in the hardened 1st Division. . . .

"About sunset of any afternoon, small knots of them could be seen trudging forward from their rear areas behind a sergeant or corporal to do their duty in the lines. Volunteers, all of them; by now the outfit had the deserved reputation of being the 'volunteeringist' in the Marine Corps. One officer was embarrassed on one occasion when, calling for volunteers, he saw his entire unit step forward before he had time to explain that this was not a dangerous mission but a mere burial detail. . . .

"Altogether, the black Marines of the 16th wrote a bright chapter at Peleliu in their race's contribution to the victorious history of the war."

Private Russell Davis, a rifleman in the 1st Marines' 2d Battalion, was digging in for the night just off White Beach One on D-Day. Years later he recalled looking back toward the shore and seeing what, to him, was a surprising and strange sight:

". . . Down along the path came a file of dark-faced men in Marine dungarees. They were tall and rugged-looking men, and their faces couldn't be distinguished in the darkness. They were the first Negro Marines I had seen in the war. They were carrying water and ammunition in from the beach, led by a huge sergeant who carried a box of ammunition on each shoulder. They dumped their supplies at the foot of the bank, and just as they did the Japanese fired a twilight salvo in on the line and everybody scattered for their holes. . . ."

One of the black Marines found himself in the same foxhole with Davis and decided to spend the night with him in the front lines. Just like his white comrades, he stood one of the watches as a full-fledged combat Marine fully entrusted to protect the lives of his newfound buddies.

2

While most of the heat-caused casualties recovered quickly and returned to action, some within a few hours, the problem of sunstroke continued in varying degrees throughout the battle. But on D-Day, and for almost a week, the shortage of drinking water became acute—and almost catastrophic. The reason for the near disaster was yet another blunder in planning the invasion.

Someone in the chain of command decided to try a new method of getting fresh water ashore to resupply the troops. At first glance, it looked like a good idea. Perhaps it was—if someone, anyone, had displayed common sense. But no one did.

Instead of bringing potable water ashore in amtracs carrying 1,000-gallon trailer tanks pulled by jeeps or trucks, or on pallets loaded with conventional 5-gallon steel jerry cans, why not bring the precious cargo to the beach in 55-gallon barrels previously used to hold gasoline or diesel fuel?

The reasoning behind the scheme had a measure of undeniable logic. The steel drums took up less valuable space on landing craft, and a few could be carried in each amtrac with assault forces. Once ashore, they could be tipped over and rolled to waterheads by shore party troops, becoming easily accessible sources to replenish supplies of drinking water.

But . . .

No effort had been made to purge the barrels of the residue of petroleum they still contained. Thus every drop of water was contaminated and literally unfit for human consumption. To drink it was an open invitation to disaster, but many hundreds of unwary Marines did despite the evil taste—and the inescapable consequences.

Half-crazed with unbearable thirst and overpowering heat, the men gulped down canteens full of the vile mixture. Within minutes, many doubled over with hellish stomach cramps. Others were hit with violent and uncontrolled coughing, vomiting, and diarrhea.

"Some stupid sonofabitch sure as hell goofed," a bitter and stiflingly sick sergeant said as he painfully crawled a few hundred feet to seek relief from his misery at Dr. Hagan's aid station. "God, how I'd like to get my hands on the fuckin' good-for-nothing bastard. So help me, I'd kill him without a second thought."

There is no known record of how many Marines were put out of action by the blunder. But the total was in the hundreds, and some were so seriously affected that they were evacuated. "How many of these recovered enough to return to duty is something I still wonder about," Hagan said years later.

Peleliu's water situation remained critical until D-Day plus five, when men from Colonel Francis Fenton's 1st Engineer Battalion found they could drill freshwater wells almost anywhere on the island. It is a miracle of no small magnitude that before then most of the men didn't succumb to the heat and thirst and were able to continue the attack.

The ordeal of one unit is recounted in an eyewitness account by Staff Sergeant Walter Conway, a Marine combat correspondent. The former reporter for the *Washington Post* was with the 5th Marines' 2d Battalion in its frontline command post on the afternoon of D-Day plus one.

It was a huge shell crater whose 20-yard top circumference sloped to a 6-foot-across bottom—an 18-inch-deep pool of murky and stagnant water with protruding chunks of coral debris.

". . . Huddled uncomfortably on one bank, seeking shade from the blistering sun and cover from Jap mortars, were Majors Richard T. Washburn of New Haven, Connecticut, and John H. Gustafson of Las Cruces, New Mexico," Conway wrote. "Both were sweat-stained and weary from thirty hours under fire. Neither spoke. Mud-spattered enlisted men dotted the sides of the hole. Some dozed. Others gulped, moistened their lips with their tongues, and looked longingly at the bottom of the hole. . . ."

The troops were members of an assault platoon that had been almost constantly in action since hitting the beach. Their few numbers, torn and dirty dungarees, and the blank look on their grimy faces were mute evidence of hard and costly fighting. It was obvious to Conway that the platoon needed replacements—and water.

Private First Class Kenneth E. Kraus, of Roxanna, Illinois, tossed up his dungaree blouse to a couple of buddies near the top of the crater. He had just washed it in the water at the bottom of the hole. "Spread it out to dry," he shouted as he emptied helmet after helmet of the dirty water over his body.

Corporal Earle L. Russell, Jr., from Clinton, Massachusetts, joined the group after helping a wounded comrade to the beachhead aid station. He dragged himself over the CP's rim and unslung his carbine, dropping down among the other men. Sweat and grime covered his face. Tattered dungarees clung to his body, soaked with perspiration.

"Water come up?" he asked.

"Sure," replied Corporal Ernest A. Sansanio of New York City. "We're purifying it down there." He pointed to the putrid pool, where Private First Class Matthew Konieczkny was dunking his bare feet. "Help yourself," Sansanio told Russell.

Ignoring the forced flippancy, Russell managed to mutter: "Jimmy just got it!"

"Where?" was the simultaneous query of half a dozen buddies.

"Through the guts."

"Bad?"

"Bad? Goddammit to hell, he's dead! I saw his body down on the beach!"

An interminable period of stunned silence was broken as Navy Lieutenant Marvin Baecker, of Lawrence, Kansas, rolled over the crater's lip. He was the twenty-eight-year-old battalion surgeon, and his appearance reflected his bone-deep exhaustion from treating the wounded on the front lines, constantly under fire. Peering at the evil-looking pool, he inched down to test whether it was safe to drink.

"How is it, Doc?" Sansanio asked. Konieczkny was sorry he'd washed his feet in it. Krauss regretted laundering his dungaree jacket.

"Well," Baecker answered, "I don't think it will kill you, but it won't have the taste of an iced Coke. You guys use plenty of halazones [water-purifying tablets], because it'll take between six and a dozen for each canteen, and give 'em time to dissolve—twenty minutes at least."

Without filling his open canteen, the doctor clawed to the top of the hole and headed back to the battalion aid station to do what he could for the constant stream of casualties.

Corporal James A. Hauer, of Fond du Lac, Wisconsin, thought for a few seconds after the surgeon left. "I think the Doc's recommendation was kinda doubtful," he said. "Guess I'll choke till the fresh water comes up."

Corporal Chesley G. Gilbert, formerly a sandlot ballplayer of Griffin, Georgia, lurched into the hole. His 6-foot-3 frame sagged to the ground. He lay facedown, dirt-encrusted dungarees oozing with sweat. This was his first break since landing, seemingly years ago. He'd been busy all the time on scouting missions, sandwiching in volunteer duty as a stretcher bearer and lugging ammunition back from the beach.

"Someone please gimme some water," he panted. No one moved. "Who's got a canteen full?" he asked, glancing slowly from man to man. Corporal Jacques C. Lewis, Gilbert's closest comrade, who hailed from San Saba, Texas, answered with a feeble attempt at humor.

"Well, now, good buddy Gil," he said, "you might phone the

purifying plant and tell 'em you're gonna find yourself another island if they don't get on the ball."

Gilbert's mirthless reply: "Yeah, I know you're a funny guy, but where's the fuckin' water?"

An Irish corporal from New York's Bronx, Tom Duffy, answered in the brogue of his parents' Emerald Isle: "Right down at ya feet where ya lookin'. Ice yaself a highball an' relax." Gilbert rolled down the crater's slope, carrying coral lumps with him, until his head and half his body were submerged in the muck.

"Anything that feels this good must be okay to drink," the huge Marine retorted as he gulped down handfuls of the water.

Chicagoan Charlie Schneider looked on in amazement. The tough, bantam-size corporal was the squad leader of a demolitions team that Gilbert had been assigned to on Cape Gloucester.

"Hey, sucker," Schneider admonished, "Doc Baecker says if ya gonna take a chance, ya gotta load it in canteens with lots of halazones or you'll grab yourself one helluva stomachful of germs."

Gilbert, unfazed by the warning, continued drinking. "Yeah," he replied. "Guess you're right—a guy can never be too careful." Then he swallowed several more scoops of water and, his thirst quenched, flung off his soaking dungaree blouse. He was snoring five minutes later, exhausted but blissfully sleeping through the noise of nearby bursts of enemy mortars.

"Jeez," commented Corporal Harold L. Park of Courtland, New York. *"That's* a Marine. I saw him work at Gloucester. He'll go through the same stink in this one and lose weight, but no Japs or germs'll ever affect his guts."

Japanese snipers, observing the traffic in and out of the command post, opened up a few minutes later. The dull thud of their bullets raised small geysers of coral dust along the hole's rim, but no one was hit. During a lull in the firing, Corporal Russell grabbed his carbine and eased over the top and vanished through the scrub foliage toward the source of the sniping.

Ten minutes later the sharp, distinctive crack of a Marine carbine replied to the brief clatter of a Japanese light machine gun. All was quiet for the next quarter hour, and then Russell vaulted back into the CP. He was carrying the enemy weapon, a Nambu automatic rifle, and a Japanese flag.

"The little yellow bastard didn't even *have* a canteen," the rambunctious Marine muttered in disgust, "and what the hell am I gonna do with this?" He held up the Nambu.

"Take it back to headquarters and see if you can swap it for a couple of cans of water," someone suggested with the logic of a combat-wise veteran who knew the value of essentials in battle.

The last rays of the brutal sun were surrendering to the welcome coolness of twilight. But within a few hundred feet of the crater, Marines were dying, and the men in the hole thanked God that their most pressing worry was the need for water. The stench of decomposing Japanese bodies was everywhere. Huge bluebottle flies feasted on the remains, then settled down in swarms on bare backs of the Marines and had dessert from the crumbs of K rations. Listless banter among the men faded and then died out entirely.

Suddenly a loud voice was heard over the spasmodic staccato of a nearby Japanese Nambu: "Water's up! Water's up! Two canteens a man. Come and get it!"

The long-awaited shouted message came from First Lieutenant Layton W. Bailey, of Dallas, Texas, who was leading a team of black Marines. He apologized as soon as he was within speaking range.

"Couldn't get it here any sooner," he said. "But we had to go through the lines, and mortars were raining on the beach—lots of amphibs knocked out. This may be a little rusty—it's had a long voyage. Use it sparingly and give Doc Baecker what he needs first." Then the lieutenant and his squad of volunteers headed back to the beach to load up again and deliver more water to other frontline Marines in desperate need.

Canteens were quickly filled. As this small group of men from the 2d Battalion, 5th Marines, gulped down the rusty water, their exhausted bodies took on new life. Picks and entrenching tools hacked away at the sides of the crater, digging foxholes for the night. Shadows lengthened, the last cigarette was snuffed out, and then there was darkness.

Guards were posted along the rim of the shell hole, each with a bullet in the chamber ready to fire. The water had soothed parched throats and revived the men's will to fight. Mortars exploded yards away, and Japanese machine-gun fire ripped through the night—but exhausted off-duty Marines slept through all the commotion.

"Early morning brought the word to move up," Sergeant Conway's story concluded. "Gear was readied. Packs were shouldered. The column started forward to a new location, warily watching for sniper fire from Nips who had infiltrated during the night. The last to leave the crater, Corporal Charley Draper, of Athens, Georgia, surveyed the coral pit, looked down at the muddy water, and sighed, 'Ah—Peleliu Spa.'

"A Jap mortar got the range and planted one in the crater—dead center—but it was a few minutes too late."

3

History recounts innumerable occasions during the American Civil War when the men in the ranks *elected* regimental commanding officers in both the Union and Confederate armies.

A military background was rarely a consideration, but some such units performed amazingly well in battle with remarkable displays of bravery by ill-trained troops brilliantly led by inexperienced superiors. The situation usually came about when a local politician, generally one of wealth and deep-rooted personal views of what constituted patriotism, had ample funds to equip and pay his mercenaries.

Most certainly none of the Marine officers on Peleliu received their commissions by ballot. Nor did the $21 monthly pay of the young volunteer Marine privates come from some individual's bank account. But the aging survivors of the Old Breed—officers or enlisted men—will tell you they would have gladly voted to decorate and promote one of Peleliu's officers to whatever level of command he thought he was qualified to fill.

His name was Paul Douglas.

He was a captain, possibly the oldest in Marine Corps history to serve in that rank in frontline combat. From beginning to end, his wartime career was unique.

Douglas was a distinguished and nationally renowned fifty-one-year-old professor of economics at the University of Chicago when he refused a direct commission to volunteer as a private on May 15, 1942. It took the personal intervention of Secretary of the Navy Frank Knox, a longtime admirer and friend, for the Marine Corps to waive its age limit and rigid physical standards and allow the rail-thin, white-maned, bespectacled academic to join up.

Not only that, but Douglas demanded that he undergo the same rigorous, dawn-to-dusk training as any other recruit in the pine forests and swamps of Parris Island. The young men, mostly robust "hot to trot" teenagers, were astounded by the determination and endurance of, in the words of one of them, "this strange and marvelous old man who never complained and did his job just as good, sometimes better, than the rest of our platoon." He asked for no favors from crusty drill instructors, and, if any were offered, no doubt he'd have unhesitatingly said, "No, thanks."

Incredibly, Douglas scored the highest rating in his platoon for rough-and-tumble bayonet fighting and nearly perfect pistol firing. He carried the outfit's guidon at graduation ceremonies, an honor bestowed by his youthful and admiring comrades as the platoon's most outstanding member.

To this day, no one else of Douglas's age has been accepted for Marine recruit training—and it is extremely doubtful that anyone accepted could make it through the brutal physical regimen, tough discipline, emotional stress, and purposely imposed hardships that were then, and still are, the trademarks of boot camp in the Corps.

After proving to himself, and countless doubters, that he had the stuff to make a fighting Marine, Douglas accepted a captain's commission. It was the idea of USMC headquarters to post him to a comfortable, innocuous, safe Stateside desk job. Secretary Knox again intervened, and Captain Douglas got his wish to join an overseas combat division.

He caught up with the 1st Division in time to serve as General Rupertus's adjutant at Cape Gloucester. He landed in the fourth wave at Peleliu as Bucky Harris's adjutant in the 5th Regiment. The now fifty-three-year-old captain immediately began writing new pages in his epic as a Marine.

The words of Sergeant James Merrifield, of San Francisco, tell part of the story:

"I have never seen anyone give more to his country than Paul Douglas," Merrifield said. "He would put a 5-gallon can of water on his back—he must have been fifty years old and most of us were eighteen or nineteen and we thought he was older than God.

"Here it was 110 degrees, his face as red as the reddest apple you have ever seen, and yet he would get up to the troops and say, 'Here, I'm bringing you some water,' and he was like God coming along. Douglas was adjutant, he was supposed to be back in the rear, and yet here he was up at the front. . . ."

Little wonder that the ex-professor quickly became known throughout the division as Gunga Din. He seemed to be everywhere on the island, always appearing when least expected and most needed.

Gene Sledge recalled an incident early in the battle when enemy artillery and mortar fire were creating havoc everywhere on the beachhead. An amtrac, carrying desperately needed water and ammunition, clanked up to where his platoon was dug in a few hundred feet from the front.

"The tractor was an older model such as I had landed in on D-Day," Sledge said, "and didn't have a drop tailgate. 'Let's go, boys,' our NCO said as he and a couple of us climbed aboard and hefted the heavy ammo boxes over the side and onto the deck.

"I saw him gaze in amazement down into the cargo area of the tractor. At the bottom, wedged under a pile of ammo boxes, we saw one of those infernal 55-gallon oil drums of water. Filled, they weighed several hundred pounds. Our NCO rested his arms on the side of the tractor and said in an exasperated tone, 'It took a bloody genius of a supply officer to do that. How in hell are we supposed to get that drum out of there?'"

Just as the sergeant's dismay reached its peak, the deadly *whisshh-shh-shh* of three incoming mortar rounds was followed by the shells exploding nearby. "Uh oh, the stuff's hit the fan now," groaned one of Sledge's companions. "Bear a hand, you guys. On the double!" the NCO yelled, followed by an anxious plea from the amtrac driver. "Look, you guys," he exhorted, "I'm gonna hafta get this tractor the hell outta here! If it gets knocked out, the lieutenant'll have my can in a crack!"

"You fellows need some help?" asked a Marine who suddenly appeared on the scene. Sledge and his comrades hadn't noticed him until he spoke. The newcomer identified himself: "I'm Captain Paul Douglas, the regimental adjutant, and I'm proud to be with you men in the 5th Marines."

"He wore green dungarees, leggings, and a cloth-covered helmet like ourselves and carried a .45 caliber automatic pistol like any mortar gunner, machine gunner, or one of our officers," Sledge remembered. "But being in combat, there wasn't any rank insignia. What astonished us was that he looked to be more than fifty years old and wore glasses—a rarity among the men on Peleliu. When he took off his helmet, we saw his gray hair."

"Gosh, Cap'n! You don't have to be up here at all, do you?" one of the men asked as he passed ammunition boxes to Douglas.

"No," the elderly captain answered, "but I always want to know how you boys up here are making out and I want to help if I can."

The men scampered for cover at the *wisshh-shh-shh* sound of three incoming mortar shells that exploded, one after the other, several yards away. They waited for another barrage, but none came.

Douglas was the first to pull himself over the amtrac's side as the shaken Marines followed to finish unloading its cargo with a new surge of energy. The cumbersome drum was hoisted overboard by a rope sling as the livid beet-faced NCO yelled out instructions, spouting a string of obscenities at the "brainless fat-assed rear-echelon bastard who thought fillin' dirty fuel barrels with drinkin' water was a good idea."

Several more mortar shells slammed down nearby shortly after the amtrac was emptied and the driver roared back toward the relative safety of the beach. The seemingly indefatigable captain helped the working party stack the heavy ammunition boxes and bade each man, "So long, good luck, and remember to keep your heads down," as he trudged down the slope.

Sledge heard a buddy ask, "What's that crazy old gray-haired guy doing up here when he could be back at regiment?" The NCO growled, "Shut up! Knock it off, you eightball! He's trying to help knuckleheads like you, and he's a damned good man."

Word of similar daily activities circulated throughout the division, ceasing only when Douglas was wounded by mortar fragments late in the campaign. Even then, he displayed what endeared him to his 1st Division comrades, especially those in the ranks: he removed his captain's bars as stretcher bearers carried him to the beach for first aid and evacuation.

The reason was a typical reflection of this grand man's philosophy. He was determined to be treated the same as any wounded enlisted Marines, and be in a ward with them on the hospital ship when they left Peleliu.

He had recovered fully in time to land in the third wave when the 1st Division spearheaded the invasion of Okinawa on April 1, 1945—Easter Sunday. He was now Major Paul Douglas, and he contributed as selflessly as before until he was again wounded. This time a Japanese machine gun cut him down and nearly took his life.

It was fourteen months before the then fifty-five-year-old Marine Corps legend was released, after numerous operations, from the Naval Medical Center in Washington. He departed with a shattered and forever useless left arm, and was retired, a highly decorated reserve lieutenant colonel, on November 1, 1946.

Despite the nationwide admiration he received for heroism as a World War II Marine, Douglas was destined to leave an even more formidable legacy of public service to the people of the United States—and to play a major role in perpetuating his beloved Marine Corps.

He returned briefly to the academic life of the University of Chicago, but soon decided to seek election to the United States Senate. A landslide victory sent him to Washington in 1948, and he was reelected by a wide margin in 1954 and 1960.

A tribute in the *Beaufort Gazette,* the newspaper read by thousands of Marines at Camp Lejeune, summarized his career on Capitol Hill. The words touched the hearts of former comrades and countless youngsters who knew the man only by reputation:

Once in the Senate, he disclosed his income publicly and refused gifts or dinners costing more than $2.50. . . . For three terms, Senator Douglas battled for truth-in-lending, public housing, civil rights, and higher minimum wages.

He was an independent man who followed his own conscience. Time and again his colleagues, Democrats and Republicans alike, lauded him as the "Conscience of the Senate." Although he was never a member of the Senate's "inner circle," he learned the ropes so quickly that the Washington press corps selected him as the nation's "Best Senator" in 1951 less than three years in office.

He never forgot the Corps, either. Until his death in September 1976, Douglas was always a "Semper Fi Marine." Behind his desk in the Senate Office Building, he kept the American flag and the Marine Corps' colors. And, during his early years as a senator, he successfully contested attempts to merge the Marines with the Army.

By his personal courage, fortitude and example to others, the

Honorable Paul H. Douglas demonstrated the personal traits so highly valued by all Marines.

Semper Fidelis, Lieutenant Colonel Douglas!

His family, friends, and university associates were amazed when he joined the Marine Corps, not only because of his age, but because he was a devout Quaker who abhorred violence of any kind. After a long struggle with his conscience, he had volunteered for Army service in 1918 but was rejected because of bad eyes.

"I became a Marine," he told Herman Kogan, a *Chicago Tribune* reporter before becoming a combat correspondent sergeant, "simply because I wanted to help bring about the return of peace as soon as possible, and being a Marine was the best way I could do it."

4

Captain Douglas spent the night of D-Day with Gordon Gayle in his battalion command post near the tip of Peleliu's airstrip. It was the major who first called him the division's Gunga Din, and his respect and admiration for Douglas were boundless.

While the expected heavy banzai charge didn't come, the Japanese constantly harassed the dug-in Marine line with mortar fire and forays from infiltrators. "None of these attacks were overwhelming in numbers or anything like that," Gayle later said, "but they kept coming all night. . . . The only thing was that the next day when daylight came, we found there were Japanese in a little clump of bushes very close to the command post but somebody had killed them. . . ."

Day Two was a scorcher. More blowtorch temperature and putrid water. Hot, heavy, and costly fighting. Heated and caustic words between Generals Rupertus and Geiger. General Smith, one of the Corps' most respected, militarily brilliant senior officers and gentlemen, looked on in silent dismay.

There were no questions about the objectives of the day's battle plan. Colonel Hanneken's 7th Marines was to resume its push south from Orange Three to secure the peninsula and several tiny unnamed atolls. Colonel Harris's 5th Regiment would do its damnedest to capture the airstrip. Colonel Puller's 1st Marines, still in deep trouble, faced another long day's struggle to knock out Japanese strongpoints in the cave-infested coral high ground north of White Beach One, an area soon to be forever remembered by the Old Breed as Bloody Nose Ridge.

People back in the States were just learning of the day-old invasion. The first word came in a terse two-sentence communiqué from Admiral Nimitz at CinCPac Headquarters in Pearl Harbor.

"At 0830 today [15 September] assault forces of the III Marine Amphibious Corps, with heavy naval and air bombardment support of the U.S. Third Fleet, successfully invaded the Palau Islands in the Western Pacific," it said. "Initial objectives were secured with a minimum of casualties." The announcement contained no further details, but within minutes, news of the landing was clattering on wire service teletypes in newsrooms of daily papers and radio stations across the country.

Japanese Imperial General Headquarters had its expectedly different version of what was happening. Radio Tokyo's morning newscast relayed it to the enemy homeland in a customary blast of propaganda:

"Our glorious forces have again slaughtered thousands of bloodthirsty American Marines in a stupid invasion attempt, this time in the Palau Islands," the broadcast said. "Commanded by valiant and brilliant Colonel Kunio Nakagawa, superb and valorous Japanese troops bravely frustrated the daring landing by 1000 hours, putting the screaming enemy hordes to flight. At 1400 hours, the ill-fated butchers attempted again to make a landing on the southwest tip of our coastline. This frantic and disorganized counterattack was also repulsed and the fiendish Yankees were put to rout once more, with the sea red with their blood."

If Radio Tokyo carried further reports on the battle for Peleliu, there is no known record of what was said. As far as the Japanese high command was concerned, the Palaus were a forgotten issue and had been for months.

From the American side, it was nearly a week before CinCPac censors permitted correspondents on the scene to write—contrary to the original communiqué saying "the initial objective was achieved with a minimum of casualties"—that Marine losses were extremely heavy. By then, the toll of killed and wounded was nearly 3,000 and the fighting was mounting in fury.

If Nakagawa heard Radio Tokyo's broadcast, he most probably accepted it stoically for what it was: unmitigated propaganda for Japanese home-front consumption. He knew the Americans could not be driven off Peleliu, and his orders were unchanged—hold it to the last man and kill as many Americans as possible in the process.

On D plus one, the Japanese commander continued the suicidal task with undeterred *bushido* determination. Half an hour after the last long minutes of darkness became the first minutes of daylight, Nakagawa signaled his heavy artillery and ash-can-size 150-millimeter mortars to commence firing. Although the shelling was intense and destructive on the beaches, most of it seemed randomly aimed at "to whom it may concern" targets, anything to hurt the invaders.

One sector, however, was singled out for special attention. Nakagawa had correctly surmised, from watching the disastrous "tankette" counterattack down the airstrip runway, that the Marines would mount an all-out drive to capture the airbase on Day Two. He intended to use every man and all the firepower he could muster to beat off the attempt and slaughter the attackers as they moved, unprotected by ground cover, across the naked, bomb-pocked, fire-raked open field.

The enemy commander was especially interested in knocking out a deep communications trench near the southwestern edge of the airstrip. His artillery observers, hidden in cliffside caves north of the airstrip, had reported a constant movement of Marines in and out of the position, an obvious sign that it was of more than casual importance to the invaders. It definitely was.

The 25-yard-long zigzag emplacement was also familiar to Nakagawa; it had been a company staging area for his troops at H-Hour. When it was overrun by surging Marines, Bucky Harris had moved in to set up the communications center and command post for his 5th Marines.

Shortly before Boyd's 1st Battalion and Gayle's 2d were scheduled to jump off in the attack to seize the airstrip, between fifteen and twenty rounds of artillery laced the trench. The results were near-catastrophic. One shell wiped out the field telephone switchboard, killing or seriously wounding nearly a dozen officers and men in the communications section.

Almost simultaneously, another slammed into Harris's CP. The colonel was buried up to his neck under the coral debris of the shattering explosion. He escaped without being seriously wounded but sustained a badly wrenched and severely painful knee, which completely immobilized him for several days.

Lieutenant Colonel Lewis W. Walt, the regiment's executive officer, was at the front in a pre-attack meeting with Major Gayle during the shelling. He found Harris lying on a stretcher when he returned, lucid but showing the effects of his injury—and loudly refusing to be evacuated.

Walt was respected throughout the division for his leadership and combat exploits in the Guadalcanal and Cape Gloucester campaigns. Harris immediately told him to take over active command of the 5th Marines and said that under the circumstances, he would depend more heavily upon Walt than might normally be the case.

Until the battle was over, they worked together as a close-knit duo, virtually as a tandem command. Walt later explained their harmonious and effective relationship.

"Harris couldn't get to the front lines," he said. "The less important decisions I made on my own. In the case of major decisions, if time was available, I talked the matter over with the colonel and asked for his decision. During the last days of the campaign our regiment was engaged on the northern end of the island and I ran the regiment from a forward command post while Colonel Harris stayed at the rear CP and I kept him informed of what was going on."

Their mutual understanding and cooperation were in sharp contrast to the bewildering aloofness that General Rupertus displayed toward General Smith, his second-in-command, and other high-ranking division officers.

As subsequent events would record, Bucky Harris was not mistaken in trusting Walt, or even in giving him freedom of action when things were rough. When he retired in 1971, Walt was assistant commandant of the Marine Corps, a four-star general with a thirty-four-year record of service surpassed by few men. Among other distinguished accomplishments, Lew Walt commanded the 5th Marines in Korea, and a decade later, his last combat duty was as the top-ranking Marine in Vietnam.

The 5th Marines began their assault to take the airstrip as planned, precisely at 8:00. A thundering bedlam of noise, followed by billowing clouds of smoke and coral dust, erupted as naval gunfire and air strikes hit the Japanese-held ridges and the burned-over undergrowth north and south of the objective.

Gordon Gayle's 2d Battalion quickly ran into trouble as it

swung south from the intersection of the airfield's runways. Not only was it being pounded by withering artillery and mortar shells, but the men were caught in open ground and taking a curtain of machine-gun and sniper fire from troops entrenched in the woods and scrub jungle to the east.

Silencing the cluster of fortified positions was deadly and close-in work that required the support of Sherman tanks before it was over. But the fiercely contested Day Two objective was reached by sundown. When Gayle's troops dug in for the night, the southern half of the airstrip belonged to the Marines. Nearly 150 Japanese bodies marked the scorched path of the advance. Twenty-seven Marines, including a company captain, had been killed or wounded.

The 1st Battalion, Robert Boyd's outfit, had faster—but not easier—going as it wheeled north to swarm the airfield's battered hangars and headquarters area. It met only light resistance from scattered pockets of ground troops dug in on the pool-table-flat field.

The 1st's major problem—and it was one of frightening and deadly concern to the men—was to make it alive through a seemingly nonstop firestorm of artillery and mortar shelling. The 115-degree heat, the lack of drinking water, the dense smoke and choking coral dust—all added to the frantic ordeal.

Gene Sledge has searing memories of the tumultuous day on the airfield: "About halfway across, I stumbled and fell forward. At that instant a large shell exploded on my left with a giant flash and a thundering roar. A fragment ricocheted off the deck and growled over my head as I went down.

"To be shelled by massed artillery and mortars is absolutely terrifying, but to be shelled in the open is terror compounded beyond belief of anyone who hasn't experienced it. The attack across Peleliu's airstrip was the worst combat experience I had during the entire war. . . ."

From the Japanese viewpoint, the shield of exploding steel took an unexpected and ironic twist. Instead of shattering the advance and putting the Marines to flight, the furious bombardment had the opposite effect: It added speed and momentum to the push. It was obvious to Boyd's men that their best hope to survive was—in the words of Technical Sergeant Benjamin Goldberg, a combat correspondent from Worcester, Massachusetts—"to get to cover off the field as fast as they could. . . .

"It was just as far and as dangerous to get back to the

jump-off point," the former sportswriter for the *Boston Globe* wrote, "so why not move ahead as Marines always do? Scampering from shell hole to shell hole, they did what was expected of them—they moved ahead. In little more than an hour, advance elements reached the main service apron and hangar area."

By late afternoon the 1st Battalion had gained its phase line for the day, the northern section of the airbase. With the 2d Battalion solidly entrenched along the southern edges of the field, the Marines controlled Peleliu's airstrip. And right on time as set down in the invasion timetable.

One can only ponder how and why some men perish and others survive such hellish action; there is no earthly way to account for it. Hard-earned combat wisdom? Unbelievably good luck? Faith and trust in a Supreme Being? What?

Perhaps a young captain, a company commander in Gayle's battalion during the airstrip attack, came as close as anyone to expressing how the Marines looked at the life-or-death puzzle. He wrote his folks at home in Michigan after Peleliu: ". . . Out here you feel your responsibility to the other people. They have become a force within you. *Esprit de corps* also helps. Your faith in God, at least mine, has helped me against fear. I only ask God out here to keep me from doing something wrong, not let me show the 'white feather' [of cowardice], to keep my men and job foremost always. . . . If anything should happen to me, don't fret because I consider myself to have been blessed to have had the life I have. Try not to worry about me. . . ."

The letter was mailed from a Navy hospital in Hawaii. The captain also said he had "sent my Purple Heart home today."

5

At 8:00 A.M., everything was suddenly quiet along the ridges inland from White Beaches One and Two. Moments before they were being raked by naval shelling and carrier-based dive-bombing and strafing attacks—all intended to pin down dug-in Japanese defenders.

Now it was time for Chesty Puller's already hard-hit 1st Marines to jump off in a fresh attempt to drive the enemy from the coral caves and fortifications of Bloody Nose Ridge.

Hollywood's moviemakers, striving for wide-screen impact,

always seem to show hundreds of shouting men surging forward, walking upright and unafraid with bayoneted rifles, in an unbroken wave toward fiercely resisting enemy positions. In reality, something entirely different happens most of the time.

Troops take advantage of every bit of protection they can find. According to "the book" of proven combat practice, men in the assault move in small and dispersed units; squads and fire teams advance, one man at a time, in low running crouches from one shell hole to another, from one burned-out enemy position to another, from the cover of one cluster of rocks or foliage to the next.

Live troops win battles, and being caught in the open is an engraved invitation to death. When a man has no cover, he doesn't stand; he crawls and hopes that he won't be hit. Only when an area is thought to be cleared of the enemy will men move in anything like a Hollywood-style formation. Even then, they are vigilant and wary and keep apart from one another.

Most of "the book" went out the window, however, the instant the 1st Marines went into action against the Japanese positions inland from White Beaches One and Two. From the very beginning, Colonel Puller's troops were in head-on assault against dug-in and well-armed enemy caves and fortifications, almost always without cover of any kind.

Marine Corps battle reports and documents largely blame Peleliu's fiendish terrain and its determined, battle-hardened, skillfully led defenders for the appalling losses suffered by Puller's regiment during the first four days of the invasion.

To maintain historical objectivity, it is necessary to record that these observations are not without foundation; that the 1st Marines' entire zone of action was almost an impregnable fortress—steep coral cliffs topped by rocky saw-toothed ridges that could be conquered only by direct frontal assault.

The view is far from unanimous, however, that Colonel Puller used his troops in a manner the situation demanded. Many men who were there—from teenage privates to young second lieutenants and seasoned combat officers, including war-wise generals—believed then and now that Puller needlessly, and perhaps wantonly, wasted lives.

That feeling seemingly is becoming more prevalent as survivors of the battle pass into and beyond middle age. A case in point:

First Lieutenant Gordon I. Swanson, from Minneapolis, was a twenty-three-year-old frontline artillery spotter on Peleliu.

He was assigned to the 1st Marines, and thus was in frequent personal contact with the colonel.

"Puller seemed to like me," Swanson wrote a friend in 1988, "although I once called him an arrogant ass. This was most unexpected by a first lieutenant to a colonel, but it was language which he understood and a label which he wore with some pride. He always seemed to be surrounded by more luck than good sense; his judgment was always questionable.

"When his book *Marine!* came off the press, he sent me one of the first copies with a pleasant handwritten note on the flyleaf. I shall always treasure it. There will never be another Chesty Puller, an observation I make with a sense of gratefulness and relief. The Defense Department needs generals who are bright and predictable. Puller was neither."

To civilian correspondents, Chesty was always "good copy"—the living legend and absolute personification of the public's view of a fearless fighting Marine determined to defeat the Japanese, single-handedly if necessary.

Newsweek's Bill Hipple was with the colonel in the 1st Marines CP as the regiment's 1st and 2d Battalions moved out to hit the ridges northeast of the airstrip on Day Two of the invasion. "You could never feel secure when you were around Chesty," Hipple recalled years later.

"He wasn't ever satisfied to just sit back and command the action, he wanted to be as close as he could to it—and lend a personal hand, even firing a few shots himself, at the slightest opportunity. He wasn't content to have his CP a few hundred feet behind the front. He wanted to be right at the front, and, so help me, that's where we were on D plus one."

A curious, tragedy-inspired relationship existed between the colonel and the correspondent. Lieutenant Colonel Samuel D. Puller, Chesty's younger brother, had been cut down by Japanese machine-gun fire on Guam. He fell dead in Hipple's arms without uttering a sound.

En route to Peleliu, they had a long talk about Sam.

"He died painlessly, didn't even know he'd been hit," Hipple reported telling Puller. "This seemed to comfort Chesty, who then, with a trace of tears, removed a corncob pipe from his clenched lips and began a half-smiling reminiscence of their happy boyhood in the faraway days and hills of Virginia, and their boisterous times together as young enlisted Marines in the 1920s."

At one point during the conversation, Hipple said, Puller

vehemently disavowed an often repeated statement he had purportedly made on Pavuvu when informed of his brother's fate: "Those who live by the sword must die by the sword." He told the correspondent: "I swear to God I didn't say any such thing!"

There is no doubt that Lewis Burwell Puller was deeply hurt by the death of Samuel Duncan Puller. Nor is there any question that it added fuel to his blazing hatred for the Japanese. Within days after receiving the tragic news, Puller ordered signs 2 feet high prominently hung in the tented mess halls of the 1st Marines. Where the paint was found is a mystery, but it was bloodred and spelled out two words: KILL JAPS!

Puller's men needed no prodding to slaughter the Japanese and inflame their hatred for the enemy. On the other hand, the hatred by Japanese troops for Marines was even greater. In cases of prisoners of war, both sides almost constantly and blatantly ignored the Geneva Convention code—which had been signed by the United States and Japan—specifying that POWs had to be treated humanely.

It was not uncommon on Guadalcanal for Marines to find the corpse of a tortured American, hanging trussed in wire from a tree with his body slashed to pieces from "bayonet practice." On Peleliu, several Marine prisoners were found clubbed to death with severed penises stuffed in their mouths. Japanese, feigning serious wounds or death, would suddenly open fire on unsuspecting Americans. Booby-trapped enemy dead were an everyday cause of Marine casualties.

There are also verified instances where Japanese, singly or in small groups with arms raised to signal surrender, were massacred by Marine machine-gun and rifle fire. It was even the practice of some Marines to loot the bodies of Japanese dead, taking anything of value—wedding rings, religious medallions, and often gold teeth or inlays.

When Gene Sledge had mothballed his Marine uniform and donned the regalia of a university professor, he wrote a candid analysis of what he believed were the underlying reasons for the often inhuman combat behavior that marked World War II in the Pacific:

> The Japanese were a fanatical enemy; that is to say, they believed in their cause with an intensity little understood by postwar Americans—and possibly many Japanese as well.
> This collective attitude, Marine and Japanese, resulted in sav-

age, ferocious fighting with no holds barred. This was not the dispassionate killing seen on other fronts or in other wars. This was a brutish, primitive hatred, as characteristic of the horror of war in the Pacific as the palm trees and the islands.

Official histories and memoirs of Marine infantrymen written after the war rarely reflect that hatred. But at the time of battle, Marines felt it deeply, bitterly, and as certainly as danger itself.

To comprehend what the troops endured then and there, one must take into full account this aspect of the Marines' war. To deny this hatred or make light of it would be as much a lie as to deny or make light of the *esprit de corps* or the intense patriotism felt by the Marines. . . .

6

Anything approaching a precise count of Japanese who fell to the 1st Marines on September 16, 1944, is impossible to determine. The total certainly was substantial, but the sorry fact is that it most likely was far, far lower than the total suffered by Puller's men.

The 2d Battalion, thirty-year-old Lieutenant Colonel Russell Honsowetz's outfit, moved out at 8:00. Although one of the youngest men in the Corps to hold such rank, Honsowetz had served with distinction under Puller in various "confrontations" with the Japanese while in China before Pearl Harbor.

Fellow officers and superiors viewed Russ Honsowetz as a "comer" with the personal courage, military know-how, selfless dedication, and instinctive leadership ability to handle any combat situation. His captains and lieutenants shared the opinion, and he had the respect of his troops; he was a hardnosed and demanding CO who always took care of them as best he could. Back on Pavuvu, after the Peleliu campaign, he was awarded the Navy Cross for valor in leading the battalion in some of the most bitter action of the invasion.

"Look, Honsowetz, I want that sonofabitchin' ridge before sundown," Puller told him just before jump-off time. "And I mean, goddammit, I *want* it!" The colonel pointed to the objective several hundred yards to the northeast, a position identified on the flawed sector map as Hill 200, so named for its elevation, as were all of Peleliu's hills.

The troops moved out along the narrow, coral-surfaced West Road that meandered 6 miles from the south end of the island to its northern tip. Led by a Sherman tank and two amtracs, they advanced some 200 to 300 yards in five minutes, taking only sporadic small-arms fire.

Then as the point of the assault pivoted west to hit the hill, the picture changed radically. What happened next can best be described with one or both of the most commonly used expressions of Marines finding themselves caught up in a deadly combat situation: "All hell broke loose!" or "The shit hit the fan!"

The precipitous slope came alive in a cyclone of resistance from heavy-machine-gun emplacements, sniper pits, hand grenades, and point-blank fire from wheeled 37-millimeter mountain guns. The enemy had waited patiently in hard-to-spot caves and dug-in coral-covered fortifications until the Marines were within easy range.

Minutes later the lead tank was disabled when three rounds of 37-millimeter shells shattered its right tracks. Almost simultaneously the thin steel sides of the amtracs were penetrated and they too were out of action. Now the infantry troops were strictly on their own.

To make matters worse, Hill 200 was a honeycomb of interconnected positions. As soon as the Marines located one source of fire, it would fall silent and its occupants would scamper through tunnels to other undiscovered caves—and the fury would come from another direction. It was a pattern of action that bedeviled Marines—and wounded and killed them—throughout the battle for Peleliu.

Hardly a yard was gained without hand-to-hand combat; close-in life-or-death struggles with clubbed rifles and thrusting bayonet blades; with rocks and knives; with fists and knees and gouging thumbs. Taller Marines grappled with shorter Japanese, their bodies entwined as Siamese twins in a grotesque, whirling mêlée of screaming men bent on killing their foe.

Nearly 200 Marines were atop the ridge by twilight, but they still were in serious trouble. The barren crest was less than 20 yards wide, and it was impossible to dig foxholes in the granitelike coral. The only cover the men had was several shallow shell craters and quickly collected low piles of rocks.

Less than 500 feet separated their hard-won outpost from another and higher enemy-held ridge—Hill 220—that kept them under almost constant machine-gun and mortar fire. It wasn't silenced until shortly before midnight by pinpointed shelling by newly landed 105-millimeter howitzers from Colonel William Harrison's 11th Marines, the division's artillery regiment.

Just as darkness shrouded the embattled hill, a field telephone wire team showed up at Honsowetz's CP on the crest. The first call came from Colonel Puller.

"How are things going?" Chesty asked.

"Not very good," Honsowetz replied. "I lost a lot of men."

Puller: "How many did you lose?"

Honsowetz: "I don't have a good count yet, but I think I lost a couple of hundred men."

"How many Japs did you kill?" The question had a stern and demanding tone.

"Well, we overran one position that had twenty-five in it. We got 'em all. There were a lot of Jap bodies around, but I don't know how many. Maybe fifty."

Puller's exasperated rejoinder: "Jesus Christ, Honsowetz, what the hell are the American people gonna think? Losing 200 fine young Marines and killing only fifty Japs! I'm gonna put you down for 500."

Unknown at the time was the fact that the 2d Battalion's costly conquest of Hill 200 was more significant than just the capture of another ridge. It denied to the Japanese the last direct observation they had of the beachhead and airstrip and thus put an end to targeted shelling that had plagued landing of troops and supplies and hampered complete occupation and reconstruction of the shell- and bomb-pocked runways.

As later developments showed, it also caused Colonel Nakagawa to move his command post from a nearby ridge to a cave several miles north. The Marines, he felt, were getting too close for comfort. The new enemy headquarters was in the heart of what ultimately became the final pocket of Japanese resistance to the conquest of the island.

The shift had an obviously serious impact on Nakagawa's already flimsy communications with other units and diminished his direct control of Peleliu's defense. Whether this shortened the battle can only be a matter of conjecture, but it certainly was no help to his well-crafted plan to hold the island and kill the hated Yankees.

Puller's 1st Battalion, commanded by Major Raymond Davis, ran into the first of a daylong sequence of savage firefights shortly after it moved out. Advancing almost due east, it came under withering attack from a huge concrete blockhouse with

4-foot-thick walls. The heavily armed fortification was large enough for a company of troops and was the hub of a major cluster of twelve deep coral pillboxes, all connected by tunnels.

The strongpoint shouldn't have been there at all on D plus one. Unlike hundreds of other hidden installations in the hills and jungles, it showed clearly on pre-invasion aerial photographs and had been marked for destruction by naval bombardment and air strikes. "Although Admiral Oldendorf had reported before D-Day that his fire support ships had run out of profitable targets, the blockhouse had been not so much as nicked, much less reduced," an official Marine Corps document states with sarcastic bluntness.

A frantic signal to the old battleship *Mississippi,* still on station to provide emergency fire support, brought a rapid response. Her 14-inch guns were on target within fifteen minutes, doing a job that should have been done days earlier.

"The blockhouse began disintegrating," an eyewitness later wrote. "The big armor-piercing and high-capacity shells crumbled the walls, and their terrific concussion killed those Japanese missed by fragmentation. Smaller naval guns, tanks, and infantry support weapons concentrated on the protecting pillboxes and presently the advance overran the position."

For whatever reason, the report fails to mention that Davis's troops had to use man-on-man force to wipe out the last enemy defenders, twenty troops sufficiently dedicated to the *bushido* code to die fighting for their "Sun of God" Emperor. Nor does it say anything about the cost to the Marines, some thirty-five of whom were killed or wounded, perhaps needlessly, because of the Navy's "oversight" (at best an inadequate word) in not obliterating the fortress before D-Day.

The 1st Battalion quickly found its troubles were just beginning. Behind the smoldering debris of the blockhouse was a dense 50-yard-deep patch of jungle, also untouched by naval shell fire. Beyond that was a steep cliff with about the same coral topography and height that confronted Honsowetz's men.

The heavy undergrowth hid shrewdly placed prepared foxholes and sniper pits. The virtually sheer incline was a maze of well-armed caves. The situation was a made-to-order battleground for the Japanese, and the only option open to Davis and his men was to do what Honsowetz and his battalion did in storming Hill 200.

And when they hit the hill, the pattern of savagery was the same. The troops crawled up the razor-sharp coral, shinnied over rocky outcroppings, plunged down into unexpected small sheer-sided gullies and crevices, dodged behind boulders—all the time under devastating fire. Most of the resistance came from small-mouthed caves—clattering bursts of heavy machine guns, thudding explosions of hand grenades, pinging but deadly sniper bullets, zapping and sinister Nambu automatic rifles.

Each eruption seemed to come from a different place. When the Marines thought they'd located a source of fire, it usually was too late. The Japanese simply had vanished, disappearing into the bowels of a cave to reappear with renewed violence from another hidden opening in the underground labyrinth.

What developed was a murderous cat-and-mouse game. When the Marines discovered a silent tunnel mouth, they waited for the Japanese to return. When the unsuspecting enemy came back, they were wiped out by rifle fire and grenades, and the entrances sealed by demolition satchels. It was a slow, frightening, and dangerous way to get the job done, and whenever a spotted cave could be bypassed, it was.

Every torturous yard of the ascent claimed more and more Marine casualties, and mounting numbers of Japanese bodies marked the bloody route to the summit. By evening, Ray Davis had the 1st Battalion's command post positioned, if precariously, atop the ridge. His troops had knocked out thirty-five fortified caves, none of which had been marked in the useless sector map made from pre-invasion reconnaissance photos. The cost was extreme: nearly 250 Marines killed or wounded.

There is a significant sequel involving Major Davis. Six years later, almost to the day, he was a lieutenant colonel with the 1st Division in Korea. As commanding officer of a different outfit, the 1st Battalion of the 7th Marines, he was awarded the Medal of Honor for beating back a series of attacks by several thousand North Korean and Chinese troops against his unit of outnumbered Marines.

But Ray Davis, who ultimately retired as a four-star general, remembered D plus one on Peleliu as "the most difficult assignment I have ever seen. . . .

". . . Company A depleted itself on the bare ridge on the right as Company C became seriously overextended on the left and was faltering. Everything we had was thrown in to fill the gaps. Remnants of Companies A and B, Engineer and Pioneer units, headquarters personnel, were formed into a meager reserve as darkness fell. Company A had moved eight hundred yards during the day, and we were able to hold on although the cost was extremely heavy."

September 16 was a far better day for Lieutenant Colonel Steve Sabol's 3d Battalion of Puller's regiment. The advance was slowed for a time by several small-arms skirmishes, but an offending cluster of lightly manned pillboxes was taken care of with rapid dispatch and very few Marine casualties.

Fortunately, the terrain didn't favor the Japanese in the 3d's sector on Day Two—no strongly fortified, cave-infested ridges, no dense jungle and scrub growth protecting dug-in enemy troops. Instead, the route of attack was along the relatively flat ground just inland from the shoreline—and Sabol's men took advantage of their good luck.

They encountered only minor resistance most of the day and, by sunset, had rolled ahead an average of 700 yards. The advance could have gone even farther, but Sabol wisely decided to stop and settle in. He didn't want the front to be overextended into a wedge where his flanks were vulnerable to a night counterattack and unable to tie in with the 5th Marines in the center of the beachhead perimeter.

7

Colonel Selden, the division's chief of staff, had to use all the military logic and personal persuasion he could think of to keep General Rupertus from landing on D-Day. It was Selden's view, shared by General Smith in his beachhead command post, that the situation ashore was still too unstable to permit exposing the commanding general and his staff.

Selden and Smith also agreed that what was most needed on the island at the time was additional troops and supplies—not more senior officers. Only after a daylong, often heated debate did Rupertus agree to a compromise. Selden and the bulk of the general's staff would land at sundown and set up a headquarters for Rupertus. He would follow early in the morning of D plus one.

It didn't take long for Selden to learn firsthand that his and General Smith's plan of action was correct. As soon as the colonel and his advance party left the *DuPage* and reached the transfer control point on the reef, they found hundreds of men in Higgins boats waiting for the few undamaged amtracs to carry them to shore.

The colonel signaled his distressing eyewitness report to Rupertus, and returned with his aides to the command ship to confront an obviously agitated major general—but one who remained outspokenly optimistic that the battle would be quickly won. And nothing short of a direct order from the Commandant of the Marine Corps, Rupertus's mentor and old friend Archie Vandegrift, would have kept the 1st Division commander from landing early in the morning. Three amtracs were bobbing at the foot of the *DuPage*'s gangway at 9:00 A.M.

At 9:50, the roaring vehicles clanked to the edge of General Smith's tank-trap CP and dropped their ramps. Major General Rupertus hobbled out, leaning heavily on a malacca cane, his broken ankle still in a cast. Colonel Selden and their aides quickly followed.

The entire command of the 1st Marine Division was now on Peleliu.

What would have been the outcome of the battle if a random barrage of Japanese "ash-can" mortars had slammed into their midst right then? One can only speculate on the disastrous consequences. In any case, it is extremely doubtful that such a frontline concentration of senior officers would be considered an acceptable practice by serious students of modern warfare—especially if the position was under direct enemy observation and taking occasional shelling.

General Rupertus, it would appear, had torn out the section of "the book" that harps on the must-do wisdom of dispersing men and equipment in *any* combat situation. While the 1st Division headquarters had a degree of protection because of its location in the deep tank trap, enemy artillery continued to harass the area for most of the following week. A couple of small nearby ammunition dumps were hit and blown sky-high, and a 105-millimeter howitzer was knocked out. But only a single shell scored on the command post, exploding in the message center and killing one man.

Rupertus exchanged perfunctory greetings with Smith as they briefly went over the situation map. Without comment, he then turned away and began talking to Selden. His actions conveyed what they were meant to, especially to General Smith: *I'm now ashore. As of now, this is my command post. This is my division and my show and I'll run both as I see fit from now on.*

After that, the assistant division commander said later, "I did a lot of traveling around the regiments and battalions, and I went in periodically to tell the general what I saw. I never sat in on any conference on planning or anything like that."

Rupertus's unbridled anxiety to get ashore was no doubt the result of what he'd seen on D-Day from his canvas-backed chair on the *DuPage*, and heard on the ship's loudspeakers that crackled constantly with radio combat circuit reports. As the day wore on, he was increasingly fearful that the assault was losing its momentum.

Something had to be done to "put more fire in the bellies" of the officers and men on the lines, the general reasoned, and it was up to him to do it. He was right about one thing. The attack was losing momentum, but mainly in Chesty Puller's sector, where the 1st Marines were being shot to pieces.

Progress elsewhere was as good as expected in most places, even better in some. There was nothing on God's earth that the general could personally do, at the moment, to alter the battle plan or speed up the advance.

Even after Rupertus personally saw close-up what Peleliu's terrain actually was like, he stoutly maintained his rosy outlook for a quick victory. "The overall feeling seemed to be that a breakthrough was imminent," a staff officer wrote. "Enemy resistance would collapse, or at worst, disintegrate as had happened on Saipan, Tinian, and Guam after a certain point had passed.

"The trouble with this reasoning was that on the other islands the collapse had occurred when U.S. troops reached favorable terrain and had been heralded by at least one suicidal banzai charge. But there were no banzais on Peleliu, and the terrain was becoming worse instead of better."

Rupertus spent most of the day studying sector maps with Selden, and talking over static-heavy field phone circuits to his regimental commanders. A lieutenant colonel on General Geiger's staff recalled the gist of the conversations. Rupertus, he said, was visibly disturbed when Chesty Puller told him of the hard times Davis's and Honsowetz's battalions were having.

"Can't they move any faster?" the general asked in a tone that was more of an order than a query. "Goddammit, Lewie, you've gotta kick ass to get results. You know that, goddammit!"

Better news from Bucky Harris in the 5th Marines CP. Both

Gayle's and Boyd's battalions had taken severe losses but were ahead of schedule; the airstrip and its complex of hangars and other installations around it were under their control.

From the southern sector, Herm Hanneken said the 7th Marines had "the situation well in hand." The regiment had met heavy resistance, the colonel reported, but he expected to secure the area by sundown.

Rupertus had just rung off from Hanneken when General Geiger appeared under the canvas tarp shielding the CP from the torrid rays of the late-afternoon sun. A look of surprise was evident on both faces.

"I didn't expect to find you here, Bill," Geiger said in a quizzical manner. He didn't seem to notice the general's gimpy leg or cane.

"Likewise, General," was Rupertus's answer. "I thought it was time for me to see what was going on."

With that, the duo moved out of earshot of the other officers and engaged in heated conversation for ten or fifteen minutes. Geiger later told his aide that the argument was over the crucial matter of when Rupertus intended to call in the Army's 81st Wildcat Division to reinforce—or possibly relieve—Chesty Puller's badly shot-up 1st Marines.

Geiger thought the move should be made then and there. Rupertus adamantly refused to do so, short of a direct order from Geiger, his superior. The problem remained in limbo for three days.

As the two generals talked, near sundown of Day Two, casualties of the 1st Regiment totaled more than 1,000 men, dead or wounded. According to "the book," losses of 15 percent are considered more than enough to relieve a regiment. Puller's had taken 33 percent in less than forty-eight hours.

Back on the beachhead, a few yards from Dr. Hagan's aid and evacuation station, Australian correspondents Denis Warner and John Brennan, of the *Sidney Bulletin,* were brewing a pot of traditionally strong tea before digging in for the night.

They were expecting their fellow Aussie Damien Parer, cameraman for *Paramount News,* to show up momentarily, so they were boiling a nightcap for three. It was laced with several ounces of brandy that Warner, veteran of five prior invasions that he was, had thoughtfully brought ashore in what he called his "personal kit to survive any landing with the Marines."

Their wait was in vain. Parer was dead, cut down in a burst

of machine-gun fire early in the day while filming the jump-off of Honsowetz's 2d Battalion.

"He was shooting tanks advancing against Japanese positions," Warner wrote in a letter to a friend. "He was actually in front of the tanks, walking backward, when he was shot. Several of us spent a good part of the third day looking for him. Brennan, who was Parer's closest friend, found the body. Sadly, someone had pulled the film out of his camera, so his last work was destroyed.

"Parer, like Brennan, was a deeply religious man. I remember him on Guam and Peleliu on his knees at dawn, praying. After that he always boiled a billy of tea. The Americans thought at first that he was nuts, but soon appreciated him for the brave man—and great photographer—that he was."

Back in Australia, Parer's death stunned the people, who mourned him much as Americans mourned Ernie Pyle when he was killed by a Japanese sniper's bullet on Ie Shima, a tiny island offshore from Okinawa during that invasion. To the Aussies, twenty-seven-year-old Damien Parer was a legend who had covered the war since 1940, both in North Africa's blazing sands and in the jungles of the South Pacific.

The Motion Picture Academy of Arts and Sciences in Los Angeles posthumously awarded the Australian an Oscar in 1944 for his "indomitable personal courage and unsurpassed professional skills in photographing American fighting men in action." It is the only time a newsreel cameraman has been so honored.

A few days after Parer's death, Marine combat correspondent Sergeant Donald A. Hallman, Sr., of Long Island City, New York, lost his left leg to the hip in a mortar attack. The thirty-nine-year-old newsman, a copy editor for the now-defunct *Brooklyn Eagle* when he volunteered, was in the assault on one of the myriad crests of Bloody Nose Ridge with a company from the 1st Marines when he was hit.

Hallman was still recovering in a naval hospital in Hawaii in late February 1945 when he was informed that his only son, a seventeen-year-old private with less than six months' service, had been killed on D-Day at Iwo Jima.

8

September 17, 1944, was a Sunday, D plus two for the Marines on Peleliu. For the Army's 81st Infantry Division, it was Fox Day, the date the Wildcats faced Japanese fire for the first time. Their objective was Angaur, approximately half Peleliu's size and some 6 miles off the island's southern tip.

In Operation Stalemate's battle plan, Major General Paul J. Mueller's 16,000-plus men were designated as the reserve force for the 1st Marine Division. Its orders were to remain afloat, ready to land reinforcements quickly if and when needed on D-Day.

Once the beachhead was established, the 81st was to assault and seize Angaur. Future use of the division depended on the performance of the unblooded troops and officers, how long it took to accomplish the mission, and the number of casualties. If all went well, various units of the division would be part of a soon-to-come invasion of Ulithi, an atoll some 300 miles due northeast of the Palaus.

Thirty-seven of the 81st's troop transports and LSTs, with a formidable escort of heavy cruisers and aircraft carriers, had stood menacingly off Babelthuap while the Marines hit Peleliu on D-Day. Several waves of amtracs, loaded with soldiers, formed lines as if about to roar toward shore—but none did. The maneuver was a feint to draw General Inoue's attention from more important events taking place 30 miles to the south.

Now it was the real thing.

H-Hour was 8:30 A.M.

General Mueller, from the bridge of his flagship, *Fremont,* watched as two regiments—designated by the Army as regimental combat teams (RCTs)—clambered down cargo nets to Higgins boats for the assault on Angaur, 3,000 yards ahead.

Unlike Peleliu, the 2,000-acre island was almost entirely flat—and no torturous reef surrounded the target. The almost square objective was about the size of an ordinary Kansas wheat farm in the States, and had excellent landing beaches on each of its sides.

Only the northeast corner, an area called Romuldo Hill, bore the faintest resemblance to Peleliu's awful terrain. And it was not infested with death-dealing caves and fortifications manned with well-armed and battle-tested Japanese. Further, all of Angaur's beaches were flat without adjacent high ground

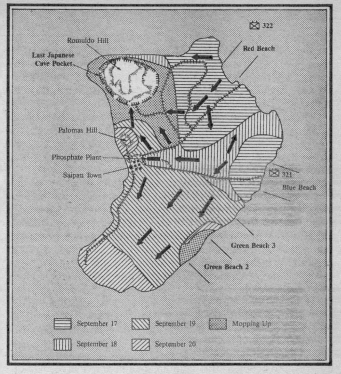

⊠ 322	
Romuldo Hill	Red Beach
Last Japanese Cave Pocket	
Palomas Hill	
Phosphate Plant	
Saipan Town	⊠ 321
	Blue Beach
	Green Beach 3
	Green Beach 2

▤ September 17	◩ September 19	▦ Mopping Up
▥ September 18	▨ September 20		

ANGAUR, SEPTEMBER 17–20, 1944

to protect them; each was seemingly made to order for an easy assault.

Major Ushio Goto, commander of the island's 1,500-man garrison, had only enough troops and firepower to defend just one possible landing area, Green Beach on the island's southeastern shore. This time pre-invasion intelligence photos paid off for the invasion forces.

So instead of hitting Green Beach, known to be fortified with several concrete-and-steel bunkers and pillboxes armed with 37-millimeter antiboat guns and .50-caliber machine guns, the 81st hit Red and Blue Beaches. They were along the island's northern shore and were virtually barren of prepared defenses.

For thirty minutes before H-Hour, the battleship *Tennessee* unleashed 857 tons of 14-inch shells on Red and Blue Beaches at point-blank range. Forty Dauntless dive-bombers from the carrier *Wasp* plastered the area with 120 500-pound explosives. And minutes before the first troops scrambled ashore, a flotilla of rocket-firing LCI landing craft let go, less than a quarter mile from the beaches, with nearly 2,000 rounds of flame-spitting 5-inch missiles.

Colonel Benjamin Venable's 322d RCT landed on Red Beach, and Colonel Robert Dark's 321st on Blue. The first amtracs were ashore at 8:35 and met only scattered small-arms fire and a few rounds of mortars, hardly enough reaction to be called heavy organized resistance.

Perhaps the Wildcats had inherited the "landing luck" of the Old Breed. Without a reef to hamper them, waves of troop-carrying Higgins boats followed at four-minute intervals. Within half an hour, three LSTs were unloading tanks, artillery, trucks, and heavy earth-moving equipment right on the beaches from their cavernous hulls.

Any thought, however, that Angaur would be an uncontested "walk-over" soon vanished. Major Goto's orders from Colonel Nakagawa were the same General Inoue had issued for the defense of Peleliu: "Make the Americans fight and die for every yard they advance, for every strongpoint. There will be no banzai attacks, and if and when the flat ground is lost, retreat to the high ground and fight to the death!"

There was understandable mass confusion among the soldiers on the beach as the regimental combat teams formed up to move inland. It was, after all, the first time they had faced the enemy in action, and it is highly probable that the easy going lulled the troops into a false impression of what the business of killing or being killed actually was all about.

Both Red and Blue Beaches were narrow, with about 100 yards of sand from the shoreline to an extremely thick jungle and formidable rain forest. "It was an obstacle so dense and tangled as to be a more impenetrable barrier than the Japanese could build," according to the 81st Division's official history of the Angaur operation.

Instead of approaching the forbidding growth in widely dispersed squads and fire teams, the still unwary soldiers headed inland abreast in platoon- and company-strength lines, crouching but moving slowly with bayonets fixed. Their delay in moving out had given Goto's troops time to take up defensive positions, not in great numbers but in sufficient force to inflict the first casualties on the men of the 81st Division.

Snipers concealed in trees picked off inviting targets as they scrambled for cover. Soon machine guns began clattering from hastily improvised bunkers. Mortars started to rain down on the beaches, not randomly fired but in definite patterns aimed at mounting piles of supplies, trucks, and bulldozers.

Although they were novices in battle, the RCTs were well trained and competently led. No one panicked when the Japanese struck back. Instead, the Wildcats did what they'd been taught Army-style to do to survive in jungle combat. They pulled back to a relatively safe distance, dispersed, found cover, dug in, called in artillery and tank support, and—when the time was right—took out the softened-up enemy positions one by one in small-unit action with rifles, grenades, and flamethrowers.

It was slow going, but this was the battle scenario for RCTs 321 and 322 on Fox Day. By sundown they had driven a 600-yard wedge inland—and found themselves in the most precarious situation the Angaur invasion was to face.

When Colonel Dark's 321st RCT dug in for the night, its perimeter was anchored on both ends of the 1,000-yard-long Blue Beach. Colonel Venable's 322nd RCT had done the same with its lines on Red Beach. The problem was that a crucial 1,000-yard gap separated the beachheads, making both vulnerable to Japanese counterattacks from the exposed flanks.

Major Goto was quick to recognize and exploit the unexpected opportunity. There was hardly a minute until dawn when a firefight wasn't crackling somewhere along the line as infiltrators probed for weak spots in the thin perimeters. The situation was made more frantic by the green American troops, understandably trigger-happy in their first nerve-racking night in combat. They shot at anything that moved—quite often at each other.

Japanese pressure was especially heavy against B and C Companies of RCT 321's 1st Battalion. It appeared several times that they might be driven into the sea, but at daybreak the entire situation was turned around.

First, some thirty carrier planes—whose pilots were old hands at flying low-level support missions for the Marines—lambasted the area in front of the endangered American lines with heavy strafing. Then, with the return of enough light to spot targets, artillery was called in, with devastating results to the Japanese. Sherman tanks shortly joined the fray, and the foot soldiers of RCTs 321 and 322 were able to resume the attack.

Fierce fighting erupted several times during the next two days when the men of the 81st ran into prepared strongpoints. It was heaviest on Fox plus one when Colonel Dark's 1st Battalion smashed against the complex of fortifications on Green Beach, where Major Goto had expected the Americans to land and had concentrated his beachhead defenses.

The area was hard to approach from the jungles and swamps, the route of RCT 321's attack, and bulldozer tanks had to carve a trail for the troops before the assault could begin. It took four hours of close-in combat before Dark's Wildcats were able to silence the interconnected maze of bunkers, pillboxes, mortar pits, and sandbagged trenches.

By sunset of the third day, Angaur had been sliced in two. The handful of survivors of the 1st Battalion of Japan's 59th Infantry Regiment were compressed into three small pockets on Romuldo Hill, there to hold out until October 19, when they were killed. Major Goto was still in command and died with his men.

So far as General Mueller was concerned, the battle for Anguar was over by midmorning of September 20, the fourth day of the operation. He signaled General Geiger on the *Mount McKinley*: "As of 1034 hours this date, target has been secured."

"Secured" didn't mean the fighting had ended—just that the Japanese were no longer deemed capable of further offensive action in sufficient strength to jeopardize the 81st Division's grip on the island.

Mueller also informed Geiger that Colonel Venable's RCT 322 would remain on Angaur to complete mop-up operations, but that the 81st Division's two other regiments "are now available for further assignment."

Geiger's response: "Maintain RCT 321 in readiness for possible immediate deployment to Peleliu. Release RCT 323 to Ulithi Attack Group." This force, commanded by Rear Admiral W.H.P. Blandy, comprised thirty-one vessels—mainly battleships, aircraft carriers, cruisers, and destroyers.

Blandy's armada arrived off Ulithi the next day and, without firing a shot, landed RCT 323 to occupy the atoll—long considered by Navy intelligence officers to be a heavily fortified Japanese naval stronghold. Instead, it had been abandoned by the enemy; its unopposed seizure is described in a Navy Archives document as "one of the great bargains of the Pacific War."

With its huge deep-water lagoon and more than fifty permanent barracks and supply buildings, Ulithi quickly became the major mid-Pacific United States base and staging area for future Navy and Marine Corps operations in the drive toward the Japanese home islands.

But Angaur? CinCPac planners wanted the island to keep the enemy from using it to shell Peleliu with heavy artillery or as a base for reinforcements against the invading Marines. Also, its flat terrain was viewed as ideal for construction of an airstrip for long-range bombers.

The 81st Division's engineer battalion finished the runways within a month. Official documents indicate that the field was used by only two planes, both crippled carrier-based fighters. As for troops to reinforce the Peleliu garrison, Major Goto's force of 1,500 men (naval intelligence had estimated it at twice that number) weren't enough to beat off the green Army troops. Heavy artillery to shell Peleliu? There was none on Angaur.

In 1989 a retired Marine general expressed his sentiments about the military significance of Angaur. "It was even more of a needless blunder than Peleliu, as useless as the tits on a boar hog," he said, "unless you consider the blooding of the Army's 81st Division a worthwhile objective."

The Marine Corps monograph on the Palaus campaign takes that view: "The three-day fight on Angaur," it asserts, "provided just what was necessary to convert well-trained, fundamentally sound regimental combat teams into a genuine combat unit. The Wildcats had met the enemy and overcome him. They had seen their own dead and wounded, and now they knew what Japanese fire sounded like. The strain had not been so long, nor casualties so severe to impair the unit's strength, while morale grew through newly confirmed confidence in itself and its leaders. In short, officers and men were ready, willing, and able. . . ."

The 81st Division's official history comes to the same conclusion: "These were now battle-tested veterans, sure of their abilities and anxious to demonstrate the prowess of combat infantrymen to the Marines."

Sergeant Jonathan G. Wagner, however, a machine gunner in RCT 321's 1st Battalion, viewed what happened on Angaur through the bleary eyes of a battle-worn and cynical GI.

"On-the-job training in this business is goddam hard and dangerous work that can be mighty expensive," he said. Casualties suffered by the 81st Division in its first combat confirmed his statement: 260 men killed in action, 1,354 wounded, and another 940 "temporarily disabled" for unspecified reasons.

Fifty-nine Japanese prisoners were taken, the only survivors of Major Goto's approximately 1,500-man force of defenders.

The only Marine known to have landed with RCT 321 on Fox Day was twenty-four-year-old Captain George P. Shultz from Swift River, Massachusetts. Officially, he was attached to the unit as its Marine Corps liaison officer, but his precise duties weren't specified. Once ashore, however, he found plenty to do.

"There was a gigantic amount of stuff unloaded on the beach," he recalled one day in June of 1986, "and there was no plan for exactly where what should go and so on. As the battle erupted, it just came in and piled up and was just sitting there. So I just took charge of it and started dispatching it, and so that basically was the Angaur landing for me."

The self-appointed beachmaster's recollections were made aboard a plush Air Force transport flying at an altitude of some 35,000 feet over the Palaus. The former Marine was then United States Secretary of State George Schulz. Accompanied by several aides and a dozen Washington correspondents, he was on a mission to the Philippines and other so-called Pacific Rim countries.

TEN

The Hills of Hades

FOR THE FIRST THREE DAYS THE BATTLE FOR PELELIU FOL-
lowed the pattern of what the Marines had come to recognize
as "conventional warfare" in the island-hopping war against
the Japanese.

It was a classic case of American naval and air power doing
everything it could to soften enemy beaches for the landing of
assault troops to establish a foothold on the objective. Once
ashore, their first objective was to set up a perimeter to hold
off the threat of a Japanese counterattack to push the invaders
back into the sea.

When this was accomplished, a constant and massive
buildup of reinforcements, armor, and supplies began stream-
ing in to expand the beachhead and provide muscle for the
all-out offensive to achieve victory. But once the relatively
small patch of flat ground around and south of the airstrip was
seized, once the push had driven across the island, the battle
took on a different and terrible dimension that was to set
Peleliu apart from all other Pacific struggles.

It is even logical to say that because of the fiendish terrain
of most of the island and the indescribable heat broken only by
monsoon rains and typhoon-force winds, the coral battleground was possibly the worst of World War II.

As D plus two dawned, the devilish landscape yet to be
conquered was about to show itself as much an obstacle to
victory as Peleliu's determined defenders. The result was prolonged and deadly guerrilla warfare, the likes and ferocity of
which no other Marine division encountered from Guadalcanal
to the war's final battle on Okinawa.

Chesty Puller's 1st Marines already had been subjected to
the realities of what was to come when they first assaulted the

low-lying ridges just inland from White Beaches One and Two. Bucky Harris's 5th Regiment and Herm Hanneken's 7th would shortly find themselves ensnarled in the same brutal predicament.

But first things first.

As General Rupertus had ordered the night before, the third day's attacks began at 8:00.

Two battalions from the 5th Marines—Boyd's 1st and Gayle's 2d—moved out to consolidate their hold on the airstrip and the adjacent complex of devastated hangars and administration buildings, where a few snipers and stragglers continued to harass the advance.

Hanneken's 7th Marines began a two-battalion drive to wipe out scattered pockets of stoutly resisting Japanese still dug in on the southern promontory of the island.

The 1st Marines assault battalions—Davis's 1st and Honsowetz's 2d—fought off fresh counterattacks, intending to strengthen the tenuous hold on Hill 200 and then take on the next ridge.

Boyd's battalion met little resistance from ground troops as it began its sweep across the northern few hundred yards of the airfield. Most of the Japanese infantry had been slaughtered or driven pell-mell into the jungle during and after the previous day's disastrous "tankette" foray.

That didn't keep Colonel Nakagawa's mortars and artillery, firing from concealed positions in the northern highlands, from doing all they could to slow the complete occupation of the airstrip's facilities. It was nearly an hour before Marine 105-millimeter howitzers, naval bombardment, and air strikes put a stop to the heavy shelling.

From then on the going was easy for the shouting, onrushing attackers. By noon, seventy-two hours after the landing, someone had hung a small American flag over the wide doors of the smoldering shambles of the roofless sandbagged cinder-block headquarters building.

By midafternoon the first elements of Seabees—men from the 33d and 73d Naval Construction Battalions—appeared with several bulldozers and road rollers. Without apparent orders from anyone, they went to work immediately to patch up the bomb- and shell-pocked runways, occasionally jumping for cover from sniper fire.

Lisle Shoemaker, the United Press correspondent, was the

first newsman on the scene, still toting the portable typewriter Bing Crosby had given him.

"The Marines' bitter struggle for this tiny sand- and coral-hilled island has been successful as far as gaining possession of a marvelous airfield which the Japs had painstakingly constructed," he wrote. ". . . The area is literally cluttered with blockhouses, pillboxes, dugouts and underground passages. . . ."

Shoemaker's dispatch said he counted more than 150 demolished Japanese planes in and around "the barely recognizable skeletons of burned-out hangars." He was surprised to find in the debris the wreckage of four American-built Douglas DC-3 commercial airliners, sold to the Japanese before the war.

Not only were most of the aircraft blown to bits, but the remnants of their aluminum fuselages and wings were corroded, their shattered steel engines rust-encrusted. All of the planes had been destroyed months before the invasion when Admiral Mitscher's Task Force 58 had ravaged Peleliu in the two days of heavy bombardment and air strikes on March 2–3.

Two Marines—twenty-four-year-old Private First Class Ziggie Ladzinski of Riverside, New Jersey, and twenty-seven-year-old Private First Class Albert F. Jensen of Philadelphia—"adopted me," Shoemaker reported.

"What kind of a Marine are you, without a gun?" Jensen demanded. The correspondent reported, "When I identified myself they immediately attached themselves as a personal bodyguard for the rest of the day."

Both men were amtrac drivers whose vehicles had been destroyed on the reef, and they had served since then as infantry troops with Boyd's battalion. The reporter noticed that Jensen was wearing strange-looking white pants and asked where he had gotten them. "They are Jap pants," the Philadelphian replied. "I lost mine on some barbed wire when I was crawling out of a pillbox. A dead Jap quartermaster is easier to deal with than a Marine supply sergeant."

The trio inspected the airfield and its buildings. Shoemaker wrote:

"The undescribable stench of Japanese dead, lying around in weird patterns of death, permeated the area. . . . A first-class radio station, complete with a small motion picture room for ranking officers, was in shambles. . . . I found the body of a Jap officer which had obviously been booby-trapped. A lone wire protruded from his shirtsleeve and extended to a bulky package sticking out underneath his shirt. . . ."

The ominous whirring noise and whomp-whomp explosions of incoming mortars sounded nearby as the newsman and the two Marines left the communications building and went their separate ways. The correspondent made note of the incident in the final paragraph of his story:

"It seemed impossible there could still be Japs near enough to man weapons after the torrent of bombs and shells that had hit the airfield, and the onslaught of the Marines who attacked it from the ground—but they did." Shoemaker told a friend years later that he never saw Ladzinski or Jensen again. "I hope they made it alive through the rest of the battle," he said.

Major Gayle's battalion, on D plus two, had more trouble with "friendly fire" than with the Japanese. First there was an off-target carrier plane strike, then Marine artillery fire that missed its mark. The route of the attack was east of the airstrip through dense jungle and a mangrove swamp toward what the sector map identified as Ngardololok, the site of a well-defended radio direction finder.

Gayle's men met only minor and ineffective resistance, most of it from isolated sniper fire, as they advanced. But hacking a path through the undergrowth was hot, backbreaking work, and heat prostration took its toll. Shortly before 11:00, the battalion's F Company was within a hundred yards of the primitive radar station but was forced to halt by a narrow causeway connecting Ngardololok with the peninsula.

Troubled by the possibility of an ambush if the Marines tried to cross the unprotected low coral bridge, Gayle called in an air strike to clear the way. Six Dauntless dive-bombers swept in at 12:45 with their .50-caliber machine guns lacing the area in a roaring low-level run. Not only did they miss the target, but much of the fire ripped into dug-in positions of stunned Marines.

The thoroughly bewildered and cursing mad battalion CO next asked for artillery support. It was half an hour before shells started landing in a nonstop fifteen-minute barrage. When it lifted, elements of F and G Companies began the perilous crossing of the causeway—only to be hit again by friendly fire.

Before the first troops reached the other side, a second and totally unexpected flight of Hellcats came diving down to strafe them, obviously believing they were Japanese. Fortunately, the machine guns were again mostly off-target and missed the Marines, and the bridgehead was established.

The memorable day of misadventure wasn't yet over for the 2d Battalion. As Gayle moved forward with E Company to cross the causeway and set up a new command post for the night, the advancing troops were hit by another downpour of Marine mortar and artillery fire. There is no record of what the bitter and angry major had to say about what must have been a single day's record for foul-ups on bedeviled Peleliu.

Most of the battalion's thirty-four casualties on D plus two resulted from friendly fire. Further, after the Marines settled in for the night, they found that the Japanese had abandoned the emplacements protecting Ngardololok along with its radio direction finder. Such are the fortunes of war, Gayle must have ruefully concluded.

2

Two battalions of the 7th Marines—Lieutenant Colonel John Gormley's 1st and Major Hunter Hurst's 3d—had plenty of difficult and dangerous work to do on D plus two. Their task was to finish the mop-up of Peleliu's southern tip and seize tiny adjacent Ngarmoked Island. The two were connected at low tide by a sand spit.

Both areas were heavily fortified and had caused major problems during the first two days of battle. Forty-eight hours of naval shelling, air strikes, artillery, and frontal assault by tank-supported Marine infantry had taken out a significant number of Japanese defenses and troops.

An estimated 300-plus Japanese had so far been killed in the sector. Marines casualties there were seventy-two, dead and wounded. Some thirty pillboxes and bunkers, four 5-inch antiboat guns, and three 75-millimeter dual-purpose anticraft weapons already had been destroyed.

Nonetheless, numerous concealed enemy strongpoints continued to fight with undiminished ferocity, especially where the 3d Battalion pushed the assault on Ngarmoked. Nineteen-year-old Private First Class Arthur J. Jackson, of Portland, Oregon, was one of the men caught up in the blistering action.

Despite his youth, Jackson was a combat veteran who had been cited for bravery on Cape Gloucester, where, under a torrent of heavy machine-gun fire from Japanese emplacements on a steep hill, he saved the life of a wounded Marine by carrying him to safety.

"Jackson always seemed to know what to do when we were in big trouble," a comrade recalled years later, "and he wasn't ever afraid to take things in his own hands to get it done. He was a gung-ho Gyrene from the word 'go' and didn't have to wait for orders to attack the Nips anywhere, anytime we were in a bad way."

The trouble confronting Jackson's platoon was far beyond bad. It was so desperate that the outfit faced the prospect of being cut to pieces, even wiped out, unless something was done—and done fast. A complex of half a dozen camouflaged pillboxes and bunkers, connected by tunnels, was the source of the deadly mess. Within seconds of each other, the outfit's recently commissioned second lieutenant commander and his senior sergeant were killed by machine-gun crossfire.

That was Jackson's now-or-never cue "to take things in his own hands to get it done." During the next hectic ninety minutes, Jackson was nothing less than a one-man Marine Corps.

The first thing he did was to ignore the withering resistance and dash ahead of the pinned-down platoon's position to the base of a large coral emplacement. Then he emptied the twenty-round magazine of his BAR into one of the bunker's narrow apertures, killing several of its occupants and startling the others so that they momentarily stopped firing.

The sudden silence gave another Marine enough time to scamper forward with two satchels—one bulging with high-explosive charges and the other with phosphorus grenades—and return safely to the lines.

Jackson knew what to do with the additional firepower—and proceeded to do it. He tossed several of the choking white-hot grenades into the bunker, followed by three chunks of fused TNT. The strongpoint blew sky-high with its thirty-five dead Japanese defenders.

There was still plenty for Jackson to do. Now, however, he had the covering firepower—bazookas, grenades, and rifles—of his comrades in the no longer pinned-down platoon. Twelve more pillboxes and bunkers were overrun as he continued the rampage. When the fighting was over, Marines counted more than fifty additional Japanese dead in the path of the youthful PFC's charge.

Jackson left Ngarmoked unscathed. But he was wounded and evacuated later in the struggle for one of the cliffs of

Bloody Nose Ridge. While recovering in a hospital on Guam, he was promoted to platoon sergeant, and he was totally fit to rejoin the 1st Division in time for the Okinawa campaign. Wounded again on May 18, 1945, he was returned to the States for treatment, and in August he was commissioned a second lieutenant.

President Harry Truman awarded the Medal of Honor to Jackson and promoted him to captain in ceremonies at the White House on October 5, 1945. The nation's highest decoration was for the action on Peleliu. It would be very difficult to find words to better recount what happened than those in the last paragraph of the accompanying citation signed by the Commander in Chief.

> Stout-hearted and indomitable despite the terrific odds, Private First Class Jackson resolutely maintained control of his platoon's movement throughout his valiant one-man assault and by his cool decision and relentless fighting spirit during the critical situation, contributed essentially to the complete annihilation of the enemy in the southern sector of the island. His gallant initiative and heroic conduct in the face of extreme peril reflect the highest credit upon Private First Class Jackson and the United States Naval Service.

Jackson's career as a Marine ended on a tragic and mysterious note in 1962 when, still a captain, he resigned from the Corps. His action resulted from being implicated in the death of one Reuben Lopez, a Cuban citizen, who had been arrested by Jackson in a restricted area of the U.S. Naval Base at Guantánamo Bay, Cuba.

The findings of an official Marine Corps inquiry into the affair have never been made public. At the time, news reports said that Lopez was shot while trying to escape and that Jackson and another officer hid his body in "an effort to prevent an international incident with the Castro government."

Jackson maintained, through the years, a resolute silence on the matter and refused to discuss it with anyone, either in public or privately with former comrades. One with whom Jackson remained in occasional contact said the hero of Ngarmoked became a mail carrier on the West Coast, where he ultimately retired.

3

Just crossing the sand spit from Peleliu to Ngarmoked was a dangerous mission for the point of the advance, troops from John Gormley's 1st Battalion. It was heavily mined and had to be cleared before the main assault began, and Jackson mounted his one-man charge.

Nearly two hours passed as Captain Frank Knoll and a squad of his demolitions experts completed the hazardous chore. He knew his business, and he had meticulously passed the know-how along to "Knoll's Knights," his crew of the 1st Engineer Battalion. Any miscue meant either instant death or, at least, a badly maimed body.

Back on Pavuvu, Knoll had been the sole occupant of a tent set up as far as possible from all others in the 7th Marines' bivouac area. The captain was by no means a loner by choice. His fellow officers found him a very congenial, articulate, well-read companion. But because he was constantly learning firsthand all he could by dismantling live mines and bombs, someone in division headquarters decided that for safety's sake, he should live in isolation.

There is no way of knowing how many times Knoll risked his life, or how many Marines he personally saved from wounds or death from land mines and booby traps, on Peleliu. It was at least a daily occurrence that was recognized by his superiors. The dauntless captain later received the Navy Cross for his valorous performance of duty, and somehow left the island without a scratch.

With the sand spit finally free of mines, the 1st Battalion's advance cranked up in full force. Four Sherman tanks, four armored amtracs, and two half-track trucks with .50-caliber machine guns led the way for B Company's infantrymen. Company A stayed put, in reserve, on the northern edge of the spit.

The Marines soon found that all their firepower was needed. They, like the 3d Battalion, had run into a hornet's nest of swarming resistance despite the shelling and air attacks Ngarmoked had taken. Instead of what they expected would be light opposition, B Company immediately came under intense mortar and machine-gun fire from small units of Japanese hidden in untouched caves and tunnel-connected dug-in positions in the jumble of rocks and coral ridges.

The terrain was so rugged that the tanks were unable to get

into position to fire until late in the struggle. Amtracs and half-tracks bogged down before they could help much, leaving only the last reserves of Gormley's battalion to push the attack. Push they did, inexorably and with the fearsome losses inherent in such combat.

Private First Class Charles H. Roan, a twenty-one-year-old farmer and part-time garage mechanic from Claude, Texas, died in the assault, sacrificing his life to save four comrades when their platoon was pinned down and partially surrounded. Every attempt to pull back to a more protected position brought on a downpour of hand grenades and heavy-machine-gun fire from enemy emplacements on the steep coral ridge the Marines were attacking.

Despite his youth and lack of rank, Roan's buddies looked to him to find a way out of the deadly situation they were in; he had made it through Cape Gloucester, and this was their first time in battle. The Marines were armed only with rifles, and Roan knew it was a lost cause unless reinforcements moved up to spring them from the deathtrap.

Help never came for the simple reason that the rest of the platoon was in the same desperate straits. Instead, the Japanese intensified the pressure with an avalanche of grenades, some flying through the air and others rolling down the rocky incline. Fragments of one tore into Roan, but missed the other men.

Moments later another of the sizzling missiles landed in the center of the group. Roan, despite his mortal wounds, managed to fling himself on the explosive and took the full impact of the blast in his stomach and chest. His comrades again escaped unharmed but instantly sprawled to the ground as if they, too, had been killed.

Two bulldozer tanks arrived on the scene half an hour later. The monsters had trundled forward, carving a path through giant boulders, to get into position to unleash point-blank cannon and machine-gun fire against the Japanese strongpoints. With the support of this armor, the surviving Marines in Roan's platoon wiped out the enemy emplacements within thirty minutes.

Shortly before 2:00, a sweat-soaked and out-of-breath runner from Gormley's battalion stumbled into Colonel Hanneken's regimental CP, in a shell hole across the sand spit from Ngarmoked.

Someone handed him a canteen of water. The young Marine's face was grimy with coral dust but without a hint of natural stubble. He gulped down several swallows and then poured the rest of the water over his matted bare head, and through swollen and parched lips, he managed to mumble out his message.

The last Japanese holdouts, he said, were trapped on a small exposed ledge and being rapidly wiped out. "Colonel Gormley told me to tell Colonel Hanneken that Ngarmoked was ours," he said.

As the welcome news was being delivered, marksmen of A and B Companies went about finishing off the doomed enemy and witnessed a strange and gruesome sight. Some Japanese were blowing their brains out with pistols. Others were plunging headfirst into the shallow sea below. When the bodies were later examined, it was found that more than a dozen of the suicides were officers, adding to the total of at least 350 Japanese killed earlier in the day.

General Rupertus was informed of developments in a terse dispatch from Colonel Hanneken to division headquarters. "At 1520 hours, our objective was taken," it said. "The 7th Marines mission on Ngarmoked is completed."

The monograph of the battle later summarized the action in these words: "A fine Japanese reinforced infantry battalion, in strongly fortified positions, had been sent to join its ancestors." The document, however, made no mention that the Marines had lost nearly 200 men, killed and wounded, in the process.

Nearly a year later, on July 21, 1945, the tree-shaded courthouse lawn of Armstrong County, Texas, was crowded with some 2,000 people sweltering in the 100-degrees-plus temperature. They had gathered in remembrance of the death of Private First Class Charles H. Roan and to witness the posthumous presentation of the Medal of Honor to his widow mother, Lillabel Roan, for the Marine's supreme sacrifice to save the lives of four comrades. A reporter from the *Fort Worth Star-Telegram* wrote of the occasion:

The ceremony was witnessed by virtually the entire population of Claude, all business having been suspended. It was delayed at the request of Mrs. Roan until another son, Chief Petty Officer J. B. Roan, a veteran of five naval operations, could be here. A third son, Private Henry C. Roan, Jr., is with the Army in the Philippines.

The award was the 25th for native sons or residents of Texas. So far as is known, it is the first presentation of a Medal of Honor ever to be made on a courthouse lawn.

4

General Smith and his staff obviously had no way of knowing, when they put together the invasion plan back on Pavuvu, which of the 1st Division's assault regiments would have the roughest assignment in the battle for Peleliu.

In the first place, they were working from air reconnaissance photos and high command intelligence forecasts that were so sadly inaccurate as to be virtually useless. Secondly, the regiments were deemed virtual equals in combat capabilities. And finally, the onerous question of how the Japanese commanders intended to use their men, armor, and fortifications to defend the target was an enigma that only time would resolve.

It was thus the luck of the draw that put Colonel Puller and his 1st Marines on White Beaches One and Two, and into murderous terrain and unbelievable Japanese resistance almost from the very moment the first wave landed.

He knew, at dawn of the battle's third day, that his regiment was in desperate shape. Puller later told Burke Davis (the author of his biography, *Marine!*) about a call he made the night before to Colonel Selden, the division chief of staff. The conversation was heated and to the point:

"Johnny, half my regiment is gone. I've got to have replacements to carry out division orders tomorrow morning."

"You know we have no replacements, Lewie."

"I told you before we came ashore that we should have at least one regiment in reserve. We're not fighting a third of the men we brought in—all these damned specialists you brought!"

"Anything wrong with your orders, Lewie?"

"No, I'm ready to go ahead, but you know my casualties are 50 percent now."

"What do you want me to do?"

"Give me some of those 17,000 men on the beach!"

"You can't have them. They're not trained infantry!"

"Give 'em to me, and by nightfall tomorrow they'll be trained infantry!"

An audible click was followed by the constant crackle and buzz characteristic of all field phones. The matter was settled for the time being, and neither Puller nor Selden could do anything about changing the situation. The 1st Marines were not alone in needing fresh manpower; so did the 5th and 7th Regiments, both of which also had taken heavy losses, if not as heavy as Puller's outfit.

The sad fact was that reinforcements *were* available from the Army's 81st Division. But General Rupertus, despite the earlier confrontation with General Geiger (who thought the Wildcats should be committed immediately), still refused to order General Mueller's troops into the struggle for Peleliu. In Rupertus's view, it was a Marine Corps operation, and his regiments—despite their problems and casualties—were capable of winning the battle on their own.

Chesty Puller was a stout advocate of man-to-man combat communications whenever possible, especially when the situation was serious. After the futile conversation with Selden, he went out immediately with a runner, stumbling over rocks in the darkness, to find the ridgeline CPs of Ray Davis's 1st Battalion and Russ Honsowetz's 2d.

The colonel passed the same order to both men: "We press the attack at 8:00 in the morning. No change. Full speed. Use every man. Any questions? Understood?"

Then he and his sergeant vanished into the night, back down the steep slope to the regimental command post. Puller slipped and fell several times during the descent, cutting himself on the sharp coral and aggravating an old shrapnel wound in his left leg—a souvenir of a Japanese mortar blast back on Guadalcanal.

Division headquarters called shortly after he returned. Selden was on the line: "Puller, you understand my orders?"

The answer was formally worded but in subdued exasperation:

"Yes, Colonel, you needn't explain further. I just came back from my battalions. We're going to take ground tomorrow without replacements, but don't forget we're going to add 10 or 15 percent to our casualties."

Honsowetz's battalion jumped off earlier than ordered, shortly after 7:30, and without pre-assault artillery or air attacks. His frontline outposts were too close to the enemy, and he thought the Japanese might be taken by surprise. As Puller had ordered, every man in the battalion was in the push. There weren't many left—just 473 officers and men still alive or unwounded from the roster of 954 who had landed less than seventy-two hours earlier.

Davis's outfit, equally riddled with casualties, mounted its attack minutes later. The day's action would be the most costly of the campaign for the 1st Marines. By nightfall both battalions had ceased to exist as organized units capable of further combat unless they received reinforcements.

Not known at the time was the fact that the disastrously undermanned assault on September 17 was against the hard core of Colonel Nakagawa's main defense line on Peleliu.

Battle maps called the area the Umurbrogols. Marines rarely used the tongue-twister designation for the saw-toothed chain of hills and mini-mountains. Stretching north from the flat land of the airstrip's headquarters complex, the barren moonscape-like coral spine of the island extended almost a third of its 6-mile length.

To the attacking troops, the Umurbrogols quickly took on a descriptive array of terribly meaningful and unforgettable names where thousands of Americans and Japanese fought, maimed, and killed one another: Bloody Nose Ridge . . . Five Sisters . . . Five Brothers . . . Death Valley . . . China Wall . . . Horseshoe Valley . . . Walt and Baldy Ridges . . . and other isolated places that can only be identified as another site of carnage in the Hills of Hell that dominated Peleliu.

5

Small bands of infiltrators had probed both Honsowetz's and Davis's ridgeline positions throughout the night, and the Japanese apparently came to believe that the Marines' toeholds were so flimsy that they could be easily wiped out the next morning. The enemy almost succeeded several times during the daylong struggle.

Immediately after moving out against the next ridge from where they had spent the anxious night, Honsowetz's lead company was hit hard and pinned down, unable to advance or pull back. Even men of the War Dog Platoon, company clerk-typists, cooks, and bakers, were thrown into the desperate attempt to hold the line and revitalize the push. They were caught in the unremitting maelstrom with the same devastating outcome—constantly mounting casualties.

The Japanese ripped into the Marines with mortars, rockets, heavy-machine-gun fire, grenades, and shelling from unsuspected large-bore naval guns hidden in the northern reaches of the Umurbrogols. In what surely was one of the understatements of the entire campaign, Honsowetz said to his executive officer, Major Charles Brush, Jr.: "It appears the Japs don't want us on this hill, much less to take the next one." Then he phoned the regimental CP and got Colonel Puller on the line.

"I told Chesty that my situation was desperate and there was no possible way I could take Hill 210 without reinforcements," Honsowetz vividly recalled more than four decades later. "Puller just repeated his orders to take the ridge, and I said 'Christ, we can't do it, the casualties are too much and we've been fighting all day and all night,' and he said, 'You sound all right, you're there. Goddammit, you get those troops in there and you take the goddamn hill.' So that was that."

Honsowetz was being crushed between the proverbial rock and a hard place, and knew it. All he could do was follow orders; somehow he had to fire up the advance and take the objective. In a crouching lope, using any cover he could find, the battalion commander carried Puller's message to his few surviving company and platoon leaders.

The men knew there was a hellish job still to be done. The answer to how the outgunned and outnumbered Marines took the objective was a bewildering development. Just as Honsowetz got the assault moving again, the enemy's heavy firepower suddenly diminished and shortly petered out.

The slopes and ridgelines no longer were being ravaged by the shattering explosions from the big naval gun emplacements up north. The violent downpour of heavy mortars disappeared as if they had fallen from a passing thunderhead squall. Long-range rockets, spitting flames and screeching as they arched through the sky, no longer slammed with deadly blasts into the area.

This didn't mean the Japanese were abandoning Hill 210, or the strongpoints on the adjacent cliffs, to the Marines. Instead, resistance from the caves, bunkers, and pillboxes was strong and as determined as ever. But now the attackers had a fighting chance to take the objective in headlong, man-on-man assault—and they went about the hazardous business of doing just that.

"There was no other way," Frank Hough wrote in the official monograph of the battle. "Clawing up and over razorback crests, shinnying coral pinnacles, plunging down into sheer-sided gullies and ravines, dodging behind boulders, by evening Honsowetz's men had gained the forward slope of another hill and were firmly, if uncomfortably, established."

Why did the Japanese lift the devastating shelling when they did, when the attack was completely bogged down and on the edge of total disaster? The answer remains a baffling subject of speculation. Was it a major tactical error that recurred with surprising and—to the Marines—fortunate frequency during the course of the invasion? Was it because of a lack of communications between Colonel Nakagawa's headquarters and the front?

Or was it another case of his and General Murai's inflexible defense plan, a hallmark of Japanese military thinking, which decreed an inviolable course of action in any given situation regardless of the outcome or consequences?

Was it because Nakagawa knew that he must conserve ammunition—that there was no prospect of replenishing his stockpile and, thus, each round must be used with maximum effect, to kill as many Americans as possible?

The battle was, after all, hardly more than seventy-two hours old. It is extremely doubtful that even Nakagawa then believed it would be nearly two months until the last shot was fired. Of a certainty, some of the invasion high command—especially General Rupertus—still felt victory would come much sooner, maybe within a week, two at the most.

An increasing number of senior officers, however, were starting to express mounting concern about what was happening, particularly about the already horrendous and constantly increasing toll of casualties. The feeling of frustration and depression was visibly strong among the commanders of ravaged assault battalions—men like Davis and Honsowetz in the 1st Marines, Boyd and Gayle in the 5th, Gormley and Hurst in the 7th.

All were decorated, battle-tested leaders of unquestioned courage and determination, and all were certain of *ultimate* success. And all of them would do what they must—follow orders.

But at what cost? What could be done to lessen the terrible bloodletting? How could Peleliu be taken otherwise?

Remarkably, morale remained high among the junior officers and troops on the lines. Their *esprit de corps,* despite the inhuman hardships and danger, reflected the purported World War I remark of an original member of the Old Breed, Sergeant Dan Daly, about to lead a trench raid against the Germans:

"All right, you wonderful bastards, let's go! You don't wanta live forever, do you?"

Now, on Day Three of the operation, the situation on Peleliu was beyond rapid remedy. Combat finesse was impossible. Nothing but head-on assault—supported whenever possible by tanks, air strikes, naval bombardment, and artillery—would work.

The struggle henceforth pitted the invading ground troops against heavy, fight-to-the-death resistance in fiendishly constricted pockets where the terrain invariably was a deadly ally of the Japanese. It became a battle of improvisation in which each offensive thrust demanded a different solution to every problem.

The 11th Marines, the division's artillery regiment, soon learned that it had to drastically change long-accepted tactics to be effective. Instead of relying on massed shelling from batteries hundreds of yards from a target, the cannoneers were forced to move single large-caliber guns as close as possible to frontline action and deliver point-blank fire.

The 75-millimeter howitzers were often manhandled, pulled and pushed into position by sweat-drenched, battle-weary infantrymen assaulting sheer cliffs defended by heavily fortified clusters of caves, bunkers, and pillboxes. "But in the end it was the man on foot with a weapon in his hand who had to take the evil ground and hold it," General Geiger said years later.

Ray Davis's 1st Battalion was in a fix virtually identical to and as desperate as that of Honsowetz's men for most of D plus two. Moving out to take Hill 205, on the 2d Battalion's right flank, Davis's assault companies and platoons were almost immediately pinned down by the heavy shelling from the northern highlands.

The daylong scenario for both outfits was the same. Only after the enemy stopped the massive high-explosives bombardment were the 1st Battalion troops able to advance. Even then, like their comrades struggling to take Hill 210, the Marines had all they could do to overrun Japanese strongpoints on the craggy slopes.

Shortly before sundown some thirty men managed to reach the narrow shell-pocked crest, still taking withering heavy-machine-gun and mortar fire from another ridge scarcely 100 yards away. They found it impossible to dig in; entrenching tools and picks were useless against the unyielding coral surface.

The best the embattled troops could do for cover was to pile rocks and debris around fragile improvised positions—and hope it would be enough for them to survive the cyclone of resistance until dawn. Then, if anyone was left, they would get reinforcements and air strikes and artillery to take over.

The day's fighting, in many respects, was a preview of most of the combat to come on Peleliu. There was seldom such a thing as a continuous line of assault. Elements of the same company, even same platoon, attacked simultaneously in every direction. Large gaps often separated them as they took on individual Japanese fortifications.

More often than not, when an attacking unit called back for an air strike or artillery bombardment, it was uncertain precisely where it was and where the help was needed. Almost all of Peleliu's ridges looked alike, and this, coupled with inaccurate maps, made it all but impossible to pinpoint where fierce combat was raging.

Bloody Nose Ridge is probably the most memorable and confusing case in point. The fact is that there was *no single* Bloody Nose Ridge on Peleliu; the identification is a historic misnomer used by Marines for *innumerable* deadly coral heights which extended for hundreds of yards north of the airstrip.

"After several days of fighting, every damned ridge looked alike," was the plausible explanation given Lisle Shoemaker by a mortar man sergeant from Ray Davis's battalion. "I'd bet a month's pay it was the same way with the Five Sisters and their goddamned Five Brothers and all the other bastard places we hit on the miserable island. Hell, they weren't even on the map until we put 'em there."

General Smith was on the prowl throughout D plus two. With a corporal runner and two sergeant bodyguards toting Thompson submachine guns, he had shuttled—sometimes under direct sniper fire and occasional brief harassing mortar barrages—between regimental command posts. In his characteristic unobtrusive and methodical way, the division's assistant commander wanted to know firsthand what was taking place along the front and what, if anything, he could do to help.

The answer, in essence, was the same from Colonels Puller, Harris, and Hanneken:

"We're in one helluva fight and we need reinforcements and all the firepower we can get to push ahead and take the high ground."

Despite the massive destruction of landing craft on the reef, despite the savage and well-organized defense of the beachhead, despite the brutal struggle of Captain Hunt's K Company to seize the Point, despite the hard-fought battles to take the airstrip and its headquarters complex, and despite the bitter combat to secure the southern tip of the island and Ngarmoked, one thing was now obvious to General Smith and the regimental commanders.

Colonel Nakagawa had from the start placed his best troops and major defenses in the torturous hills of the Umurbrogols. There was absolutely no chance for a quick victory, they agreed, and the worst of the campaign, along with inevitably mounting casualties, was yet to come.

If the developments of the first seventy-two hours had any impact on General Rupertus's bewildering optimistic outlook for a rapid conquest of Peleliu, he kept it to himself. Shortly after 9:00 he called the regimental command posts with orders for D plus three. They were the same as before:

"Resume the attack with maximum effort in all sectors at 0800 hours on 18 September."

General Smith wondered if Rupertus realized that Chesty Puller's 1st Marines already had 1,236 confirmed casualties. The outfit's three-day casualties were just six less than all 1st Division fatalities during the 123 days on Guadalcanal, and only eleven fewer than the entire division's toll of dead and wounded in 131 days of combat at Cape Gloucester.

He was certain General Geiger wasn't aware of the intolerable situation. Otherwise he would be doing something drastic about it—even if it meant relieving the colonel of his command and pulling the regiment out of the lines, an unprecedented move in Marine Corps history.

6

While the men of the Old Breed took perverse pride in calling themselves "raggedy-assed Marines," their self-imposed deprecating description wasn't even close to how they looked after three days on Peleliu.

Their appearance was, in all likelihood, the grimiest, most evil-looking, stinking, and nonmilitary of any division at any time or place in the Pacific war. Except for a lucky scattered few high-ranking officers and aides, those who had spent most of the time afloat and little if any on the island, not a man wore anything faintly resembling a GI uniform.

Green dungarees were turned sooty gray from the coral ash, and ripped and torn from diving for cover or scampering over sharp rocks that were everywhere on the flat ground and ridges. Streaks of gray marked the salty path of sweat down the back of blouses and across shoulders where packs and rifles were carried.

Stains of unsuppressed urine surrounded crotches and trickled down pants legs. Hind ends showed splotches of uncontrolled and odorous bowel movements. Leggings had long been abandoned. Trouser legs were shortened, ripped almost to the knees or cut off with combat knives. Skivvy underwear shirts and drawers were discarded, blankets and ponchos thrown away.

Some men—even Chesty Puller—were stripped to the waist. Soles and sides of usually laceless combat boots of most men had been pierced by razor-edged chunks of coral. Camouflaged canvas helmet covers were draped, Arab-like, to protect necks from sunburn. Hair resembled heavy patches of steel wool. Smudged faces had the blackened look of miners emerging from a double shift in deep coal pits. Eyes were bloodshot and bleary from the fiendish combination of blazing sun, constantly swirling dust, and debris—and omnipresent fear.

The men were always thirsty and spoke through parched and swollen lips in raspy, hesitating voices like zombies. None had eaten more than a few bites of K or C rations since hitting the beach.

Tom Lea captured the awful essence of the men's appearance and emotional state in a widely reproduced painting called *The Thousand-Yard Stare*. It shows a Marine with Bloody Nose Ridge in the background, staring blankly ahead, seemingly unable to comprehend his surroundings. The artist-writer's notes, made on his sketch pad during the battle, recount his subject's individual ordeal. But it is also an indelible portrait of what many troops looked and felt like on Peleliu.

"Last evening he came down from the hills," Lea wrote. "Told to get some sleep, he found a shell hole and slumped into it. He's awake now. First light has given his gray face eerie color. He left the States thirty-one months ago. He was wounded in his first campaign. He has had tropical diseases. There is no food or water in the hills except what you carry. He half-sleeps at night and gouges Japs out of holes all day. Two-thirds of his company has been killed or wounded but he is still standing. So he will return to attack this morning. How much can a human being endure?"

"I can assure you that an 'excursion' to Bloody Nose wasn't like a picnic on Coney Island," Paul V. Lewis of Frenchtown, New Jersey, wryly commented forty-five years later. He had been a nineteen-year-old private first class scout-sniper in one of the companies with Colonel Davis's battalion in the 1st Regiment. He, like all of the unit's retired survivors, said he was "lucky as hell to have made it through the campaign in one piece.

"There were just seventy-four men left when we came off the lines at 1300 hours on September 23," he recalled. "We were all that was left of nearly 400 who landed on D-Day." Like many 1st Marines veterans, officers and enlisted, he placed the blame for the haunting losses on the regimental commander.

"Chesty Puller should never have passed the rank of second lieutenant," sixty-four-year-old Lewis said with decades-old rancor. "He went to Peleliu to get the Big Medal"—the Medal of Honor—"and if he had to get us all killed to get it he was going to do so, just so long as he was still there at the end."

Richard Fisher, of Bellevue, Washington, expressed a similar bitter reaction in a 1985 letter to another retired member of the Old Breed. Like Lewis, he had been a scout-sniper; he was a twenty-two-year-old sergeant assigned to division headquarters and had been one of the "Alamo Scouts" who landed three times on missions to reconnoiter Cape Gloucester before that invasion.

"Chesty Puller was a warmonger," Fisher wrote. "One of his problems was he believed his image. God, he wanted Peleliu—and he got it—because the Marine Corps was getting ready to rotate him home and he wanted his first regimental command, the 1st Marines. . . . All battles are 'training exercises' for men like Puller, and it was just another rung up his ladder—just like the Canal and Cape Gloucester—another 'training exercise' for the next battle. . . . Puller was a man who could not live long without war. . . ."

All three of his battalion commanders—Raymond Davis, Russell Honsowetz, and Stephen Sabol—maintained, through the years, a discreetly noncommittal public silence on their views of Puller's handling of the regiment. In private, however, they have been critical of what one described as his "failure to recognize soon enough that we were a shot-to-pieces outfit while still ordering us to do impossible things with the worn-out, pitifully few men we still had."

Gordon D. Gayle, the major who commanded the 2d Battalion of the 5th Marines, talked about the colonel in a 1987 interview with Frederick K. Dashiell, a highly respected Washington newsman who had been a Marine combat correspondent in the invasions of Guam and Iwo Jima.

A retired brigadier general, acclaimed military academician, and Marine Corps historian, Gayle told the journalist:

"Puller was probably the best man we had to go up against a stone wall. He should have had more firepower from the Navy. It was not nearly what it should have been, but Puller got the job done." When asked his personal feelings about the controversial colonel, General Gayle responded: "I shouldn't talk about that. I'd rather keep them to myself."

General Robert E. Cushman, Commandant of the Marine Corps in the mid-1970s, once candidly discussed Puller with a longtime friend who had served with Cushman when he was a lieutenant colonel battalion commander in the 3d Division on Iwo Jima.

"Lewie was probably the best combat officer the Marine Corps ever had," the general said, "but he wasn't able to understand anything but 'attack! attack!' He was beyond his element in commanding any unit larger than a company—maybe a battalion—where he could keep his hands on everything and be right in the middle of it."

Lewis Burwell Puller lived by a self-inspired code of honor, one so contradictory and complex that it defied categorizing. He was devoted—beyond the imagination of men who remembered him in battle—to his high school sweetheart wife, Virginia, and their two toddler daughters. Whether in combat, aboard ship headed for an invasion, or at base camp between campaigns, he wrote daily letters—sometimes only a few hastily scribbled lines when in action—home to Saluda, Virginia. They were tenderly worded, romantic, and reassuring, as if penned by a studious poet.

Prayer and God were seldom mentioned. His attitude toward chaplains was respectful on the surface, but only a notch above his openly expressed disdain for Navy brass. Battlefield padres, the colonel said on several occasions, "are unnecessary distractions to troops in the brutality of combat." War was Chesty Puller's religion, a fact that his family knew and accepted, however reluctantly.

"Have no fear, My Darling Wife," he once wrote when the outcome at Guadalcanal was in doubt, "everything will come out all right. Your faith and our love will see to that."

"Puller becomes so angry sometimes that words seem to stick in his throat and he has to cool off, but he is very fair and every man knows it," Navy Lieutenant Edward L. Smith, the colonel's battalion surgeon on Guadalcanal, once said.

Except for his indisputable—often wantonly reckless—personal bravery in battle, the Old Warrior's greatest forte as a combat leader was his long-accumulated knowledge of how *individual* Marines felt about themselves and the Marine Corps—and he knew how to deal with the situation.

If it required hard-nosed discipline, he had no peers in dishing it out. If a friendly man-to-man chat would do the job, he could handle it. When compassion or understanding was needed, he had an open mind. Regardless of the outcome, however, he unremittingly demanded that all his men—officers and troops—follow his orders without question, just as he did those of his superiors.

Among Puller's detractors there is a deeply held conviction that he harbored not an iota of feeling about the fate of the men he commanded. But there is substantial evidence to the contrary that he possessed profound concern for them as *individuals*. As Marines, however, he viewed them as he saw himself: as expendable weapons of war.

Once on Cape Gloucester he came across a young private in a foxhole during a spirited scrimmage. The stubble-free youth, exhausted and quivering with fear, was huddled stone-faced and looking blankly into space with the unmistakable gaze of total demoralization. It was minutes before the disoriented teenager recognized Puller.

"Colonel," he managed to mumble, "we gotta get the hell outta here."

"That's no way to talk, old man," was Puller's soft-spoken, fatherly response. "Old man" was the colonel's conventional way of addressing any subordinate, regardless of rank, in normal conversation. He led the youngster a few yards to the rear, out of hearing range of nearby Marines, and they squatted and talked for ten or fifteen minutes.

"Look, old man, I wanta go home, too. I'm not getting any younger. Hell, I'm forty-five years old, you know that? I got a family at home. I know this dump is no good, but neither of us is going home until we lick these bastards. We've gotta help make our folks safe back home. I'll try to get you some hot chow up here, old man."

The private went back to his hole with a feeling that at least someone in the hellish jungle was aware of his existence and cared about what happened to him.

An incident that occurred on Guadalcanal left its mark on the 1st Marines. It involved Puller, a newly arrived second lieutenant from the States, and a wizened private whose tattered dungarees and gaunt face and frame attested to lengthy duty in the jungles and hills. He found the man at rigid attention, constantly saluting like a wound-up toy soldier as the beardless shavetail faced him, hands on hips.

"What goes on here, old man?" the colonel politely asked the officer.

"This Marine, sir. He didn't salute me as we passed, and I've ordered him to salute a hundred times."

Without changing expression or tone of voice, Puller said: "You're right, lieutenant, so right. But you know that an officer must return every salute he receives. Now let me see you get to it and do your share."

Puller watched until the count was completed. Then, without a word, he went about his business. The episode warmed the hearts of the men in the ranks. It also was a strong message to newly commissioned spit-and-polish officers unfamiliar with the realities of a combat zone. Puller also made points with the troops with a firm directive:

"Whenever we're training in the field at chow time, or in reserve in battle, privates will be fed first, then the noncoms, and the officers last of all."

He was adamant and forceful on another matter that was the

foundation of his philosophy that Marines were, by intent and training, a breed of men different from other servicemen.

"No officer's life is worth more than any man in the ranks," he solemnly declared. "An officer may have more effect on the fighting, but if he does his duty, so far as I can see, he must be up front to see what's actually going on with the troops.

"They'd find a replacement for me if I got hit. I've never seen a Marine outfit fall apart for the lack of any one man. I don't want you to go out under the guns just for show. It's only the idiots and green kids who think they are bulletproof. But if you don't show some courage, your other officers won't either, and the kids will hang back. It's that kind of outfit that's always in trouble. . . ."

Puller didn't always abide by his dictum of the indispensability of any one man. During a heavy Japanese counterattack on Guadalcanal, his battalion command post took several direct mortar hits. He himself was struck by seven shell fragments, but loudly and profanely refused medical attention until he collapsed from loss of blood. The corpsman on the scene took one look at the gushing wounds and began hastily writing a red tag denoting a casualty requiring immediate evacuation and surgery.

"Take that damned label and paste it on a bottle!" Puller bellowed. "I remain in command here!"

Such was his obvious attitude at daybreak of D plus three on Peleliu. Shimmering heat waves already had begun to radiate from the glaring coral, through which could be seen the harsh, stripped outlines of Bloody Nose Ridge and the barren, forbidding hills beyond.

Barely able to stand because of a badly swollen and obviously infected leg that still carried a large chunk of mortar from the episode on Guadalcanal, Puller made it clear that he was still in command of the remnants of the 1st Marine Regiment—and hadn't the slightest intention of giving it up.

Robert "Pepper" Martin, of *Time* magazine, was one newsman who openly admired Puller's élan and *esprit de corps.* But he always was careful to maintain the objectivity of a respected journalist by diligently reporting the colonel's flamboyant eccentricities.

Martin spent the night in a tarpaulin-covered shell hole a few yards from Puller's CP. He described the scene some ninety minutes after the D plus three attack began:

It was a scorching hot day and Puller was stripped to the waist with nothing more than a piece of tin and a poncho to give him some shade. He was smoking his battered pipe; characteristically he held the pipe between his incisors and talked out of the side of his mouth.

His CP was located where the bluffs [of Bloody Nose Ridge] came very close to the road. This defilade was necessary because the Japanese were laying down considerable mortar fire, and considerable small-arms fire was passing overhead.

While I was at the CP some Japanese snipers worked down to a position north of the CP where they could fire down on it. Puller organized a patrol and sent them out to get the snipers. In a few minutes there were bursts of fire and shortly after that the patrol returned. There was no more sniper fire.

The field phone buzzed. The colonel listened and growled into it: "We're still going but some of my companies are damned small." A Jap mortar opened up and the men around the colonel flattened out. The CO himself did not change position. He stuck out his chest and spat: "The bastards!"

Martin's story showed up on Peleliu a few days later in *Time*'s mini-sized weekly Pacific war zone edition. Its twenty-four pages were printed in Honolulu on tissue-thin paper and flown by courier planes along with official documents to the battlefronts and rear-echelon areas.

The column was headlined "Man of War" and carried a photo of the 1st Marines' commander stripped to the waist in his CP. General Rupertus was livid when he saw it, and immediately made his feelings known.

"Puller," he all but shouted on the field phone, "you've got the best publicity bureau in the Marine Corps!"

The colonel stoutly denied any responsibility. But when the general hung up, he carefully folded the story and placed it in the back cover of his ever-present pocket edition of Caesar's *Gallic Wars*.

The problem wasn't that Rupertus objected to press coverage of the Marine Corps. He was piqued because there was no mention of him in the story, an affront to his status as commanding general of the 1st Marine Division and his hoped-for appointment as the next Marine Corps Commandant when General Vandegrift retired.

In an obvious personally concocted ploy to help achieve his ambition to succeed Vandegrift, a nine-page double-spaced profile of Rupertus appeared at Marine Corps headquarters just a month before D-Day of Operation Stalemate. The article was, from start to finish, what Hollywood publicity agents call a "puff piece."

It extolled Rupertus's "unquestioned virtues and background as a supremely courageous combat-tested leader, brilliant battle planner, and military tactician who is deeply respected by his officers and admired and well liked by the troops." The some 1,700 words carried the byline of combat correspondent Sergeant George McMillan.

Conscientious and highly respected journalist-author that he was, McMillan later said he had "written the thing under direct orders and there wasn't anything I could do but follow them." A photocopy of the original dispatch bears the official stamp and signature of the "Chief Censor, U.S. Pacific Fleet," and a similar approval from CinCPac's "Public Relations Division, U.S. Marine Corps." A handwritten note appears below the censors' chops:

> Note to Hdqrs: The following piece is intended for Sunday magazines, and it is suggested to be released to them as soon as possible after the outfit goes into its next action. I wrote it with a hopeful eye on the *N.Y. Times* Sunday mag, but if they don't like it, certainly the *Washington Star* or *Post* should. Pix will have to be used from Hdqrs files for exceptional reasons. The general has approved the article, with changes he made on this manuscript.
>
> McMillan

For reasons never made public, the story was not released for publication. Long after V-J Day, however, McMillan asked retired Brigadier General Robert L. Denig, director of Marine Corps public relations during the war, what happened to it.

"I don't really remember," Denig recalled with a sly grin. "But I think it was one of those times when sound judgment prevailed. If some civilian correspondent wanted to write about Rupertus—or any other Marine from private to general—that was his business. But we weren't a personal publicity outfit for any one person; that wasn't our job, and Archie Vandegrift knew it."

7

Technical Sergeant Joseph L. Alli was one of the combat correspondents. At twenty-six, he had left his job as a police reporter on the *Buffalo Evening News,* and he had been with the 1st Division since Guadalcanal.

Captain Everett P. Pope was the twenty-five-year-old commander of C Company in the 1st Battalion of Chesty Puller's 1st Marines. He had been commissioned a Marine Reserve second lieutenant in June 1941, after graduating *magna cum laude* from Bowdoin College in Brunswick, Maine, with Phi Beta Kappa honors in French.

The scholarly shavetail, whose postwar aim was an academic career at his alma mater, caught up with the 1st Division in time to lead a machine-gun platoon during the Solomons campaign. On Cape Gloucester, he had led a fourteen-man patrol on a mop-up sweep that killed twenty Japanese and captured twelve.

The paths of Alli and Pope crossed for the first time during the fourth day on Peleliu. Pope's job was to lead his men in an attack on a zigzag ridge adjacent to Hills 205 and 210, where Honsowetz's and Davis's men had been all but annihilated. Alli was along to report about the action that occurred on what the sector map designated Hill 100.

"To Pope and his troops, it was Bloody Nose Ridge or one of the Five Sisters or Five Brothers, depending on the man you talked to," Alli wrote. "Regardless of what you called it, it meant another grinding, hot, brutal day of hard fighting, heavy losses, and trouble from the word 'go.'"

Like most of the companies in the 1st Marines, C Company by now was one in name only. Of the 242 officers and men who had landed on D-Day, only Captain Pope and ninety troops remained to carry on the fight; the others had been killed or wounded seriously enough to be evacuated.

Nonetheless, the outfit moved out as ordered shortly before noon. The approach to the base of the hill was through a small swamp. But the advance was almost immediately pinned down by heavy-machine-gun fire from two camouflaged pillboxes about 50 yards across the slimy pond.

Pope judiciously decided to try another route, a narrow road that crossed the sinkhole by a causeway. While C Company belonged to Ray Davis's 1st Battalion, it had been shifted to the

2d Battalion for the day's mission. Thus the company CO called Russ Honsowetz's CP to discuss with the colonel the change in plans and to ask for tank support.

Pope's men stayed put, using whatever cover they could find, still taking strong resistance and frequent casualties for more than two hours. It was late afternoon before four Shermans roared onto the scene, carving a trail in the burned-over stubbled brush as they roared forward to lead the way across the low-lying coral bridge.

"It was one of those bad days when everything went wrong," Alli's story said. "The first tank slipped over the side of the causeway and was immobilized. The second tried to pull it out, but slid over the other side. Neither could move, blocking the passage to the other Shermans."

This left Captain Pope and C Company with two unpromising options: endure the remorseless enemy fire until help came to retrieve the disabled tanks, or gamble on the chance of making it across the causeway in man-by-man sprints. Pope decided the dangerous footrace was the best idea, all things considered, and the unexpected impromptu maneuver caught the enemy completely by surprise; not one man was hit during the frantic dash.

The charge carried to the foot of the hill, where the Marines paused to count heads, catch their breaths, and regroup. Pope and about two dozen of his men then assaulted the rocky slope, supported with only mortar and machine-gun fire from across the swamp.

The push reached the crest within ten minutes.

Whatever jubilation the Marines felt quickly turned into dismay and concern. They weren't atop Hill 100, where they first thought they were, but on a long isolated ridge where their position was dominated by a higher and heavily armed enemy strongpoint less than 50 yards away.

There were a multitude of reasons that C Company had swarmed the wrong hill: inaccurate maps, the similar appearance of the barren ridges in the Umurbrogols, and the always hectic confusion of battle. Explanations meant nothing to Pope and his men. All they knew or cared about was that they were facing a deadly ordeal with the odds solidly against them as twilight approached.

This time Pope had no options. The depleted remnants of C Company were surrounded, cut off from any hope of reinforcements before dawn. If they were to survive the night, they had to do it on their own.

From almost point-blank range, Japanese machine guns, mortars, and light artillery opened up on the besieged Marines from the nearby peaks. Immediately after darkness fell the enemy began ground attacks, first in small infiltrator bands, and, when these failed, in groups of twenty or twenty-five who tried to storm the ridge.

The Marines beat back each assault, but at a dreadful cost. Not only had the number of defenders been reduced to an exhausted and pitiful few, but they were lightly armed. The only weapons they had were one light .30-caliber machine gun, several 1918-vintage Browning automatic rifles, two Thompson submachine guns, Garand M-1 rifles, and a limited supply of hand grenades.

"When the grenades ran low, we threw three or four rocks and then a grenade," one of the survivors told Alli. "The Japs didn't know which was which, and this, thank God, kept a lot of 'em pinned down and afraid to attack."

The only firepower support C Company got that night was from a mortar platoon at the foot of the ridge. The help was more than welcomed and contributed much to keeping Pope's thinly held outposts from being overrun.

"We figured we fired more than 3,000 rounds that day and night," a then twenty-two-year-old private first class, Barnett "Barney" Bell, of Canton, Georgia, recalled forty-five years later. "We knew Captain Pope needed all the help he could get, and we did our best to provide it."

At one point, Bell said, "our sergeant asked for a man to find the battalion CP and ask Colonel Honsowetz direct if they could get some help up to C Company." Bell volunteered for the duty. "I found the colonel in a kind of plank lean-to," the Georgian remembered. "There were rifle rounds and shells coming from everywhere, and all he kept saying was 'Don't bunch up.' I said, 'Colonel, Captain Pope needs help bad on the ridge,' and he said, 'No way, son.' I hated that 'son' stuff, so I answered, 'Bullshit,' and left before anything else was said."

By sunrise the Marines were beating off the enemy with bare fists, combat knives, and rocks, and even hurling ammunition boxes at them. Finally only eight riflemen remained. Daylight brought a resumption of heavy Japanese artillery fire, and Captain Pope was ordered to somehow withdraw.

Under the cover of a dense smoke screen and heavy artillery

shelling, the men came down from the ridge, crawling, slithering, rolling—any way they could make it. The Japanese occupied the summit within minutes, set up several 155-millimeter mortars, and quickly unleashed a firestorm bombardment on the Marines below.

Whether Alli's dispatch from the field had any bearing on the ultimate award of the Medal of Honor to Captain Everett P. Pope is unknown and questionable. But the combat correspondent was close enough to the epic action to see it all unfold, and to write about it for the people back home.

The coveted decoration to Pope brought with it a promotion to major, and an accompanying citation signed by President Roosevelt. The document read in part:

> For conspicuous gallantry and intrepidity above and beyond the call of duty, Captain Pope rallied his men . . . and remained on the exposed hill determined to hold through the night. Attacked continuously with grenades, machine guns and rifles from three sides and twice subjected to suicidal attacks during the night, he and his valiant men fiercely beat back or destroyed the enemy. . . . His valiant leadership against devastating odds while protecting the units below from heavy Japanese attack reflects the highest credit upon Captain Pope and the United States Naval Service.

Four of Company C's officers and men received the Navy Cross, the Marine Corps' second-highest decoration, for their heroism on the hilltop outpost. The Japanese considered the ridge so important that it was stoutly defended until it was finally seized on October 3, two weeks after Pope and his men first stormed the summit. Not until then, because of the constant and fierce fighting, was it possible to recover the bodies of Marines killed in the savage action.

There is a final footnote to the battle for Peleliu so far as Captain Pope is concerned. It is a happy one for him, but also a tragic reminder of what the victory cost.

He was the only company commander or platoon leader in his battalion who was neither killed nor seriously wounded during the invasion.

ELEVEN

A Battle Gone Amok?

PELELIU WAS A VERY CROWDED ISLAND BY D PLUS FOUR, probably the most densely populated piece of real estate of comparable size anywhere in the Pacific. Nearly 45,000 men—American and Japanese—were on the less than 8 square miles of hellish hot coral. All had the same purpose: to kill.

United States forces outnumbered the Japanese almost four to one. But as far as long-recognized manpower requirements for a successful amphibious operation were concerned, the figures were grossly misleading.

Fewer than 10,000 of the Americans were Marine combat troops; many were in battle for the first time, and others were so battered from five days of savage action that, in other campaigns, they would have been pulled from the lines for a break in the relentless ordeal.

What General Rupertus refused to acknowledge—or admit it if he did—was that the 1st Division's assault regiments were numerically inadequate to carry out their assignment without reinforcements from the Army's 81st Division.

The accepted Marine Corps doctrine, developed through years of prewar training maneuvers and proven in earlier Pacific combat landings, was that a three-to-one ratio was mandatory for an invasion: three Marine assault troops for each Japanese defender of the objective.

In addition, a special obstacle confronting Operation Stalemate was the way General Murai and Colonel Nakagawa had masterfully planned Peleliu's defense to take advantage of the island's fiendish terrain. Entrenched in well-armed and fortified positions, almost always hidden in caves or dugouts, a few determined Japanese could hold out against and inflict sickening losses on much larger numbers of attacking Americans.

Except for Nakagawa's disastrous tank-led charge across the airstrip on D-Day, the Marines rarely encountered an exposed and above-ground force of more than a platoon of thirty or forty Japanese troops.

The fact that upward of 20,000 other Americans were ashore was obviously reassuring to the hard-pressed units on the front lines. It meant that overwhelming United States military might was there, ready to support the fighting where, when, and if possible. But the inescapable reality was that most of this awesome force—except for the artillerymen of the 11th Marines and DUKW and amtrac crewmen—were classified as noncombatants; they were rear-echelon people with only a bare minimum of infantry training beyond that received in boot camp.

Nonetheless, General Rupertus's orders to his dead-tired, shot-up line outfits were basically unchanged for the fifth day of the invasion: "All infantry units will resume the attack with maximum effort in all sectors at 0830 hours on 19 September." He was still optimistic, despite mounting contrary evidence, that a climactic battle-ending breakthrough would come soon if, in his words, "Puller, Hanneken, and Harris would hurry up the advance."

D plus four was another day of grueling but minimal gains for the infantry. The 1st Marines resumed the assault against the cliffs of Bloody Nose Ridge. The 5th pushed some 300 yards into the rugged high ground north of the airstrip against spasms of strong opposition. The 7th finished the mop-up of Ngarmoked and then cleared out several pockets of minor resistance in a mangrove swamp that blocked the route to virtually unmolested Purple Beach, 2 miles across the island from where the D-Day landings were made.

Casualties continued to mount, but most of them were felled by thirst, dehydration, or fatigue, victims of the 120-degree-plus heat who were soon able to return to duty. Only Chesty Puller's troops on Bloody Nose Ridge were hit hard by enemy fire, loosing nearly a hundred more men, killed and wounded.

The fifth day of battle, as later events verified, marked the beginning of many developments that would influence the future conduct of the campaign—and spark much of the controversy that still persists four and a half decades later.

For one thing, General Geiger's simmering trepidations about the way Rupertus was directing the assault surfaced in a heated confrontation between the two commanders. There were two basic points of disagreement:

Why did Rupertus continue to order the infantry regiments to "hurry up" despite atrocious and, in some instances, what Geiger felt were unwarranted casualties? Why did Rupertus remain so adamantly firm in his refusal to commit the Army's 81st Division, the operation's sole remaining reserve force, to the struggle?

Geiger left unsaid his mounting concern over Rupertus's physical condition and emotional state. His overriding concern, pure and simple, was whether the 1st Marine Division would emerge from the campaign as an outfit capable of spearheading a future amphibious assault, the invasion of Okinawa, which was already in the preliminary planning stage at CinCPac headquarters in Pearl Harbor.

Geiger was convinced that unless Rupertus changed his thinking, sooner or later he would have to exert his authority as commanding general of the III Marine Amphibious Corps—even if it meant relieving the 1st Division's commanding general while in combat, a drastic action without precedent in Marine Corps history.

Despite the vexatious and unresolved command situation, both generals were, of a certainty, reassured by developments on the small but strategically important part of Peleliu that was now firmly in American hands, the beachhead and airstrip.

Shore parties of black Marines from Lieutenant Colonel Robert Ballance's 1st Pioneer Battalion and bulldozer operators from Colonel Francis Fenton's 1st Engineer Battalion, working nonstop since D-plus one, had cleared large sections of the original landing areas.

The 2,500-yard-long beachhead was no longer a junkyard of amtrac hulks and other demolished equipment—DUKW amphibian trucks, earth-moving machines, jeeps, and trailers. The shell-pocked grayish coral sands no longer were strewn with helter-skelter piles of ammunition and supplies. Five clearly marked medical aid and evacuation stations were transferring the wounded to shipboard hospitals without interminable and painful delays.

To say that the beachhead was even moderately safe, however, would be far from true. Every few minutes one area or another was hit by a random round of mortars or several artillery shells. The whir or whine of incoming barrages was usually sufficient warning for men to scamper for cover from the explosions; few were killed or seriously wounded.

When the acrid smoke lifted and chunks of coral debris stopped falling, it was only moments until, in the words of Private First Class Franklin Jackson, a bulldozer operator from Birmingham, Alabama, "it was back to business as usual."

Order replaced chaos as supply dumps were dispersed to sites designated by Ballance's beachmasters, blaring directions through high-powered bullhorns.

But the lack of amtracs and DUKWs, caused by the D-Day carnage on the reef, hampered a steady ship-to-shore flow of vital needs of battle. The inevitable result was an often serious shortage of ammunition for artillery batteries, mortar outfits, and front-line troops.

The problem was overcome on D plus five by Navy UDT frogmen, a specially trained team of underwater demolitions experts, who blasted several passages through the reef. After that the big, blunt-nosed LSTs plowed straight to Purple Beach, opened their huge hinged bows, and unloaded cargoes—men, weapons, supplies, equipment—directly on land.

Perhaps the most welcome sign of progress to the troops was that unpolluted drinking water was now available without depending on supplies from ships beyond the reef. It gushed in unlimited quantities from half a dozen wells drilled by Marine engineers, and 500-gallon trailers, pulled by jeeps or loaded on amtracs, regularly carried it to waterheads just behind the front lines.

Not everything happening on the beach was a welcome sight.

In an area, once a palm grove, not far inland from Orange Beach Two, just beyond the southwest boundary of the airfield, gravediggers worked from dawn to dusk. They buried the dead in accordance with Marine Corps regulations: "Three feet from center line of body to center line of body, fifty bodies to a row, 3 feet between rows."

Each grave was listed on a master location chart with the man's name, rank, serial number, and unit. Prepainted wooden crosses and slablike markers, cut to specifications by a lumber company in the States, came bundled for efficient handling and were erected and stenciled with the dead man's name. In cases where bodies were so mutilated that positive identification was impossible, the graves were marked "UNKNOWN."

2

There is no known record of the name of the first American pilot to land on Peleliu's airstrip, but his plane was a carrier-based Grumman F4F whose engine had lost power during a strafing attack on Bloody Nose Ridge. The crippled Wildcat fighter made a straight-in approach from the north and bounced several times before rolling to a stop near the center of the field.

It was shortly after 11:00 A.M., September 19, and the area had been under sometimes heavy artillery fire most of the morning. But the shelling had petered out bit by bit as the Japanese gunners shifted their attention to the infantry attacks.

Surprisingly, enemy reaction remained minor when the plane landed; these were only a few rounds of mortars, which missed the target by several hundred yards. Seabees from the Navy's 33d Construction Battalion, laboring to patch up the bomb-pocked runways, attached a rope to the landing hook on the Wildcat's tail and pulled it to the tarmac of the demolished Japanese hangars.

Four hundred Seabees had landed with the early waves of the assault on D-Day. Because of the disastrous traffic jam on the reef, however, their equipment remained offshore on LSTs until the morning of D plus three, a delay that resulted in death for seven of the men, and wounds to nineteen more who were serving as volunteer stretcher bearers.

Many of the others, armed with carbines and rifles picked up on the beach, had moved side by side with the 5th Marines to help capture the airfield. Fortunately for the Navy pilot, a few of their bulldozers and road scrapers had shown up in time for the hardworking sailors to get about 500 yards of the runways in good enough shape for his emergency landing.

The urgency of their work became more evident just after 3:00 when three grime-covered amtracs roared, throttles wide open, over the ridge from White Beach Two.

"Hey, you guys!" the driver of the lead vehicle yelled. "We got some fuckin' big crates for you. I think they're airplanes. Unload 'em quick so we can get the hell outta here." The sweat-soaked, visibly fatigued operator's anxiety was amply justified.

Since sunup he'd made seven trips carrying cargo and men from the beach and returning with wounded Marines. And each mission across the open ground—dubbed Mortar Valley or Purple Heart Run by amtrac crews—had drawn heavy enemy shelling, a fact clearly evident from near-miss fragment dents in the armored sides of his battered vehicle. When someone asked him how the machine was still operating, he replied, "I guess she's runnin' now because she's so excited."

Captain Wallace J. Slappey had been sweating out the arrival of the "fuckin' big crates" since slogging across the field nearly twenty-four hours earlier. He was commanding officer of VMO-3, the official designation of the 1st Division's own "air force" of seven small unarmed artillery spotter planes.

The "Piperschmitts" and "Messercubs" made the voyage from Pavuvu aboard an LST. Mechanics had removed wings, tail assemblies, and landing gear from the two-seater fuselages and then carefully packed them in wooden containers for the long trip to Peleliu. VMO-3's ground crewmen had done the job to perfection. The planes were undamaged, not even a slight tear in the fabric covering, and were reassembled and ready for flight in a matter of hours.

Carrier-based aerial observers had performed yeoman duty in calling in artillery and naval bombardment until now. But their planes flew too fast and too high to do the demanding low and slow flying job that Slappey's Marine spotters were trained for to support the infantry. Henceforth, with the Piperschmitts and Messercubs circling only a few hundred feet above the ridges, the number of times supporting fire—artillery, mortars, and air strikes—hit the wrong targets dropped substantially, a gratifying statistic for the attacking ground troops.

Seabees and Marine engineers had done more than make significant headway in getting the runways ready for the arrival of Marine fighter planes and dive-bombers. They also had cleared the bombed-out Japanese headquarters building of much of its rubble and had roofed over part of it with panels of metal salvaged from the demolished hangars.

General Rupertus was noticeably pleased with this development, so much so that he voiced one of his rare compliments.

"You and your men are to be commended on the fine work you are doing," he told Navy Lieutenant Jerome Darman, a former building contractor from Chicago, the Seabee unit's commanding officer. "This will make an excellent division headquarters."

The general was especially laudatory when he learned that one of Darman's enterprising crew had repaired a Japanese generator, which produced enough electricity to light three rooms and provide power for the CP's radio communications gear.

By early afternoon, Rupertus and his senior staff aides had occupied the sandbagged cinder-block structure. It would be the headquarters of the 1st Marine Division until General Mueller and his 81st Army Division ultimately took over to finish off organized resistance by Colonel Nakagawa's last-stand defenders.

General Smith, however, remained in the same tank-trap CP he'd set up on D-Day. Nothing had changed in Rupertus's strange attitude toward the assistant division commander; nor would it ever be different throughout their bewildering association.

"I'll let you know when I need you," one of Rupertus's aides recalled the general telling Smith at the time. "You stay here and do your job and I'll do mine from the division HQ in the Jap building."

3

Even before the first of VMO-3's planes was given a fire support spotting mission, Bucky Harris asked Captain Slappey if he would provide him with a pilot and plane for a short flight. The 5th Regiment's commander wanted a firsthand close-up aerial view of Peleliu's evil terrain.

The 5th Marines, since landing, had come up against their share of strong and costly enemy resistance while smashing across the island—particularly during the D-Day enemy tank attack. To a degree, however, they had been lucky; most of the action was on the flat land around the airstrip.

Now Harris's assault battalions were about to hit the high ground, and so the meticulous planner-strategist made the low-level reconnaissance in the Piperschmitt. Only then, he felt, could he determine the best way to use his troops—and take minimum casualties—in attacking the hundreds of Japanese strongpoints that honeycombed the island's torturous Umurbrogol spine.

"I was appalled at the sight of those ridges from the air," Harris told Gene Sledge years later. "Sheer coral walls with caves everywhere, box canyons, crevices, rock-strewn cliffs, and all defended by well-hidden Japs. I knew then that would be no breakthrough.

"I told Rupertus and Puller what I had seen, and suggested they fly over and see for themselves. They just smiled and said they had maps. I knew we were in for a bloody siege."

The contretemps didn't end there, according to Harris. During the next four weeks, Rupertus constantly needled the colonel "to hurry up the operation." Harris invariably responded: "I'm lavish with my ammunition, but stingy with my men's lives."

The final count of the division's combat losses reflected the truth of the statement as well as Harris's tactical wisdom. Although the 5th Marines encountered their share of savage fighting, especially in the treacherous northern ridges of the Umurbrogals, their casualties were the lowest of the division's infantry regiments.

The relationship between Rupertus and Harris took numerous twists as the battle wore on. Some were staff confrontations over division strategy and the use of the 5th Marines in carrying it out.

Harris recalled one such incident: "General Rupertus came to our CP one morning and looked at the operations map that Colonel Walt and I had been studying. Then the general said, 'I've just been over talking to Colonel Harrison [commander of the division's artillery regiment], and he told me that he had fired 75 percent of his ammunition in support of the 5th Marines.'

"I couldn't help grinning and remarking that Walt and I had been checking our map and found that the 5th had taken 70 percent of the division's objectives, so it looked like Colonel Harrison still owed us 5 percent more. Unseen by any of us, General Geiger had come in quietly and had overheard our conversation.

"He spoke up and said that when he went to school, he had learned that in war there was a lot of shooting and that those who shot the most and the best were normally the winners. He then added that he always came to my CP because I was always shooting and seemed to be the only one that had gotten somewhere in so doing.

"General Rupertus remarked: 'Bucky can have all the artillery support he wants.' Then he took his leave without another word."

In the hindsight of history, a later meeting between Rupertus and Harris has a stark significance as an indication of the general's emotional state that raises serious and still unanswered questions about his fitness to command the 1st Marine Division on Peleliu.

"Early in the morning of October 5 I had a phone call from the division commander asking me to come to his headquarters at once," Harris said years later. "I got in my jeep and went immediately. When I arrived I was told to come in. There was no one else present.

"Tears were coursing down the general's cheeks when he said, 'Harris, I'm at the end of my rope. Two of my fine regiments are in ruins. You usually seem to know what to do, and get it done. I'm going to turn over to you everything we have left. This is strictly between us.' I went back to my CP a very thoughtful man."

So far as can be determined, Harris never revealed the incredible episode to anyone until 1981, when he told Gene Sledge about it. Nor did he and Rupertus ever discuss the occasion again. To both, it was something they obviously wished had never happened.

The inescapable fact is that, assuming Rupertus was in control of his mental faculties and meant what he said to Harris, the general was without authority to turn over command of the division to the 5th Marines' colonel. That was a decision that only could be made by General Geiger, who was unaware of the incident. And he undoubtedly, under the circumstances, would have sought the concurrence of his superiors, possibly as high as Admiral Nimitz and even General Vandegrift, before taking the unprecedented move.

Colonel Harold O. Deakin, the general's G-1, had a distressingly similar experience with the visibly depressed division commander during the same period. He recalled it in a long and candid interview taped in 1973 for Marine Corps archives:

". . . Rupertus and I were sitting on his bunk, alone, and he had his head in his hands and he said, 'This thing has just about got me beat.' I hadn't been, at that point, what you'd call a friend of Rupertus's, but I found myself with my arm around his shoulder comforting him, and telling him, 'Now, General, everything is going to work out.'

"I was kind of a staff officer, half chaplain, and, I guess, all Deakin. . . . He expected Peleliu to be a snap, you see, and when it didn't turn out to be a snap, he found the going rough, like everyone else. . . ."

Howard Handleman, the International News Service correspondent, had an encounter with Rupertus worthy of mention if only to further indicate the general's peculiar state.

"I was heading back from the front on D plus four or five," the reporter said, "when I stopped at the division CP. I told Rupertus I'd seen lots of dead Marines during the day. He insisted there were only a few Marine casualties, and added: 'You can't make an omelette without breaking the eggs.'"

As Handleman left to find an amtrac ride to the *Mount McKinley* to write and file his copy, he saw a case of whiskey under the general's cot. It was quite natural for him to wonder if Rupertus was a heavy drinker. But he saw nothing to be gained by pursuing the matter and thus let it drop.

In 1987, Dick Dashiell brought up the subject in an interview with retired Brigadier General Gordon Gayle. "Alcohol was not his problem," Gayle replied, adding that it characterized Rupertus "only in a sense." Dashiell said he did not elaborate except to say the general occasionally sent the division's regimental and battalion commanders several bottles of scotch or bourbon to share the limited supply with combat officers.

Gene Sledge answered a letter in 1989 asking what he knew, if anything, about Rupertus's use of alcohol. The reply was flippant but with reflective overtones.

"I had not heard that Rupertus kept a case of booze under his cot," the former private first class and then professor-author wrote. "He should have used more of it and we might have been better off, because the unit commanders could have used their discretion to save lives in situations they understood and he didn't; he kept saying, 'Hurry it up.'"

4

Many senior officers involved in Operation Stalemate—Marines, Navy, and Army—openly expressed, at one time or another, the opinion that Roy S. Geiger and William H. Rupertus had but one thing in common: Both were dedicated and ambitious Marine Corps major generals.

Otherwise, they were as different in physical appearance as the comic strip characters Mutt and Jeff. Their temperaments were opposed to the point of controlled but obvious personal dislike—sometimes bordering on mistrust. They viewed military strategy and tactics, and treatment of subordinates, in irreconcilable ways.

Geiger was one of a kind in the roster of Marine Corps generals, a commander equally proficient at the controls of an airplane in combat and in a frontline foxhole CP with the infantry. He was a bear of a man—husky shoulders, a round face with sharp features, deep blue eyes, and close-cropped white hair. He was usually soft-spoken, but could roar like a bullhorn when angry. As one of his former staff officers, retired Brigadier General Frederick P. Henderson, put it:

"Geiger looked and acted like a general who always knew what he was doing and why he was doing it. He could be stern and curt—sometimes to a degree that some people considered ruthless—when the situation demanded. He spared neither himself nor his subordinates when the chips were down." Henderson, obviously no admirer of Rupertus, outspokenly viewed him as "a physical and mental pygmy who should have been relieved of command of the 1st Division on Peleliu."

Archie Vandegrift and Roy Geiger were commissioned second lieutenants together in 1909, graduating in the same class from what the Marine Corps then called its School of Application at Parris Island. They remained close friends, although their careers took separate directions in climbing the ladder to high command.

Geiger was the third "Flying Leatherneck" to have earned pilot's wings. As a captain, he led a joint Army–Marine Corps squadron of twin-engined biplane bombers in France during World War I. He flew two-seater Curtiss Jennies in Central America in the 1920s and was still regarded primarily as an "aviation man" when Pearl Harbor was attacked.

Through the years, Geiger was a hard-driving pioneer of the concept of low-level air support for Marine infantry. To develop and refine the then revolutionary strategy, the pilot spent much time with ground troops in training maneuvers. This was the genesis of his understanding of the problems of what he admiringly called "the *real* Marine Corps."

Working with infantry officers, he learned firsthand the intricacies of planning and executing amphibious assault operations. From then on, Marine aviation had only one purpose in Geiger's mind: to support the ground troops.

Superior officers as high as the Joint Chiefs of Staff recognized Geiger's talent for handling joint commands, for coordinating and leading in battle units with diverse tactical training backgrounds and strategic concepts. The ultimate confirmation of this came on June 18, 1945, when Army Lieutenant General Simon Bolivar Buckner was killed by Japanese artillery on Okinawa. Geiger was given command of Buckner's Tenth Army.

The 200,000-man combined Army and Marine Corps operation was fighting what was destined to be the last land battle of World War II. The Tenth Army consisted of the 1st and 6th Marine Divisions and the 27th, 77th, and 99th Army Divisions. It was—and remains—the largest force ever commanded by a Marine.

Since their initial D plus one encounter in the 1st Division's tank-trap CP, relations between Rupertus and Geiger were on a collision course. This was evident to staff officers of both generals, who were powerless to do anything about the situation. Adding to the problem, in the mind of Lieutenant Colonel Lewis J. Fields, Rupertus's G-1, was Geiger's constant prowling of the front lines.

"General Geiger was a fearless man," Fields recalled after his retirement as a lieutenant general in 1970. "We always had to worry about him. He'd get out and go climbing up mountains, up the hills, right up to the front, and talk to the guys.

"If you put your head around a rock, the chances were that you'd get plugged between the eyes. Marines were getting killed daily like that. But he'd go out there and do it, and we worried ourselves to death about him. We didn't want any corps commander getting shot, particularly him. . . ."

Shortly before noon of D plus six, September 21, Geiger appeared at the 1st Marines' CP with Frederick Henderson and two sergeant bodyguards armed with cocked Thompson submachine guns.

Chesty Puller was on the phone, profanely barking "hurry up" orders to Russ Honsowetz's all but annihilated 2d Battalion, which was assaulting another of the nameless crests of Bloody Nose Ridge. The scene was virtually the same as the one described in Pepper Martin's *Time* magazine story: the colonel stripped to the waist, dungarees smudged with coral grime, without a cap or helmet, boots unlaced, and his leg so badly swollen that he could barely walk.

The command post was at the base of a cliff about half a mile south of a small village identified on maps as Garekoru. It was approximately halfway up the eastern shore of the island and marked the point of the division's farthest northern push in a week of fighting.

As Geiger approached the colonel, several mortars dropped a few hundred feet away, something that apparently happened with such frequency that no one in the CP bothered to take cover. The clatter of heavy-machine-gun fire and occasional explosions of hand grenades could clearly be heard from the ridge under attack by Honsowetz's men. As usual, Puller was as close to the action as he could be.

"What can I do for you, General?" the colonel asked as the visitor crouched beside him.

"Just thought I'd drop in and see how things were going," Geiger replied. "Let's talk in private." There was a noticeable edge of concern in his voice as they moved out of earshot of the other Marines. Thus there is no firsthand account of the conversation between the visibly upset general and the fiery regimental commander. The only account of witnesses was that the exchange was heated and brief.

However, according to historian Harry A. Gailey, Geiger—when he left some fifteen minutes later—"came to the conclusion that Puller was out of touch with reality." While there is substantial evidence to verify the inherent truth of the statement, Professor Gailey never identified its source.

Geiger hailed a passing amtrac carrying wounded Marines to the beach and, with Henderson and their armed escorts, rode down the narrow coral north-south road to division headquarters at the airstrip.

The time had come for the inevitable showdown with Rupertus.

"It wasn't what you'd call a really stormy session, although it had some very tense moments," Colonel Deakin recalled. "Johnny Selden, Jeff Fields, and the general were going over the situation map when Geiger showed up and asked to see the latest casualty reports from Lewie Puller's outfit."

The general scrutinized them with slow deliberation, but he made no immediate comment as Rupertus, Selden, Fields, and Deakin stood silently at his side. The figures confirmed his judgment and worst fears. The 1st Marines no longer existed as a combat regiment; it was an organization only on paper, without enough manpower to be called an assault force.

Since D-Day, in less than 200 hours, the regiment had lost 1,672 men, killed and wounded. The percentage breakdown graphically told the appalling story—the heaviest losses ever suffered by a regiment in Marine Corps history.

Ray Davis's 1st Battalion casualties were 71 percent. Only seventy-four men were left in its nine rifle platoons, and every lieutenant platoon leader in the battalion had been killed or wounded. Russ Honsowetz's 2d Battalion had lost 56 percent of its complement, Steve Sabol's 3d Battalion 55 percent.

Unless the survivors were pulled from the lines as soon as possible, Geiger realized beyond question, the skeleton units faced total extinction. Fields, who retired as a lieutenant general in 1970, recalled the grim Geiger-Rupertus confrontation. Speaking of the 1st Regiment, he said:

"They weren't fire-eaters anymore. They had to be replaced if we could find someone to replace them. Geiger wanted to use one of the 81st Division's regiment of Army men. But here, of course, we came into personalities.

"First, Colonel Puller would never admit defeat. He was that kind of guy. . . . He hated the Japanese and he wouldn't say that he needed the help of *any* regiment. General Rupertus didn't want an Army regiment, so, of course, he said no. . . ."

Geiger had made his decision before the conference began, and was rapidly losing patience over Rupertus's obstinate, bewildering, nonsensical position. He listened for five or ten minutes before "Silent Lew" spoke up.

"I felt we needed fresh troops," Fields said, "so I told General Geiger we should bring in the Army. He then turned to Rupertus, and said he felt the same way, and told him to act immediately."

There is no record of the reaction of the 1st Division's volatile commander to his G-1's flagrant disregard of military protocol in speaking out to Geiger. But Geiger was the commanding general of the III Marine Amphibious Corps, and, as such, was Rupertus's superior officer; Rupertus thus could do nothing but comply with Geiger's orders to bring in Army reinforcements.

To emphasize his certainty that Chesty Puller and the 1st Marines were totally spent and unfit for further combat under any circumstances, Geiger went further. He directed that all of the regiment's survivors, officers and men, were to be evacuated as quickly as possible to the division's base camp on Pavuvu.

At 1625 hours on September 21, an urgent dispatch was flashed to General Mueller's headquarters on Angaur:

MUELLER FROM GEIGER XXX URGENTLY REQUEST RCT 321
IMMEDIATE TRANSFER FROM ANGAUR AND ASSIGNMENT TO
COMMANDING GENERAL 1ST MAR DIV PELELIU HQ XXX REPLY
SOONEST XXX HQ III AMPHIB CORPS XXX

The matter was settled. The battle for Peleliu was about to enter its next and ultimately final stage. Early in the morning of the 22nd, Colonel Robert Dark's RCT began boarding six LSTs, and they were ashore on Orange Beach Two by noon the next day.

Shortly after 3:00, the Army's RCT 321 officially replaced the 1st Marine Regiment in the battle for Peleliu. Dark's first move was perhaps indicative of the wide gulf that separated the combat philosophy and attitude of the Army and Marine Corps. He took one look at Chesty Puller's forward command post and ordered it moved 1,000 yards to the rear. The colonel thought the 1st Marines' CP was too close to the fighting, and put his command unnecessarily in danger of an enemy attack.

Colonel Lewis Fields made no secret of his disdain for the Army's way of operating in combat. "They were fresh troops all right," was his dour comment, "but they didn't have the vim and vigor of a Marine outfit. They landed and for days sat on their duffs, and didn't do much except occupy ground we'd already taken. . . ."

Haggard and parched, discouraged and disenchanted, hungry to the point of near collapse, bleary-eyed with almost intolerable combat fatigue, shredded dungarees vile with urine and defecation, the 1st Marines made their torturous, stumbling way across the island to Purple Beach. There, in what was Peleliu's closest approximation of a rest area, they remained for another week before embarking for Pavuvu.

George McMillan talked to one of the men. "We're not a regiment," he mumbled through swollen and sunburned lips. "We're the *survivors* of a regiment."

Gene Sledge was in the 5th Marines bivouac area on Purple Beach as the first men of Puller's regiment appeared. "I saw some familiar faces as the three weary battalions trudged past us," he remembered, "but I was shocked at the absence of so many others I knew in the regiment. 'How many men left in your company?' I asked an old Camp Elliott buddy. He looked at me with bloodshot eyes and choked as he said, 'Twenty is all that's left in the whole company, Sledgehammer. They nearly wiped us out.' "

True to character, out of touch with reality or not, Chesty Puller was still determined to carry on the fight. The troops hardly had settled in when he told them they would go back into action after a three-day rest. The outlandish order was canceled by a division staff officer as soon as he heard about it.

"Some patrols were sent out to search for bypassed Japanese," McMillan later wrote, "but most of the men did only three things in the days they were on Purple Beach: eat, sleep, and look for buddies, check to see who was wounded, who was dead—and who was alive."

Today's survivors of the Old Breed, especially those who were on Peleliu, point to what happened there to Chesty Puller and the 1st Marines as indisputable proof that everything came "the hard way" to the 1st Marine Division in World War II—from beginning to end.

"Even getting off the goddamn island wasn't easy," then Private First Class Henry Wynne, of Rochester, New York, remembered more than four decades later. "It was raining like all hell and the surf and ocean swells were so rough that we didn't think we could make it to the ships waiting to take us back to Pavuvu."

The embarkation was, indeed, arduous and nerve-racking, especially for gaunt, battle-weary, drenched-to-the-skin men. They had to make a brutal climb up the cargo net of a beached LST, make their way to the stern, and clamber down to several DUKW amphibious trucks bobbing violently in the choppy ocean.

Two hospital-equipped transports, *Pinckney* and *Tyron,* were 1,000 yards offshore, waiting to return what was left of the regiment to the division's base camp in the palm groves of Macquitti Bay. Three of the DUKWs swamped before reaching the ships, but, fortunately, no one was lost.

What certainly was one Marine's capstone of an incredibly horrible ordeal came just after he somehow managed to climb still another cargo net to the deck of the *Pinckney*. He was approached by an eager, clean, close-shaven, immaculately dressed young Navy officer:

"Got any souvenirs to trade?"

The soaked, exhausted, combat-battered, bewildered Marine stood in silent controlled meditation for a few moments. He was empty-handed, and reached back and patted his own rear end.

"I brought my ass outta there, Swabbie. That's my souvenir of Peleliu."

Colonel Puller was among the last to board ship before the destroyer-escorted convoy sailed at dawn of October 2. He was carrying a souvenir—not from Peleliu, but the mortar fragment from Guadalcanal embedded in his left leg. The limb was swollen so much that his thigh was almost twice its normal size, and the throbbing pain was constant. He could walk only by draping an arm around the shoulder of someone for support.

Doctors took one look and hurried him to the operating room. Ranting like a banshee, he finally submitted to a local anesthetic. The surgeon, Commander Herbert Patterson of Long Beach, California, went to the bone and removed a chunk of steel about an inch long and a quarter inch wide in an operation lasting nearly two hours.

Six days later, on October 8, the indomitable colonel—ignoring the advice and admonitions of doctors—hoisted himself from his bunk and hobbled about, unaided, for several minutes. The next day, in fresh khakis and with his famed chest held high, he was able to walk down the ship's gangway to the base camp on Pavuvu.

Although he didn't know it then, World War II was over for forty-six-year-old Lewis Burwell Puller—but not his flamboyant and controversial career as a Marine Corps officer and legendary military figure. By the time he had fully recovered from the shipboard operation and was pronounced fit for return to active duty, the Japanese had surrendered.

In July 1950, he was back in battle, again as a regimental commander with the 1st Marine Division in Korea. Even after his retirement as a lieutenant general on November 1, 1955, he remained active in Marine Corps affairs. In 1966, with the United States deeply enmeshed in the Vietnam conflict, his request for a return to active combat duty was turned down because of his age.

While the then sixty-eight-year-old general had no direct involvement in the costly drawn-out struggle, it brought deep tragedy to the Puller family—just as it did to thousands of others throughout the nation.

On October 11, 1968, twenty-three-year-old Second Lieutenant Lewis B. Puller, Jr., triggered a booby-trapped Vietcong land mine. The blast caused the loss of six fingers and the amputation of his legs—one to his right hip, the other to just above his left knee. Young Puller, the general's only son, was a platoon leader in the 1st Marines, the regiment his father commanded on Peleliu.

Whether Chesty Puller was too aggressive on Peleliu, whether he wantonly wasted lives as "expendable weapons of war," is a question that never will be answered to the satisfaction of his adherents or critics. But there can be no doubt that the 1st Marines, constantly prodded by their commander from his frontline CP, contributed beyond any reasonable expectations to the final victory.

A paragraph from the Marine Corps monograph of the battle officially documents—in cold, revealing, unembellished statistics—what the regiment did in five days of head-on combat:

"In accomplishing its mission to this point (September 21), it had killed an estimated 3,942 Japanese (nearly a third of Colonel Nakagawa's garrison) and reduced the following major enemy positions and installations: ten defended coral ridges, three large blockhouses, twenty-two pillboxes, thirteen antitank guns, and 144 defended caves."

General Smith, never known to overstate the facts and often critical of Puller's push-push tactics, commented:

"Lewie banged his head against the opposition. I went over the ground he captured, and I didn't see how human beings captured it, but they did. He believed in momentum . . . just keep on hitting and trying to keep up the momentum until he'd overrun the whole thing. . . . There was no finesse about it, but there was gallantry and determination. . . ."

5

September 21 ended the first week on Peleliu. It was, in some aspects, both the best and worst time of the entire battle for the 1st Division, a fact sometimes difficult for survivors to reconcile with their memories of the struggle. To most of the troops, it was a period of unrelenting hardship and carnage, the meanest ordeal of their lives.

The plus factors were measured strictly in textbook terms of military accomplishments. General Smith summarized them in a postwar tape-recorded interview for Marine Corps archives:

Seven days after the landing, all of the southern end of Peleliu was in our hands, as well as the high ground immediately dominating the airfield. All the beaches that were ever used were in use.

There was room for the proper deployment of all the artillery. Unloading was unhampered except by the weather and hydrographic conditions. The airfield was available and essential base development work was underway.

Frank Hough further accentuated the positive in the official monograph of the campaign. "Furthermore," he wrote, "the Japanese potential for effective counteraction had been destroyed with the elimination of an estimated two-thirds of their strength." Both evaluations, however, had notably significant and sad flaws.

Colonel Nakagawa's remaining troops were solidly entrenched in the hidden caves and fortifications of the Umurbrogols. There, in the barren cliffs and crevices of the Five Sisters and Five Brothers, of Death Valley and the China Wall, half a dozen Japanese could and did hold out for days, even weeks, against platoon- and company-strength assaults by Marines and the Army's RCT 321.

In what can only be construed as a gratuitous commendation to Rupertus on the status of the campaign on D plus six, the monograph also stated: "In that all of Peleliu that possessed any strategic value had been secured, the commanding general's early prediction of quick conquest had not fallen so short of literal realization."

Rupertus's subsequent enigmatic and emotional conversations with Colonels Deakin and Harris reflected, beyond a shadow of doubt, the general's belated and reluctant acceptance of the fact that a battle-ending breakthrough was impossible.

While General Smith's statement was basically honest, it put the best face on what Hough's monograph described as "tactical results of great importance achieved in a solid week of hard fighting." Left unsaid was that much of the ground captured was comparatively flat, where superior Navy and Marine Corps firepower was most effective.

Nor were the effects of the terrible casualties given justified emphasis: 3,946 Marines killed or wounded in approximately 170 hours of combat—one man every two and a half minutes night and day. Not only had Chesty Puller's 1st Marines ceased to exist as a fighting regiment, but Bucky Harris's 5th and Herm Hanneken's 7th were drained far below manpower levels that, according to "the book," were absolutely necessary for front-line action.

An official Marine Corps document expresses, in surprising candor, the high command's outlook at the end of the first week of the battle:

> Organized resistance, clearly, was far from an end. But even at this stage, no one not gifted with clairvoyance would have predicted that two more months were destined to elapse before it would end.

6

The first night of the invasion's second week brought two things to Peleliu: the first monsoon rain to hit the island since the Marines landed, and an attempt by the Japanese to reinforce Colonel Nakagawa's garrison.

The cooling downpour was unexpected and welcomed. The enemy action was neither. The last thing the Americans wanted was more Japanese to fight, but the invasion high command had been concerned about the possibility since D-Day.

Daily reconnaissance flights by Navy carrier planes had confirmed pre-invasion intelligence reports that General Inoue had a large force of reserves—possibly 25,000 troops—on Babelthuap. He apparently still believed the "big island" of the Palaus, some 30 miles north of Peleliu, was an imminent invasion target and so far hadn't sent fresh manpower into the battle.

Why Inoue decided to send reinforcements was never ascertained, and there are several versions of what actually happened.

The logbook of the destroyer *H. L. Edwards,* on picket duty off Akarakoro Point at Peleliu's northernmost tip, recorded the approach of several barges shortly before midnight on September 23. Because of the rain and darkness it was impossible to determine their exact number, but it was estimated at between ten and fifteen.

The commanding officer of the destroyer wrote that "the enemy craft were promptly brought under fire by naval vessels and Marine artillery, which claimed the destruction of seven."

The 1st Division's battle diary described what apparently was a second attempt to land reinforcements:

"At 0245 on the 24th another group was taken under fire; eight were observed to explode, and ten wrecks were observed on the reefs after daybreak. According to a captured survivor, the convoy included thirteen barges and a motor sampan, all of which were believed destroyed."

Colonel Nakagawa had a far different version of the episode. He messaged General Inoue: "The advance detachment made a successful landing at 0520 under command of First Lieutenant Murahori. . . . Of the main body, nine barges arrived safely but six were shelled and burned while taking the wrong landing route. Most of the personnel on these were able to land by walking through the shallow waters. . . ."

Nakagawa made no mention of losses, possibly a deliberate omission to encourage General Inoue to send further reinforcements using the same route. If that was the colonel's hope, it was fruitless. Inoue had made his first and last move to bolster Peleliu's defenses, a fact obviously unknown to the invaders. As it had been since the beginning, the island was, to the general, a lost cause except as a killing ground for as many Americans as possible before Nakagawa's garrison was annihilated.

Marine intelligence officers estimated that the Japanese had succeeded in landing from 300 to 600 fresh troops. Under ordinary circumstances, the numbers would cause little anxiety. But now it was a new factor to be reckoned with because of the desperately understrength, weary, frustrated 5th and 7th Marines—and the unknown combat capabilities of the Army's untested RCT 321 to press the attack.

The possibility of still more Japanese reinforcements being hurled into the struggle added substantially to the distress and indecision of General Rupertus. General Geiger earlier had discussed with the 1st Division commander the threat of Japanese attempts to land more men, and was quick to grasp the mounting seriousness of the current situation.

Geiger acted immediately to head off a further recurrence of enemy troop-landing expeditions by ordering increased Navy picket boats off Akarakoro Point and beefed-up aerial observation of Babelthuap. Then he and Rupertus, back at division headquarters, set to work with staff members on a permanent solution to the problem.

In short order, they came up with the battle plan that was

the blueprint of the rest of the campaign. In essence, it was what Geiger had had in the back of his mind since D plus two when the airstrip was captured. The idea was to build up the airstrip complex area with heavy artillery and operational aircraft facilities while Marine and Army assault units moved to the northern tip of the island, using the Japanese-built coral-topped East Road and West Road as the main routes of attack.

Once Akarakoro Point was reached, Ngesebus Island—connected to Peleliu by a 500-yard-long causeway—would be seized. Not only would its capture end the threat of more enemy reinforcements, but it would give the Americans another airstrip, a fighter plane base with a hard-surfaced 1,000-yard-long runway, three relatively undamaged hangars, and six permanent barracks.

After this was accomplished, the full thrust of the offensive would be aimed at isolating the high grounds of the Umurbrogols, the north-south spine of Peleliu where an estimated 1,500 survivors of Nakagawa's garrison had burrowed in. By splitting these defenders into individual pockets of resistance, the final phase of the battle could then begin.

The long-acknowledged differences in training, discipline, tactics, and combat philosophies of the Marine Corps and Army were evident the first day Colonel Dark's RCT 321 went into combat to carry out the final-phase plan.

Following twenty minutes of heavy naval bombardment and air strikes on the ridges that paralleled the West Road, Dark's 1st Battalion moved north toward Garekoru village. It reached the objective, some half a mile from the jump-off point, without drawing enemy fire.

The colonel then halted the advance and ordered a patrol forward to scout for Japanese strongpoints. It returned half an hour later with a report that in pushing ahead nearly 1,000 yards, it spotted several enemy positions on the cliffs but had encountered no resistance. By then it was late afternoon, and instead of pushing ahead as the favorable reconnaissance would seemingly justify, Dark ordered the battalion to dig in for the night and resume the attack the next day.

What Dark had failed to consider—or possibly didn't know—was that his 2d and 3d Battalions, which had been protecting his eastern flank from the ridges, were no longer there. They had run into what the RCT's war diary described as "fairly heavy Japanese fire" and had left the high ground for the much easier going along the West Road with the rest of the regiment of Wildcats.

Fortunately for RCT 321, Major Hunter Hurst's 3d Battalion of the 7th Marines had been ordered to follow Dark's troops along the road and maintain contact with the Army units on the ridges.

Hurst could hardly believe his eyes when he saw the soldiers scrambling down the slopes, leaving the flank of the advance completely exposed. He realized that unless something was done fast, the door was wide open for the Japanese to reinforce their troops on the crest—and then swarm down in a probably strong and devastating counterattack.

To plug the gap and prevent possible disastrous losses to Dark's apparently unwary troops, Hurst ordered his battalion to assault the hill. The Marines took the objective in the heaviest fighting that day on the island, and lost twenty-seven killed and wounded in the process. The major was bitter, his fuming anger at the flash point, when he reported the episode to 1st Division headquarters. He thought then, as he did long after the battle, that it was Colonel Dark's responsibility to order his own troops to recapture and hold the ridge they had abandoned.

"That's the Wildcat Division of pussycats all the way," General Rupertus reputedly remarked when he was informed of the affair. "Now I can tell Geiger, 'I told you so. That's why I didn't want the Army involved in this in the first place.'"

Whether he repeated the statement to the III Corps commander is not known. Nor is there a documented account of Colonel Dark's reaction to what could have been a disaster to RCT 321 in its first action on Peleliu if Major Hurst and his Marines hadn't been on the scene.

No purpose is served in reiterating the interservice rivalry, sometimes outright contempt, that existed then between the Marine Corps and the Army. It is universally known, and only clouds the issue of their relationship in Operation Stalemate.

When the invasion was planned, the 81st Infantry Division was given four specific assignments: to capture Angaur, serve as a reserve force to be used where and when ordered, mop up the remnants of diehard Japanese defenders after Peleliu was declared secure, and serve as the occupying garrison after the Marines left the Palaus.

In short, the role of General Mueller's Wildcats was secondary in the overall scheme of things. Thus, in all probability, the division would not have been committed to the Peleliu assault if the 1st Marine Regiment hadn't been shot to pieces.

There definitely was no lack of individual acts of uncommon heroism among the officers and men of the 81st.

Technical Sergeant Joseph A. Miller was one of them. Armed only with a Browning automatic rifle, he stood exposed to enemy fire to cover the withdrawal of his company from a ridge swarming with Japanese. When they made it safely down the slope, Miller carried a wounded comrade down the slope.

Later the same day, he mounted the ridge in a one-man assault. He held the position alone for some twenty hours, killed twenty Japanese during the lengthy ordeal, and was awarded a spot commission to second lieutenant for his bravery.

Then there was Private George M. Bachman, a member of RCT 321's engineer battalion.

One night during the push toward Ngesebus he spotted a case of white phosphorus grenades burning on a truck parked in the unit's bivouac area. The vehicle also carried a ton of high-explosive demolition charges, six 55-gallon drums of flamethrower fuel, and several hundred volatile percussion caps. Realizing that the whole load could blow sky-high at any moment, Bachman vaulted into the smoldering tarpaulin-covered vehicle and threw the spewing crate as far as he could.

Then, with bare hands, the twenty-year-old private beat out the remaining flames. His unhesitating fearless act of courage undoubtedly saved the lives of many comrades and earned for him the coveted Soldier's Medal for bravery.

Lieutenant Colonel Raymond S. Gates, a 1940 graduate of the U.S. Military Academy at West Point, was commander of RCT 321's 1st Battalion. Marines who saw him in action thought he had all the qualifications of full-fledged membership in the Old Breed: fearless, dedicated, combat-savvy, and considerate of his men.

Whenever his outfit was on the line, Gates constantly moved from position to position, keeping a personal handle on the situation regardless of danger. On one of many missions in the drive to isolate the Umurbrogols, Gates was in an outpost with several men when someone triggered a booby trap. He was among the casualties, but refused to leave until all the other wounded were safely evacuated under heavy enemy small-arms and machine-gun fire.

Time and again Gates remained at the front, directing his

men in assaults against caves and pillboxes and risking his life to rescue the wounded. Late in the campaign, in one of these encounters, the battalion commander was killed, shot in the head by a sniper's bullet.

Colonel Gates was the senior officer of the 81st Division lost in combat. He was posthumously awarded the Distinguished Service Cross. Except for the Medal of Honor, it is the highest decoration the Army can bestow for valor.

Sergeant Clayton E. Shockley and Private First Class Jack R. Musolf showed that bravery wasn't always confined to front-line combat. The two men, members of the 81st Division's signal company, were troubleshooting a telephone line in a rear-echelon area of Purple Beach.

Shockley noticed that the wire disappeared abruptly into a swamp. Hand over hand, he followed it until he discovered five heavily armed Japanese hidden in a bypassed cluster of dense burned-over mangrove tree stumps. He promptly killed one of the enemy with a burst of carbine fire.

The survivors responded with a barrage of hand grenades as Shockley scampered back to his jeep for more ammunition. Then he and Muslof darted through the grenade blasts and assaulted the position head-on. In short order three more Japanese were killed and the fifth was wounded. The two so-called noncombatant soldiers were awarded the Silver Star for valor.

As was the case with the men of the 1st Marine Division, countless similar acts of bravery by soldiers of the 81st Army Division went unnoticed except by those directly involved in the action.

"Just living through the sonofabitchin' battle was enough for me," Marine Corporal Robertson Forbes, of Trenton, Missouri, said. "I didn't need a medal, especially a Purple Heart, to remind me of how lucky *anyone*—Dogface or Leatherneck—had to be to survive."

Rarely have more truthful words been spoken.

TWELVE

Countdown to Victory

D-DAY PLUS TWELVE, SEPTEMBER 27, WAS A DAY TO BE remembered.

At 8:00 in the morning the Stars and Stripes were formally raised over the cinder-block headquarters building of 1st Marine Division headquarters at the northern edge of the airstrip.

Generals Geiger, Rupertus, and Smith—standing side by side at ramrod attention with Colonels Puller, Harris, and Hanneken and high-ranking aides—saluted as the flag went up, snapping in the hot, dusty wind. The rumble of falling artillery was clearly audible from the highlands a few thousand feet to the north, where the assault troops of RCT 321 and the 5th and 7th Marines were about to jump off in the day's attack.

There were no speeches, and although members of the division band served as honor guard for the occasion, there was no traditional playing of "The Star-Spangled Banner" and "The Marine Corps Hymn." Instruments had been left behind on Pavuvu, and the musicians were serving as guards for the division CP and filling in as infantry at the front, as well as stretcher bearers.

To the gaggle of rear-echelon enlisted men who witnessed the event, it meant that the brass, at least, felt the time was definitely approaching when the island would be officially declared secure. The officers and troops pushing the drive in and around the Umurbrogols had a different view. If anything, Japanese resistance was stiffening and the hardest and bloodiest combat was ahead for those still able to fight.

If Colonel Nakagawa saw the ceremonies, he did nothing to interrupt them. Although the airfield was within range of his big mortars and artillery he apparently saw no point in revealing his well-concealed emplacements or wasting precious ammunition in futile gestures of defiance.

The Japanese commander's strategy remained unchanged: Let the stupid Americans come to him and he would wipe them out, man by man, until the last of his troops fell. He continued to send out nightly suicide squads, laden with demolition charges, in attempts to infiltrate the airfield and headquarters complex to do whatever damage they could. But none made it, and the Marines' and Seabees' buildup of the facilities moved rapidly ahead.

Nearly 4,000 feet of the north-south runway was operational, and the nucleus of the Marines' own combat air power had arrived near sunset on September 24 to put it to use. The initial flight—eight long-range, radar-equipped F6F-3N Grumman Hellcat night fighters—had flown in from Guam.

Brigadier General James T. "Nuts" Moore, commander of the 2d Marine Air Wing, was at the controls of the first plane to touch down. His primary flight training instructor in the 1920s had been then Major Roy Geiger, and he was among the early pilots of Geiger's Cactus Air Force on Guadalcanal.

Bill Hipple, the *Newsweek* reporter, once asked Moore how he got his nickname. "When I applied for aviation duty, my fellow second looies wanted to know why," the general replied. "I said 'I don't really know, so just call me Nuts.' "

Admiral Nimitz's CinCPac headquarters in Pearl Harbor listed "MAB [Marine Air Base] Peleliu in operational status" the day before the flag was raised. That was when Major Robert F. "Cowboy" Stout's squadron of twenty-four F4U fighter-bombers, flying from the carrier *Lexington* 50 miles at sea, landed on the island.

Officially designated as VMF-114, Stout's pilots and their distinctive aircraft, heavily armed, fast-climbing, highly maneuverable, 400-mile-an-hour, blunt-nosed, gull-winged Chance-Vought Corsairs, went immediately to work. Flying low-level bombing and strafing support missions for ground troops, VMF-114 and another two dozen F6F Hellcats—from Major John Fitting, Jr.'s VMF-216, which flew in from the *Wasp* two days later—were of incalculable importance in the final phase of the campaign.

Now that General Moore's 2d MAW was on Peleliu with some sixty combat aircraft, the invasion's Navy high command felt the Marines had sufficient air power of their own to take care of any possible Japanese air or naval strikes. Thus the *Lexing-*

ton and *Wasp,* the last of the carriers assigned to Operation Stalemate, were relieved and steamed away to join MacArthur's armada off the Philippines.

The Marines, from Generals Geiger and Rupertus to teenage replacement privates, were grateful for the Navy's air support. They fully realized the landing—and the progress made so far—would have been impossible without it. But the men in the assault units felt more confident, more secure, when *their* planes and *their* pilots took over.

The reasoning was understandable. From primary flight training to combat, Marine pilots constantly were imbued with Roy Geiger's dictum that was also the Corps' officially recognized policy: "The sole purpose of Marine aviation is to support the infantry."

Even after getting their wings, most pilots were required to spend time training with ground troops to call in close air support during infantry maneuvers. The objective was obvious: to give the fliers firsthand knowledge of what it felt like to be, as General Moore once put it, "down in the dirt with the 'working classes' of combat Marines when air firepower was badly needed."

"These guys weren't just high-flyin' airplane jockeys," twenty-year-old Private First Class Nolen Marbrey of Brooksville, Florida, remembered. "They knew from personal experience how it felt to be pinned down by enemy fire and how much the troops depended on them when the goin' was rough."

William Boniface, a combat correspondent sergeant from Bel Air, Maryland, who had been a *Baltimore Sun* reporter, described one mission by four of VMF-114's Corsair pilots:

"The engines of the beautiful gull-winged planes roared, whined, and strained as they peeled off and plummeted down in single file from an altitude of about 5,000 feet. They held their fire until they were as low as 1,000 feet, and then opened up. They plastered the ridgeline next to where a company of the 1st Battalion of the 5th Marines was pinned down under heavy-machine-gun and mortar fire, hitting the enemy emplacements with strafing, bombs, and rockets.

"The effect was awesome as dirt, sand, chunks of coral, and debris spewed into the air. We were sure, time and again, that a pilot was pulling out too late and would crash as he came in close enough for us to see his face, not more than 50 feet above us. But none did as they zoomed skyward, circled around, and made more low-level passes until all the Japanese positions were silenced, blown to bits with their occupants and weapons. . . ."

Perhaps the most memorable thing to Marine pilots on Peleliu was the extremely close location of hidden and heavily fortified Japanese strongpoints less than 1,000 yards from the northern end of the airstrip's main runway.

"The target was so damned near that when we made our first strike on September 26, fragments from one of the 1,000-pound bombs we dropped ended up back on the airfield," Cowboy Stout recalled. "In the weeks to come, we hit the area with everything we had but weren't ever able to knock it out." VMF-114's lack of success was easily explainable—the Japanese were just too well concealed, a fact borne out by an astounding event that would not take place until long after the war was over.

The objective was a 100-square-yard pocket on the crest of Bloody Nose Ridge. Concentrated there was a honeycomb of impossible-to-pinpoint, concrete-reinforced multilevel caves and underground blockhouses with 6-foot-thick cement ceilings and walls. They provided the Japanese with direct observation of the massive buildup on the occupied part of the island, but it is doubtful that the bypassed outposts were in communication with Colonel Nakagawa's headquarters deep in the Umurbrogol highlands.

Whatever the enemy saw had little effect on the Japanese commander's plans to defend the island, especially since he already had conceded that southern Peleliu was lost to the Americans. This failed, however, to stop occasionally heavy and most likely unauthorized mortar and howitzer bombardments on the nearby airbase and the 1st Division's headquarters complex, which was rapidly becoming a mammoth and well-organized supply depot.

The shelling was largely ineffective—more harassing to the nerves than threatening to the battle's outcome—but it was a nuisance that General Moore wanted removed once and for all. His orders to that effect resulted in a series of what certainly must be recorded as the shortest bomb runs in the history of aviation warfare.

Corsair pilots were over the target, with half-ton bombs unloaded, less than *fifteen seconds* after takeoff. "We didn't even have time to raise the landing gear before the mission was over," Colonel Caleb F. Bailey, the MAG-11 commander, told Gene Sherman, the *Los Angeles Times* correspondent. "Then we'd make a tight turn, land, rearm, and do it again. . . ."

From dawn to dusk on September 30, Corsair pilots dropped fifty 1,000-pound bombs on the pocket. They also smothered it with two dozen unfused napalm tanks that were ignited by ground troops with phosphorus grenades and flamethrowers. The blasts rumbled like an earthquake and sent clouds of billowing grayish smoke and debris so high that they were seen everywhere on the island.

There was no sign of Japanese activity there for the rest of the battle. But there is a sequel that stretches imagination to the ultimate limits of belief. It is the definitive episode that characterized the virtual impregnability of many of Peleliu's defenses and the supreme determination of Colonel Nakagawa's troops to fight on despite overwhelming American military might.

On April 21, 1947, more than twenty months after V-J Day, Lieutenant Tadamichi Yamaguchi and twenty-six of his troops finally came down from the pocket on Bloody Nose Ridge to surrender.

For nearly three years, Yamaguchi and his guerrillas had held out there, convinced that the Marines had merely overrun the Palaus and that Japanese forces, temporarily pushed back in that part of the Pacific, would return to recapture Peleliu. They not only managed to survive by scrounging food, medicine, and other supplies during frequent one- or two-man midnight forays on nearby unguarded supply dumps, but they had thrived.

Captain L. O. Fox, commanding officer of the eighty-man Marine garrison of what by then was known as NOB (Naval Operating Base) Peleliu, was ultimately informed of the small but regular raids. He thought at first that they were cases of traditional "moonlight requisitioning" by U.S. occupation forces, but his thinking changed when a Japanese soldier's dirty but unbloody cap and tunic—obviously not souvenirs stashed by an American—were discovered in a Quonset hut stockpiled with rations, some of which were missing.

An urgent dispatch to the prisoner-of-war compound on Guam resulted in Navy intelligence headquarters flying Admiral Hainan Sumikawa immediately to Peleliu. Accompanied by Marine guards in two jeeps, one equipped with a powerful loudspeaker, the captured admiral scouted the island constantly blaring orders for Yamaguchi and his troops to surrender, since Japan had lost the war to the Americans. It was futile and without purpose to hold out any longer, he kept repeating.

When the last twenty-seven of Colonel Nakagawa's estimated 13,500-man Peleliu garrison emerged from their redoubt on Bloody Nose Ridge, Captain Fox led a patrol of his men into the depths of the stronghold the survivors had occupied for more than 1,000 days of war and peace.

Little wonder that the position was undamaged by the hundreds of tons of naval shelling and aerial bombardment that had hit the 100-square-yard area just north of the airstrip. It was at least 100 feet below the solid coral surface, a concrete-walled fortress impervious to attack.

"The place was well stocked with rations and medical supplies and even had running water," Chief Warrant Officer Jack Goodall, Fox's provost marshal, said. "It was lighted with kerosene lamps, and there was plenty of ammunition and weapons and everyone had a bunk. We even found several boxes of Kleenex."

The Japanese were given clean white civilian clothing, tennis shoes, and soap and towels, and allowed to soak in showers, a luxury they hadn't experienced since before the island was invaded. Then they were returned to Japan, not as prisoners of war but as "disarmed military personnel of the former enemy."

"They never had it so good in the Jap army," Staff Sergeant E. V. Sturgeon, one of Goodall's MPs, observed. "I wish we'd been treated that well." Goodall spoke from experience. He was a former POW, captured when the Japanese overran Wake Island in early 1942, and had spent thirty-three months in a stockade in northern Japan before being liberated at war's end.

2

"There were actually *two* Pelelius after the first two weeks of the battle," General Smith observed a decade later in a long conversation with an Associated Press correspondent he had first met in Korea when Smith commanded the 1st Marine Division.

By then, in September 1955, he was a sixty-three-year-old

retired four-star general, one of the most respected Marines of all time.

To those fortunate enough to have known him personally, the slight, soft-spoken, erudite 1916 graduate (with a *cum laude* degree in philosophy) from the Berkeley campus of the University of California remains the epitome of a gentleman, as well as a leader of unsurpassed military acumen and brilliance. The same opinion is shared by historians and students of his thirty-eight-year career as a Marine Corps officer.

"One Peleliu was the flat ground we had captured on the southern third of the island," Smith said. "There we went about the job, all but unmolested, we'd been sent to do—seize the airstrip, and bring in our men and planes so that the Japanese couldn't use the island to interfere with MacArthur's operations in the Philippines.

"The *other* Peleliu began at Bloody Nose Ridge and extended northward through the Umurbrogols to Ngesebus Island. This was a brutally different extra-inning ball game, one where the score was kept in the number of ridges taken and how many Marines were killed or wounded in the seemingly endless process."

Among the general's most admired traits was that he seldom, if ever, was openly critical of the actions or decisions of his fellow officers, superior or subordinate. Smith thus never spoke out in public about the Palau campaign's high command decisions.

But he later told several close friends that, as a retired brigadier general recalled, "he often wondered why we didn't simply leave the highlands to the Japanese, keep shelling and bombing them from offshore and the part of Peleliu we held until there were too few left to continue the fight."

By D plus thirteen, September 28, "Peleliu South"—so designated in a news story written by Captain Earl Wilson, 2d MAW's public relations officer—had taken on the look of a bustling, fully functioning combat-zone Marine base.

The airstrip's control tower, perched atop what had been the Japanese radio transmitter building, was handling takeoffs and landings by Corsairs and Hellcats flying more than fifty ground support missions a day. Seabees and Marine engineers were erecting the first Quonset barracks and mess halls for mounting numbers of noncombatant rear-echelon personnel.

A central post office was set up in the canvas-covered shell of a small bombed-out shack next to the division HQ. A R4D

Navy Douglas transport was regularly flying couriers with urgent dispatches, along with incoming and outgoing sacks of V-mail, to and from Guam.

Seabees erected a movie screen not far from the patched-up causeway leading to Ngarmoked Island. The fact that it was only a few hundred feet from the ever-expanding cemetery seemed not to bother any of the nightly viewers. They were more upset by the noise of exploding artillery and mortars where heavy fighting was going on up north; the din often obscured the music and dialogue of the film being shown. Navy shore parties and bivouacked units of the Wildcat Division, more accustomed than the Marines to the amenities of civilized life, wondered why it was taking so long for a USO troupe to show up with live entertainment.

Nearly 50,000 tons of supplies had been off-loaded from cargo ships and LSTs and dispersed in well-organized supply dumps. Stockpiles grew daily, especially after a pontoon causeway was floated from the reef to where Orange Beaches One and Two came together. The heavy steel dock enabled three LSTs to unload at once, and their cargoes quickly moved to shore.

One of the major concerns of the invasion planners was the possibility of heavy Japanese aerial attacks or a powerful hit-and-run, lightning-fast naval strike *after* the beachhead was established. The apprehension was understandable; the constantly accumulating tonnage of war matériel and thousands of behind-the-lines Americans were a magnetic target.

To guard against the threat, Peleliu South—by D plus twelve—was probably the most heavily armed and protected American outpost in the Pacific. Admiral Oldendorf's battleships *Mississippi* and *Maryland* remained on station 10 miles offshore with the cruisers *Denver* and *Columbus* and six destroyer escorts. Wide-ranging submarines prowled a 1,000-square-mile area as an early-warning network against marauding enemy naval task forces. MAG-11's long-range, radar-equipped Hellcats, armed with bombs and machine guns, flew round-the-clock patrols covering a 300-mile radius to intercept air strikes. Cowboy Stout's and Cal Bailey's squadrons of fifty-plus Corsairs and Hellcats were always on the alert to shoot down any Japanese planes able to penetrate the screen.

Only two did. Both were Jake bombers, lumbering, ancient, noisy, twin-engined, lightly armed, slow-moving planes that apparently made the fifteen-minute flight from Babelthuap in an ill-conceived, if not stupid and meaningless, midnight foray.

One dropped several hand grenades on an unoccupied ridge in the Umurbrogols. Pamphlets urging the Marines to surrender floated to earth from the other. Both were easy, flaming victims of quick-triggered Hellcat pilots.

Six battalions of artillery were emplaced and calibrated to lay down nonstop barrages anywhere on the island, or to fire on any adventurous Japanese warships that appeared offshore. Their combined firepower numbered nearly 150 pieces. One battalion of three four-gun batteries were awesome 155-millimeter "Long Toms" that could hit a pinpointed target 15 miles away; the others were shorter-range but potent 75s and 105s—the basic artillery weapons of all Marine divisions.

Since the Japanese fleet made no attempts to shell Peleliu and the enemy did not try to recapture the island, the sole work of the cannoneers was to support the ground troops in the assault. This kept the artillerymen busy—very, very busy.

A report compiled for some obscure reason at CinCPac headquarters after the battle told the story in cold statistics that, beyond words, graphically reflected the fury of the action.

In all, Marine artillerymen fired 133,000 rounds of shells during the thirty-five days their guns were in action: 13,000 from the 155s, 65,000 from the 75s, and 55,000 from the 105s. Calculated on a minute-by-minute, twenty-four-hours-a-day basis, lanyards were pulled at a rate of one every twenty-three seconds.

Marine and Seabee bulldozer operators carved a network of roads for amtracs and trucks to haul, on a regular schedule, whatever was needed by the troops to dumps just behind the front. Most often, the return trips carried bodies of men killed in action.

Improvised beachhead first aid and evacuation stations, like Dr. Hagan's exposed D-Day shell hole, were replaced by four completely equipped and fully manned field hospitals. Each had prefabricated operating rooms where major surgery was performed by teams of experts from Navy Commander Emil E. Napp's 1st Medical Battalion.

On October 4, D plus nineteen, big twin-engined Curtiss Commando hospital planes from VMR-952 began regular air evacuation of the most seriously wounded. In the next five days, 247 men were flown to Guam for special treatment unavailable on Peleliu. The four-hour journey was made more bearable by the presence of what grateful Marines called "Flight Angels"—nurses from the Navy's Nurse's Corps.

From then until the fighting was over, the majority of casualties who had lost limbs, been blinded, or suffered life-threatening internal wounds were evacuated by air. The less seriously hurt left on one of the big hospital ships, *Bountiful* or *Solace,* for recuperation in Hawaii or Australia.

On the front lines, the unremitting struggle first to rescue and then to save the lives of the wounded was the unchanging and dangerous jobs of corpsmen, stretcher bearers, and Navy doctors.

The battlefield surgeons usually were young Navy Reserve lieutenants called to active duty with little experience beyond that gained as hospital interns. Almost always under enemy fire, and working with little more than a satchel of basic surgical instruments, they constantly performed unbelievable miracles.

Stopping the hemorrhaging of fountains of blood, administering plasma, applying splints to damaged limbs, injecting pain-killing morphine, the medics did everything they could to enable seriously shot-up Marines to survive and then be taken to the rear for hospitalization or evacuation.

The valiant, mercy-minded men paid a very high price for their selfless dedication to fallen comrades. Serried crosses in Peleliu's cemetery ultimately bore the names of six doctors, ninety-seven corpsmen, and nearly 200 stretcher bearers.

Among the constantly lengthening rows of markers in the burial ground was one stenciled "PFC JOHN D. NEW." He had been an instant celebrity in his hometown of Mobile, Alabama, four months after his seventeenth birthday.

When the apprentice machinist in a paper mill heard the news of the Pearl Harbor attack on the radio, he jumped on his bicycle and pedaled as fast as he could to the Marine Corps recruiting station to volunteer. It was closed, but the teenage patriot was not deterred. He leaned his bike against the building and sat down beside it, patiently waiting—sometimes dozing—all that night for someone to show up in the morning.

On December 8, 1941, John D. New was sworn in as the first person from the city to join up to fight the Japanese, a story duly reported, along with a photo of the swearing-in ceremony, on the front page of the afternoon edition of the *Press-Register.*

Private First Class New was one of the pioneers of the new generation of the Old Breed. He was with a mortar platoon on Guadalcanal and Cape Gloucester. He was doing the same thing on Peleliu, by then a salty Old Hand with the 2d Battalion of the 7th Marines who had celebrated his nineteenth birthday on Pavuvu by getting tipsy on a batch of "jungle juice" scrounged up by his buddies.

What the husky, blue-eyed, brownish-haired Mobilian did on September 25, 1944, would again make headlines back home—but for a tragically different reason.

Shortly after noon, New and two other men had strung wire to the crest of a small ridge north of Garekoru village. They were calling in mortar fire to support the advance north for the planned assault on Ngesebus Island, and went about their job unmolested for nearly half an hour.

Then, from a concealed bypassed cave below their position, a Japanese popped out with two hand grenades, one in each hand. Before the Marines could react, he hurled both almost simultaneously. One missed its target. The other didn't. It landed, still sputtering and about to explode, two feet away.

"Private First Class New instantly perceived the dire peril and, with utter disregard for his own safety, unhesitatingly flung himself upon the grenade and absorbed the full impact of the explosion, thus saving the lives of the two other Marines but resulting in his being mortally wounded."

The words were included in the citation, signed by President Truman, which accompanied the presentation to his widowed mother of PFC New's posthumous award of the Medal of Honor.

The ceremonies were held at the White House on December 8, 1945. It was four years to the day after the youth volunteered to serve his country proudly and valorously as a Marine—a member of the Old Breed forever remembered by his comrades.

3

Few major attacks came off as successfully as hoped in the battle for Peleliu. The amphibious assault on Ngesebus Island was a notable and gratifying exception.

Not only was the operation carried out as planned, but it was a classic textbook performance, a near-perfect display of how to coordinate and use all of the ingredients—naval, air, artillery, and ground troops—to pull off a combat landing with minimum losses.

Teamwork and expertise were the undeniable keys, beginning with the joint planning of Bucky Harris and Lew Walt, the CO and executive officer of the 5th Marines. Both knew their stuff and how to use the combined knowledge they adroitly shared. The basic scheme was Harris's. Walt's responsibility was to execute it.

Ngesebus's tiny size—it was less than 2,500 yards long from tip to tip and about half that wide—was not indicative of its importance to the overall strategy for ultimate victory on Peleliu.

In American hands, the island would effectively block any future landing of large Japanese reinforcements from Babelthuap. It also was the site of a small airstrip that could be developed for fighter plane use. But more important, Ngesebus would give U.S. troops control of northern Peleliu and thus isolate the Japanese in their dwindling and hard-pressed pocket in the Umurbrogols.

Unlike Generals Geiger and Smith, who daily dropped in unexpectedly at regimental and battalion command posts "to see how things are going," Rupertus rarely ventured from division headquarters. The division commander, however, had a surprisingly different viewpoint as H-Hour approached for the assault on Ngesebus Island.

In retrospect, Rupertus's change of mind can be questioned as foolhardy and without purpose, another example of his often baffling actions from beginning to end of Operation Stalemate. He decided not only to witness the attack personally but to make a party of it. According to Frank Hough's official chronicle of the campaign:

"Because it promised to provide a good show, high officers from the various elements, including the transports, command ships, and fire support vessels, were invited to view it from a vantage point which provided safety and even a certain amount of comfort. They were not disappointed."

Apparently no one had given consideration to the potential for disaster if a random, lucky Japanese artillery shell or "ashcan" mortar had fallen in their midst. The possibility certainly existed, because Japanese defenses on Ngesebus were known to include at least two large naval guns, several 75-millimeter artillery pieces, and numerous mortar emplacements.

Ngesebus was 700 yards from Peleliu and could be assaulted in two ways. One was for the attack to cross a narrow coral causeway in file, a route obviously out of the question, since the exposed troops would be slaughtered piecemeal as they moved out.

The other and workable option, Harris and Walt decided, was to land a single tank-supported battalion—with three assault companies abreast—across a 100-yard-wide reef approximately a mile long, and establish a beachhead.

"It was D-Day all over again," commented Admiral Oldendorf, one of General Rupertus's group of observers.

Marines clambering aboard the first wave of amtracs agreed. "I wonder if we'll get another battle star for this landing?" one man asked a buddy.

H-Hour was 9:00 A.M., September 28, the fourteenth day of the invasion.

Precisely at 8:00 the battleship *Mississippi* and the cruisers *Denver* and *Columbus* opened fire from point-blank range. For the next forty minutes they unloaded a saturation softening-up bombardment on the generally flat island and an inland ridge. The 100-foot cave-pocked elevation was the only terrain that even slightly resembled Peleliu's torturous high ground.

Twenty minutes before H-Hour, the naval shelling lifted and the Corsairs of Cowboy Stout's VMF-114 took over. Anxious troops were crammed shoulder to shoulder on some thirty landing craft waiting for the signal to cross the reef. They cheered, waved, and raised clenched fists in jubilation at what they saw.

Private First Class Gene Sledge, whose K Company was involved in the action, remembered the sights and sounds of the tumultuous scene.

"The huge naval shells rumbled like freight cars as they arched overhead, clearly visible, and exploded in giant, thunderous blasts," he wrote, "and our Marine pilots outdid themselves.

"Never during the war did I see fighter pilots take such risks by not pulling out of their dives until the very last instant. But, expert pilots that they were, they gave the beach a brutal pounding without mishap to plane or pilot. We talked about their spectacular flying even after the battle ended."

Major John Gustafson's 3d Battalion of the 5th Marines was the attack force. Thirteen amphibious Sherman tanks—each mounting a 75-millimeter cannon and twin .50-caliber machine guns—were first in line. Their mission was to lay down cover for the four following lines of troop-carrying amtracs that hit the beach at three-minute intervals.

The assault wave jumped off at 9:05 A.M. and was across the reef six minutes later. By 9:30, all attack units—troops, tanks, and support weapons—were ashore. "From that point on," the 1st Division's battle diary recorded, "infantry and armor performed with a ruthless efficiency unequaled in any previous Pacific operation."

Lew Walt, the overall on-the-spot commander of the operation, was more prosaic, albeit most laudatory, in his analysis of the assault and capture of Ngesebus. The no-nonsense, battle-savvy colonel wrote in his action report:

> The landing was highly successful. Some fifty of the enemy were killed or captured in the pillboxes on the beach without having so much as a chance to fire a shot at our approaching waves.
>
> The fighter planes did a remarkable job of strafing the beach up to the time our leading wave was 30 yards from the water line. A Japanese officer captured in the beach positions stated that the strafing was the most terrifying experience he had been through and that they had been allowed no opportunity to defend the shore.
>
> Major Gustafson and the officers under his command used excellent tactics and made maximum use of supporting arms.

The 3d Battalion CO later elaborated, writing:

> It should be emphasized that with the terrain most suitable for an infantry-tank attack, with both elements coordinating perfectly, the operation was *made to appear* easy. The tanks should get a great deal of credit, but, on the other hand, the tank commanders later said they never experienced such coordination from the infantry.

Gustafson's "made to appear" phrase was a precise and bitter reflection of Walt's view, especially in light of subsequent statements by General Rupertus. The division commander told news correspondents and upper-echelon brass that he was pleased with the success of the operation, but described enemy opposition in such belittling words as "light," "slight," and "meager."

If the resistance on Ngesebus is compared to the massive

and costly Japanese resistance on D-Day and the extreme difficulties and heavy losses sustained in the continuing assault
in the Umurbrogols, there was an obvious element of truth in
Rupertus's observation. The inescapable fact, however, was
that Ngesebus was defended by 500 well-led enemy troops,
nearly all of them in caves and strongly prepared positions.

Somewhat surprisingly, the official Marine Corps monograph contradicts Rupertus's characterization. The 209-page
document states:

"It was hardly 'light' opposition for a single battalion already
badly depleted. The truth is that a skillful adaptation of tactics
and weapons to terrain, plus unusually fine teamwork, caused
a potentially difficult situation to be carried through so quickly
and effectively. . . ."

As in all battles, some ground troops invariably are lucky
enough to find the going easier, and less dangerous and costly,
than others. Ngesebus was no different, as Gene Sledge and K
Company quickly realized.

The amtrac carrying the Alabama youth and his comrades
landed without opposition as the thunder of naval bombardment and air strikes cleared the way. But as they scrambled
from the protection of the armor and reached the airstrip's
edge, the situation changed radically. A Nambu light machine
gun opened up forcing them to lunge for cover. That signaled
the start of a violent firefight with an undetermined number of
Japanese entrenched in a bunker on a nearby ridge and in
several sniper pits in the area.

"A buddy and I huddled behind a coral rock as the machine-
gun slugs ripped viciously overhead," Sledge said. "He was on
my right. Because the rock was so small, we pressed shoulder
to shoulder, hugging it for protection. Suddenly there was a
sickening crack like someone snapping a large stick." It was a
shot from a bypassed sniper.

"My friend screamed, 'Oh God, I'm hit!' and lurched over on
to his right side. He grabbed his left elbow, groaning and grim-
macing with pain as he thrashed around kicking up dust. I
dragged him around to the other side of the rock as the Nambu
bullets whizzed overhead."

Sledge yelled for a corpsman and, almost simultaneously,
saw two Marines approaching. He pointed toward the source
of the Nambu fire and the men quickly hailed a tank advancing
from the beach. Just as a stretcher team arrived to carry
Sledge's wounded buddy to safety, the two Marines reap-

peared waving as one shouted, "We got the bastard, he ain't gonna shoot nobody else."

But the fierce mêlée was far from over. Nambu fire and hand grenades still were coming from Japanese inside the bunker.

Sledge and two comrades, John Redifer and Vincent Santos, somehow made their way to the top of the fortification and began dropping grenades through an open ventilator shaft. Some of the missives exploded with a muffled deadly sound, but the Japanese threw others out of a ground-level aperture before they could detonate.

Corporal R. V. Burgin ordered the three Marines from the bunker's roof with a shout: "Let's get the hell outta here and get a tank to help knock the damned thing out." When the armed amtrac arrived, it fired three 75-millimeter shells into the bunker.

Then, in Sledge's words, "someone remarked that if the fragments hadn't killed those inside, the concussion surely had. But before the dust even settled, I saw a Japanese soldier appear at the blasted opening. He was grim determination personified as he drew back his arm to throw a grenade at us.

"My carbine was already up. When he appeared, I lined up my sights on his chest and began squeezing off shots. As the first bullet hit him, his face contorted in agony. His knees buckled. The grenade slipped from his grasp. All the men near me, including the amtrac machine gunner, had seen him and began firing. The soldier collapsed in the fusilade, and the grenade went off at his feet. Even in the midst of these fast-moving events, I looked down at my carbine with sober reflection.

"I had just killed a man at close range. That I had seen clearly the pain on his face when my bullets hit him came as a jolt. It suddenly made the war a very personal affair. The expression on the man's face filled me with shame and then disgust for the war and all the misery it was causing.

"My combat experience thus far made me realize that such sentiments for an enemy soldier were the maudlin meditations of a fool. Look at me, a member of the 5th Marine Regiment—one of the oldest, finest, and toughest regiments in the Marine Corps—feeling ashamed because I had shot a damned foe before he could throw a grenade at me! I felt like a fool and was thankful my buddies couldn't read my thoughts."

Major Gustafson's men had overrun most of Ngesebus by sundown, and the island was declared secure at 5:00 the next afternoon. It was a few minutes more than thirty hours after the first wave of Marines swarmed ashore.

To say that the 3d Battalion of the 5th Marines lost "only" forty-eight troops—fifteen killed and thirty-three wounded—is to demean the devotion to duty and sacrifices made to take the piece of coral. Every man who emerged unhurt considered himself blessed, and each grieved for the loss of comrades, some of whom had been foxhole-sharing buddies since Guadalcanal.

"There ain't no such a thing as 'only a few casualties,' " a weary, bleary-eyed sergeant from I Company said. "Even *one* man hit is a helluva price to pay, 'specially when ya think the guy could be yourself or your best friend."

The importance Colonel Nakagawa placed on Ngesebus was evident. He had garrisoned it with elite troops, mostly veterans of the Kwantung Army's conquest of North China, and he expected it to hold out much longer than it did—and to kill or maim more Americans than it did.

Beyond doubt, the heavy prelanding naval shelling and the close-in strafing and bombing by VMF-114 were welcome factors in softening up the beaches. But when push came to shove, and the heavy support fire lifted, Ngesebus was like all other battles in the Pacific. The dirty, nitty-gritty, life-or-death job of digging out and subduing the Japanese fell to the infantry, the proudly self-proclaimed "working class" of the Marine Corps.

Marines killed 440 of the defenders and captured twenty-three *after* the landing. The losses were the heaviest inflicted on the Japanese by one battalion, understrength as it was, in any single engagement during the struggle for Peleliu.

By sundown of September 29, D plus fourteen, soldiers from RCT 321's 2d Battalion had crossed the causeway to relieve Gus Gustafson's weary assault force and complete the final mop-up of the supposedly few remaining bypassed enemy positions.

The slightly more than 600 survivors of Companies I, K, and L—they had lost nearly a third of their men since D-Day—waded through the shallow water to the reef and dragged themselves aboard waiting Higgins boats. It was well past dark when they arrived in the area near Ngardololok, inland from Purple Beach on Peleliu's eastern shore, where the remnants of Chesty Puller's 1st Marines were waiting to be evacuated to the division's base camp on Pavuvu.

"We were all beat up and tired as hell," Private First Class Ed Baranyi of Highland Heights, Ohio, recalled forty-five years later. "But it was the best thing I remember about the battle. There was hot chow, the first we had since D-Day, and we bivouacked where we felt we could sleep safe from Nip infiltrators or a surprise mortar and machine-gun attack."

Bucky Harris, Lew Walt, and Gus Gustafson were justifiably proud of what the 5th Marines had accomplished on Ngesebus—but one aspect of the operation was ironically disappointing. The captured airstrip was surfaced with sand so soft that it was useless, a fact that was meaningless to the occupying troops of RCT 321.

Within a week some of the soldiers were living in tents with plywood decks, eating hot food three times daily, watching nightly movies, and taking showers. Sadly, their idyll was destined to be very temporary. Heavy fighting, some of it the most savage and costly of the campaign, was still ahead for General Mueller's Wildcat Division—just as it was for the badly mauled Marines of Bucky Harris's 5th Regiment and Herman Hanneken's 7th.

4

September 30 was D plus fifteen, the third Saturday of the "quickie" invasion predicted by General Rupertus. Shortly after noon he declared that "organized resistance has ended on Ngesebus and all of northern Peleliu has been secured."

The general's announcement, however, was premature. It was, according to a footnote in the official Marine Corps chronology of the battle, "another instance where the terms 'organized resistance' and 'secured' are apt to be deceptive." The document continues: "By the time they [RCT 321's 2d Battalion] finished mopping up this [Ngesebus] area they were convinced that they had been through a major battle."

General Mueller's personal history of the 81st Division views the final sweep in a less dramatic manner, saying simply: "Determined resistance, eventually overcome, was offered by Japanese holding Courtemanche Ridge (the island's only high ground)." No details of the action are given, nor is mention made of the fact that one soldier was killed and three wounded by a booby-trap hand grenade in the three-day operation.

"If northern Peleliu was secured on D plus seventeen, no one bothered to tell the Japs on Radar Hill," Lieutenant Colonel Robert A. Boyd observed later.

With less than 500 men left in his 1st Battalion, 5th Marines, Boyd attacked the well-fortified dome-shaped citadel shortly after 2:00. It rose abruptly to an elevation of nearly 200 feet above the flat jungle and a mangrove swamp, several hundred yards south of Akarakoro Point, and was the dominating high ground of the island's northernmost sector.

In Japanese hands, heavy mortars, rockets, and artillery on Radar Hill could play havoc with the occupation of Ngesebus. The stronghold also was the last major obstacle blocking the climactic drive to surround Colonel Nakagawa's only remaining large concentration of diehard troops entrenched in the countless hidden blockhouses, pillboxes, and caves of the Umurbrogols.

Boyd's men charged two sides of the steep, rocky slopes with everything they had—rifles, bazookas, flamethrowers, demolition charges. It was slow, cautious going as position after position was taken out. The ascent was a curious combination of sometimes savage fighting and virtually no opposition.

"The area was infested with Japanese, many of them in prepared positions where they fought to the death," the 1st Battalion's war diary said of the action. "But surprisingly few of them fought with the skill and determination the Marines had learned to expect from Japanese combat infantrymen. . . . A handful surrendered, but many simply hid, abjectly awaiting death with little effort to defend themselves or kill the attacking Marines. . . ."

By late afternoon, several patrols and a team of telephone wiremen were on the summit, where they took cover behind coral rocks to wait for the other assault troops. Along with Colonel Boyd, they were on the scene within an hour and set up the battalion's forward command post.

Muffled sounds of Japanese moving around in a labyrinth of bypassed caves were audible throughout the night. Otherwise, all was quiet on Radar Hill except for occasional random and ineffective harassing mortar fire and the infrequent clatter of machine guns and hand-grenade explosions coming from an area about 500 yards to the north.

Major Gordon Gayle's 2d Battalion had been there since early morning, engaged in a heated attack to wipe out an estimated 200 hard-fighting enemy troops. Some were holed up in the rubble of what had been a phosphate refinery, the others in caves on a ridge behind it.

Gayle's men had the situation well in hand. But like their 1st Battalion comrades on Radar Hill, they were waiting for dawn before finishing the job. During the night, however, their plans were changed, a move that totally pleased all hands. Instead of mounting new ground attacks, always hard and dangerous work, both battalions were ordered to pull back at daybreak.

The decision was made by Bucky Harris following a post-midnight phone call from Lew Walt at the 5th Marines forward CP, located in a captured Japanese bunker a few hundred yards from Radar Hill.

"Let's bring up some heavy artillery in the morning and let them wind this thing up, once and for all," the regimental commander told his executive officer. Walt later recalled that the order substantiated a post-battle observation by Colonel Selden, the division's chief of staff. "Harris," Selden had said, "used supporting fires more fully and wisely than any of our regimental commanders on Peleliu."

A 155-millimeter "Long Tom" and its crew showed up at dawn, and the big weapon was soon firing in a previously unheard-of way, an unorthodox technique that would prove invaluable in the days immediately to come as the drive to conquer Peleliu reached its climax. Designed to hit pinpointed objectives miles away, the cannon was aimed at targets less than 300 yards from its sandbagged emplacement.

The range was so short that the crew had to take cover from the fragmentation of their own bursts. One shell after another silenced an objective, either on Radar Hill, on the phosphate plant, or in the caves overlooking it.

"Nips could be seen trying to crawl out through the rubble knocked down by the shell bursts," an eyewitness said. "One round set off a munitions cache inside the cave system on Radar Hill which blew through the principal cave mouth in three successive blasts, the last with a large smoke ring."

Shortly after noon the field phone rang in Bucky Harris's command post near Garekoru village. The colonel picked up the receiver and smiled at the welcome news from his second-in-command.

"We've run out of targets," Lew Walt said. "You can tell Rupertus he was right, but maybe a trifle early in his announcement. Peleliu North *is* secure and there's no sign of further resistance, organized or otherwise."

Before long a churning cloud of dust signaled the approach of a hastily assembled convoy of trucks, DUKWs, and amtracs rumbling north on the shell-pocked East Road. They parked, motors still running, near the Long Tom gun emplacement. One by one, the vehicles were loaded with weary Marines.

Some were so exhausted that buddies had to help them. Others smiled wanly to themselves, grateful to be leaving the front alive and unhurt. A few men shuffled like zombies, their faces encrusted with coral grime, and their eyes glazed in an uncomprehending stare.

There was little conversation, no give-and-take banter, as the men of the 1st and 2d Battalions made the bumpy trip to the Ngardololok rest area to bivouac with their previously relieved 3d Battalion comrades.

The officers and men of the 5th Marines had every reason to be proud of what they had accomplished in seizing Ngesebus and giving an honest meaning to the word "secured" by wiping out the last Japanese strongpoints and resistance in northern Peleliu.

However, it was after V-J Day when a few military analysts and historians took time to study closely what actually happened during the "forgotten battle." Only then did Bucky Harris, Lew Walt, and the 5th Marine Regiment receive the tribute they deserved for their unsurpassed contribution to the ultimate victory in the Palaus campaign.

The outfit's assault battalions had driven a wedge across the island on D-Day and were a dominant factor in beating back the enemy's tank-supported counterattack across the airstrip that afternoon. The 5th had then secured the complex of hangars and buildings that became the command headquarters and operational nerve center of the combined ground-air offensive to conquer the island. It had done its share of heavy fighting in the northward push before attacking Ngesebus.

In four and a half days, beginning at H-Hour on Ngesebus, the 5th Marines and its supporting elements had killed 1,572 Japanese troops, taken seventy-two prisoners, and seized or destroyed upward of 300 fortified positions. The cost to the Marines was less than could normally be expected in such sustained combat: eighty-seven killed and 217 wounded.

The strategic importance of Ngesebus's capture and the elimination of Japanese resistance on Peleliu's northern tip cannot be overemphasized. As stated in the monograph of the battle:

"Thereafter the Japanese potential for jeopardizing island security on any considerable scale ceased to exist. The sole object was to make the conquest as costly and time-consuming as possible; to kill for the mere sake of killing, and to pin down U.S. troops against their employment."

With southern Peleliu irretrievably in American hands, the remnants of Colonel Nakagawa's formidable defense system was now confined to a pocket of heavily armed caves and fortifications in the center of the island's fiendish Umurbrogols. It was here that he had planned, long before D-Day, to make his fight-to-the-death final stand.

Thus by October 5, D plus twenty, the invasion had become, in the words of the 1st Division's official account of the campaign, "a battle of attrition—a slow, slugging, yard-by-yard struggle to blast the enemy from his last remaining stronghold in the high ground."

In three weeks of constant assault, the 1st Marine Division had lost 5,044 men—843 killed, 3,845 wounded, and 356 missing. A reasonably accurate tabulation compiled by division intelligence officers listed 9,076 Japanese dead and 140 prisoners, mostly Korean and Okinawan civilian laborers rather than combat troops.

The stage was set for the final phase of Operation Stalemate.

THIRTEEN

The Final Phase

OCTOBER 5, D PLUS TWENTY.

American forces had an unbreakable hold on more than 90 percent of Peleliu. Marine intelligence officers estimated that all but 1,500 Japanese troops had been killed outright or sealed in caves without hope of survival.

Thus, according to "the book" of accepted military theory, achieving final victory should be a relatively simple operation with a minimum of casualties. Sadly, this was not to be the case, for several crucial reasons.

While Colonel Nakagawa's remaining defenders were greatly outnumbered by Marines and soldiers, the island's terrain still was the enemy's most potent ally. The unconquered area was roughly 900 yards long and 400 yards wide—less than half the size of New York's Yankee Stadium and its parking lot. But the Japanese last-stand redoubt was located in what was the absolute worst of all of Peleliu's awful landscape. It was an unsurpassed conglomeration of rocky spines, a contorted mass of decayed coral and scrub undergrowth strewn with rubble, crags, crevices, 200-foot-tall sheer cliffs, and barren, narrow, saw-toothed ridges.

Nakagawa knew every nook and cranny of the area as well as he did the centuries-old garden of his home in Kyoto, Japan's ancient capital and traditional Valhalla of the empire's samurai warriors. He not only had used his knowledge of the terrain to make it as impregnable as any fortress imaginable, but also had carefully held back his most experienced, battle-hardened, highly disciplined troops and trusted officers to stand and die in its last-ditch defenses, a plan he had concocted soon after arriving on Peleliu for the first time.

The southern boundary of the deadly enclave was just

beyond Bloody Nose Ridge, less than a mile north of 1st Division headquarters and the burgeoning airstrip complex of planes and supply stockpiles. Any thought that the objective—it quickly became known and is still remembered as "the Pocket"—was deliberately bypassed is far from fact.

Chesty Puller's 1st Marines repeatedly had tried at heavy cost to overrun the area since D plus two. Captain Pope had earned his Medal of Honor in one of the futile attacks. Even as the final push began, bodies of twelve men from Pope's C Company were still unrecovered; heaps of dungaree-clad decomposed flesh sprawled along the ridge where they had been cut down. Repeated attempts to retrieve the dead had been fruitless, resulting only in more casualties—evidence of the enemy's savage determination to hold every yard of the area.

General Rupertus ordered Colonel Hanneken's 7th Marines to spearhead what the Old Breed of World War I would probably have called "the big push"—the final offensive to take the Pocket and finally end the struggle for Peleliu. The reason for using the 7th was obvious: At the time the regiment was the *only* outfit available to mount the attack.

Colonel Harris's 5th Marines were in reserve at Ngardololok, resting and refitting from the Ngesebus operation and taking out the last stubborn resistance on Radar Hill and around the phosphate plant. Colonel Dark's RCT 321 soldiers were mopping up Ngesebus or otherwise occupied in destroying troublesome bypassed enemy positions along the West Road north of Garekoru village.

In the frantic days to come, however, both regiments were thrown into the struggle and suffered hundreds of new casualties. As Colonel Hanneken and his troops quickly found, the task was too much for one exhausted, battered, half-strength Marine outfit to handle.

Two unexpected developments further complicated the situation. One was the weather, a three-day roaring typhoon that halted the landing of additional ammunition and supplies needed to feed the insatiable appetite of battle.

The other was a bewildering decision by General Rupertus. He ordered the 1st Tank Battalion's remaining dozen Shermans back to Pavuvu in the same convoy with the shot-up 1st Marines. For the rest of the campaign, the only armored support the Americans had came from the Army's 710th Tank Battalion, whose only combat experience was during the two-day action on Angaur. Even General Smith, normally reluctant to criticize anyone, said that sending away the Marine armor so early was "a bad mistake and the tanks were sorely missed when heavy mobile firepower was so important."

The change in weather was welcomed at first. Rainsqualls cooled the blast-furnace temperature, for the first time since D-Day, to a livable 80 degrees and took the parched taste from the mouths of the troops. The succor was short-lived and soon cast a cloud of gray gloom across the island. Dust-encrusted dungarees turned stiff, hard, and heavy as a plaster-of-paris statue. Protecting weapons so they would fire in the downpour was a menacing problem.

Within hours the winds reached hurricane force and whipped up 30 foot waves that crashed along the shoreline. Purple Beach, by now the main seaborne supply artery for the invasion, was especially hard hit. Two LSTs unloading cargo on a pontoon causeway off Orange Beach were driven ashore and heavily damaged.

Peleliu was isolated for the next three days from the offshore fleet of cargo vessels as the turbulent seas made it impossible for landing craft, large or small, to make it to the beachhead. Ammunition shortages developed with frightening speed—bullets for rifles and machine guns, shells for tanks, artillery, and mortars. There were C rations for only four days on the island, and chow was reduced to two soggy servings a day.

The malevolence of nature was understandably something the high command could not plan for in advance. But even after the storm's destructive force had passed and supplies could again be landed, shortages persisted. Remaining stockpiles of everything were meager pending the storm-delayed arrival of additional cargo ships, several days away.

While not desperate, the situation was serious enough for General Geiger to radio an urgent dispatch to CinCPac's newly established forward headquarters on Guam. The message wasted no words of explanation, saying only: "We need supplies of all kinds and we need them now." Admiral Raymond Spruance, Nimitz's soft-spoken "can do" right hand, was in command. His reaction was customary: immediate and effective.

Within hours the first transport planes of an airlift, unprecedented in size in the Pacific, were loaded and en route to Peleliu, some 600 miles away. In all, seventy-five Marine Curtiss Commandos and Navy Douglas Skytrains were used in the emergency supply operation, many making numerous flights.

In addition to several tons of ammunition, manifests showed the delivery of 42,000 cardboard cartons of "ten-in-one" rations, each container with enough food to provide a meal for ten men. Much-needed fresh clothing was included: 1,000 sets of dungarees, 5,000 pairs of socks, and 1,000 pairs of shoes.

The weather and supply shortages temporarily slowed the tempo of the fighting and made it more difficult. But there was no halt in the determined American struggle to eliminate the Pocket. Nor in the fanaticism of the Japanese to hold it.

2

Many things about the Pocket were deceptive, at least to a cursory observer. "In broad daylight one could stand at the mouth of Horseshoe Valley," Frank Hough wrote, "and study at leisure the precipitous slopes and sheer cliffs that were its walls. It was eerie. You could almost physically feel the weightless presence of hundreds of hostile eyes watching you. Yet there was no sign of the enemy: no movement, no shots; only a lonely silence."

Small patrols of Marines occasionally moved around with impunity. But violence erupted whenever they unwarily approached a strategic outpost or enough troops ventured into the area to provide an exposed and profitable target. Then a fury of fire of all kinds—small arms, machine guns, mortars, artillery—rained down in a deadly cascade from countless well-hidden caves.

There were just two routes to approach the Pocket. Both were well guarded and extremely hazardous.

One was a narrow rubble-strewn road from the southeast that crossed an open causeway into Horseshoe Valley. It could be used with difficulty by infantry-supporting tanks and LVTs mounting 75-millimeter cannon and twin .50 caliber machine guns.

The other attack route was over a chain of sheer cliffs and steep ridges that formed the northern barrier, obstacles that could be overcome only by men on foot with weapons they could carry. Approaching the Pocket merely meant, Marines were quick to discover, that their major problems were still ahead. Once inside the vaguely defined perimeter, the troops were ensnared in what was virtually a monstrous trap—and the only way to escape was to wipe out the enemy.

The east wall was a knavish combination of two connected, almost perpendicular coral heights. Marines called them Walt Ridge and Boyd Ridge, for Lieutenant Colonels Lew Walt and Bob Boyd, who had led earlier futile and costly attempts by the 5th Marines battalions to overrun them.

The parallel buttress, some 1,200 feet to the west, was dominated in the center by the China Wall. The 200-yard-long, 200-foot-tall cliff was flanked at each end by the foreboding Five Sisters and Five Brothers, barren, grotesque stalagmites that were battered but suffered little real damage from hundreds of rounds of naval and artillery shells and countless bombing and strafing attacks from VMF-114's Corsairs.

Baldy Ridge was the Pocket's northern bastion, not a solitary strongpoint but the hub of dozens of steep, heavily armed hills and deep fortified crevices. While the approach across the causeway from the south was unobstructed by perilously close high ground, it was within easy range of artillery and mortars from enemy positions. Any heavy movement of attacking armor or troops touched off fast and furious fire from three directions.

The fundamental, awesome, costly difficulty that confronted the Americans in eliminating the Pocket was basic. Despite the overwhelming United States superiority in *overall* firepower—naval shelling, artillery, air strikes, tanks, armored LVTs—the action was fought largely on terms dictated by the Japanese, which prolonged the campaign and added to the toll of killed and wounded Americans.

Months after the battle, a joint Army-Navy team of intelligence officers from CinCPac headquarters conducted a survey of the area. They found that nearly a third of all the fortified caves on Peleliu were concentrated in the Pocket, a killing ground that was approximately six or seven city blocks long and three or four wide.

The caves varied in size and firepower. Some held only two or three Japanese; others were deceptively large with small openings. Colonel Nakagawa's original headquarters was an example, as Marines discovered after he abandoned it, apparently on D plus four, and moved to a deep hole in one of the Five Brothers.

The mouth was hidden in a cluster of boulders and was so narrow that only one man at a time could enter or leave. The cave had several levels, including one with a balcony where the enemy commander could observe the activities of his staff working in a concrete-reinforced room just below. In the words of a report made by a division intelligence officer who examined the enemy nerve center:

"The installation had most of the comforts and conveniences of permanent quarters: wooden decks, electric lighting, radio and telephone communications equipment, a well-equipped galley, and partitioned quarters with built-in bunks."

On one occasion a ten-man patrol from the 5th Marines' L Company killed six enemy troops defending the heavily armed camouflaged mouth of a cliffside position some 70 yards up the China Wall. The attackers cautiously ventured inside and found an enormous cavern crowded with eighty surprised Japanese. Before the enemy could react, they were annihilated by automatic-weapons fire, grenades, and flamethrowers. Despite a furious firefight to wipe out the troops guarding the entrance, it was one of the rare times when all the Marines emerged unscathed from a head-on assault against a major strongpoint in the Pocket.

Revetments of logs, coral-filled oil drums, and concrete pillboxes protected most of the entrances. Some had heavy steel doors that could be swung open to push out artillery pieces, mortars, or dual-purpose rapid-firing antiaircraft guns cranked down for point-blank fire. The armor pieces unleashed barrages for a very short time, and then were quickly pulled back behind their shields before Marines could spot the source or answer the fire.

Massed artillery fire could keep Japanese pinned inside caves until it lifted. Then the enemy would bolt out and man dug-in positions, ready, willing, and able to fight off assaulting ground troops. Major J. R. Chaisson, a battery commander in the 11th Marines, recalled firing 1,000 rounds from the outfit's 75-millimeter howitzers into a 200-square-yard area on Baldy Ridge:

"It rattled the teeth of the Japs," he said, "but caused only a temporary letup in resistance without appreciably disturbing anything below the foliage and coral topsoil." The main contribution of most artillery, according to ground troops, was to burn away dense scrub growth and expose hidden emplacements. Cannon proved their greatest worth when single guns were manhandled up a ridge to as close as 50 yards from a target. Only point-blank high-explosive fire demolished strongpoints and wiped out their defenders without subjecting assaulting riflemen to fierce opposition.

Sherman tanks, with armor-piercing 75-millimeter cannon rounds and twin .50-caliber machine guns, were a great asset, if they could get in position to help. So were special steel-plated LVT-A amtracs that mounted newly developed flame-throwers—a weapon used in combat for the first time on Peleliu—that could squirt a stream of sizzling, death-dealing fire 200 feet.

Second MAW's Corsair and Hellcat pilots flew treetop-level support missions from sunrise to sunset every day, doing all they could to knock out known or suspected Japanese defenses. Their efforts always provided an aerial circus—a noisy and spectacular display of great daring, fantastic flying skills, and determination to make the going easier for the hard-pressed infantry.

On one occasion, Cowboy Stout's VMF-114 unloaded forty 500-pound bombs in a twenty-minute attack on a 100-square-yard area along Walt Ridge. But like most air strikes in the Pocket, it was distressingly unsuccessful—except to raise the morale of the ground troops.

The infantrymen—Army and Marine—were always grateful for any and all help they could get from whatever source. But they knew that in the ultimate showdown only they, the incon-spicuous foot soldiers, the "working class" in all conflicts since the Stone Age dawn of tribal warfare, would have the dirty job of taking out the last organized resistance and ending the battle.

That was the way victory was achieved in the Pocket.

3

Major E. Hunter Hurst's 3d Battalion of the 7th Marines was the spearhead of the push to take out Colonel Nakagawa's last Gibraltar-like fortifications in the Pocket. Like their regimental comrades and their counterparts in Bucky Harris's 5th Marines, Hurst's men were battle-weary, shot-up, and under-standably apprehensive.

Slightly more than half of the battalion's 958 officers and men who landed on D-Day were still alive and unwounded.

Now the survivors faced another ordeal that was certain, they were convinced, to claim more heavy casualties.

As ordered by General Rupertus, the assault jumped off shortly after 9:00 in the cloudy, humid, stiflingly hot morning of October 5, D plus twenty. A lingering blanket of acrid gray smoke and coral dust covered the area, evidence of a pre-attack twenty-minute shelling by 155-millimeter Long Tom artillery firing from emplacements below the airstrip, and a string of low-level strafing and bombing runs by VMF-114's Corsairs.

Baldy Ridge, the steep-sloped 200-feet-high bastion that formed the Pocket's northern wall, was the objective. Not only was it formidable and threatening in appearance, but the only approach was guarded by three unnamed dome-shaped hills, each about 90 feet tall, and a 100-foot peak identified on maps as Knob Three. All five bristled with hidden heavily armed caves, camouflaged bunkers, and concrete pillboxes.

Major Hurst doubted that his bone-tired troops, determined as they still were, could take Baldy Ridge that day. But when men of K Company stormed the first three hills with surprising ease and very few casualties, he decided to leave a small holding force on them and go to work on Knob Three.

Technical Sergeant Jeremiah O'Leary was with Hurst in his command post, a shallow trench at the renewed attack's jump-off point.

"At 1115 hours, forty-eight men of L Company moved out from their positions to assault Knob Three," the twenty-five-year-old combat correspondent, a reporter for the *Washington Star* when he enlisted, wrote. "Commanded by 230-pound Second Lieutenant James E. Dunn, of Duluth, Minnesota, the platoon encircled the butte by moving through a ravine with 100-foot walls into which a tank had tried unsuccessfully to advance earlier in the morning."

The Marines immediately were hit with heavy small-arms fire from Japanese in another draw that ran perpendicular to the one through which they were attempting to advance. Two of Dunn's men were wounded and carried to the rear as the others scampered on, one and two at a time, to the base of the knob.

There were three ways to scale the hill. One was up a gradual but exposed slope where the platoon was sure to be smothered by all kinds of resistance from the Japanese on Baldy Ridge. The second was an all-out charge up the slopes of the knob itself. Or they could try to reach the objective by moving along a narrow ledge that extended upward from one of the three captured small hills held by the small force from K Company.

"Men went up all three routes," O'Leary reported, "clinging to roots and vines, clambering over rock faults and crevices. When they reached the top they lay on their bellies on the sharp, serrated coral, scattered here and there with scrub brush. All around them was a forest of spines and crags as high, or higher, than the height they occupied. 'Old Baldy' looked down on them menacingly. Uncharted ravines isolated them on all sides from the rest of the Umurbrogol. . . ."

Lieutenant Dunn and forty-five men were atop Knob Three. Surprisingly, only two of the platoon had been wounded during the ascent. The situation took on an ominous look as soon as the Marines began to scout for cover and consolidate their tenuous position.

The first hint of major problems came when a PFC was shot through the head by a single shot from a sniper's spider trap. That apparently was the signal for the Japanese to open up with heavy-machine-gun fire from numerous caves on towering Baldy and in the cliffs of ridges a stone's throw away.

Three Marines were killed instantly as the enemy turned up the heat of the resistance. Everyone scrambled frantically for whatever protection he could find.

"Men were getting hit all over the face of the hill," O'Leary wrote. "The heavy chug-chug-chug of antitank guns was punctuated by the swift rattle of Nambus. Bullets tore Lieutenant Dunn from his grip on the cliffside where he was trying to withdraw his men to safer positions, and he fell to his death on the ravine floor many feet below."

The platoon was trapped in a cunningly devised ambush. The Japanese had deliberately *let* the attackers get to the exposed top of Knob Three with a minimum show of concern. The Marines unwittingly had taken the bait and were paying the price, methodically being annihilated, man by man. The slaughter was a classic example of Colonel Nakagawa's insidious defense plan at work.

"The wounded crawled behind rocks or just lay motionless, bullets hitting them again and again," O'Leary's account said. "Others cried for help and begged their comrades not to leave them behind. Medical corpsmen worked valiantly to drag men to the protection of the ledge. One of them stood up and yelled: 'Take it easy! Bandage each other. Get out a few at a time.' He was shot and killed."

Some wounded men, others still unhurt, dropped their weapons. It was impossible to lower themselves from the hill without using both hands. The descent was tragic for many. Several were riddled by machine-gun fire and plummeted, dead, to the sharp rocks below; others slipped and fell, suffering deep cuts and broken arms and legs when they hit the jagged coral bottom of the ravine.

Captain James V. "Jamo" Shanley, commander of L Company, was heartsick but virtually helpless at what he saw happening to the platoon. He was immensely well liked and highly respected by his men. Not only had Shanley earned the Navy Cross for saving the lives of three of them on Cape Gloucester, but all hands admired his leadership and understanding of the problems and hardships faced by the GIs and junior grade lieutenants. Everyone in L Company affectionately and openly called him Jamo except in the presence of higher-ranking officers.

The only possible immediate relief, the captain realized, had to come from K Company outposts on the three small hills below. If they could somehow dampen the fury of the enemy firestorm, then maybe there was a chance that the remnants of the ambushed platoon could make it to cover and survive.

"For God's sake, smoke up that hill!" he yelled.

The shouted plea was hardly audible over the noise of the Japanese fire, although the distance separating the two Marine positions was little more than that between first and second base of a baseball diamond. The difference was that the ground was not flat and was cluttered with violently reacting Japanese defenses. Shanley also was on the field phone, calling for tank support.

Rifle-fired smoke grenades from K Company shortly began to lay down scattered patches of cover. But there was no sign of the Sherman; it was still bogged down in the impassable coral rocks of the ravine where it had been stalled since the attack jumped off.

"When the billows of phosphorus settled down on the ledge," O'Leary's dispatch said, "some men simply dropped themselves from it, taking the chance of injury from the fall. Five were successful and crawled under the immobile tank for shelter."

Ten men were still trapped on the ledge, including six

wounded, who were being treated by a corpsman and guarded by three unscathed buddies. Higher up on the knob's crest were three more shot-up Marines who the Japanese must have thought were dead. The wounded urged the uninjured to jump.

"You've done all you can for us," one said. "Now get the hell outta here!" The words were uttered with all the force of a command he could muster. And when the next volley of smoke grenades enveloped the ledge, the unwounded did what otherwise might have seemed the ultimate display of cruelty—they rolled their fallen comrades over the edge. They could think of no other way their fallen buddies had even a remote chance to survive.

Five of the casualties tumbled down the slope like formless rag dolls. The other man's feet were tangled in some brush, and he hung headfirst and exposed to enemy fire until one of the unwounded freed him. Arms around each other, they slid to the floor of the ravine, where waiting Marines carried all seven to the battalion aid station.

Then the three men still atop Knob Three tried to come down from the barren deathtrap. One of them was killed the instant he started a dash for the ledge. The other two made it to the base of the hill, but both were hit by machine-gun fire. The less seriously wounded grasped his slumped comrade, supporting him as they attempted to cross the last few yards of an open draw to the beckoning safety of the entrapped tank.

The clattering burst of a Nambu cut them down before they made it.

Captain Shanley watched as bullets continued to rip menacingly just inches over the fallen, now crawling Marines. The sight was more than he could take without doing something about it.

"Although a lieutenant tried to hold him, Jamo darted from cover into the draw," O'Leary's story said. "He swept one of the men into his arms, carried him back to the Sherman, laid him tenderly in the tank's lee, and ran out into the fire-swept open ground again for the other. He didn't reach him."

The wasplike whistling whir of an incoming mortar sent onlookers sprawling for any protection they could find. The shell exploded a few feet from Shanley. Its sizzling steel fragments shredded his body from head to feet. The captain was literally blown to pieces, dead before he knew what hit him.

That was not the end of the tragic episode. Shanley's executive officer and best friend, First Lieutenant Harold Collins, rushed out when he saw the captain fall in the sickening gray smoke and coral debris.

"He had just reached Jamo when the chug-chug of an antitank gun was heard. The lieutenant fell at Jamo's side, dead."

This was the last paragraph of the Marine combat correspondent's dispatch. Because of censorship restrictions, it was weeks before the story was released for publication back home.

By then Peleliu was a forgotten battle, and the account of the epic self-sacrifice and gallantry of Lieutenant Dunn's platoon and of Captain Shanley, the valorous commanding officer of L Company, 3d Battalion, 7th Marines, was largely unnoticed by the press and public.

Shortly after 5:30 in the afternoon of October 5 a runner carried a terse message to Major Hurst's command post. It reported the deaths of Shanley, Collins, and Dunn and said that only eleven men remained of the forty-eight who had mounted the probing attack against Baldy Ridge.

The savage, costly fight had been three hours and fifteen minutes of carnage, and the Marines seemingly were no closer to taking Old Baldy than when the assault began. The impression General Rupertus and his staff got that night from looking at the casualty figures and sector map was that the engagement was entirely one-sided in favor of the Japanese.

The assumption was only partially correct. While Captain Shanley and Lieutenants Dunn and Collins had been killed and just eleven men of the assault platoon were still alive, the attack was not fruitless. More than a dozen strongly fortified Japanese positions had been destroyed and at least a hundred enemy killed, proof that Old Baldy was vulnerable, that the north wall of the Umurbrogol pocket could be taken—perhaps with fewer losses—now that the approach to the summit had been softened up.

The Japanese defenders still on and around Baldy Ridge had a different view of the situation. They knew it was impossible to hold out for more than a few days at most against the overwhelming combined firepower—artillery, naval bombardment, aircraft attacks, and tanks—of the Americans.

But the Japanese also knew that exhausted but determined Marine infantrymen would, in the end, have to finish the job the hard way: by close-in, head-on, man-to-man assault. The enemy was prepared and determined to collect a heavy price for each yard gained until the last shot was fired.

The survivors of K and L Companies, now less than 400 officers and men, were acutely aware of what they faced as they dug in at twilight.

They expected a night of violence, of infiltrators probing for weak spots in the thin Marine perimeter in the ravine below Knob Three, of attacks on lightly manned outposts on the surrounding slopes—or a massed assault to overrun what was left of Hunter Hurst's 3d Battalion, 7th Marines.

Two PFCs, Wesley Phelps and Richard C. Kraus, were among the concerned K Company troops. Both would be dead by dawn the next day, sacrificing their lives to save those of comrades.

Beginning at Guadalcanal and ending at Okinawa, the uncommon bravery of nineteen members of the Old Breed earned the Medal of Honor. Phelps and Kraus were the last of eight to be awarded the nation's highest decoration, albeit posthumously, for their supreme valor on Peleliu.

Private First Class Phelps had been called up for military service in April 1943 by the Selective Service Board of Butler County, Kentucky. The circumstances were unusual, to say the least.

The then nineteen-year-old youth worked 70 acres of land in the hardscrabble rocky hills along the Ohio River. Not only were most farmers given draft deferments at the time, but Phelps was also the sole support of ailing parents; his father was so infirm that he was unable to leave the house.

Nevertheless, Wesley Phelps was drafted. At the induction center in Indianapolis, Indiana, he promptly volunteered for duty in the Marine Corps instead of serving as a soldier or sailor.

Immediately after boot camp, he was shipped overseas as a replacement and joined the 1st Division two weeks before the Cape Gloucester invasion. Despite his lack of combat training, he made it through three of the campaign's sharpest scrimmages and was promoted to PFC with a letter of commendation for "outstanding performance of duty."

Phelps landed in the third wave to hit Orange Beach Two. His closest buddy, Private First Class Paul Moore, was in the same amtrac. Moore came from a 1,000-acre wheat farm in Kansas. He volunteered in 1942, he had told Phelps, "to get the hell away from the damned boredom and hard work, have some fun, and see what the rest of the world was like."

Both were machine gunners and had been in countless desperate situations together since D-Day. But so far, in nearly three weeks of almost constant combat, both had escaped being wounded.

Now Phelps and Private First Class Richard Shipley were in a foxhole, manning a light .30-caliber machine gun on K Company's perimeter. Moore was a few yards away in another machine-gun position with Corporal Robert Grise. All was surprisingly—but suspiciously—quiet along the line until almost midnight, when the Japanese attacked in force.

One by one and in small groups, nearly a hundred enemy troops had moved silently from the ledge below Knob Three to hit the Marine outposts. The Japanese maintained discipline even then, slipping almost without a sound into the Marine lines, not as a screaming banzai horde but in organized units bent on wiping out what was left of K Company.

Suddenly a Japanese parachute flare lit the landscape in an eerie greenish pattern. Some of the enemy opened up with Nambu semiautomatic rifles. Others fired pistols and hurled hand grenades as they lunged toward the startled but alert Marines.

Within seconds the scene was typical of literally hundreds of furious man-on-man mêlées fought on Peleliu. Phelps had emptied his weapon and was reloading it with another belt of ammunition, his last, when he heard the thud and hiss of a grenade.

"Look out, Shipley! Grenade!" he managed to shout, hoping to hurl it from their foxhole before it exploded. But he knew he was too late. Without a second thought, the Kentucky farm boy rolled over on the grenade and took the full force of its blast.

Shipley escaped with a small scratch from a spent fragment, finished reloading their machine gun, and continued the fight. The lifeless body of the man who had saved his life was beside him, sprawled in a puddle of blood.

Moore and Grise, who had witnessed the action, immediately lugged their weapon to the edge of the foxhole. The three men, with two machine guns, beat back repeated attacks until dawn. Phelps and eleven other Marines were killed in the nightlong mêlée.

When reinforcements from L Company came up, they counted fifty-two Japanese dead in the rubble of the ravine where Phelps had given his life to save Shipley and help stave off the enemy attack.

On April 26, 1946, more than nine months after V-J Day, Mrs.

Axel Phelps was presented with her son's posthumous Medal of Honor. The hero's father was still too ill to attend the ceremonies held on the lawn of the Butler County Courthouse at Rosine, Kentucky, a few miles from the Phelps farm.

In the somber but proud gathering of several hundred persons were Paul Moore, Phelps's wheat farmer buddy, by then a civilian, and Corporal Grise. Both had witnessed Phelps's supreme act of valor, and the Marine Corps had assigned Grise to write a news story about the Peleliu episode and the Medal of Honor presentation.

Grise said Phelps had initially been proposed for a posthumous Navy Cross. "However," he wrote, "Major General Pedro A. del Valle, who replaced Major General Rupertus as 1st Division commander after Peleliu, recommended the Medal of Honor as a more fitting decoration for this act of self-sacrifice."

Grise's story ended on a more personal note: "Along with his tearful condolences, Paul Moore gave Mrs. Phelps a check for $150. It was, he said, to pay back money Phelps had loaned him to cover losses in a dice game on Pavuvu."

Private First Class Kraus had been overseas just three months when he landed on Peleliu. The eighteen-year-old Minneapolis youth was an amtrac driver whose landing craft was among those demolished on D-Day.

Since then he had been a stretcher bearer with the 1st Medical Battalion. He had lost count of how many wounded men he had helped bring back, most often under enemy fire, from the front. He only knew he was desperately weary and lucky beyond belief to be still alive and unwounded.

Shortly after daybreak, Kraus volunteered to join three other men to retrieve a seriously hurt K Company corporal who had been hit by machine-gun fire in the previous night's fury in the ravine where Phelps sacrificed his life.

As the team approached the wounded Marine, it came under a fusillade of machine-gun and mortar fire and was forced to lunge for cover. The men were pinned down for nearly half an hour before the Japanese took on another target and things quieted down. They waited a few more minutes before warily moving out again.

The stretcher bearers had advanced only a few yards when one spotted two men, wearing Marine dungarees, approaching them in a running crouch. Something about the way they moved made Kraus suspicious, and he shouted a demand for the day's password.

The answer was pidgin English: "Now you die, stupid Yankees!" The Marines heard the defiant yell just as a hand grenade landed in their midst, less than a foot in front of Kraus.

Like Phelps, Kraus did what all Marines were—and are to this day—expected to do in such a situation. He flung himself on the explosive, took the roaring impact of its blast in his stomach and chest, and was instantly killed. Believing the grenade had annihilated the four "stupid Yankees," both Japanese vanished in the burned-over undergrowth.

Mrs. Edwin Olsen, Kraus's mother, was presented her son's posthumous Medal of Honor on July 20, 1945. Several hundred saddened but grateful and proud Minneapolis residents attended the ceremonies held in a downtown park. The last paragraph of the citation, signed by President Truman, expressed the thoughts of comrades Kraus had hardly the time to get to know in his three months with the Old Breed:

> . . . By his prompt action and great personal valor in the face of almost certain death, PFC Kraus saved the lives of his three companions, and his loyal spirit of self-sacrifice reflects the highest credit upon himself and the U.S. Naval Service. He gallantly gave his life for his comrades.

4

The assault on Baldy Ridge was the last time Major Hurst's battalion saw action on Peleliu. It was, in fact, the final combat of the campaign for the 7th Marine Regiment.

Colonel Hanneken's 7th Marines, like Chesty Puller's 1st, had shot their wad. "Purely and simply, there were no longer enough men in the outfit to continue the fight," General Smith told a friend, a former Associated Press correspondent, in a long conversation years later.

"Those still on their feet—whether in Johnny Gormley's 1st, Spence Berger's 2d, or Hunt Hurst's 3d Battalion—were beyond mere exhaustion," he said. "They were shot to pieces, beat to a pulp, all of them physically—and many of them mentally—fatigued to where the 'thousand-yard stare' was a common expression on their faces."

The plight of the regiment and the urgent need for pulling it from the lines had been, for several days, a matter of cutting concern to General Geiger. Whenever he broached the subject to General Rupertus, however, the answer was the same:

"Give 'em a little more time," the division commander said in effect, "and they'll take the Pocket and the battle will be over."

Finally—on October 6, D plus twenty-one—Rupertus conceded that the 7th Marines was finished as a regiment capable of further action. He decided to relieve the unit after receiving the message of the previous day's costly and unsuccessful attack on Old Baldy and a detailed staff report on the regiment's casualties.

Of the 3,217 officers and men who landed on D-Day, 1,486 had been killed or wounded. Colonel Selden figured that it amounted to 46.2 percent of its total complement, more than three times the percentage recognized in "the book" as the absolute limit of losses allowable for a regiment to be combat-effective and remain on the lines.

Rupertus's order reached Colonel Hanneken's command post shortly after noon and immediately was relayed to the battalion CPs. No time was lost in getting the welcome news to the companies, platoons, and troops manning isolated outposts.

Within half an hour, battle-weary Marines began arriving—one by one and in small groups—at a designated assembly area near the rubble of Garekoru village, the headquarters of Colonel Dark's Army RCT 321. Aware that a few Japanese snipers still were taking potshots from hidden spider traps on nearby cliffs, they wisely dispersed and found cover wherever they could. And there the depleted remnants of the 7th Marines waited for further orders to move out to wherever they were going.

Two hours passed before there was any indication of their destination.

"Maybe they're waiting till they get hot chow ready and our sacks made up so we can sleep on a full stomach," a bedraggled corporal from Boyd's battalion said.

"No way," his half-dozing buddy answered wearily. "It's the same old routine bullshit of 'hurry up and wait,' and you can bet your draggin' ass that we'll eat C rations, if anything, and we'll sleep in another hole in the ground."

The first sign of movement was a billowing cloud of dust and the roaring sound of an armored amtrac moving north on the West Road toward Garekoru at full speed. Immediately behind were six four-wheel-drive Army trucks, with jeeps, mounting heavy machine guns, interspersed among the troop-carrier vehicles. The convoy was taking no chance of running into an ambush without enough firepower to fight its way through.

"Load up, Marines!" the lead truck driver yelled loud enough to be heard over the din. "This time you ride, courtesy of the United States Army." It was totally unexpected; the men had thought that, as usual, they would have to somehow summon the energy to trudge wherever they went.

A Peleliu version of gridlock developed as Marines clambered aboard the canvas-covered trucks, but the vehicles managed to turn around and head south. The convoy came and went four times before the last men of the 7th Marines were carried to their new bivouac area on Ngarmoked Island, 3 miles away.

There was no hot chow for them that night, only ten-in-one rations. But they did sleep in safety in tents previously used by units of Colonel Dark's RCT 321. More important and supremely welcomed was an official announcement the next morning from Colonel Hanneken.

"Pass the word to all hands," he told his weary battalion commanders, "that it's all over for the 7th Marines on Peleliu. We have orders from division headquarters to go back to Pavuvu as soon as transportation is available."

Two ships appeared offshore three days later—the Navy AKA *Sea Sturgeon* and an old Dutch merchantman, the *Sloterdyke*—and the survivors of the 7th Marine Regiment embarked. As Peleliu disappeared below the horizon, a dour sergeant from Hunter Hurst's battalion, a survivor of the attack on Baldy Ridge, stood at the stern of the *Sea Sturgeon*.

He looked back at the island and mumbled: "Nothing Atoll."

5

The 7th's departure left just one Marine infantry regiment on Peleliu—Colonel Harris's 5th—to carry on the struggle to eliminate the Pocket in the Umurbrogols. Even as Hurst's battalion was, man by man, moving from its positions at the base of Baldy, Major Gordon Gayle's 2d Battalion of the 5th had moved through its lines to again assault the ridge.

The push began with close-up heavy artillery bombardment and was supported by three cannon-firing tanks, weapons unavailable until bulldozer-equipped Shermans had carved approaches through the narrow coral ravines at the foot of the steep slopes. In a classic example of the Bucky Harris dictum of being lavish with firepower and stingy with the lives of his men, Baldy Ridge was seized by Gayle's battalion in seventy-two hours of often intense fighting. Marine casualties were less than two dozen, mostly wounded, while enemy killed were estimated at four times that number.

Major "Gus" Gustafson's 3d Battalion probed for soft spots in a maze of hard-to-spot coral-and-concrete bunkers in the rocky, burned-over flat ground some 300 yards south of Baldy. Some maps identified the area as Wildcat Bowl; on others it was called Horseshoe Valley. The 3d's ultimate objective, once it penetrated these defenses, was to silence a steady torrent of opposition from the Five Brothers.

But there were no soft spots, as K Company found when it mounted its attack. With heavy support from the 11th Regiment's 75-millimeter howitzers, Army tanks, and flamethrowing Marine amtracs, the assault got to a shallow pond within 100 yards of the Brothers on D plus twenty-one—but no further. The Marines were forced to pull back by a constant stream of machine-gun crossfire, mortars, and shelling from antitank guns that honeycombed the sheer cliffs.

L Company ran into a similar firestorm when it tried to gain a foothold on the virtually perpendicular sides of the China Wall. A curtain of fire ripped into the assault units from all directions, and casualties were moderately heavy in both companies, which already were at half strength. The struggle, however, was not without substantial and irreplaceable losses to the enemy; an estimated seventy-five Japanese were killed by Marine riflemen, and at least a dozen caves were seared and blasted shut by the flame-spouting LVTs and Sherman tanks with an unknown number of defenders trapped inside.

In three days of heavy action, Lieutenant Colonel Robert Boyd's 1st Battalion fought its way to the crests of Walt Ridge and Boyd Ridge, the latter named for the outfit's CO after an earlier unsuccessful attack. This gave the Marines control of the Pocket's east wall and tightened the pressure on Colonel Nakagawa's surrounded, constantly diminishing, but still stoutly resisting enclave.

Since the 7th Marines were pulled from the lines, Bucky Harris's regiment had been the only Americans attacking the Japanese in the Umurbrogols. Advances were unspectacular but methodically logical, a deliberate and determined scenario to take as few additional casualties as possible in hacking away at the last enemy strongpoints in Peleliu's most brutal terrain.

This was the way Colonel Harris believed, as he had from the beginning, the battle should be fought, how it could best and most quickly be won with minimum losses. Besides, he reasoned, what more could be expected from a battered regiment that had been almost constantly in head-on combat for three weeks?

Nonetheless, General Rupertus was on the phone several times a day to Harris's or Lew Walt's command post, prodding, ordering, demanding the impossible:

"Hurry it up! Goddammit, don't let the advance stall! Don't lose your momentum!"

There was just one reason for the calls: Rupertus's overriding desire to wipe out the Pocket and end organized Japanese resistance before turning Peleliu over to the Army. All he wanted the 81st Division to do was to mop up and occupy the island after the 1st Division had conquered it.

To the 5th Marines, however, the fighting was nothing short of an endless nightmare. They were too tired, too saddened by the loss of buddies, too sick of their own stench, too hot and hungry and thirsty to notice that the battle *was* coming to an end.

They were simply too exhausted and unobserving to recognize that the Japanese troops they now spotted were always fewer in numbers, and often reacted more slowly and with less fury and firepower when attacked. But as far as the Marines on the front were concerned, the enemy's fanatical determination and willingness to die for the Emperor and the warrior's ancient code of *bushido* were largely unabated, although their physical plight was even worse than that of the Americans.

Most of Colonel Nakagawa's troops had lived since D-Day deep underground, where the air they breathed was always stale and short of oxygen. They were constantly thirsty, without drinking water except that collected in makeshift cisterns or murky puddles during rainsqualls. A single bowl of rice and a few chunks of dried fish made up the daily per-man food ration.

Nerves were frayed from the incessant thunderclap explosions of naval shelling, artillery bombardment, and air attacks. The heat and humidity of the caves magnified the sickening stench of feces, untreated and festering wounds, decomposing

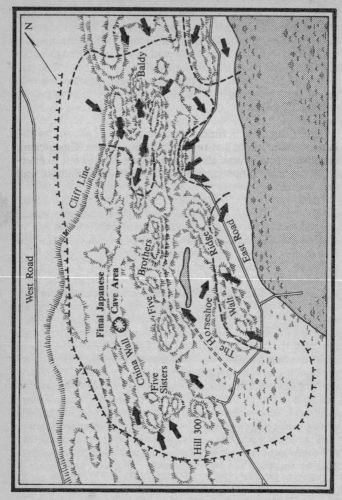

MARINE ADVANCES IN THE UMURBROGOL

bodies of the dead, and decaying garbage, all a feasting ground for hordes of maggots and huge blowflies. The smoke of cordite and gunpowder added to the haze of the caves, dimly lighted in most cases by sputtering kerosene miner's lamps.

"I still hate the little yellow bastards, but they were damned good fighters," remembered sixty-eight-year-old Herbert L. Mizner, of Chicago. "I don't know how they took it, but they did and still fought like sonsabitches all the way." Mizner was an eighteen-year-old PFC flamethrower operator in the 5th Marines, and had counted fifty-two Japanese bodies in a blasted and incinerated multimouthed tunnel near the base of one of the Five Brothers.

By October 10, D plus twenty-five, the 5th Marines' push to eliminate the baneful Umurbrogol pocket had become for the Japanese a matter of last-resort guerrilla warfare. The ancient, simplistic strategy was all Colonel Nagakawa had left to effectively use his meager remaining weapons, ammunition, and manpower to wound and kill Americans.

Except by personally moving from position to position in the dead of night, the Japanese commander had no way to communicate with his scattered units. Telephone lines between the outposts and his headquarters had long been wiped out. He was, however, still in contact with General Inoue on Koror by both radio and an underwater cable.

Nakagawa had anticipated the destruction of his communications network on Peleliu and had purposely made last-stand orders part of his defense plan. Specifically, he had authorized individual unit commanders—regardless of rank or size of the force they led—to act independently to hold out as long as possible. Their ultimate duty, the colonel emphasized, was to inflict as much damage as they could on the Americans before the last Japanese was killed, fulfilling his duty to the Emperor and the Land of the Rising Sun.

Infiltrators, individuals and in small teams, were—along with snipers—the major source of trouble and casualties for the Americans during the rest of the battle. There were, however, several fairly large-scale and costly skirmishes yet to come—as the Army's 81st Division found to its dismay when it relieved the Old Breed to mop up and occupy the island.

6

Except for the continuing struggle in the Pocket, off-duty personnel now moved almost anywhere on Peleliu without much fear for their safety. Many got more than they bargained for.

"Noncombatant souvenir hunters and the morbidly curious

were turning out in such hordes as to constitute nearly as great a nuisance as Japanese infiltrators," Frank Hough recalled. "They were mainly aviation ground personnel, sailors ashore from the transports, and rear-echelon service troops with nothing better to do. In most cases, it was their first operation and they had apparently been given a big snow job that all Japs died with a jeweled sword in hand."

Major Joseph E. Buckley, the 7th Marines' weapons company CO, had his own way of handling the intrusive visitors. Any men found in his area without good reason were promptly seized, handed rifles, and placed in the line. "If they behaved themselves, I notified their unit commanders of their whereabouts and present employment," he said. "Otherwise, I didn't bother, and they were carried as AWOL as long as I chose to hold them."

Frontline Marines didn't much care whether the "rear-echelon Charlies" got themselves hurt; they considered the whole lot stupid to be where the fighting was going on when they didn't have to be. The trouble was that every time someone was wounded on the nonsensical expeditions, weary and battered men had to face enemy fire to rescue him.

Many Marines who had no business being forward weren't motivated by curiosity or the farfetched possibility of finding a samurai sword. Scores left the safety of rear areas with the sole purpose of lending a hand to embattled comrades, voluntarily bringing up supplies, serving as stretcher bearers, helping man depleted outposts.

Said Lieutenant Colonel Spencer Berger, CO of the 7th Marines' 2d Battalion: "I believe the unknown officers and men from the Marine air units, who slipped away from the airstrip and plagued me daily to let them help 'in some way,' deserve real credit for what they did."

Robert Sherrod, the *Time* magazine correspondent, who landed with Marine assault waves in more invasions than any other newsman in the Pacific, echoed Berger's observation in his definitive *History of Marine Corps Aviation in World War II*:

"Many of the men of the 2d Marine Air Wing served as volunteer stretcher bearers, gravediggers, and doing other jobs not usually associated with airplanes. Considering their complete lack of training for such duties and status as noncombatant troops, the aviation men performed exceedingly well on the lines and at a heavy cost. Ten were killed and sixty-seven wounded in ground action on Peleliu."

Colonel Joseph F. Hankins was one of the rear-echelon men who wanted to do more than official duties called for. His desire to lend a hand at the front cost him his life; he was the highest-ranking Marine killed on Peleliu.

Hankins had been a battalion commander in the 1st Marines on Cape Gloucester. In recognition of courage and leadership, he was promoted and named division provost marshal as well as the commanding officer of the headquarters battalion. Both jobs demanded more routine paperwork than anything else, an assignment far from the liking of a man who thought he could better serve the Marine Corps by leading troops in combat.

The colonel had become increasingly concerned by serious problems encountered by men in his military police company who were helping maintain security on the West Road, the main artery used by trucks and amtracs to supply the 5th Marines' assault in the Umurbrogols and the Army's RCT 321 bivouacked on Ngesebus Island. For several days the MPs had been harassed by sniper fire from nearby ridges and hit at night by small bands of infiltrators.

Without informing Rupertus or any of the general's aides, Hankins told his executive officer that he wanted personally to see what could be done about the situation. An expert sharp-shooter who had been a member of many elite peacetime Marine Corps competitive rifle teams, he armed himself with an M-1 and a set of binoculars.

"I'm gonna do a little countersnipin' on my own," he said, jumping into a jeep that sped away in a cloud of coral dust.

Less than five minutes later, Hankins rounded a bend in the road and found what could hardly be imagined on Peleliu: a traffic jam. An amtrac somehow had become immobilized and was sideways across the entire width of the narrow road. Several trucks were jammed, bumper to bumper, right behind it.

Under normal circumstances, the mess could be cleared up in minutes—but this was a deadly different matter. The vehicles were caught in searing but spasmodic crossfire from Japanese snipers scattered behind boulders on a steep nearby hill. Drivers and crews had abandoned the LVT and trucks, scrambling for the protection of the reverse slope of the road. The sight of a colonel climbing calmly from his jeep sparked the men to emerge as fast as they could from their cover.

Standing upright in the middle of the road, Hankins shouted commands and gave hand signals that, between pings of sniper fire, unsnarled the roadblock. The convoy had just started to move again, northward toward Garekoru Village, when a single shot from the ridge ripped through Hankins's chest.

He was killed instantly. From then until the last American left Peleliu, the scene of the tragic episode was called Dead Man's Curve.

7

On D plus twenty-two, the day the 5th Marines began its final drive against the Pocket, Admiral Nimitz reached the conclusion that the battle for Peleliu was over. His decision was based on a careful analysis of the latest intelligence reports flown by courier plane from the *Mount McKinley* and an exchange of radio messages with Admiral Halsey.

The communiqué issued by CinCPac detailed developments in the Palaus and, without specifically saying so, left little doubt that victory had been achieved. Back home the drawn-out, costly struggle again made the front pages of newspapers everywhere. The Associated Press story by Rembert James said:

PEARL HARBOR, Oct. 7 (AP)—American marines and soldiers invading the Palaus have killed 12,211 Japanese and captured 224 since Sept. 15, the day of the landings, the Navy announced today in a communiqué.

On the airbase island of Peleliu, 11,083 Japanese have been slain and 214 captured but the enemy still was clinging to one pocket of resistance on Umurbrogol Mountain. Today's communiqué said American tanks and artillery had reduced the pocket yesterday.

It was announced earlier (on Oct. 5) that 1,012 American fighting men had been killed, 6,100 wounded, and 280 missing since the beginning of military operations in the Palaus. Up to that time, CinCPac said, 11,043 Japanese were killed and 187 taken prisoner.

Today's announcement made no mention of additional American casualties since the Oct. 5 communiqué.

However, a high-ranking Navy censor ventured the analysis that "based on the number of known Japanese dead, you can logically assume that the enemy garrison has been virtually, if not totally, wiped out. . . ."

Anyone with a knowledge of the number of combat troops that composed a Marine division, had he read between the lines of the communiqué, could have sensed what the high command on Peleliu acutely knew: The 1st Marine Division had been shot to pieces and could no longer be considered a functioning assault force.

Nonetheless, and despite Admiral Nimitz's communiqué, the fighting to eliminate the Pocket continued. The 5th Marines chipped away at the enemy around Baldy Ridge and among the cliffs of the China Wall and the Five Brothers. A few more enemy positions were overrun each day, but the push had run out of steam. Like the 1st and 7th Marines, Bucky Harris's regiment no longer had enough men to sustain the advance, but casualties still increased.

"It becomes a common occurrence," an Old Breed veteran observed, "that in a long campaign men tend to get more careless about taking cover the longer the fight goes on, partly because of fatigue and partly, I suppose, due to a 'don't give a damn' feeling of futility and fatalism."

He was an Old China Hand who knew what he was talking about, a much-decorated and three-times-wounded infantry captain who had risen through the ranks to command companies on Guadalcanal and Cape Gloucester before hitting Peleliu with the 5th Marines. In all, 358 company captains and lieutenants were killed during the Palaus campaign. He wasn't among them, although he was again badly shot up and given a medical discharge after he recovered from the amputation of his left leg.

General Geiger spent most of his time aboard the *Mount McKinley* during the final days of the battle. There was little he could do whenever he went ashore except to urge General Rupertus to relieve the 5th Marines and replace them with fully manned, tank-supported, fresh Army regimental combat teams already on Peleliu, Ngesebus, and Angaur.

Each time Geiger mentioned the subject, Rupertus passed it off, saying, in effect, that he was still in command of the 1st Marine Division and that what he did with the 5th Regiment was his decision, and his alone, to make. Geiger held his patience but realized, albeit reluctantly, that there were just two means to resolve their impasse.

One way was to relieve Rupertus of his command, something that had never been done to a Marine Corps general in combat and an action that would create monumental turmoil at headquarters in Washington. The other was to issue a direct order to Rupertus to relieve the 5th Marines with soldiers from General Mueller's 81st Wildcat Division.

To relieve Rupertus would most certainly end his military career. To go over his head by ordering the Army to replace the 5th Marines would, at the very least, seriously jeopardize the division commander's future in the Marine Corps.

More to the point, in Geiger's mind, was his belief that the battle was all but over; that it was only a matter of days, perhaps even hours, until the last Japanese strongholds were overrun in the Pocket and the island entirely in American hands. To impose his rank, to exercise his command status, at this stage of the conflict would accomplish very little and, he suspected, might be considered by some fellow generals as a misguided and even spiteful action rather than a sound strategic decision.

The contretemps became moot on October 12, D plus twenty-seven. At 9:30 A.M. a radio-teletyped dispatch from CinCPac's Pearl Harbor headquarters was received by Admiral Wilkinson, the invasion's overall on-the-spot commander, on the *Mount McKinley*. The message directed Wilkinson to return immediately to Hawaii for a pressing new assignment.

His designated replacement was Admiral Fort, who had been responsible for getting the invasion armada to Peleliu and landing the Marines on the beachhead. Fort's first order of business, CinCPac said, was "to declare the 'Assault Phase' of the campaign finished, and to forthwith direct the relief of the 1stMarDiv by 81st Army Division units to assume final mop-up and occupation duties on Peleliu and adjacent captured islands."

The newly appointed commander of Operation Stalemate went ashore and personally relayed his instructions to Generals Geiger and Rupertus at 1st Division headquarters. Both received the news without a visible display of emotion.

"I'm glad it's finally over and the Marines can leave," one of Geiger's aides later quoted the general as saying. He said Rupertus's comment was three words: "I am too."

Two days later, Colonel Dark's RCT 321 began taking over the 5th Marines' positions on Baldy Ridge, among the cliffs of the China Wall, and in the crevices and perpendicular slopes of the Five Brothers and adjacent Five Sisters.

The 5th's casualties were less, but only slightly, than those of the 1st and 7th Marines. The regiment's H-Hour roster was 3,117 officers and men. In twenty-nine days, it had lost 1,309, killed and wounded—42 percent of the landing force. Pre-invasion questions about Bucky Harris's ability to lead troops in combat had proved groundless. Not only was his regiment in combat longer than its counterparts, but it had taken nearly twice the area captured by Puller's and Hanneken's troops.

Army trucks and DUKWs carried the 5th's survivors to RCT 321's former bivouac area near the demolished phosphate plant and on Ngesebus Island to wait for ships to take them back to Pavuvu. The stay was pleasant beyond all expectations. The Marines found that the Dogfaces had left behind plywood-decked tents, running showers, an equipped cookhouse, and a screen for nightly movies.

Colonel Venable's RCT 322 was ordered from Angaur to garrison Ngarmoked Island and southern Peleliu's flat ground, an area that included block-square supply dumps, the constantly busy airstrip and newly constructed hangars, and the island's headquarters and communications complex.

LSTs boated the regiment and its equipment to the pontoon causeway dock on Orange Beach Two. Within days the soldiers had settled into the routine of an occupying force that expected to be on the island for an extended time. To make the stay as comfortable and civilized as possible, they erected a miniature tent city complete with showers, screened mess hall, and a combination quartermaster–PX–post office in a Quonset hut—and, of course, a movie screen. Below it was a small stage built in expectation of the arrival of a USO entertainment troupe in the not too distant future.

It was not all fun and games, however, for the Army troops. Intermittent rumbles of artillery shells exploding in the Umurbrogols meant that the "Wildcats" of RCT 322 were still at work against isolated hold-out Japanese positions in the Pocket, something that would continue for five more weeks.

The few hundred Marines of the 5th Regiment were unconcerned about what was happening at the front. They were just resting and killing time in boredom and anticipation, waiting for ships so they could leave behind what was, to all hands, the horrible nightmare of what had happened to them and their comrades on a man-killing hellhole island.

8

October 30, 1944.

D-Day plus thirty-five.

At high noon, without a ceremony of any kind, General Geiger passed Marine Corps command of Peleliu and the conquered islands of the Palaus to Army General Mueller and his 81st Division. It was five weeks, almost to the hour, since the first waves of Marine assault troops had gained a toehold on Peleliu's beaches in what their commanding general had confidently—but so mistakenly—predicted would be a "quickie" operation.

Generals Geiger and Rupertus, along with their top aides, left the island shortly after 2:00, bound for Guadalcanal. They traveled first-class. Admiral Halsey had sent a converted four-engined B-24 Liberator bomber for the seven-hour flight.

General Smith was left behind as the liaison with General Mueller during the transition from Marine to Army command. Rupertus maintained his bewildering aloof and disrespectful attitude toward the assistant division commander to the end. When Smith asked by name for two staff officers to assist in working with the Army, Rupertus sarcastically refused.

Colonel Harold Deakin was one of the men Smith requested. He later recalled the awkward farewell: ". . . And I guess you want a jeep driver, and you've already got a cook," Deakin quoted Rupertus as saying. Deakin continued, "Finally it was decided that Major George Gober, an assistant G-4, would stay, but that was all. . . ."

There is no record of Rupertus and Smith ever meeting again.

But Oliver P. Smith, always the epitome of a conscientious and competent officer and head-to-toe gentleman, did the job in a manner that would do credit to a fully staffed liaison team. It was almost a month before he and Gober left for Pavuvu with the last contingent of the Old Breed, an artillery battalion.

They made the ten-day voyage on a crowded, uncomfortable 6-knot "rust-bucket" Liberty ship. None of the passengers minded. To them, leaving Peleliu in one piece, by whatever means, was all that mattered.

The survivors of the 5th Marines felt the same way when, in the overcast dawn of the day the Army took over on Peleliu, the AKA transport *Sea Runner* and two converted troop-carrying destroyers appeared beyond the reef off Ngesebus Island. The troops were rested enough by then to form up and march in units to amtracs waiting to carry them to the Pavuvu-bound ships.

Major Gordon Gayle, CO of the regiment's 2d Battalion, recalled the embarkation on a tragic note. Of the 953 men who were with the outfit on D-Day, 60 percent of its officers and 40 percent of the troops had been killed or wounded. That, in itself, was more than sufficient cause for Gayle's deep feelings of remorse and regret. But the bitter, harsh, unforgettable memory of the losses was made even more intolerable by the fact that one of his men was the last combat Marine to die on Peleliu.

". . . While our troops were lined up waiting to get into the boats, one man had this .45 'Tommy' gun and he had his hand on the handle," Gayle told Marine Corps historian Benis Frank years later. "Somebody bumped his elbow and he pushed the bolt forward or pushed it back. When it slammed forward, it shot the man in front of him right through the belly and killed him." A white cross—with the accidentally slain Marine's name stenciled on it—marked the last grave dug in Peleliu's cemetery for the Old Breed.

Sorrowfully, however, there would be 110 more for soldiers killed between then and November 27, when the Wildcats silenced the last enemy strongpoint in the Pocket. The 81st Division paid a high price for its bitter exposure to battle. On Angaur, Ngesebus, and Peleliu, it suffered 2,433 casualties— 370 killed, 2,041 wounded, and twenty-two missing.

Colonel Nakagawa kept his vow to fight to the inevitable end. At 10:30 in the morning of November 25, seventy-two days after the invasion began, he sent his final message to General Inoue on Babelthuap: "All is over on Peleliu." Nothing was left of the 13,000-plus garrison, he said, but fifty unwounded and seventy wounded troops with a few hand grenades and twenty rounds of ammunition for each man.

Major General Murai was still at the colonel's side. His role in the fighting remains a mystery, but he apparently was satisfied to leave command of Peleliu's defense to his subordinate, and to offer advice only when it was requested. Whatever the arrangement, it had worked exceedingly well.

The generals and admirals who commanded the operation— and especially the regimental and battalion officers who led the infantry, both Marines and Army—concurred in the assessment. The disposition of Japanese troops, the choice of defensive positions, the fury and cost of the battle were all the proof they needed that they had run up against—and ultimately defeated—an extremely well-disciplined enemy force commanded by a leader of unquestionable military talent and personal bravery.

Nakagawa burned the beribboned ceremonial colors of his longtime command, the 2d Infantry Regiment of the Kwantung Army, immediately after sending the battle's-end message to Inoue. Then he and Murai disemboweled themselves with ancient jeweled daggers in the traditional last rites of Japanese samurai warriors. When Imperial General Headquarters in Tokyo learned of their deaths, War Minister General Hideki Tojo posthumously promoted both to lieutenant generals.

Fewer than 300 of Peleliu's garrison survived the campaign, mostly noncombatant navy construction battalion workers or forced-labor Koreans. But the Japanese who did the fighting were, in the words of a sergeant from the 7th Marines, "a tough bunch of little bastards and it took a helluva lot to kill 'em." He spoke not only of the courage and determination of his 1st Division comrades, but of the great amount of American firepower and ammunition needed to achieve victory.

Records and statistics compiled by the anonymous and always busy CinCPac "bean counters" recorded that, on an average, 1,589.5 rounds of heavy and light ammunition were used to kill *one* Japanese on Peleliu. For reasons impossible to comprehend, at least by a layman, the figures were further broken down. They showed that to kill *each* of the 13,000-plus Japanese on the island, it took:

> 1,331 rounds of .30-caliber bullets
> 152 rounds of .45-caliber bullets
> 69 rounds of .50-caliber bullets
> 9 rounds of 60-millimeter mortar shells
> 5 rounds of 81-millimeter mortar shells
> 1 rifle grenade
> 10 hand grenades
> 6 rounds of 75-millimeter howitzer shells
> 5 rounds of 105-millimeter cannon shells
> 1 ½ rounds of 155-millimeter Long Tom shells

Firepower, awesome as it was, was not what won the battle. If anyone were to read everything written about the Palaus campaign, it is safe to wager that nothing could be found to surpass the words of the 1st Marine Division's Presidential Unit Citation to capsulize what happened during the epic struggle. It reads:

> For extraordinary heroism in action against enemy Japanese forces at Peleliu and Ngesebus from September 15 to 29, 1944. Landing over a treacherous coral reef against hostile mortar and artillery fire, the 1st Marine Division, Reinforced, seized a narrow, heavily mined beachhead and advanced foot by foot in the face of relentless enfilade fire through rain forests and mangrove swamps toward the airstrip, the key to the enemy defenses of the southern Palaus.
>
> Opposed all the way by thoroughly disciplined, veteran Japanese troops heavily entrenched in caves and in reinforced concrete pillboxes which honeycombed the high ground throughout the island, the officers and men of the Division fought with undiminished spirit and courage despite heavy losses, exhausting heat and difficult terrain, seizing and holding a highly strategic air and land base for future operations in the Western Pacific.
>
> By their individual acts of heroism, their aggressiveness and fortitude, the men of the 1st Marine Division upheld the highest traditions of the United States Naval Service.

But two all-important facts must be added to put the battle in tragic historical focus. One is the haunting, terrible total of 6,336 1st Marine Division casualties: 1,121 killed, 5,142 wounded, and seventy-three missing. The other is an even greater tragedy: Peleliu should have been bypassed and never invaded at all.

Epilogue

THE OLD BREED RETURNED TO PAVUVU IN SMALL CONVOYS of two or three transports at a time escorted by destroyers. As the ships moved slowly from the gentle swells of the Pacific into the tranquil waters of Macquitti Bay, rails were lined with troops.

"I guess I'm glad to see Pavuvu this time," one man said.

From shipboard, the island appeared much the same as when the invasion armada embarked for the Palaus nearly two months earlier. But with the exception of the never-ending nuisance of the rats and land crabs, the base camp had undergone massive and mostly welcome changes.

The first created dumbfounded surprise.

As the Marines landed on the beach, they saw something they could hardly believe. Six petite, smiling young *American women,* wearing gray jumpsuits emblazoned with Red Cross insignia, were busy handing out chilled grapefruit juice in paper cups.

That was just the beginning.

While the division was gone, Seabees and Marine engineers had bulldozed and scraped a network of hard-packed coral roads throughout the encampment. They also had rolled a 15-acre parade ground along the road that still served as the island's airstrip. No longer would companies and platoons become entangled with each other in training exercises, close-order drills, or unit inspections.

The biggest improvement, the greatest boost to morale, for the troops was in basic, civilized living conditions. Most of the leaky cast-off Army tents had been replaced with plywood-decked new ones with electric lights. Every company area had showers; many had a laundry. Chow was plentiful, but usually something concocted by cooks from gallon cans of traditional GI rations.

Each battalion had a screened mess hall that was lighted at night—a club of a sort where men played cards, wrote letters, and held gabfests, read nearly current magazines, comic books, and specially printed Armed Forces paperback editions of best-selling books.

Beer rations were issued regularly: three cans per man per week. A well-stocked post exchange was in operation. There was plenty of equipment for organized sports competition: baseball, volleyball, basketball, boxing—even horseshoe tournaments. Swimming in Macquitti Bay and sunbathing on its beaches was a daily routine for many men. And, of course, there were always nightly movies. And even Coca-Cola and, occasionally, ice cream.

For the first couple of weeks, before the division settled into a regimen of refitting and training for its next campaign, most men spent much time visiting other outfits, searching out old friends. They shared whatever was available: a cigar, cigarettes, candy bar, chewing gum—a can of beer or a canteen of "jungle juice" if the hosts had any.

"You really didn't know," a corporal told George McMillan, "until you got back to Pavuvu how many of your buddies were gone. Up to then, you kept telling yourself that they'd turn up on Pavuvu, that they had been only slightly wounded, or not wounded at all, just lost from their units. But at Pavuvu, you couldn't fool yourself any longer."

Scattered throughout the division were 4,493 enlisted men and fifty-seven officers, replacements who had arrived during the battle. A few hundred were Old Salts—some veterans of the 1st Division—who had recovered from wounds received in earlier campaigns and been sent overseas again to face the enemy in future combat. Most of the troops, however, were teenage draftees who had volunteered for Marine Corps duty.

Among the "new" officers was Major General Pedro Augusto del Valle, Rupertus's successor as commanding general of the 1st Marine Division. In reality, it was a homecoming for the Puerto Rico–born general. He was a graduate of the United States Naval Academy and had commanded Marine detachments on battleships and cruisers during World War I.

When General Vandegrift received orders to activate the pre–Pearl Harbor "force in readiness" that became the 1st

Division, then Colonel del Valle was one of the first of the cadre of officers he personally selected to help do the job.

On Guadalcanal he commanded the 11th Marines, the outfit's artillery regiment, and was awarded the Legion of Merit by Admiral Halsey "for bravery, outstanding performance of duty, and high combat morale characteristic of units under his command." When Vandegrift was named Marine Corps Commandant, del Valle went to Quantico, and served as the president of the Marine Corps Equipment Board.

Now, on Pavuvu, the troops credited the new division commander for the changes just as they blamed Rupertus for the awful conditions before the Palaus campaign. The same feeling, according to Colonel Deakin, was prevalent among all levels of the division's officers and enlisted men.

". . . The spirit of the division changed overnight," he said in a tape-recorded postwar interview for Marine Corps archives. "What a wonderful leader! The best leader in the Marine Corps I ever saw. . . . Pedro had no superior, and, in my opinion, should have been Commandant when he retired. . . ."

Despite the obvious improvements that made Pavuvu a tidy, efficient, well-organized base camp, the rejuvenated division still faced monumental problems in preparing for its next operation. The island's 600 acres of *usable* terrain was far too little for the large-scale combat training and maneuvers required.

General del Valle's solution was to ship battalions, one or two at a time, 60 miles to Guadalcanal, where there was enough ground for the units—including tanks and artillery—to work themselves into a state of combat readiness. When the time came to embark for the invasion of Okinawa, the 1st Marine Division was again the "Fighting First" and ready, as Deakin said, "to whip its weight in wild tigers."

The division's infantry regiment COs on Peleliu—Colonels Puller, Harris, and Hanneken—were relieved of their commands and flown to the States for long-overdue leave. They all expected to again be leading assault troops in the ultimate invasion of Japan, but the dropping of atomic bombs on Hiroshima and Nagasaki—and V-J Day—intervened.

Colonels Deakin and Honsowetz went to Okinawa as General del Valle's G-1 and G-3 staff officers. They were largely responsible for ramrodding the planning and execution of the division's impressive contribution to victory in the final ground battle of World War II.

Six of Peleliu's infantry battalion COs—Spencer Berger, John

Gustafson, Hunter Hurst, Stephen Sabol, Austin Shofner, and John Gormley—were back in action on Okinawa. They commanded the same battalions they had led in the Palaus—but just a few of their subordinate company captains and lieutenant platoon leaders were veterans. Like the very young draftee troops, most were youthful replacements—"ninety-day wonders"—fresh from three months in officer training school at Quantico, Virginia.

Brigadier General Louis R. Jones succeeded O. P. Smith as the division's assistant commander. General Rupertus's much-abused foil was given a new billet with General Buckner for Okinawa. In his customary unobtrusive, soft-spoken, extremely competent manner, he was Marine deputy chief of staff to the commanding general of the United States Tenth Army—the 250,000-man force that included the 1st Division and the newly formed 6th Marine Division that conquered Okinawa.

Shortly after General Rupertus arrived on Guadalcanal with General Geiger, he received special dispatch orders to report to USMC headquarters in Washington. He arrived on October 29, and met privately with his old friend Archie Vandegrift.

There is no record of what was said during Rupertus's meeting with the Commandant. However, one of Vandegrift's top aides said years later that the general told him that he "had no choice but to relieve Rupertus of his command and expressed his sorrowful displeasure and regrets over the way things turned out, and the heavy losses suffered, in the Palaus."

Vandegrift's memoirs contains a brief paragraph that also indicates that the session was not entirely pleasant:

". . . I knew the Peleliu campaign must nearly have exhausted him. He, of course, did not see things my way, but he quieted down a little when I gave him command of the Marine Corps Schools heretofore run under my direct aegis."

The tight-knit inner circle of USMC headquarters brass was quick to recognize the new assignment for what it actually was. To them, it was without doubt a "tombstone billet" signaling the demise of Bill Rupertus's thirty-one-year climb up the ladder of command, an ascent he had hoped would end with his wearing the coveted four stars of Marine Corps Commandant.

Vandegrift further soothed the feelings of the man considered by many high-ranking officers his protégé and hand-picked successor by awarding him the Distinguished Service Medal. The citation read in part:

Landing his powerful fighting 1st Division against the fierce opposition of constant artillery and mortar fire from the high ground and devastating fire from firmly entrenched pillboxes and concealed positions adjacent to the beaches, Major General Rupertus gallantly maneuvered his command over swamps, rocky and precipitous slopes and through dense jungle growth in a relentless advance, resolutely withstanding repeated counterattacks to annihilate a fanatically determined enemy or drive him back into a defensive pocket in the centrally located hills in the center of the island. . . .

Most of the Old Breed had a far different view of Rupertus's contribution to Peleliu's conquest. To more than a few of them, especially combat officers, the award of the medal was a totally unwarranted but understandable action by Vandegrift— final formal recognition of his friendship with Rupertus during the more than three decades they served together in the Marine Corps.

Vandegrift's assessment in his biography that "the Peleliu campaign must nearly have exhausted" Rupertus need not have used the qualifying word "nearly." "Completely exhausted" would have been more accurate, it soon became apparent, to describe the general's condition.

During a routine checkup at the Bethesda Naval Hospital in suburban Washington, doctors discovered that Rupertus had developed a serious, life-threatening heart problem.

On March 24, 1945, the general attended a small dinner party at Washington's Navy Yard. The host was Colonel R. C. Kilmartin, commander of the base's Marine barracks and a close friend since the 1920s, when they served together in Central America.

Shortly after 9:30, without uttering a sound, Rupertus fell to the floor on the doorstep to his quarters. A Navy doctor on duty at the nearby dispensary was on the scene within minutes. There was nothing he could do except say that Rupertus was dead, stricken with a massive coronary attack. He was fifty-five years old.

Two days later, at 11:00 A.M., William Harrison Rupertus, Major General, United States Marine Corps, was buried with full military honors in the Arlington National Cemetery. The gravesite was on a gentle hillside slope facing USMC headquarters a few hundred yards away. Colonel Kilmartin was the only pallbearer not a general. The others were General Vandegrift, two major generals, and two brigadiers.

Ten thousand miles away in the South Pacific, on Pavuvu and Guadalcanal, advance elements of the 1st Marine Division were embarking for the battle of Okinawa. The assault waves hit the beaches shortly after 9:00 on sun-drenched Easter Sunday morning, April 1, 1945. It was the fourth invasion for the Old Breed, a record unsurpassed by any division, Marine or Army, during World War II.

After V-J Day, most Marine divisions were broken up into smaller units occupying Japan and other captured islands—but not the 1st. Under a new commander, Major General DeWitt Peck, it was sent en masse to North China to make sure that the half-million-strong force of heavily armed Japanese still there accepted the terms of the empire's unconditional surrender.

2

Nearly 2,000 Marines and Seabees were still on Peleliu a year after the last battered units of the 1st Division had returned to Pavuvu and, rejuvenated, had invaded Okinawa.

Almost until V-J Day, the Corsairs and Hellcats of General "Nuts" Moore's 2d MAW flew daily harassing strafing and bombing missions against Japanese installations on Koror, Babelthuap, and small atolls in the northern Palaus. During the arduous weeks it took General Mueller's 81st Division to mop up the Umurbrogol pocket, Marine fliers provided low-level air support for virtually every attack.

" 'Another milk run,' " Robert Sherrod wrote, "was the characterization generally given by Marine pilots to the strikes from Peleliu on the other Palaus."

But some of the targets—particularly those on Koror and Babelthuap—were heavily armed with antiaircraft batteries manned by expert gun crews. Although none of the sorties were challenged by enemy interceptor aircraft, eighteen Marine airmen were shot down by ack-ack fire from late October to early June.

One of those killed was the redoubtable Major Robert "Cowboy" Stout, VMF-114's flamboyant, fearless, extremely competent, highly respected commanding officer.

Colonel Caleb Bailey's long-range, heavily armed, radar-equipped F6F-3N Hellcats swept thousands of miles in night and day patrols, scouting for Japanese naval vessels, surface or submarines, which might have intentions to hit the American bastion with hit-and-run shelling. None did.

The Navy's 33d Construction Battalion of 1,052 enlisted men and twenty-eight officers worked from sunrise to sunset. With their steam shovels, bulldozers, road rollers, and heavy cranes, they lengthened and paved the airstrip's runways, built permanent hangars, erected giant 50,000-gallon steel fuel tanks, and constructed dozens of buildings and other facilities needed for large-scale offensive naval and air operations against the Japanese.

The field was big enough, when it was finished, to handle giant 3,000-mile-range B-29 bombers just beginning to arrive in the Pacific to commence the devastating destruction of Japan's major cities and war production centers. Well-protected submarine docks were constructed inside the reef at the southern tip of Ngarmoked Island. Kossol Passage was swept clear of mines to provide suitable anchorages for battleships, cruisers, and aircraft carriers.

None of the facilities were ever used for their intended purposes. Simply put, the war had bypassed Peleliu before it was conquered.

Even on D-Day, when General MacArthur's forces landed unopposed on Morotai, it was obvious that his campaign to retake the Philippines was not threatened in the least by Japanese air or naval power from the Palaus.

The Marianas—Saipan, Tinian, and Guam—had been captured in late June and early July by the 2d, 3d, and 4th Marine Divisions in an unexpectedly swift but costly campaign. Between them, the three islands already had operational runways for all the B-29 Superforts that would ever be used to defeat the Japanese Empire.

The uncontested seizure of Ulithi and Yap gave Admiral Halsey's mighty rampaging Third Fleet a gigantic, well-protected anchorage while he and Admiral Nimitz decided where to strike next. Ulithi also became the staging area for the armadas of troop transports and naval support—battlewagons, carriers, cruisers, destroyers, and other ships—needed to invade and conquer Iwo Jima and Okinawa.

Halsey's task forces occasionally steamed past within sight of Peleliu, coming or going from increasingly massive and devastating raids on targets in the Philippines or Formosa. But they never used the anchorage in Kossol Passage, nor did any of the ships stop to take on fuel from the mammoth storage tanks or replenish storage lockers with shells from the acres of ammunition dumps.

By late December, only twenty-four Corsairs were stationed on the airstrip, all the air power CinCPac thought necessary to ward off highly improbable enemy naval or air strikes on Peleliu. The other planes, pilots, and ground crewmen had long since left to support General MacArthur's campaign in the Philippines, to join naval task forces for carrier duty, or to operate from bases in the Marianas.

The prime objective of Peleliu's invasion thus became little more than a backwater noncombatant airfield, a superbly equipped refueling and rest stop for transports flying between the Mariana Islands and the Philippines. A few planes, including long-range bombers and carrier fighters, used it for emergency landings.

"Sometimes we were very busy," Colonel Karl Day, commanding officer of MAB (Marine Air Base) Peleliu, said. "But we were always able to handle the job without sweat." He recalled that on January 11–12, 1945, 176 transient aircraft stayed overnight. The facilities were more than adequate to house and feed their 1,240 passengers and flight crewmen.

When Jackson L. Hendricks, a retired sixty-four-year-old sergeant from Bucky Harris's 5th Marines, somehow came across the figures in 1988, he wryly commented: "Maybe Peleliu was of some use after all—but only as a gas station and motel that cost a helluva lot of deaths and misery."

In early February 1945, all but one battalion of General Mueller's 81st Army Division left Peleliu for a base camp near Noumea on New Caledonia. The some 900 troops who remained were considered a more than adequate garrison force for the island.

On V-J Day, the Wildcats were on Leyte in the Philippines training for the invasion of Japan. With the only battle they would ever fight behind them, they were ordered on September 25 to occupation duty on the Japanese island of Honshu.

General Mueller served as Military Governor, and commander of the 81st, until the division was deactivated on January 20, 1946. The general was ordered to Tokyo, where he became General MacArthur's chief of staff—an exalted and extremely influential post he filled with distinction.

3

Peleliu.

Early November 1990.

The island appears unchanged from the way it looked before the pre-invasion bombardment blasted and burned away the dense primeval foliage that concealed the man-killing terrain of Bloody Nose Ridge and the rest of the Umurbrogols.

Except for the 3,000-yard-long main runway of the airstrip, there are few conspicuous reminders of what happened in the fall of 1944. Most other landmarks have long since been smothered by a lush tropical growth so thick that even natives must know where to look to find relics of the battle.

More than anything else, Peleliu today is what it was before World War II—a reef-fringed backwater atoll with little value or use to anyone except its some 500 inhabitants.

All of them live in three villages along the northern beaches across the narrow split of water from Ngesebus. Most of the houses are two- or three-room shacks built from coral blocks or metal siding salvaged from abandoned wartime Quonset huts. Only a few have electricity or running water.

There is no public school system, but a Seventh-Day Adventist church serves as a classroom for preteenagers and is also the center of the island's religious and community activities. Some half a dozen general stores sell canned food, American-style blue jeans and multicolored cotton dresses, hardware, and other needs.

Just as the battle for Peleliu is either forgotten or unknown by most Americans, so are the island's present long-standing and perplexing official ties with the United States.

On August 15, 1947, exactly two years after V-J Day, the United Nations General Assembly unanimously approved a mandate making all of the Palaus a U.S. Trust Territory. The UN action also gave the same status to some 2,000 other Central and Western Pacific islands and atolls seized and occupied by the Japanese during the war.

All of the Trust Territories except the Palaus have set their own separate governmental courses in elections supervised by the UN. Some are the world's smallest democracies, tiny clusters of sparsely populated atolls with less land than a medium-size American city. Others voted to return hereditary tribal chieftains to their thrones, perfectly content to live in centuries-old fiefdoms.

Guam, the largest of the Central Pacific islands and a U.S. possession since the Spanish-American War, opted to resume and strengthen its close ties with Uncle Sam. It became a United States Commonwealth Territory with its own constitution, an elected governor and legislature, and a nonvoting representative in Congress back in Washington.

The Palaus, however, are a different matter—a complex, expensive, unresolved matter that has caused official Washington constant concern and cost American taxpayers more than $500 million during the past four decades.

Most of the money has been used to finance a multitude of ill-advised and notably unsuccessful "development programs" to make what is now officially known as the Republic of Belau into a remote showcase of democracy and free enterprise.

The end of the largess is not in sight. In early 1990, the United States added another $12 million to the bill—cash that accounts for 95 percent of Belau's annual official budget. Since nearly half of the islands' employed citizens are on the government payroll, the significance of the continuing grants is obvious to the archipelago's prosperity, if not its economic survival.

Except for income from Japanese tourists and illegally grown and exported marijuana—most of it from Peleliu—the U.S. Treasury alone keeps the Republic of Belau from bankruptcy.

America's foreign and military policies are deeply enmeshed in the current state of affairs. In some ways, it is an amazing flashback to the consideration that supposedly prompted Marine Lieutenant Colonel "Pete" Ellis's mysterious and fatal mission to the Palaus in 1923: the strategic military importance of the island chain to the defense of U.S. interests in the Far East.

The Department of Defense has proclaimed the privilege of "eminent domain" to build and maintain huge naval, air, and ground force installations on the islands. Military planners want them as "fall-back positions" in the event that the Philippine government refuses to renew leases on massive American bases on Luzon when an existing treaty expires in 1992.

Angaur would become a mammoth Air Force complex with facilities capable of handling hundreds of aircraft—giant transports, supersonic jet fighters, and 6,000-mile-range nuclear-armed bombers. The Navy would use Koror as a port for atomic-powered Trident submarines armed with nuclear missiles and torpedoes. Half of Babelthuap would become a permanent 15,000-acre training camp and base for Marine and Army ground troops.

Congress has approved an annual payment of $428,000 for a fifteen-year renewable lease on the land, and the Pentagon has set aside several billion dollars to build the facilities. But the proposal is in limbo, rejected seven times since 1983 by the Republic of Belau's House of Delegates and confirmed in each instance by a referendum of the islands' some 3,500 eligible voters.

The core of the thorny issue is the demand of the Belauans for what they call a "Compact of Free Association." It denies the United States authority to base atomic-powered naval vessels at Koror or maintain stockpiles of nuclear weapons anywhere in the islands.

"No one on Capitol Hill seems interested in refashioning the compact to make it more attractive to Belau," Allen Stayman, staff director of the Senate committee that oversees relations with the islands, said in March 1990. "The issue is buried in Congress. Instead, action will be limited to haggling over continuing aid grants."

Officials on Koror, the self-styled republic's capital, estimate that approximately a hundred American citizens live there. Virtually all are listed as "technical advisers" employed by federal agencies in Washington.

A handful of others work for Air Micronesia, a subsidiary of Continental Airlines, which provides daily island-hopping Boeing 727 jetliner service to and from Guam with stops at Yap and Ulithi. Flights usually are well booked with Japanese tourists or honeymooners—some 25,000 annually—who use "Air Mike" for the final leg of journeys from Tokyo via Guam.

Despite the inability to resolve the Compact of Free Association muddle, the United States maintains—to use the term in a manner verging on the ludicrous—"an active military presence in the islands." It consists of thirteen members of a Navy construction battalion.

"The Seabees work all over the place," said a Washington spokesman for the Naval Facilities Engineering Command. "They help build schools and hospitals, dig drainage ditches and water-catching cisterns—community service projects like that." The officer added that he had "no information about any plans to construct U.S. military bases."

And so what about Peleliu?

Pentagon planners consider it, and the ancient airstrip now half covered with scrub jungle, without an iota of military value in their strategic scenario.

Belauan government officials largely ignore the island as useless for anything except the illegal growth and clandestine export of high-grade marijuana.

Agents of the U.S. Drug Enforcement Administration on Guam contend that several high-ranking authorities on Koror not only are fully aware of what is going on, but also are deeply involved in it. According to DEA's investigators, they share in the multimillion-dollar annual income from smuggling the exotic weed by long-range executive-type jets from Peleliu's main runway to the Hawaiian Islands and points as distant as California.

The highest echelons of the Republic of Belau, according to American officials, also have been linked to massive cases of fraud. One involved a $40 million scheme with a now-bankrupt British combine to build an electric generating plant on Koror, a facility capable of producing more than twice the amount of power that would be necessary even if the United States went ahead with uncertain future plans for a giant military complex on the islands.

There is no documented trace of what happened to $20 million of the total funds, all borrowed from New York banks and Wall Street financial interests. But the entire loan was guaranteed by the U.S. Treasury and State Department, and ultimately was paid with American taxpayer dollars. A lengthy probe by the Federal Bureau of Investigation was inconclusive. However, Haruo Remelik, the republic's first president who was elected in 1985, reputedly received a multimillion-dollar payoff for his role in the affair. He was assassinated a few months later and was succeeded by Lazarus Salil, a close friend and political ally. Salil was in office for less than a year when he committed suicide. He left no note explaining his action, but FBI sources believe Salil also was involved in the fraud.

4

The last bodies of Americans killed during the invasion were exhumed from the cemetery in 1952 and returned to the States for final burial in plots selected by their next of kin. Some chose Arlington National Cemetery; others selected closer sites to be near the graves of their dead.

Once or twice a year, a small Japanese cruise ship anchors for a few days at what now is called Camp Beck Dock on Ngarmoked Island. The passengers are widows and families of Colonel Nakagawa's troops on pilgrimages to honor their dead in services held at a small Shinto shrine at the base of Bloody Nose Ridge.

Very few Americans ever visit Peleliu.

The island is both unknown and without historic significance to most who were born or became adults after V-J Day. Thus they have no interest in making the trip, not even those who live on Koror.

To most elderly survivors of the Old Breed, it is either too far away from home or an awful place of horrible memories they would like to forget but can't.

Everett Shults, the retired master sergeant from Lakeview, Washington, is one of a handful of 1st Division veterans who has returned to Peleliu. He has made the long voyage twice, both times with the dedicated intention of seeing that a suitable memorial was erected to honor the Marines whose lives were sacrificed in the conquest of the island.

Colonel Russell Honsowetz, now retired in Alamo, California, is another who went back for the same reason. With the help of other 1st Division Old Hands, the mission was accomplished.

"We chose a location on a low cliff on the southern end of Bloody Nose Ridge," Honsowetz recalled. The site was one of sad recollections for the man who had earned the Navy Cross as the commanding officer of the 2d Battalion, 1st Marines, in repeated and costly assaults on the steep, barren, heavily defended coral bluffs inland from White Beach Two.

The yard-wide, 4-foot-high red granite monument was dedicated on October 7, 1984, by a small contingent of the division's Peleliu veterans, some accompanied by their spouses.

Master Sergeant Shults presided over the brief ceremonies. It was almost forty years to the day after the final push began to eliminate the last pocket of Japanese resistance in the Umurbrogols. Few words were spoken. The memorial's engraved epitaph said in stark simplicity all that was deemed necessary and appropriate:

IN MEMORY OF THE MARINES
WHO GAVE THEIR LIVES IN THE SEIZURE
OF PELELIU AND NGESEBUS ISLAND
FROM THE JAPANESE DURING THE
PERIOD 15TH SEPTEMBER THROUGH
15TH OCTOBER 1944.

Centered above the words is the globe-and-anchor Marine Corps emblem. The diamond-shaped insignia of the 1st Marine Division—a perpendicular red figure 1 with the word "Guadalcanal" emblazoned in white against a coral-blue background of five stars representing the Southern Cross—is engraved on the left corner at the bottom of the tribute.

The Stars and Stripes snap in the constant hot breeze atop a 10-foot flagstaff that crowns the memorial. It can be seen across the island. The Belau-roving Seabees have carved steps up the steep coral cliff and keep the surrounding area clear of encroaching jungle growth.

Only a handful of Americans have visited the monument. It is highly improbable that many more ever will.

What matters most to the survivors of the terrible, needless struggle is the knowledge that the memorial is there, and they will forever remember their buddies who died to achieve victory in the Pacific war's "forgotten battle."

Author's Note

The late Don Whitehead was an Associated Press correspondent who was awarded two Pulitzer Prizes for distinguished frontline combat reporting.

The first was for his graphic coverage of the United States Army's surge across Hitler's Germany in World War II. The other was for a series of brilliant dispatches written while with the 1st Marine Division, surrounded and outnumbered, battling the Chinese at the Chosin Reservoir in the subzero cold of Korea.

Don later became an author of such best-selling books as *The FBI Story*. But except for his on-the-spot reporting of men in combat, he hardly ever wrote a word about war, much less a book.

The last time we met, in the spring of 1973, I asked him why he had never published his recollections of the two historic conflicts. He was silent for what seemed several minutes, probing his psyche for just the right words. Then, in the Southern drawl of his Kentucky hill country origins, he said:

"There's too much to tell and, I'm afraid, too few to listen. Besides, I don't know where I'd be able to stop once I got started."

Don Whitehead's dilemma, alas, became mine in attempting to tell the story of the conquest of Peleliu. The result owes more to what other people did than to my putting words on paper. First, of course, were the people—from privates to generals and admirals—involved in the battle. Their actions, quite naturally, are the basis of the story.

Searching out much of what happened would have been impossible without the selfless interest and assistance of more than a hundred survivors. In personal interviews and lengthy telephone conversations and letters, they provided firsthand recollections and observations of the historic struggle.

Henry Berry eloquently expressed a kaleidoscopic montage of their thoughts in his book *Semper Fi, Mac*:

> Now they remember it all—the bloody beachheads, the jungles, the hilltops they paid so dearly for, the buddies they lost, the amazing courage and shocking foul-ups they saw—in a time and a war when patriotism and tradition weren't things you just talked about. They were things you fought and died for.

Almost every person who was on the island had experiences worthy of inclusion in this chronicle of the battle, and all of their recollections contributed greatly to the eyewitness essence of the final manuscript. Regrettably, the deeds of many people and units cannot be fully told despite their undeniable importance to victory in the Palaus.

The explanation is something that every author must reluctantly face: Any book can cover just so much ground, particularly one about a monumental battle where so much happened to so many men in so many places at the same time.

To my everlasting sorrow, I have come to know personally only a few of the Old Breed who fought on Peleliu. It is highly unlikely, too, that I will ever meet and swap war stories with many more in the future.

One of those I never met is Gordon I. Swanson. He was a twenty-four-year-old first lieutenant on Peleliu. Today he is a professor in the College of Education at the University of Minnesota in St. Paul. He wrote me on October 21, 1987:

> One cannot possibly describe the sense of community which joins a group of men whose destiny is held together by mutual support. A few hours together under fire is the best way to discover some special kinds of leadership and courage. It is still difficult for me to believe how much stamina Marines can display under stress and how much energy is left for compassion at the end of the trek. No single observer saw the whole. If you were able to describe it, nobody would believe it. . . .

There was, I've been told by historian Benis M. Frank, a tradition in the pre–World War I Marine Corps. It originated following the war with Spain in 1898 when a small contingent of Leathernecks, taking heavy casualties, overcame an enemy force three times their number in a savage engagement on Samar Island in the Philippines.

After that, whenever a survivor of the struggle entered a roomful of Marines, someone would invariably jump to attention and loudly proclaim:

"Stand, gentlemen. He served at Samar!"

Those of the Old Breed who were on Peleliu deserve the same tribute. It is beyond my ability to find adequate words to express my gratitude to those who contributed to this book. The least I can do to show my appreciation is to inform readers who they were:

James Anderson, Cameron, Wisconsin; Eric H. Archer, Berkeley, California; Louis J. Bacher, Artesia, New Mexico; Ed Baranyi, Highland Heights, Ohio; B. A. Bell, Canton, Georgia; Jess C. Bowman, Houston, Texas; Clay Boyd, Portland, Oregon; H. P. Church, Oliver Springs, Texas; Donald Clark, Forestville, California; W. A. Coons, Springfield, Oregon; John T. Crim, Jr., Kilgore, Texas; Braswell D. Deen, Jr., Atlanta, Georgia; Koiner Dixie, Lakeland, Florida; D. A. Duffus, New York City; H. J. Dupont, Port Arthur, Texas; Richard Fisher, Bellevue, Washington; Fred K. Fox, Austin, Texas; T. F. Freeman, Palm Springs, California; Carl Fulgenzi, Riveria Beach, Florida.

John R. Green, Mobile, Alabama; Otha L. Grishman, Sequin, Texas; Fred E. Harris, Madisonville, Kentucky; Herbert B. Huffman, New Carlisle, Ohio; John F. Hughes, Ridgewood, New Jersey; Larry Hurst, Pearland, Texas; Joseph R. Lacoy, Concord, New Hampshire; Herbert F. Lehmann, Euclid, Ohio; Paul V. Lewis, Frenchtown, New Jersey; Don MacIvor, Yuba City, California; Nolen Marbrey, Brooksville, Florida; Bill Marston, North Valley Stream, New York; Jack McCombs, Palm Beach Gardens, Florida; C. B. McMullen, Live Oak, Florida; Charles Monrose, New Orleans, Louisiana; W. Paul Moore, Princeton, Kansas; Jeff L. Morgan, Houston, Texas; Michael Mosemak, Jacksonville, North Carolina; Joseph J. Moskalczak, Blakely, Pennsylvania; Richard Mulholland, Chester, New Jersey; Raymond Murray, East Aurora, New York.

Charles M. Nees, Carlisle, Pennsylvania; Charles H. Owen, Lafayette, Georgia; S. W. Phillips, Warwick, Rhode Island; DuWayne A. Philo, San Marcos, California; Albert F. Reutlinger, Louisville, Kentucky; Robert Richeson, Graham, Texas; John B. Rodenhausen, Warrington, Pennsylvania; Larry Sheridan,

Vista, California: W. A. Streick, North Ridge, California; Ben Sussman, Sherman Oaks, California; George R. Sweeney, Holiday, Florida; William A. Taylor, Bassett, Virginia; Thomas C. Teuscher, Havelock, North Carolina; Ray C. Teusher, Ocala, Florida; Lloyd L. Verran, Greenville, Tennessee; George Williams, Wenonah, New Jersey; and Lee Zitko, San Pedro, California.

Two members of the Old Breed wrote memoirs of their experiences on Peleliu.

One was the late George P. Hunt, whose brilliant postwar career in journalism ended with his retirement as managing editor of *Life* magazine.

The other is former Private First Class Eugene B. Sledge. After V-J Day, he returned to his hometown—Mobile, Alabama—where he chose teaching as his life's work. The mortarman on Peleliu recently retired after some three decades of distinguished service as Dr. Sledge, Ph.D, professor of biology at the University of Montevallo.

George Hunt's *Coral Comes High* and Gene Sledge's *With The Old Breed at Peleliu and Okinawa* are recognized as classic works by literary critics and universally acclaimed by World War II Marines for, in the words of one, "telling what life *really* was like and how men died" on the forsaken islands and in the brutal battles of the Pacific.

With their gracious consent, I have used graphic segments of both books to recount meaningful personal accounts of the horrors of Peleliu. My debt to them is beyond measure, not only for the use of their words, but also for providing previously unpublished accounts of incidents that added significantly to a better understanding of the actions of General Rupertus, Colonel Puller, and other officers and men who fought on Peleliu.

The contributions of two of my fellow Marine Corps combat correspondent sergeants, Frederick K. Dashiell and the late George McMillan, must also be acknowledged for their importance in what ultimately became this paean to the men of the 1st Marine Division.

George's incomparable World War II history of the division, *The Old Breed,* was of unique value as an eyewitness source of what made it the fighting force that it was, not only on Peleliu but beginning before Pearl Harbor and ending in North China after V-J Day.

Dashiell, known as Dick to the ever-diminishing ranks of our Pacific war buddies, is now a semiretired journalist in Washington. For more than four decades, he has been acknowledged by his colleagues as one of the most dedicated and respected editors and reporters covering the fast-breaking, often historic news that constantly flows from the nation's capital.

Without Dick's knowledge of where to find elusive answers to troubling questions, without his determined ability to search out and confirm little-known but crucial facts, it would have been difficult indeed to write this book. Whenever I was stumped, I called Dick and he quickly bailed me out. Every author should be so fortunate, but there is only one Frederick K. Dashiell.

There also is a group of men who deserve special mention: the Marine combat photographers who daily risked their lives to take many of the pictures that illustrate this book. Most of them have never before been published, nor—due to an odd Marine Corps policy—have the names of the photographers accompanied their work. WWII cameramen were usually assigned to the intelligence sections of combat units and their pictures were made, not for release to the public, but as an official restricted-in-use photographic record of a campaign.

Lisle Shoemaker and I first met in a shell hole on the black sands of Iwo Jima on D-Day of that invasion. It was his second landing on a blazing beachhead, and my first. We kept in touch through the years and became close friends.

He left United Press after V-J Day and ultimately retired as editor in chief of the *Desert Sun* in Palm Springs, California. His Peleliu collection of combat photos, yellowed newspaper clippings, hastily scribbled notes, and person-to-person recollections of the Palaus operation was of inestimable use in bringing to parts of this book an otherwise impossible personal touch.

I also met Howard Handleman, the International News Service correspondent, under what can only be described as unpleasant circumstances. We both landed in the early assault waves when the 1st Marine Division invaded Inchon, Korea, in 1950. We, too, developed a still enduring friendship. Howard, who was foreign editor of *U.S. News & World Report* when he retired, contributed his Peleliu files and recollections, and they have been liberally used in the same way as Shoemaker's.

Bill Hipple, the *Newsweek* correspondent, was an acquaintance before World War II when he was on the staff of the Associated Press and I was a cub reporter for United Press in Chicago. It is impossible to miss Bill's revealing input, some of it published for the first time, in what became this book. In postwar years, he became the public relations vice president of American Airlines in Los Angeles, where he died of cancer in 1988.

Now, despite the dilemma posed by Don Whitehead, I believe I know where to stop putting words to paper and recognize that what I have written is a *fait accompli.*

B.D.R.
Somerset, New Jersey, 1993

Bibliography

Bateson, Charles. *The War with Japan.* Lansing, Michigan: Michigan State University Press, 1968.

Belote, James H., and Belote, William. *Titans of the Seas.* New York: Harper & Row, 1975.

Bishop, Jim. *FDR's Last Year.* New York: Morrow, 1947.

Cant, Gilbert. *The Great Pacific Victory.* New York: John Day, 1945.

Costello, John. *The Pacific War.* New York: Rawson, Wade, 1981.

Craig, William. *The Fall of Japan.* New York: Dial, 1967.

Davis, Burke. *Marine! The Life of Lieutenant General Lewis B. (Chesty) Puller.* Boston: Little, Brown, 1962.

Douglas, Paul H. *In the Fullness of Time.* New York: Harcourt Brace Jovanovich, 1971.

Dower, John W. *War Without Mercy.* New York: Pantheon, 1986.

Frank, Richard B. *Guadalcanal.* New York: Random House, 1990.

Gailey, Harry A. *Peleliu: 1944.* Annapolis, Md.: Nautical & Aviation Publishing Company of America, 1983.

Garand, George W., and Strobridge, Truman R. *Western Pacific Operations: History of U.S. Marine Corps Operations in World War II.* Vol. 4. Washington, D.C.: Historical Branch, U.S. Marine Corps, 1971.

Halsey, William F., and Bryan, Jay, III. *Admiral Halsey's Story.* New York: McGraw-Hill, 1947.

Hayes, Grace Person. *The History of the Joint Chiefs of Staff in World War II: The War Against Japan.* Washington, D.C.: Historical Section, Joint Chiefs of Staff, 1953.

Hough, Frank O. *Peleliu.* Washington, D.C.: Historical Division, U.S. Marine Corps, 1950.

————. *The Island War.* Philadelphia: Lippincott, 1947.

Hoyt, Edwin P. *How They Won the War in the Pacific.* New York: Weybright & Talley, 1970.

Hunt, George P. *Coral Comes High.* New York: Harper & Brothers, 1947.

———. "Honorable Discharge." New York: *Fortune,* November 1947.

Iseley, Jeter A., and Crowl, Philip A. *The U.S. Marines and Amphibious War.* Princeton, N.J.: Princeton University Press, 1951.

Jensen, Oliver. *Carrier War.* New York: Simon & Schuster, 1945.

Kennard, Richard C. *Combat Letters Home.* Bryn Mawr, Pa.: Dorrance, 1985.

Kirby, Major General S. Woodburn. *The War Against Japan.* London: Her Majesty's Stationery Office, 1965.

Layton, Rear Admiral Edwin T., with Captain Roger Pineau and John Costello. *And I Was There.* New York: Morrow, 1982.

Leckie, Robert. *Helmet for My Pillow.* New York: Random House, 1957.

———. *Strong Men Armed.* New York: Random House, 1962.

McMillan, George. *The Old Breed: A History of the First Marine Division in World War II.* Washington, D.C.: Infantry Journal Press, 1949.

Manchester, William. *Goodbye, Darkness.* Boston: Little, Brown, 1979.

———. *American Caesar.* Boston: Little, Brown, 1982.

Merrill, James J. *A Sailor's Admiral: A Biography of William F. Halsey.* New York: Doubleday, 1976.

Morison, Samuel Eliot. *History of United States Naval Operations in World War II.* Boston: Little, Brown, 1960.

———. *The Two-Ocean Navy.* Boston: Little, Brown, 1963.

Mueller, General Paul J. *The 81st Wildcat Division in World War II.* Washington, D.C.: Infantry Journal Press, 1948.

Murphy, Jack. *History of the U.S. Marines.* Greenwich, Conn.: Exeter Books, 1984.

O'Sheel, Patrick, and Cook, Gene. *Semper Fidelis.* New York: William Sloan Associates, 1948.

Potter, E. B. *Bull Halsey.* Annapolis, Md.: Naval Institute Press, 1985.

Pratt, Fletcher. *The Marine's War.* New York: William Sloan Associates, 1948.

Price, Willard. *Japan's Islands of Mystery.* New York: John Day, 1944.

Sherrod, Robert. *History of Marine Corps Aviation in World War II.* Washington, D.C.: Combat Forces Press, 1952.

Siefring, Thomas A. *History of the United States Marines.* London, England: Bison Books, 1979.

Simmons, Edwin. *The United States Marines, 1775–1975.* New York: Viking, 1974.

Sledge, Eugene B. *With The Old Breed at Peleliu and Okinawa.* Novato, Calif.: Presidio Press, 1981.

Smith, General Holland M., and Finch, Percy. *Coral and Brass.* New York: Scribner's, 1949.

Smith, S. E., ed. *The United States Marine Corps in World War II.* New York: Random House, 1969.

Spector, Ronald H. *Eagle Against the Sun.* New York: Free Press, 1985.

Stanley, David. *Micronesia Handbook.* Chico, Calif.: Moon Publications, 1989.

Toland, John. *The Rising Sun.* New York: Random House, 1970.

Vandegrift, A. A., as told to Robert A. Asprey. *Once a Marine: The Memoirs of General A. A. Vandegrift.* New York: Norton, 1964.

Zimmerman, John L. "The Marine's First Spy." Philadelphia: *Saturday Evening Post,* November 23, 1946.

Index

About the Author

Bill D. Ross began his career as a newsman in 1938 on a weekly paper in Cherokee, Iowa, after graduating from high school in Kansas City, Missouri. He was in Washington, D.C., in the late summer of 1944, awaiting military transportation to England as a United Press reporter covering the war in Europe, but instead joined the Marine Corps as a combat correspondent. Less than six months later he was a sergeant on the beachhead at Iwo Jima on D-Day, February 19, 1945. After V-J Day he volunteered for an additional six months' service with the 1st Marine Division in North China. In 1946 he became a member of the Washington staff of Associated Press, and went to Korea in July 1950 as an AP correspondent, landing with the first wave of Marines at Inchon in what became a two-year tour of duty in Korea and Japan. Mr. Ross subsequently became a public relations and advertising executive in New York, and later wrote for metropolitan newspapers, as well as national magazines, television, and motion pictures. His first book, *Iwo Jima: Legacy of Valor,* was published in 1985. He is presently working on a history of the battles for Wake and Midway islands in the Pacific, and on a chronicle of print-media correspondents and photographers, and their radio and pioneer television newsmen counterparts who reported from the battlefronts of World War II and Korea. Mr. Ross also has been commissioned by the Marine Corps Historical Center to write two volumes of a new series recounting all Marine campaigns during World War II. The collection is scheduled for publication in the fall of 1995 to commemorate the fiftieth anniversary of V-J Day. His books will cover the invasions of New Britain and Iwo Jima.